A Nation of Statesmen

Civilization of the American Indian Series

A Nation of Statesmen

*The Political Culture
of the
Stockbridge-Munsee Mohicans,
1815–1972*

James W. Oberly

University of Oklahoma Press : Norman

Also by James W. Oberly

(with Louise Merriam) *United States History: A Bibliography of the New Writings on American History* (Manchester, 1995)
Sixty-Million Acres: American Veterans and the Public Lands before the Civil War (Kent, Ohio, 1990)

Publication of this book is made possible in part through the generous contributions of the University of Wisconsin–Eau Claire Foundation and the law firm of Von Briesen, Purtell & Roper.

Library of Congress Cataloging-in-Publication Data

Oberly, James Warren, 1954–
    A nation of statesmen : the political culture of the Stockbridge-Munsee Mohicans, 1815–1972 / James W. Oberly.
        p. cm. — (Civilization of the American Indian series; vol. 252)
    Includes bibiographical references and index.
    ISBN 0-8061-3675-8 (alk. paper)
    1. Mohegan Indians—Politics and government.   2. Stockbridge and Munsee Tribe of Indians—Politics and government.   3. Indians of North America—Wisconsin—Politics and government.   4. Political culture—Wisconsin—History.   I. Title: Political culture of the Stockbridge-Munsee Mohicans, 1815–1972.   II. Title.   III. Series.

E99.M83O22 2005
306.2'089'9734—dc22

                                                                        2004059879

A Nation of Statesmen is Volume 252 in the Civilization of the American Indian Series.

Contents

Maps

Tables and Figures

TABLES

FIGURES

Preface and Acknowledgments

This book began in late 1997 with an invitation from the Stockbridge-Munsee Legal Department to conduct research for the Stockbridge-Munsee Community concerning a boundary dispute in Shawano County, Wisconsin. The tribe's attorneys asked me to apply my expertise in the history of nineteenth- and twentieth-century public land policy to locate relevant primary source documents and prepare a research report. More than seven years later, that narrow task has become a political history of the Stockbridge-Munsee Band of Mohicans in Wisconsin.

Along the way one moment stands out. I recall a preliminary hearing in U.S. District Court in October 1998 where I presented my research report and testified on direct and cross-examination. The courtroom was packed with tribal members and with their white neighbors (opponents in the litigation) from Shawano County, each group having made the three-hour drive south to Milwaukee to attend the week-long hearing. The attorneys, the judge, the clerk, and I, at the front of the courtroom, had copies of my report and the exhibits I had helped to prepare. But the hundred or so observers whose lives would be greatly affected by the outcome had no report, no documents, no exhibits—only the oral testimony. How different this was from my classroom at the University of Wisconsin–Eau Claire (UWEC), where I show images on three overhead screens from a networked computer projector. In class, my students and I can read, analyze, and discuss together the primary sources. Above all, my students can ask questions when they do not understand something. In the courtroom, only those with a formal need to know had this access. And the only person who asked a question without knowing the answer in advance was the judge. I decided that the legal system had missed a teaching opportunity with a highly motivated and interested audience. I hope that this book, and the documentary record on which it is based, will be helpful to those who want to continue to learn about the history that I talked about that week in Milwaukee.

The scholar of nineteenth- and twentieth-century Mohican political history is faced with an almost overwhelming archival record and set of oral histories. The collections of the Stockbridge-Munsee Historical Library Museum on the tribe's reservation are the essential starting point. The fluency of Mohican political leaders in written English makes this an unusual tribe among American Indians. The student of the Mohicans does not need to rely on government Indian agents for information on the tribe's thinking; quite the contrary, the tribe's leaders were capable of speaking and writing for themselves. As much as possible, this book attempts to air the voices of the Mohicans themselves as they sometimes cooperated with and sometimes struggled against the United States, neighboring Indian tribes, and their white and black neighbors in the making of their own political history.

I wish to thank the Stockbridge-Munsee Tribal Councils since 1998 for their support of this project, particularly Robert Chicks, tribal chairman, Sterling Schreiber, tribal vice-chairman, and Terrie Terrio, tribal treasurer. I also want to thank the members of the Stockbridge-Munsee Historical Committee, including chair Dorothy Davids, Sheila Miller Powless, Theresa Miller Puskarenko, Eunice Stick, Doug Miller, Molly Miller, Leah Joy Miller, Ruth Gudinas, and David Wrone, for reading drafts of this work and for making me welcome as an occasional guest at their semimonthly meetings. Sheila Powless, Arlee Davids, and Sherry White also spent numerous hours helping me to work through the excellent holdings of documents and oral histories in the Stockbridge-Munsee Historical Library Museum.

I am grateful to the Stockbridge-Munsee Legal Department, including staff attorneys Paul Stenzel, Sharon Greene-Gretzinger, and Doug Huck, for discussing tribal history with me and for reading the manuscript in full and sharing their comments. The Legal Department arranged "mobile oral history" days in 2000 and 2001 during which elders toured the reservation in a van and shared memories about people and places and activities in the 1910s, 1920s, and 1930s, such as hunting, fishing, berry picking, swimming, and tobogganing. I especially want to thank elders Virginia "Gin" Johnson, Bernice Miller Pigeon, the late Priscilla Church, the late Walter Jacobs, Virgil Murphy, and Clarence Chicks. The participation on the oral history tours of UWEC student cartographers Colleen Orzech, Barb Featherly, Jed Durni, and Bob Passow enabled us to gather the information that led to the preparation of some of the maps in this book.

In addition to the members of the Stockbridge-Munsee Legal Department, I also want to acknowledge how much I learned from Brian Pierson, the tribe's outside counsel with the law firm of von Briesen, Purtell & Roper. Also, the questions posed by Wisconsin assistant attorney generals Charles Hoornstra, John Greene, and Thomas Dosch forced me to think about every document I discovered and every assertion I made. I learned from the research of the expert witnesses Charles Cleland of Michigan State University for the tribe, Lawrence Kelly of North Texas State University, and the late James Clifton for the state of Wisconsin.

After completing my contract obligation to the tribe, I was able to present some of the ideas in this book at various forums, starting with the University of Minnesota's Early American History Workshop. I thank Lisa Norling, John Howe, Rus Menard, and the other regular workshop members, especially Chad Ronnander, Brad Jarvis, and Kate Thomas, for their invitations to discuss my work, and David Wilkins of the Political Science and American Indian Studies Departments at the University of Minnesota for his help and interest. I also benefited from comments at a forum at the Minnesota Population Center, directed by Steve Ruggles, as well as the use of the IPUMS files for the United States in 1900 for comparative purposes. My colleagues Myron Gutman, Eric Austin, Mary Vardigan, Hank Heitowit, Bill Hobby, Kambidima Wotela, Patricia Blackman, Hugo Horta, Peter Bratt, Shinichi Aizawa, Jonatan Svanlund, Kristi Balzer, Phil D'Anieri, Yael Proaktor, Svenja Wiese, Jeff Beemer, Bahar Akman, Akira Watanabe, Tracy Roof, Shuang Chen, David Mitchell, and Michal Paneth-Peleg of the Inter-University Consortium for Political and Social Research were welcoming during my recent summer stays in Ann Arbor, when I had the spare time to work in the collections of the Bentley Library on the early history of the Michigan Territory. I appreciate the invitation to talk about Mohican history from the Native American Students Association at UWEC during American Indian Awareness Week in 2002. Thanks to UWEC colleagues Larry Martin, Mike Hilger, Ron Satz, Richard St. Germaine, and Louise Edwards-Simpson of the American Indian Studies Program. Patricia Stovey and Peter Shrake graciously shared their research on Wisconsin Indian history with me. My History Department colleagues at UWEC, especially Robert Gough and Steven Gosch, and my history colleague at the University of Wisconsin–La Crosse, Martin Zanger, have enhanced my teaching and learning over the past two decades. And I want to acknowledge that I borrowed the concept "nation of firsts" from my History Department colleague Kate Lang. She finds it a strong presence in the records of the eleventh-century caliphate; I find it a millennium later in the records of the Mohican Nation.

Preparing for presentations at the Native American Institute at Albany, New York, at the "Many Trails of the Mohican Nation" conference at Bowler, Wisconsin, and to the Fellows of the Newberry Library helped me to conceptualize the organization of the material. I wish to thank Helen Hornbeck Tanner, James Grossman, and Sara Austin at the Newberry and especially Loretta Fowler for her help when we were both in residence at the Newberry. Lion G. Miles of Stockbridge, Massachusetts, Shirley Dunn of East Greenbush, New York, and Martin Zank of Eau Claire, Wisconsin, have given very generously of their time and knowledge on this project.

A 2002 fellowship at the Newberry Library, a sabbatical leave granted during the spring 2002 semester by the Regents of the University of Wisconsin System, and support from the University of Wisconsin System Institute on Race and Ethnicity and the UWEC Office of University Research gave me the time and resources to work on this project in 2002 and 2003. The staff archivists at the National Archives in Washington, D.C., and in Chicago have been very helpful over the years, especially Scott Forsythe, Glenn Fowler, and Kimberly Green in Chicago. The archivists of the Wisconsin Historical Society have also done a great deal for this project, especially Sue Ginter Watson at the Area Research Center (ARC), University of Wisconsin–River Falls, and Deborah Anderson of the ARC, University of Wisconsin–Green Bay. Ruth Wachter Nelson at the ARC, University of Wisconsin–Stevens Point helped with the Melvin Laird

Papers. Rick Pifer, Larry Lynch, Heather Muir, and Rita Sorkness at the ARC, UWEC, offered much help over the years.

Four colleagues read this entire book in manuscript: Richard Niemi and Mary Young, both of the University of Rochester, and David Wrone of the University of Wisconsin–Stevens Point and the College of the Menominee Nation, and Martin Zank of Eau Claire, Wisconsin. I am very grateful for their help. I also wish to express my gratitude to the anonymous referees who read the manuscript for the University of Oklahoma Press and suggested valuable corrections, improvements, and changes, as did my editors, Alice Stanton and Sheila Berg. Any errors of fact in this book are the responsibility of the author.

I with to thank my traveling seminar colleagues of Interstate-94 for their friendship and support: Gerry Conner, Mike Dorsher, Bob Sampson, and Louise Edwards-Simpson. Finally, I wish to thank Louise Merriam, Will Oberly, Nick Oberly, and Peter Oberly for their love and support as I worked on *A Nation of Statesmen*.

A Nation of Statesmen

Abbreviations

ARCIA   Annual Report of the Commissioner of Indian Affairs
BIA   Bureau of Indian Affairs
CCC-ID   Civilian Conservation Corps–Indian Division
CCF   Central Classified Files of the Office of Indian Affairs
CWA   Civil Works Administration
FERA   Federal Emergency Relief Administration
FSA   Farm Security Administration
GLITC   Great Lakes Inter-Tribal Council
GLO   General Land Office
H.R.   House of Representatives Bill
ICC   Indian Claims Commission
I.R.A.   Indian Rights Association
IRA   Indian Reorganization Act of 1934
LR-GB   Letters Received from the Green Bay Agency of the Office of Indian Affairs
NCAI   National Congress of American Indians
OIA   Office of Indian Affairs
RA   Resettlement Administration
S.B.   Senate Bill
SMHLM   Stockbridge-Munsee Historical Library Museum
SPP   Stockbridge Purchase Project
TPUS   Territorial Papers of the United States
WCC   Wisconsin Conservation Commission
WHC   Wisconsin Historical Collections
WPA   Works Progress Administration

CHAPTER 1

A Nation of Firsts

A Brief Mohican Political History

James Fennimore Cooper's *Last of the Mohicans* and the films of the same name brought the Mohican Indians to the attention of the American public. Cooper's 1828 novel featured the exploits of a white frontiersman, Hawkeye, and his two Mohican companions, Chingachook and his son, Uncas. The novel is set in colonial New York against the grand events of the English surrender of Fort Ticonderoga to combined French-Indian forces. Hawkeye and the two Mohicans manage to safeguard the lives of two English maidens, Alice Munro and Corinne Munro. Chingachook and Uncas are portrayed as men of few words, as simple "children of the forest" or "noble savages," in contrast to some of the Iroquois and mixed-race characters in the book. At the book's conclusion, Chingachook dies and his life is celebrated by the few living members of the tribe at its ancestral village in the upper Hudson Valley. The fictional Mohicans of Chingachook and Uncas were a doomed people, soon to be overwhelmed by English settlement. Cooper himself observed in a footnote that at that time, 1828, the Mohicans were "scattered across the Great West." In Cooper's America, the Mohicans of the Hudson Valley disappeared from history, and Chingachook and Uncas were the last of a noble breed.[1]

At about the time Cooper was working on *The Last of the Mohicans*, the Mohicans themselves were embarking on yet another geographic removal from New York to Massachusetts and Connecticut in the 1730s and 1740s and then to central New York State among the Oneida Indians after the American Revolution. By the early 1820s the Mohicans were compelled to leave the Oneida lands for the Great West, specifically, the area around Green Bay in the Michigan Territory. The Mohicans lived on after Cooper dismissed them as a vanished race.[2]

The American literary world may have viewed the Mohicans as a vanished race, but Congress, the executive branch, and the judiciary of the U.S. government knew differently. From the Washington administration of the early Republic through the Clinton administration at the end of the twentieth century, the Mohicans almost continually pressed issues of government-to-government business with the United States. A count of the documents listed in the congressional serial set yields more than sixty separate reports to the House and Senate on Stockbridge-Munsee Mohican affairs in New York and Wisconsin. A tally of the laws of the United States, the *Statutes at Large*, shows that the executive negotiated and the Senate ratified five treaties with the Stockbridge-Munsees between 1794 and 1856. That roster does not include four other treaty negotiations that resulted in signed treaties but that the Senate refused to ratify. The same search of the *Statutes at Large* reveals an additional ten congressional acts passed between 1843 and 1972 that relate to Stockbridge-Munsee business. And that list excludes three bills passed by both houses but vetoed by the president and not reconsidered by the Congress. Finally, the Stockbridge-Munsees regularly have appeared as plaintiffs, defendants, or interested parties in lawsuits in the federal courts. Four of those cases made their way to the U.S. Supreme Court for argument and decision.

A fitting counter-Cooper bit of drama represents how the Stockbridge-Munsee Mohicans see themselves today. In 2001 NBC's *The West Wing* broadcast an episode titled "The Indians in the Lobby." In the telecast two Stockbridge-Munsee tribal officials appear at the White House on the Wednesday before Thanksgiving and demand to see the president on a long-delayed Interior Department matter. The two Mohicans vow to stand in the White House lobby until their issue is addressed by the president and his staff. We learn that the tribe has waited fifteen years for a simple decision from the Interior Department. The tribal chair and tribal attorney—the two Indians in the lobby—also recite a long history of removals, broken treaties, and land loss on their Wisconsin reservation. At the end of a long day during which the two tribal leaders stand silently (not unlike

Chingachook and Uncas might have done), the president's communications director works out a compromise whereby the Executive Department will end the fifteen-year stalemate on the land-to-trust issue. In wonder, the communications director asks the two Mohicans how they can be so patient yet so persistent. "We have no choice," answers the tribal attorney. The survival of the Mohican Nation has depended on patience, persistence, and engagement in politics.[3]

In fact, in one way or another, the Stockbridge-Munsee Band of Mohicans has been pursuing a claim against the United States and the states of New York, Massachusetts, and Wisconsin since the mid-1780s. But *The West Wing* captured a significant element of Mohican politics, the seemingly never-ending quest for justice from the United States and several states and local governments to make right some of the wrongs of nineteenth-century federal Indian policy.

Anthropologists say that the term "Mohican" characterized the seventeeth-century union of three groups of Indian villages in what is now the Hudson River Valley of New York State: the "Mahicans," the Wappingers, and the Housatonics. Both "Mohican" and "Mahican" are variants on "Moh-he-con-nuck," which means "people of the waters that are never still," a reference to the tidal Hudson River. Similarly, the term "Munsee" refers to a group of Delaware Indians who lived on the west bank of the Hudson River in the Minisink River valley of the Catskill Mountains. The Mohican language is an Algonquian dialect and was spoken until the 1930s. The Munsee language is one of three Delaware dialects and is still spoken by Canadian and Oklahoma Munsees.[4]

The confederacy of the two native groups might properly be called "Mohican-Munsee," except that no one uses that term. In the first half of the eighteenth century, the Mohicans fragmented into groups that moved in different directions. Some moved west into the Susquehanna Valley; some moved to live among Moravian missionaries on the east bank of the Hudson River. The main stem of the Mohicans also moved east to the Housatonic Valley of Massachusetts and Connecticut and developed a new home village named Stockbridge. That village name has stuck as a synonym for "Mohican." For the first thirty years in Wisconsin, the two groups were referred to as the Stockbridge and Munsee Tribes of Indians, indicating some separation. Since 1856 the United States has dubbed them hyphenated Native Americans, the confederacy of the Stockbridge-Munsees.[5]

"Stockbridge-Munsees," "Stockbridges," "Mohicans," and sometimes "Stockbridge-Munsee Mohicans" are terms that members of the group used somewhat interchangeably in the nineteenth and twentieth centuries. But those names refer to ethnic identity, not to the political organization of the group. The nomenclature for such political forms originated with the nineteenth-century ethnologist Lewis Henry Morgan, who wrote in his study of the Iroquois Confederacy about the sequence of political develop-ment from "bands" to "tribes" to "kingdoms" to "nations." Morgan con-sidered these forms in hierarchical fashion, from simplest to most com-plex. The Stockbridge-Munsees, however, have confounded Morgan's typology in the way that they refer to themselves. Throughout the nineteenth century the Stockbridge-Munsees called themselves a nation, not a tribe or band. Toward the end of the nineteenth century and during the first third of the twentieth, the Stockbridge-Munsees referred to themselves as a tribe. Since 1937 these Indian people have called them-selves the Stockbridge-Munsee Community. I attempt to follow the poli-tical usage preferred by the people themselves; thus the discussion about the nineteenth century uses the term "nation" and about the twentieth century, "tribe" and "community."[6]

Stockbridge-Munsee politics have taken place on three levels. The first is the internation level, or government-to-government relations between tribes and the United States. Conducting treaty diplomacy with the United States, or after the end of the treaty era lobbying Congress and the Bureau of Indian Affairs, was the most important level of politics practiced by the Stockbridge-Munsees. During the first half of the nineteenth century, this internation diplomacy was closely connected to the federal policy of Indian removal. Between 1785 and 1856 the number of Mohican removals was as great as any American Indian tribe in the United States (map 1). The Mohicans left Massachusetts, then New York, and they made two addi-tional removals within Wisconsin, not to mention contemplating but not acting on proposed removals to Iowa and Minnesota. One dissident faction left Wisconsin for Kansas, from which that band was relocated to Indian Territory, now Oklahoma. Each of these removals and relocations caused hardship to the Mohicans. And each injustice energized the Mohican leaders to seek a remedy or correction for the wrong done their people. Correcting those injustices has been the central theme of Mohican politics for almost two centuries. The struggle for justice in the form of claims

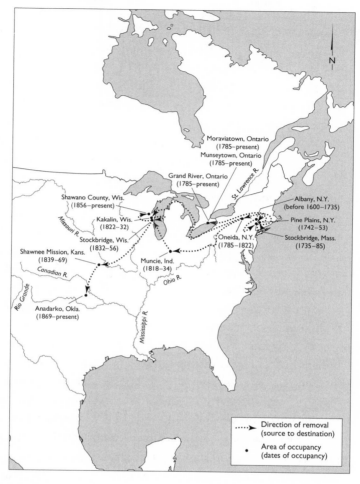

Map 1.
Removals of the
Stockbridges
and Munsees in
North America,
1735–1869

against the United States and the various states gave meaning and purpose
to the tribal identity of the Mohican Nation.

The second level of Mohican political history involved cooperation and
sometimes disagreement between the Stockbridge-Munsee Mohicans and
other American Indian tribes both in New York and in Wisconsin. The
Stockbridges moved from Massachusetts to live beside the Oneidas of
New York in 1785 after the American Revolution and stayed with them in
central New York until the great removal to Wisconsin in the 1820s. The
Stockbridges were even more closely tied to the Brothertown Indians, a
confederation of southern New England and Long Island tribes that also
lived with the Oneidas after the Revolution. The Stockbridges, the Munsees,

the St. Regis Mohawks, the Brothertowns, and the Oneidas worked together to create a united front of "New York Indians" in 1820, 1821, and 1822 to deal with the Menominee and Ho-Chunk Indians of the Green Bay area. The New York Indians drafted a treaty with the Wisconsin tribes that transferred all the Wisconsin lands to the care of the New York Indians. The New York Indians told their Menominee and Ho-Chunk counterparts that extensive dealings with the "long fingernails" of the Americans made the New Yorkers better equipped to defend an Indian homeland in Wisconsin against the United States. The Menominees were not persuaded and only grudgingly on two separate occasions ceded and relinquished land for the Stockbridges.[7]

In 1831, after a decade of intertribal disputes, the Menominees made a large cession to the United States of lands bordering Lake Michigan. Out of this cession, the Oneidas won control of a half-million-acre tract in northeastern Wisconsin that was intended to be a homeland for other Indians still in New York State. The Stockbridge-Munsees resisted relocating to the "New York Indian Tract" and instead convinced the United States to reserve two townships out of the public domain on the east side of Lake Winnebago for their use. Similarly, the Brothertown Indians had a single township reserved for their use, located adjacent to the Stockbridge-Munsee reservation. In 1839 Congress passed a statute that dissolved the Brothertown Indian Reservation, and that same year the Stockbridge-Munsee Indian Reservation was halved in size by a treaty. The remaining reserved township was soon dissolved by Congress, then restored to reservation status by Congress, then ceded back to the United States by the Stockbridge-Munsees in 1848. For some years, and not for the first or last time, the Stockbridge-Munsees occupied a tract in which they had lost title. Since 1856 the Stockbridge-Munsees have lived on a reservation adjacent to the Menominees. Many Stockbridges have worked as loggers in the Menominee forests and at the Menominee sawmill at Neopit, just north of the Stockbridge reservation. Many Menominees came to the Stockbridge reservation in the 1910s and 1920s to obtain alcohol from Stockbridgers who ran illegal saloons. In more recent years, the two tribal governments each bid for the purchase of a golf course and for land parcels on the Stockbridge-Munsee Reservation.[8]

The third level of Mohican political history is intratribal, or the internal contest for power among families within the Mohican Nation. The

Stockbridge-Munsees have had more than their share of factional and "party" disputes over the past 180 years. Untangling the roots of party differences in the tribe is another task for the historian of Mohican politics, one that requires what might be described as "deep genealogy" to make sense of the alliances and ruptures between the tribe's great families.[9]

In the 1820s the Congregational minister John Sergeant bemoaned the appearance of a "party spirit" at New Stockbridge so severe that he predicted it would lead to the Mohicans' ruin. In the mid-1830s federal officials reported that the Mohicans of Stockbridge-on-the-Lake divided into two groups, an "Emigrant Party" and a "Wiskonsin [sic] Party." In the 1840s the Stockbridges divided once again into a Citizens Party and an Indian Party. In 1856 the Commissioner of Indian Affairs sought a treaty that would bring together all Stockbridges and Munsees, regardless of "party." So many observers and participants in Stockbridge-Munsee affairs used the term "party" that the historian must analyze that term. Political scientists understand a political party in a democracy as an organization that seeks political office through contesting and winning elections, that mobilizes a constituency to that end, and, once in power, that implements stated policies and distributes resources that meet with the approbation of the voters that put the party into power. In the American two-party system of winner-takes-all elections, the political party consists of leaders and supporters who define themselves as members of one party and decidedly not of the other. The transmission of party identification from parents to children over the generations constitutes a party system. The American political scene at the beginning of the nineteenth century was one of elite factions, cliques, and juntos, but not until the mid-1830s did a genuine mass-based party system of Democrats and Whigs emerge in every state in the Union.

In the years the Mohicans lived at Stockbridge-on-the-Lake in Calumet County, Wisconsin, a two-party system emerged with some but not all the features of the Democrats and Whigs. Stockbridge-Munsee parties divided on ideological grounds over the question of how to respond to U.S. demands for Indian removal from Wisconsin. The membership of the Stockbridge-Munsee parties also had different social bases, much like the Democrats and Whigs. Stockbridge-Munsee parents transmitted their party allegiance to their children. When in power, Stockbridge-Munsee parties attempted to implement policies that benefited their members, to such an extent that leaders sometimes resembled party bosses interested primarily in providing patronage to their members. Most intriguing was the post–Civil War overlap between the party system of Citizens and Indians in the Stockbridge-Munsee tribe and Democrats and Republicans in Wisconsin.

The two-party system of Democrats and Whigs, and later the Democrats and Republicans, accepted the possibility that they might lose an election, and they accepted the place of a loyal opposition. When the Whigs lost an election, they could regroup and contest the next one. When the Democrats won, they did not choose as their first action the disfranchisement of the Whigs. The great exception to the national practice occurred after the Civil War, when white Southern Democrats used murder and intimidation to destroy what they perceived as an alien political system of black suffrage and Republican Party rule. In the 1890s the Southern Democrats had written new state constitutions that effectively disfranchised their black opponents as well as their poor white ones. Thereafter, politics was a matter of factions, cliques, and juntos in the white Democratic Party. Nineteenth-century Stockbridge-Munsee politics was southern in this sense: after 1843 one party did not recognize the legitimacy of the other, and when in power, the ruling Indian Party usually had as its first priority the disfranchisement of its Citizens Party opponents. Yet in the twentieth century the Stockbridge-Munsees were largely able to put aside party differences and work together to defend and strengthen their reservation in Shawano County, Wisconsin. Politics did not end, but on crucial issues such as allotment, constitutional government, and working to place land into federal trust, the descendants of the Citizens Party and Indian Party were able to work together.[10]

This political history of the Stockbridge-Munsees has largely gone unremarked among scholars. There is no book-length treatment of the tribe's history in Wisconsin. Among historians, only Joseph Schaefer in the 1930s and John Savagian in the 1990s have written chapter-length studies of two episodes of Wisconsin Mohican history. Schaefer wrote about the loss of the Stockbridge Reservation on Lake Winnebago in the 1840s, and Savagian wrote that the tribe enjoyed a revival under the Indian Reorganization Act (IRA) of the 1930s. Only two anthropologists have undertaken any detailed study of the Stockbridge-Munsees in Wisconsin, one in the 1920s and one in the 1960s. By contrast, there is an extensive scholarship on the history of the Mohicans in seventeenth- and eighteenth-century New York and New England.[11] The paucity of detailed studies of the Wisconsin Stockbridge-Munsees was telling when the editors of the Smithsonian Institution's *Handbook of North American Indians* set about looking for a synthesis of Mohican history and culture. T. J. Brasser's 1976 article in volume 15 of the *Handbook* largely covered the tribe's past in New York and New England and paid little attention to the Wisconsin history of the tribe.[12]

PERIODS OF THE STOCKBRIDGE-MUNSEE POLITY

The first task of the historian is to organize the past into discrete periods. The term I use for organizing Mohican history into historical eras is "polity," defined in Webster's *Revised Unabridged Dictionary* (1913) as "the form or constitution of the civil government of a nation or state; the framework or organization by which the various departments of government are combined into a systematic whole." I divide Stockbridge-Munsee history in Wisconsin into seven discrete periods, characterized by the changes in the form of local, tribal government and politics as practiced by the Mohicans: (1) 1815–32, the era of the New York polity, when the main body of the tribe, together with its institutions, was transferred from central New York to the intertribal village at Grand Kakalin in Wisconsin; (2) 1833–55, the period of the Calumet County polity, established at the new Stockbridge-by-the-Lake settlement, which featured a new, written republican constitution; (3) 1856–70, the Shawano County polity, established at the new Mo-he-con-nuck on the Red River, characterized by a democratic-republican constitution; (4) 1871–92, the restoration of the Quinney, or Indian, Party polity, characterized by an alliance of one faction with the powerful Republican Party group of politicans-businessmen known as the "Pine Ring"; (5) 1893–1934, the Allotment era polity of the Tribal Business Committee and the unofficial Mohican Club; (6) 1934–48, the era of the Indian New Deal characterized by a new constitution and corporate charter and federally purchased land base; and (7) 1948–72, which saw emergence of a mature tribal council form of government after World War II that successfully resisted termination and built an intertribal alliance with other Wisconsin tribes.

After organizing the past into discrete periods, the historian must justify this organization by identifying the critical points of change in time and explaining why these changes occurred when they did.

The New York Polity, to the War of 1812 and After

The first historical period of Mohican politics is the tribe's decision at New Stockbridge, New York, in the years after the War of 1812 to remove to Wisconsin. The tribe had a formal organization in 1819 that was later mockingly imitated by the New York City Democratic Party at its Tammany Hall. The tribe was led by a head "sachem," or civil chief, who claimed his leadership on the basis of heredity and clan membership. In 1819 the sachem was Solomon U. Hendricks, son of Capt. Hendrick Aupaumut and a descendant of the Mohicans who had moved from the Hudson Valley to the Housatonic Valley of western Massachusetts and Connecticut in the eighteenth century. The sachem of the tribe was assisted by three senior councilors—all men—as well as an "Owl," or speaker, and a "Runner," or messenger. Less formally, Sachem Hendricks had to acknowledge the diplomatic role of a "Hero," or war chief in the tribe. That role was filled for nearly half a century by his father, Captain Aupamut. Sachem Hendricks, and later Sachem John Metoxen, oversaw the Stockbridge role in the New York Indians' negotiations with the Menominees and Ho-Chunks for land in the Green Bay region. The hereditary leadership continued when the tribe acquired a treaty-based reservation on the east shore of Lake Winnebago in Wisconsin.[13]

The Quinney Republic in Wisconsin, 1833–1855

John W. Quinney, the descendant of a former sachem at the tribe's Massachusetts home, emerged in the early 1830s as a leader in Wisconsin. Born in New York State in 1797, he removed to Wisconsin in 1829 with other Quinney family members. His sister Electa soon achieved distinction as the first schoolteacher in the Wisconsin portion of the Michigan Territory. Quinney rose rapidly to leadership in the tribe. As the elected sachem, he made nine trips from Green Bay to Washington, D.C., as the Stockbridge Nation's chief diplomat in treaty dealings with the United States.

According to the historian Herman Viola, Quinney spent so much time at the federal Indian Office on his tribe's business that War Department officials honored him with having his portrait painted and hung in a prominent position. Quinney drafted a new written constitution for the tribe in 1837 that marked both a significant change in governance and the second historical period of Mohican politics in Wisconsin. Quinney's constitution abolished hereditary selection and replaced it with democratic election. He maintained the titles sachem and councilor but otherwise remade the Stockbridges into a Jacksonian polity with frequent elections and nonstop politicking. Quinney served several nonconsecutive terms as sachem of the tribe under the 1837 constitution, a period noteworthy for the congressional abolition of the tribe in 1843, a reversal of that decision in 1846, and, in 1847, the framing of a new state constitution for Wisconsin that specifically included the Stockbridges as citizens with the right to vote and access to state courts and thereby subject to state power. Quinney also negotiated a treaty in 1848 that called for the removal of the tribe to Minnesota.[14]

The Democratic Polity of the Citizens Party, 1856–1870

In the immediate aftermath of his death in 1855, Quinney's opponents—known since the early 1840s as the Citizens Party—negotiated a new treaty with the United States that called for removal not from Lake Winnebago to Minnesota but to the nearby Menominee Reservation on the Wolf River. The insurgents, led by a Hendricks descendant, established their new settlement in frontier Shawano County and then scrapped the Quinney constitution for a new constitution in 1857. That document governed tribal politics for the next fifteen years, a third period in the Wisconsin history of the Mohicans that was marked by incessant fighting between the Quinney and Hendricks parties, with the Quinneys and their relatives prevailing by the end of the period. In addition to disagreements over policy, a deep fault line opened over intratribal race perceptions. The Quinney Party disdained the African-Indian origins of the Citizens Party members.[15]

The Restoration Polity of the Indian Party and the Pine Ring, 1871–1892

The Quinney faction, or Indian Party, sought outside help in 1870 to overthrow the Citizens Party and to have their rivals expelled from the tribe. The Indian Party leadership did not stop until it convinced Congress to pass an act in 1871 achieving that goal. The first action of the restored Quinney polity was to repeal the 1857 Citizens Party constitution and reinstate John W. Quinney's 1837 charter. The price the Indian Party paid for internal victory was that Congress put up for sale three-fourths of the land parcels on the Shawano County reservation, the best tracts of which were grabbed by the "Pine Ring" lumbermen. The Stockbridge-Munsees were the first Wisconsin tribe to determine how to make use of their timberland patrimony. The Indian Party leadership rejected a Citizens Party proposal that the tribe begin its own logging and lumbering enterprise, a path that the neighboring Menominee tribe chose decades later. For the rest of the 1870s and 1880s, the Indian Party subsisted on modest annuity payments from the proceeds of the timber and fought off every effort at tribal restoration by the Citizens Party.

The Stockbridge leader of the Citizens Party faction was John C. Adams, son of Electa Quinney Adams and nephew of John W. Quinney. Adams left the Stockbridge Reservation to attend college at Lawrence University and completed his studies at the same time that the Pine Ring made its timber grab. Despite his maternal lineage, Adams cast his political lot with the opponents of the Indian Party. He spent more than twenty years lobbying the Indian Office and Congress to overturn an 1871 law that adversely affected the tribe's welfare, as Adams saw it. Congress considered Adams's draft bill every session from 1876 to 1893, when it finally passed. The Indian Office conducted numerous investigations of the problems Adams described, especially the high-handed manner in which one faction of the tribe held and used power. At one point, an exasperated Indian Office special agent wrote that the Stockbridge-Munsees "cannot be classified as Indians." Instead, "the men are all either politicians or 'Statesmen' and the almost sole occupation of the entire male portion of the tribe is politics."[16]

The Struggle for Sovereignty in the Era of Allotment and Assimilation, 1893–1933

In 1893 the Indian Office dissolved the Constitution of 1871 and abolished the tribal government that was run by Quinney descendants, who increasingly bore the surname Miller. In its place the Commissioner of Indian Affairs appointed a new "Tribal Business Committee" to represent the tribe's interests in dealings with the United States. The Tribal Business Committee, with quite limited powers, did its best over the next forty years to lead the tribe. The Stockbridge leader Carlton (Carl) Miller spent more than two decades leading the tribe after it lost its lands and was attempting to regain a land base in Wisconsin with federal help. The private Society of Mohicans fraternal organization led by Carl Miller on the Stockbridge-Munsee reservation ran parallel to the Tribal Business Committee in conducting politics during this period of Mohican history in Wisconsin. These were decades when the Tribal Business Committee and the Society of Mohicans struggled to direct the education of the tribe's young people. Numerous Mohican children went to federal and private boarding schools off the reservation. Others went to a local federal Indian day school. The majority attended an on-reservation Lutheran mission school. The tribe embraced Puritan Congregationalism in the 1730s and Presbyterianism in the 1830s and were evangelized by German Lutherans after 1900. Some members of the tribe became active in the 1920s in a pan-Indian movement of onetime New York Indians who sought international recognition from the League of Nations and also a large judgment against New York State for past treaty violations.

The Mohicans of the Indian New Deal, 1934–1948

After the collapse of the so-called League of the Six Nations in the early 1930s, Miller turned the tribe's attention to the new opportunities emanating from the federal government's "Indian New Deal." Miller organized a vote among the Stockbridge-Munsees of 166 to 1 in December 1934 in favor of accepting the new Indian Reorganization Act. Next the tribe's leaders set about writing a new constitution to govern the tribe. The Mohicans went through numerous drafts of a constitution before they finally won approval from the Interior Department in 1937 for their new tribal government. This marked a decisive break with the government-to-government relations conducted by the old Tribal Business Committee and ushered in a new period of Mohican political history in Wisconsin. The document approved by the secretary of the interior resembled very closely the standard IRA-era constitution of Indian tribes. It set forth membership standards, areas of tribal sovereignty, and provisions for the election of a tribal council.[17]

Securing the Homeland against Termination, 1948–1974

For twenty-six years Arvid E. Miller, Carl's son, served as the tribe's elected chairman. In that capacity, Miller led the tribe in its fight against federal termination and for the acquisition of additional lands within its reservation boundaries. He also led all Wisconsin tribes in the organization of a pan-Indian lobbying group, the Great Lakes Inter-Tribal Council.

During each of these seven periods, the Mohicans engaged in active internation, intertribal, and intratribal politics. Each historical period also had a dominant person who led a governing coalition and represented the tribe to the United States and to other Indian tribes. The sachem, or tribal chair, was always a man, but he usually depended on a coalition led by religious women of the tribe and on the support of extended families.

The form of tribal government during each of these seven periods owed its shape to both internal and external factors. The Mohicans enjoyed considerable autonomy in the early and mid-nineteenth century but lost control of the form of tribal government to U.S. officials at the end of the nineteenth century and into the twentieth century. At several times since 1820 the structure of Mohican politics broke down completely. The pressure of outside federal and private market power ruptured tribal consensus. Tribal members sometimes abandoned discussion for threats, evictions, and even arson against one another. Yet the tribe has persevered, patched up its differences, and maintained as firm a defense of tribal sovereignty as possible.

The form of politics frequently changed, particularly with constitutions and governing mechanisms, but tribal survival and advancement has been central to Mohican politics. Scholars and tribal members alike tend to use the term "sovereignty" to describe the cluster of issues concerned with tribal survival and advancement. And despite the changes in political forms, and sometimes political divisions, other basic issues of Stockbridge-Munsee politics have been long-lived. One of the foremost issues in all seven historical periods is the question of tribal and community membership.

Similarly, landownership, tribal employment, law and order, and disbursal of tribal funds have been the stuff of local tribal politics for almost two centuries.

In each historical period of Stockbridge-Munsee polity, I examine a set of the perennial contested issues that made for politics. For the first such constant issue—membership in the tribe and community—I ask a set of questions: Who is a member? Is membership determined by maternal descent or paternal descent or both? Who makes the rules of membership? Does membership include full standing in the polity, or is it limited by age and gender? For the issue of lands and homeland, I ask a different set of questions: Who decides where the tribe will live? Who decides on removal and where to relocate? Who decides on the form in which the homelands will be held, that is, communally or individually? How did the Stockbridge-Munsees understand their Wisconsin reservations? Also, how are members treated who do not live on the homelands? No political history would be complete without addressing the topic of tribal funds and tribal jobs. The tribe has had accounts with the U.S. Treasury since the 1820s. Moreover, the tribe has almost continually pressed monetary claims against the United States and the states of New York and Massachusetts since the 1820s. Who decided to pursue those claims? Who received cash payments and on what basis? Who decided on the allocation of funds? Similarly, when the tribe hired its own members for employment, who got the jobs? The issue of law and order, or more precisely, jurisdiction over criminal and civil matters on the Stockbridge-Munsee homelands, was a frequent issue in tribal politics. Who administered justice, the tribe or outsiders? Who exercised the power of life and death and incarceration? How did competing jurisdictions understand the laws applying to tribal members?

The Mohicans define themselves today in large part as the people who refused to vanish. Instead of dying out in 1757, as Cooper treated them in prose, the community continues its American Indian identity in Wisconsin. From the modern Mohican point of view, there is no "last" of the Mohicans, and if the community has its way, there never will be. Furthermore, the community sees itself as an Indian nation of firsts, not lasts. The Mohicans can claim "first" status in a number of ways. They have maintained a continuous identity as an Indian people for nearly four hundred years, despite constant contact and political relations with Europe and later the United States. That is a span of time longer than any other Eastern

Algonquin people. The Mohicans were also the first to experience numerous initiatives in U.S. federal Indian policy. The Mohicans were among the first tribes to acquire fluency in the English language, creating a rich documentary record. The Stockbridges and Munsees were also two of the first tribes to embrace Christianity and reshape it to fit their own experiences. Each of the "great awakenings" in American religious and social history has particularly touched the Mohicans.[18]

In addition, the tribe experienced earlier than most other American Indian tribes the pressures of forced assimilation through mission posts and boarding schools. The tribe was one of the first to suffer land loss through flawed federal policies, including the allotment process, whereby communally owned tribal landholdings were dissolved in favor of individual Indian land parcels. In 1934 they were the first to seek a new tribal government under the Indian Reorganization Act, and in more recent years, the Stockbridge-Munsees have been in the vanguard of efforts across Indian Country to make use of new casino revenues to rebuild and revitalize tribal infrastructure and culture.

The most basic truth of the history of the Stockbridge-Munsee Mohicans is that the tribe would not have survived as a nation of Chingachooks and Uncases. Such a nation would not have had the political skills to confront each new challenge. To the contrary, the Mohicans produced generations of leaders who have engaged in every form of politics. The form and substance of Mohican politics from the War of 1812 to the present is the subject of this book. Politics has been a primary occupation of the tribe at least since the War of 1812, and the Stockbridge-Munsees truly are a nation of statesmen. I take that label literally as a description of Mohican history—the pursuit of politics and statecraft—and I explain their ethnic survival as an American Indian people through their ceaseless engagement with politics, on all levels.

CHAPTER 2

The Paternalist Policy of the Great Fathers, 1815–1832

After the American Revolution, the Mohicans chose to leave their homes in Stockbridge, Massachusetts, for central New York, where they lived alongside the Oneida Indians. The Stockbridge Mohicans had two names for their new homeland, New Stockbridge, in honor of their old Berkshire home, and "Moh-he-con-nuk," the name they always gave to their primary settlement. The reasons for the removal from Massachusetts involved land loss to whites and the loss of political power in the town of Stockbridge.[1]

In addition to welcoming the Stockbridge Indians among themselves, the Oneidas opened their lands to the amalgamated New England–New York tribe of Brothertown Indians under the leadership of Rev. Samson Occum. The Stockbridges brought their own missionary with them to the Oneida homelands, Rev. John Sergeant II, son of the first Puritan missionary to the tribe, who arrived in Stockbridge in 1736. The younger Sergeant began his mission at Stockbridge in 1775 and stayed with the tribe during the tumultuous times of the Revolution in New England and New York.[2]

The Stockbridge and Brothertown tribes spent less than forty years at New Stockbridge. Reverend Occum left a record of the migration of 1784 from Connecticut to the Oneida lands until his death in 1792. Reverend Sergeant kept a journal off and on during the more than three decades he lived at New Stockbridge. Rev. Jedediah Morse, yet another Massachusetts divine interested in the Christian Indians, made two visits to New Stockbridge, one in 1796 and one in 1820, that provide some information about the Stockbridges, Brothertowners, and Oneidas. And from the tribal leaders themselves, there is an episodic record of correspondence and other writings, especially from their leader, Capt. Hendrick Aupaumut, a Revolutionary War veteran who had earned an officer's commission with the U.S. Army. The United States maintained distant relations with the Stockbridge and Munsee tribes, negotiating one treaty with them in New York State in 1794. New York State had more direct political relations with the tribes. From these scattered accounts, it is possible to reconstruct a sense of the New York polity.[3]

About 120 Stockbridges left Massachusetts for the Oneida lands in 1785. Even before the Stockbridges left the Housatonic Valley, the Brothertown Indians had left scattered villages on Long Island and in Connecticut and Rhode Island. In 1796 Reverend Morse and another cleric, Jeremy Belknap, counted 300 Stockbridges, 150 Brothertowners, and 628 Oneidas living in central New York. When Morse returned to New Stockbridge on official War Department business in 1820, he found about a 50 percent increase in the population of Oneidas and Stockbridges, the latter now numbering 438. Reverend Morse did not consider that the population was flourishing, but that may have been in contrast to the extraordinary growth in the white populations of New England and New York at the end of the eighteenth and beginning of the nineteenth century. It is significant that the Stockbridges established enough political, economic, and social stability between 1785 and 1820 that their population increased. Clearly, this was no vanishing tribe of Indians.[4]

The Stockbridges began their new lives in New York with the 1785 planting and harvest. At first, the tribe had no landownership rights among the Oneidas. An intertribal agreement between the Oneidas and the Stockbridges was signed at Fort Schuyler, New York, in 1788, granting the Mohicans a thirty-six-square-mile (23,040-acre) tract. Immediately after assuming control of their township, the Stockbridges must have scrambled to feed themselves by a combination of barter and purchase. A receipt from July 1789 shows the "Sachems and Councillors" acquiring 150 bushels of Indian corn, which they would "honorably pay in October next in Gingseng Roots."[5]

The Mohicans of New Stockbridge dealt with the state of New York primarily on criminal justice and law enforcement matters. Hendrick

Aupaumut made frequent trips to the state legislature sitting at Albany asking for special laws on behalf of the Stockbridges. For example, in 1797 he asked for a state law criminalizing the sale of alcohol in the state to Indians. Yet living under state jurisdiction could be very frustrating for the Stockbridges. In 1815 a Stockbridge named John W. Jacobs was a victim of "cold blood murder" by a white man, and four years after the crime, the Stockbridges complained to Gov. DeWitt Clinton about the failure of the state to live up to its promises of the 1780s about protecting Indians from crime perpetrated by whites.[6]

The ethnic mix at New Stockbridge became more complicated, at least when reported in the English language, when the Brotherton Band of Delaware Indians (a separate tribe from the southern New England Brothertowners) left New Jersey in 1802 and moved north to live among the Stockbridges. After the move, the Stockbridges petitioned the New York legislature for the construction of two schools to accommodate one hundred Stockbridge and newly arrived Brothertown Indians. The Stockbridges asked for instructors, either "white men or that of our own colour who may be found capable of teaching a school."[7] Throughout the early nineteenth century, scattered families of New York, New Jersey, and New England Indians sought refuge at New Stockbridge and Oneida. Many of these refugee Indians were of mixed Native-African-English-Dutch descent. The Stockbridges opened their homes and lands to these migrants and often adopted them into the tribe.[8]

When the Reverends Belknap and Morse made their visit to New Stockbridge in 1796 they found that the tribe retained possession of the full thirty-six square miles of land. However, this was divided into individually owned parcels, in fee simple as the two clerics reported, although not quite accurately; there was one restriction: tribal members could not sell their land parcels to whites. The reason for dividing common lands into individual parcels—a policy later called allotment—was to encourage individual Indian men to pursue field-crop agriculture. Belknap and Morse reported that in 1796 "two-thirds of men and nine-tenths of women" were productive workers among the Stockbridges. Most significant, the Reverends Belknap and Morse noted meeting Captain Aupaumut, the war hero of the tribe, plowing his fields behind his own team of oxen.[9]

At Oneida, the New England ministers did not find conditions that met with their approval. The Oneida Indian men ridiculed the Stockbridges and Brothertowners for "scratching the soil like hedge-hogs" and, point-edly, for behaving like women. Still, one-third of the Stockbridge men pursued an older economy of "fishing and fowling" and hunting. This one-third of the male population also chose to make money off their lands by leasing them to whites, which circumvented the prohibition on outright land sales but probably violated its spirit. In 1796 the Stockbridges were in the midst of an enormously important social change. Two-thirds of the men had reconceived their gender roles to include settled agriculture and stock-raising—on parcels they owned—as proper men's work. The mis-sionaries were trying to convince Stockbridge women to take up the work of New York farmwives, namely, textile and food production, not basket or bead making. The Brothertowners also had gone through this shift in gender roles, but the Oneidas had not. According to Belknap and Morse, the Oneidas approvingly viewed the Christian God as having given white men the plow for farming and red men the bow and arrow for hunting.[10]

By 1820, when Morse returned for an inspection visit, he found the Stockbridges "more advanced in the knowledge of our language, and in civilization, than any Indians in our country." By the term "civilization," Morse meant the whole set of religious beliefs, family and gender roles, educational attainment, and material culture that characterized northern whites. Yet despite the population increase from 300 to 438, Morse reported without comment that the lands owned by Stockbridges had declined in total area to just 17,000 acres. According to John N. Davidson's interviews with Stockbridge descendants in the 1890s, the state of New York bought 4,500 acres from individual Indians in 1813. Between Morse's two visits, the tribal land base, even if in individual ownership, had shrunk by one-fourth. An increasing population and a shrinking land base was not a good formula for long-term community stability.[11]

Regarding organized religion, many Stockbridges in the 1780s preferred listening to the Mohegan Reverend Occum preach than to their own Reverend Sergeant. This rivalry may be attributed in part to the arrival of the former at the Oneida site before the latter. For more than a year, the Stockbridge advance emigrants listened to Reverend Occum preach and found his lessons preferable to those of their old minister. Reverend Occum believed the great migration west from New England to New York had strong biblical parallels. On leaving Connecticut, he preached a sermon drawing on the descriptions of the Israelites leaving Egypt. Later, at Oneida, he dreamed that the great English evangelist George Whitefield came to him in a dream. He wrote: "[Whitefield] put his face to my face, and rub'd his face to mine and Said, 'I'm glad, that you preach the Excellency of Jesus Christ.'" The dream became even more unusual when Whitefield, in preaching to the assembled Indians, "[b]arked like a Dog with a Thundering Voice."[12]

The rivalry between the Brothertown and Stockbridge missions ended with Occum's death in 1792. Thereafter Reverend Sergeant ministered to both flocks as one mission. What is striking is how few Stockbridges were admitted into full membership in the church and how unbalanced the gender ratio was among them. Membership in the church reflected older Puritan norms, when it was suspicious of those seeking membership and insisted on a long trial of "profession" and an examination on the fine points of Scripture before the congregation. Few Stockbridges could meet the test. Reverends Belknap and Morse noted in 1796 that only five men and twenty-five women were church members, and of that group, two of the men were suspended for drunkenness and one of the women for disorderly conduct. If the total population of New Stockbridge was 300 people, just 27 full church members was a small percentage of even the adult population of the tribe. As late as 1818 at New Stockbridge, Reverend Sergeant could count only four men and ten women as church members. Other accounts, however, indicate that the entire community was expected to attend worship services, which Reverend Sergeant preached in both Mohican and English. The gender imbalance in church membership is consistent with similar patterns from Puritan and, later, Congregational New England. It is also consistent with the older Mohican cultural pattern of matrilineal authority. The anthropologist Ted J. Brasser ventured that the influence of what he called "principal women" was felt in the church and in the alliances that the women made with and through their sons, wives, and brothers.[13]

The Congregationalists did not have a monopoly on religious instruction among the Stockbridges and Brothertowners. The Society of Friends took an active interest in spreading their beliefs among the Indians and offered scholarships to Stockbridge youth who attended boarding schools in Pennsylvania and New York. For example, the future Stockbridge leaders John W. Quinney and Solomon U. Hendricks attended a Quaker boarding school in Westchester County, New York, between 1810 and 1813. Women

Friends made a special effort at outreach to Stockbridge women, going so far as to help to establish the Female Society for Providing Good Morals, Industry and Manufactures among the women of the tribe.[14]

The male leaders of the Stockbridge tribe took part in treaty negotiations with the Washington administration in 1794. The main negotiations were between the United States and the remaining Iroquois tribes in New York State that were friendly to American power. Most of the old Iroquois Confederacy had sided with Great Britain during the Revolutionary War, but the Oneidas and Stockbridges had been on the U.S. side. In small increments the Stockbridges became revised in federal eyes as part of the League of the Six Nations, even though the tribe had been a seventeenth-century adversary of the Mohawks. The Stockbridges were a signatory to the treaty of Canandaigua, which, among other items, provided for a payment of $4,500 in perpetuity to the Six Nations. The Stockbridges were not specifically guaranteed payment in the Canandaigua treaty, at least in the federal view, but in subsequent years the tribe made numerous efforts to secure payment under the treaty, finally gaining success in 1843.[15]

A counterinterpretation of the Stockbridges as Six Nations member was offered by the historian Alan Taylor. In a 1996 article about Hendrick Aupaumut's career, he found an anti-Iroquois, and particularly an anti-Oneida strain, in Aupaumut's speeches and letters. Taylor maintains that Aupaumut's dealings with the trans-Ohio tribes in the years 1791–93 are best understood as an attempt to help the western Indians but also to help his own Mohicans become more independent of the Oneidas in New York and to gain favor with the United States to press old land claims. Taylor has Aupaumut look into the future in 1791 and determine that the New Stockbridge location could not be maintained for the Mohicans. "If further removal west was inevitable," Taylor wrote of Aupaumut, "he meant to manage its pace, location, and circumstances in order to preserve the Mohican nation."[16]

A picture of the New York polity begins to emerge. The Stockbridges lived in a rural township with a population density of eight to twelve people per square mile. Perhaps fifty families lived in single-family frame houses. The clan system of Mohican organization had been discarded in the 1730s at Stockbridge, and instead political leadership was expressed through township officeholding and external diplomacy with the Oneidas, Brother-towners, trans-Ohio tribes, and United States. The Mohicans became accustomed to living in an intertribal and multiethnic area. Individual migrants and sometimes their families from other tribes could find a new tribal home at New Stockbridge among the Mohicans. Women dominated the church and together with their husbands, sons, and brothers redefined masculine identity to include agriculture and stock-raising. The male heads of families such as the Hendrickses, Quinneys, Konkapots, and Metoxens had ruled at Stockbridge, Massachusetts, and continued to hold sway at New Stockbridge, New York. Each of these families produced a sachem at New Stockbridge.[17]

The rural community that the Mohicans built at New Stockbridge was unstable in the long run, however. The growing population and shrinking land base meant that the tribe would have to acquire more territory elsewhere if it wanted to pass along a landed inheritance to the next generation. More immediately, the Oneida lands of central New York came under great pressure between 1785 and 1820 from New York State and private interests who wanted to bring capitalism to the area. Taylor sees Aupaumut preparing his people to leave New Stockbridge after just a few years of residence among the Oneidas. The historian Laurence Hauptman writes about a "conspiracy of interests" to remove the Oneidas, Senecas, Stockbridges, and Brothertowners.[18]

The War of 1812 provided the Stockbridges with new opportunities for military service to the United States. A score of men from New Stockbridge served four months in the New York militia in 1814. Despite their loyal wartime service, the pro-U.S. New York Indians found themselves in a weakened position. The state was intent on clearing Indian title to lands for reasons of securing the border with British North America, and also to obtain transportation corridors for contemplated roads and canals. Private land companies wanted to remove the Indians around Oneida so that whites could take up the lands. Under this pressure, the Stockbridges as a tribe decided after the close of the war to remove themselves once again.[19]

The first intended destination for the tribe was the Indiana Territory, to join Delaware, Munsee, and Miami Bands of Indians near present-day Muncie, Indiana, in the upper White River Valley. Before 1783, when the trans-Ohio country was under British sovereignty, the Miami Nation extended a welcome to the various New York tribes, including the Delawares, Mohicans, and Munsees, to join them in the White River country. Some bands of mixed Delawares, Munsees, and Mohicans joined the

Miamis in the confused aftermath of the Revolution. This migration to the White River Valley was a part of the forming and re-forming of intertribal Indian groups in the trans-Ohio region. The generosity of the Miamis to the New York tribes was confirmed in land cession treaties of 1805 and 1809 that were signed with the United States.[20]

The Stockbridges of Massachusetts and later of New York kept alive the memory of the Miami offer. The White River area was well known to Sachem Aupaumut, who had made diplomatic visits to the trans-Ohio region in the 1790s and 1800s before the outbreak of the War of 1812. Aupaumut visited the White River villages in 1802, and, according to one account, preached the Christian gospel to eight hundred gathered Delaware Indians. He called on old memories of cooperation between the various Algonquian-speaking people and used what Taylor calls a mix of diplomacy, history, and genealogy to tie the interests of the Mohicans to those of the western Indian nations. He called the Shawnees "younger brothers." He referred to the Miamis as "fathers" and to the Delawares as "grandfathers," recalling a seventeenth-century alliance between the Mohicans and Delawares back in New Netherlands.[21] Most important, Aupaumut secured confirmation from President Thomas Jefferson in December 1808 of the Stockbridge joint occupancy rights in the Delaware-Miami lands in the Indiana Territory. President Jefferson and Secretary of War Henry Dearborn received a written account from Aupaumut and an oral confirmation from one of the Miami leaders in late 1808 and then acknowledged the reports. As the Mohicans later recounted their own actions and those of Jefferson and Dearborn:

> A part of our nation . . . removed to these lands and possessed them, with the Delawares and Munsees, and made large improvements on them at great expense to the nation, to prepare them for us. . . . It was put into writing, on parchment[,] . . . and was sealed with the seal of your nation, and subscribed and witnessed by our father, Thomas Jefferson, and Henry Dearborn, one of your chief counsellors.[22]

At the time of Aupaumut's 1802 visit, half a dozen Mohican families had accepted the offer of the Delawares to move among them. It might be an exaggeration to say that those six families had been working for fifteen years to prepare the White River lands for the great body of the Mohicans, but the connection was certainly remembered in 1817, when two new families left New Stockbridge to join the Delaware-Munsee-Mohican settlement on the White River.

In 1818 the tribe authorized John Metoxen to lead a party of seventy-five Stockbridges to relocate to the White River lands and secure a place for all the scattered Mohicans. Alas for the poor Stockbridges, the Delawares and Miamis had just concluded a land cession treaty with the United States in October 1818 by which they ceded and relinquished all rights to their lands on the White River to the United State. According to the U.S. Indian agent to the Miamis and Delawares, the Mohicans in New Stockbridge were invited to attend the treaty council at St. Mary's, Ohio, but the tribe declined, preferring instead to send written instructions to the Delawares to sell no land to the United States and to hold a 400-square-mile tract for the New Stockbridge Mohicans. Unfortunately for the Mohicans, the U.S. Indian agent refused to transmit their instructions to the Delawares, who in the absence of Mohican negotiators signed a land cession treaty with the United States and prepared to move to the trans-Missouri territory, in present-day Kansas. The Indian agent encouraged the Delawares to invite the Mohicans of New Stockbridge to move to the trans-Missouri lands. In the agent's words, "I think their best interests will be promoted by so doing. They cannot be preserved in what is called reservations. The intemperate use of ardent spirits is destroying them rapidly."[23]

The idea of a new Moh-he-con-nuk on the White River disappeared with the Delaware land cession treaty of 1818. The Metoxen band of Stockbridges lived among the Ohio and Indiana intertribal and multiethnic villages for several years, with no money for returning to New York and uncertain prospects of a new permanent home in the West. An 1819 report placed them at Picqua, Ohio, with "not one Dollar amongst the whole of them." They later moved to Shawneetown, Ohio, where they were reported to be "in a Starving Condition."[24]

It is striking to read the contemporary accounts of the Mohicans of New Stockbridge about their plans for leading the proposed alliance of Delawares and Munsees and Miamis, Potawatomis, and others in the trans-Ohio region. The messianic and revitalization sentiments are clear, as Aupaumut and the head men at New Stockbridge wrote of their plans:

> In the last year our nation looked with pain on the situation of our brethren in the west. We saw them lying in darkness and Paganism,

and believed that our God called upon us to send among them a colony of our nation, in which was built up a church of our Lord and Saviour, that we might be the means of civilizing and christianizing them, and doing them great good. . . . We hoped to aid greatly in spreading over this whole island, even to the great western waters, the fruits of religion and civilization, that all our red brethren might partake of them and be made happy, our God adored, and his kingdom advanced.[25]

The Mohicans of New Stockbridge launched a lobbying campaign in 1819 for Congress to reverse its approval of the St. Mary's treaty but without success. The Mohicans proved tenancious, however. For the next twenty years, they held to their claim to a part of the proceeds the United States paid for the White River land cession.

After learning about the failure of the White River expedition, the Mohicans of New Stockbridge turned their attention in a new direction, toward the trans–Lake Michigan country, which the sachem, Solomon U. Hendricks, saw as a likely destination for all the New York Indians, not just the Stockbridges. Hendricks emphasized the unhealthy state of life at New Stockbridge as a result of the increasing presence of white whiskey sellers and drunken white neighbors. Hendricks argued that the moral regeneration of the tribe depended on physical removal to the West, out of the reach of whites and their liquor.[26]

As was contemplated in the White River plans, the Mohicans of New Stockbridge would "Christianize" and "civilize" the aboriginal tribes to the territory west of Lake Michigan. The two terms carried overlapping symbolic meanings. "Christianize" meant to accept but adapt Protestantism from a white missionary but worship in the Mohican language. One of the great cultural projects of the first decade at New Stockbridge was undertaken by Joseph Quinney and Hendrick Aupaumut in translating the Puritan 1648 "Westminster Assembly's Shorter Catechism" into Mohican. The involvement in the Quinney translation project was almost a hereditary role in the tribe. Quinney's grandfather had served as the first translator of John Sergeant's sermons at Stockbridge, Massachusetts, in the 1730s. To "Christianize" also meant to practice temperance and avoid whiskey. In 1818 Reverend Sergeant founded the Temperance Society at New Stockbridge, which quickly gained more members than the church itself.[27]

The term "civilize," as used to describe the Stockbridges and by the Stockbridges themselves meant a complex set of behaviors and attitudes. The idea of hierarchies of civilization gained currency in the eighteenth century as a replacement for the older dichotomy believer/heathen. According to the philosophers of the Scottish Enlightenment, societies could be classified on four ascending levels of civilization: (1) "rude," or barbarian, ones that lived by the chase and by war and plunder; (2) "pastoral" ones that depended on the tending of livestock herds over the commons for support; (3) agricultural ones that respected the division of lands into private property; and (4) urban ones such as Edinburgh itself where the arts and sciences could fluorish. Americans, especially Jeffersonians, did not always accept the idea of the fourth stage as the highest, but they venerated settled agriculture practiced by men on their own plots of land as a mark of civilization. Thus in 1796 when the Reverends Belknap and Morse saw Hendrick Aupaumut plowing his fields behind his own team of oxen, they beheld a man of civilization. The other side of the gendered understanding of civilized society was that women labored at home, especially in textile and food production. They did not grow field crops but instead practiced horticultural gardening.[28]

Americans of the early Republic looked on most American Indians as "rude" or "wild," and therefore uncivilized. The exceptions, such as the "Five Civilized Nations" of the South or the Mohicans of New Stockbridge, were viewed differently. They might still be forced to remove to the West, ostensibly for fear that they would become addicted to white alcohol and other vices and thereby fall down the ladder of civilization. But the civilized Indian tribes could also be used as missionary societies in their own right among the western tribes. This plan existed in embryonic form in the White River emigration scheme, but it came full flower in the trans–Lake Michigan plan of the 1820s.

The Stockbridge missionary Sergeant took up the plan and used his connections in the network of New England missionaries to lobby the federal government for the plan. In 1820 the War Department appointed Reverend Morse—the New Stockbridge chronicler of 1796—to make a 3,000-mile journey from New Haven to Green Bay and back to report on conditions in Indian Country. It took Morse more than three months to cover the distance, and he spent more than two weeks scouting Green Bay as a likely location for the New York tribes. The Morse Report, submitted in 1820 but not printed widely until 1822, contemplated a new Indian territory bounded by Lake Michigan on the east, Lake Superior on the north, the Illinois Territory border on the south, and the Mississippi River on the west. In short, the expected Indian homeland closely overlapped what later became the territory and state of Wisconsin. This was to be a racialized territory for Indians alone. Morse advised the secretary of war, "Let regulations be made to prohibit the introduction of white settlers within the limits of this territory."[29] There would be no tide of white land seekers pressing against Indian villages. There would be no white whiskey sellers to undo the work of the Christianizers and civilizers. And the physical geography of the proposed territory would be a guarantee. As one Stockbridge supporter, Rev. Calvin Colton, wrote grandiloquently: "The white man will never go there. He will never desire these lands. They are too far off. And besides, there is a natural boundary, the Great Lakes to defend you ever from such incursions."[30]

The territorial governor of Michigan, Lewis Cass, also signed on to the Morse plan in late 1820—but for reasons of law and order and national security rather than from a desire for Christianizing and civilizing. In November 1820 Cass wrote to Secretary of War John C. Calhoun advising against an attempt to secure a land cession from the Menominees:

> The effect therefore of extinguishing Indian title to this large tract of land, independent of pecuniary stipulations, which may be made, is, that it is thrown open to every adventurer, who may choose to enter it. . . . But there is another consideration of much weight upon this subject. I have reason to believe that the Six Nations from New York would select a part of this Country for their residence, and the policy of permitting them to do it, cannot be doubted. . . . It is very desirable to place them in that Country. Their habits & the strong pecuniary ties, which bind them to the United States would ensure their fidelity, and they would act as a check upon the Winnebagoes, the worst affected of any Indians upon our borders.[31]

In a remarkably short time, the trans–Lake Michigan territory around Green Bay came under the close scrutiny of U.S. political leaders. Nominally, the United States had acquired sovereignty to the region at the 1783 Peace of Paris agreement with Great Britain. On the ground, the Menominees and Ho-Chunks living west of Lake Michigan were clearly allied with British North America. During the War of 1812, the United States was driven out of Chicago and Prairie du Chien; there was no garrison at Green Bay to drive out. Instead the Indians and French-Indian Métis of the region helped their British and Indian neighbors in Michigan to attack and capture the American fort at Mackinac in 1812 and to hold it throughout the war.[32]

In the aftermath of the war, the United States embarked on a diplomatic effort to repair relations with the Indian nations of the old Northwest. To disrupt relations between the Menominees and Ho-Chunks with British North America, U.S. policy makers decided to establish a fort at Green Bay. Acting Secretary of War Alexander Dallas made plans in June 1815 for "an Indian agency on the Fox River, in the neighbourhood of Green Bay . . . that the establishment, so formed, shall be a military station." Dallas continued, "A display of the power of the United States in that remote quarter would be productive of Salutary effects upon the minds of the Indians."[33]

A new U.S. Indian agent, Col. John Bowyer, arrived at the Bay to oversee relations with the Menominees and the Ho-Chunks and to establish an agency at the Army's new Fort Howard post at the mouth of the Fox River. For several years, the army was content to occupy Fort Howard without seeking to acquire title to the surrounding lands. In 1819 Colonel Bowyer sought to sign a treaty with the Menominees and Ho-Chunks in which the tribes would cede lands on both sides of the Fox River for fourteen miles. The Menominees and Ho-Chunks did not favor this idea, and neither did Secretary Calhoun in Washington. The economy-minded secretary wrote to Bowyer: "The department is not desirous of obtaining a cession of this tract of country, unless it can be done at a very moderate expense." And the tribes stated that they allowed Colonel Bowyer the small tract on which the fort sat but no more.[34]

Thus the timing of Morse's 1820 report coincided with a federal decision not to pursue large-scale purchases of land from the Menominees and Ho-Chunks. After receipt of Reverend Morse's enthusiastic report about the possibilities of the Green Bay area, the Monroe administration was receptive to the possibility of an intertribal Indian removal from New York westward. That summer of 1820 the Menominees expressed their displeasure with Colonel Bowyer's would-be treaty and made clear that they would not cede the Fox River waterway. They also made clear their unhappiness about the idea of the New York Indians moving to the Menominee homeland. Still, Morse, Sergeant, and others interested in the plan saw the advantages of sending Christian Indians to the Menominee and Ho-Chunk homelands as an example of preferred religious, social, and political behavior for the Wisconsin tribes. No greater contrast existed, thought Reverend Morse, between the Christian Mohicans and their "wild" brethren.[35]

The French-speaking settlers at Green Bay, known at the time as Canadians or French-Indians and by scholars today as Métis, had their own qualms about the proposed in-migration of New York Indians. The Métis had thought their land titles were secured by the 1795 Jay treaty between the United States and Great Britain. An 1807 act of Congress confirmed the legality of their holdings. But now, in 1820, they besieged Congress and the administration with petitions, memorials, and letters demanding acknowledgment of their land claims that suddenly were endangered by Colonel Bowyer's treaty making. In 1820 Congress passed legislation authorizing the appointment of special commissioners to examine the title claims of French-speaking settlers at various points in the Northwest, including Green Bay. The commissioners journeyed to the Bay, took testimony, made a plat map of the claims, and reported back to Congress in 1823. What Congress knew as the "French private claims" soon came into conflict with the claims of the New York Indians and with the claims of the army garrison at Fort Howard in one of the most complicated land title tangles in the history of the early Republic.[36]

What happened after the failure of the Bowyer treaty of 1819 did not follow the usual pattern of U.S. handling of Indian land questions. The overlap between sovereignty and ownership in the United States was understood in a definite way after ratification of the Constitution in 1787. The United States claimed sovereignty over the territory ceded to it by Great Britain in 1783; however, the United States respected Indian occupancy of lands in the United States. "Indian Country" was that part of the United States where the land had not passed from Indian occupancy. And furthermore, after passage of the 1790 Non-Intercourse Act, only the United States had the legal right to buy title to Indian land and thereby end the Indian right of occupancy.[37] Federal officials from the beginning of the Washington administration understood that a binding land cession treaty was needed to transfer title of Indian Country to the United States. The lands would then enter the public domain, which after

1812 had its own agency, the General Land Office, to manage the survey and sale and transfer of title into private ownership. Thus early in the history of the Republic the United States established this sequential pattern of the westward movement: internation land cession treaty, survey of the public domain, sale of the public lands, conveyance of title to private property, settlement. The federal government was the indispensable middleman in the process; the alternative was whites invading Indian Country for mineral riches, for farmland, or for other reasons, and experience showed that such illegal invasions and occupations inevitably led to conflict and bloodshed. Despite thirty years of experience with this process, the United States fumbled the negotiations for obtaining land from the Menominees and Ho-Chunks and for guaranteeing the rights of the Métis at Green Bay. Instead of the War Department instructing Colonel Bowyer to renegotiate the abortive treaty of 1819 so as to accommodate the New York Indians, the administration left the New York Indians to make their own best deal.[38]

In summer 1821 a delegation of fourteen New York Indians negotiated with the Menominees and Ho-Chunks. Six of the fourteen were Stockbridges: Wahaunowaunmust (Solomon U. Hendrick), Wausaunah (Jacob Konkapot), Wenowaomang (Abner Hendrick), Chiksokin (Jacob Chicks), Naukahwah (Robert Konkapot), and Katakonkapont (Rufus Turkey). The dual listing of the Stockbridge delegates' names in Algonquian and English is testimony to their ability to serve as brokers between two cultures. Albert Ellis, a white man, accompanied the Six Nations leader, a St. Regis Mohawk minister named Eleazar Williams. Governor Cass from Detroit sent his personal secretary, C. C. Trowbridge, along on the mission and also instructed the new Indian agent at Green Bay to assist the New York tribes. The Wisconsin tribes expressed reluctance to accommodate potentially thousands of New York Indians, so instead an agreement was reached whereby the New York tribes would have a wide swath of land on the Fox River, midway between Green Bay and Lake Winnebago. The formal treaty language required the Menominees and Ho-Chunks to "Cede, Release, and QuitClaim" the lands "forever," to the New York Indians, reserving only the right to hunt and fish on the ceded territory. For this tract, the New York tribes paid $500 down and promised $1,500 the next year. The Stockbridge part of the delegation put up most of the money.[39]

The 1821 land cession was highly unusual because it was from two Indian tribes to an Indian confederacy. Still, the New York tribes were not done attempting to acquire a landed domain in the Menominee homeland. They decided that the 1821 agreement "did not contain sufficient room for the convenient settlement of the several tribes concerned in it." The next summer, 1822, Reverend Williams and the Stockbridge and Six Nations delegates returned to Green Bay to negotiate a larger land cession from the Menominees and Ho-Chunks. Unlike in 1821, this New York Indian delegation to Green Bay included a representative of the Munsees, who asked to join in the proposed move to the West.[40]

The Ho-Chunks wanted no part of any treaty with the New York tribes and promptly walked out of the initial August 1822 meeting at Green Bay. The Menominees, however, reached an understanding with the New York Indian delegates. On September 22, 1822, the Menominees signed an agreement to share their lands in common with the New York tribes and in return accepted an offering of $1,000 in gifts at the treaty signing, with another $2,000 in gifts pledged over the following two years. Aside from the gifts given, the New York Indian plan was similar to the old White River understanding: lands of the host tribe would be shared in common with the incoming New York Indians and could not be alienated to the United States without joint agreement.[41]

The Stockbridge members of the New York Indian delegation of 1822 spoke with the Menominees in a form of the Algonquian language that both peoples understood. The Mohicans called the Menominees their "grandchildren" and frequently reminded their hosts that the onetime Outagamie ("Fox") residents of the Green Bay region had invited the Mohicans to live among them in the 1730s. The call of old ties apparently helped to smooth the discussions in summer 1822. In addition, the New York Indian delegates stressed that they had experience with the whites. As one told the Menominees and Ho-Chunks, "The knives of the pale men were sharp and their nails were long and when fastened upon the lands of the Indians, they went deep and held fast."[42]

The New York tribes told the Menominees that they—the New York Indians—knew how to prevent those long fingernails from any future takings of Menominee lands. In effect, the Mohicans and the other New York tribes were acting in a fashion diametrically opposed to what the United States and the American Board of Foreign Missions had anticipated. Instead of passing American values to the Wisconsin tribes, the New

York Indians sought to help the Menominees, at least, hold onto their lands in common against the Americans. Alan Taylor discerned the same pattern in Hendrick Aupaumut's behavior thirty years before, when he tried to negotiate an agreement between the United States and the trans-Ohio tribes, especially the Delawares. Aupaumut told the Delawares in 1793, "You will be able to hold your lands to the latest generation." Taylor observed that the Americans thought they were using Aupaumut to advance their own territorial interests; however, Aupaumut "believed that he was using them to secure Indian persistence."[43]

The problem with the 1822 intertribal treaty lay in its interpretation. Did sharing lands in common mean that the Menominees would co-own their tract of seven million or so acres in present-day Wisconsin with the New York Indians? Or did it mean that the Menominees merely consented to allow the New York tribes to move to lands occupied by the Menominees and "build their fires" among them? The New York Indians thought they had purchased co-ownership rights to seven million acres at a price of just four cents per 100 acres. The Menominees thought they had acquired $3,000 in gifts in return for a magnanimous offer to let the New Yorkers live in their homelands.

The differing interpretations soon led to a dispute. By 1823 the Menominees had repudiated the New York Indian understanding of the agreement. And back in New York, most of the Six Nations also repudiated their negotiators, not because of the terms of the deal, but because most of the Six Nations did not want to leave New York. Only the Stockbridges were determined to move to the Green Bay region, to be joined by groups of Oneidas and Munsees. The main body of Six Nations Indians remained in New York after 1822 or moved west into British North America, in present-day Ontario.

The Métis settlers at Green Bay protested the 1822 treaty and pointed out the flaws of the intertribal agreement. They signed a mass petition on February 4, 1823, against the agreement, then followed that with additional, frequent remonstrances to the president and Congress against the plan for the migration of the New York Indians. The Métis noted that Rev. Eleazar Williams had no authority to negotiate for the Six Nations, that the Menominees who signed the treaty had no authority to do so, and that the United States was not a signatory party to the treaty. A November 1823 petition from the Green Bay Métis read:

En Septembre 1822 le Ministre Williams conclu un traite Entre les Stockbridges qu'il representoit Et les Follesavoines et Puants, il en Statua lui meme les clauses, sans la participation de ces deux nations, qui n'y furent representi par aucune personne instruit, Etablie a cet Effet la saine partie de la nation follesavoine S'y est refuse et les puants revoquant en doute, que leurs intentions aiente ete exprimees dans la traite Ecrit; parce qu'ils N'ont pu obtenir un interprette de leur Choix. Le traite ainsi trace tel que le Ministre Williams la trouve avantageux a Ses dessiens a ete signe par quelque Miserables rebuts de la nation follesavoine: temoigne par le militaire qui N'etoit pas present, Ce qui a ete observe par un des officiers.[44]

The Stockbridges immediately countered the French-speaking settlers at the Bay, asking Reverend Morse to use his influence with the War Department to have the claims of the New York Indians upheld and the plan for the intertribal territory at Green Bay sustained. Despite the protests from the Métis at Green Bay, President Monroe gave his assent in March 1823 to the Menominee–New York Indian agreeement. He concurred with the New York Indians on their understanding of co-ownership of the Menominee lands, but he limited the area shared to lands north and west of the Fox River, "that quantity being deemed sufficient for the use" of the New York Indians. And for the rest of the Monroe administration, the War Department officially supported the claims of the New York Indians.[45]

Once the Mohicans decided to leave New Stockbridge, they increased the pace of land cession agreements with New York State. The two parties signed half a dozen agreements between 1822 and 1830 to transfer owner-ship to the state of land parcels in New Stockbridge. Each group that left New Stockbridge for Green Bay sold another parcel as a means of financ-ing the emigration. Reverend Sergeant noted that the tribal landholdings were reduced to just "5 or 6,000 a[cres] of land left" in January 1824, a reduction of two-thirds from Morse's visit in 1820.[46]

The first Stockbridge settlers in the Green Bay region selected a site in fall 1822 on the east bank of the Fox River where the rocks and rapids impeded boat navigation farther upstream to Lake Winnebago (map 2). The Métis name for the site was Grand Kakalin, known today as Kaukauna. This site guaranteed to bring lots of traffic past them and also had commercial possibilities as a transshipment point and as a mill site.

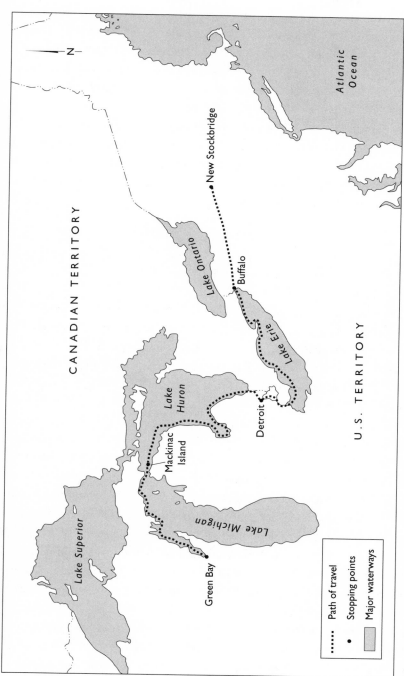

Map 2. Stockbridge-Munsee migration, 1822–1830: New Stockbridge to Green Bay

The Mextoxen group of Stockbridges, which had traveled throughout Indiana and Ohio, joined the settlement at Grand Kakalin in 1823. So, too, did another group of Stockbridges, some Munsees, and a small number of Oneidas, who removed to the Fox River Valley in 1823. This amalgamated party chose a settlement nearby at Little Kakalin (present-day Little Chute).[47]

In September 1823, back at New Stockbridge, the Mohicans entered into yet another intertribal treaty, this time with the neighboring Brothertown Indians. The September 23 agreement provided for the Brothertown Indians to pay the Stockbridge $500 for the right "to be considered as a component part of the Muhheconnuck or Stockbridge nation to all the lands comprehended within and described in the two treatees [sic] made at Green Bay." In 1824 and 1825 more of the New York Indians arrived at Green Bay, notably a group of Oneidas who took up a settlement along Duck Creek, on the west side of the Fox River, six miles from the army post at Fort Howard.[48]

Emigration to Green Bay could be a haphazard (and hazardous) undertaking. Among the 1823 emigrants were about fifty men, according to Reverend Sergeant, and they carried only enough food for one month. When they arrived at Green Bay, they had to provide for their own food and "live on fish and wild meat thro the winter."[49] The Mohicans and the other New York migrants called the new settlement at Grand Kakalin "Statesburg." Reverend Sergeant did not make the trip with his Mohican congregation; he died in New York in September 1824. For several years, the only minister to the New York tribes in the new Wisconsin settlements was the erratic Rev. Eleazar Williams. Then, in 1827, the Scottish Board of Foreign Missions agreed to underwrite a Presbyterian mission to the Stockbridges, Munsees, and assorted other peoples at Statesburg-on-the-Fox. Rev. Jesse Miner took up the first mission ministry in 1828, but death cut short his calling in 1829. His replacement, Rev. Cutting Marsh, served from 1830 through 1848. Under Reverend Miner's supervision, the Stockbridges constructed a log church that housed as many as three hundred worshippers. Many years later, the young son of Reverend Miner recalled the white men of Green Bay who journeyed to the Grand Kakalin to help John Metoxen build the mission house, especially a young man named Daniel Whitney who had just begun a career in business and politics in the Michigan Territory.[50] The Stockbridges of Statesburg also began the first public school in the trans–Lake Michigan region in 1828, taught by a Stockbridge woman, Electa Quinney.[51]

The War Department asked its agent for periodic population estimates of the Indians in the Green Bay region. Colonel Brevoort, the Indian agent at Green Bay in 1825, reported that there were exactly 2,408 Menominees and 4,003 Ho-Chunks in his jurisdiction. He did not report the population of the New York Indian migrants. An 1828 population count by the Green Bay agent listed 270 Stockbridges at Grand Kakalin, 70 Oneidas at Duck Creek, and an unknown number of Brothertowners at Little Kakalin. By contrast, in New York State the populations were 300 Stockbridges still at New Stockbridge, 1,100 Oneidas, 360 Brothertowners, and 300 St. Regis Mohawks. These were the tribes that had started migrating to the Green Bay region. (See map 3.) Another 3,000 Senecas and Tuscaroras still lived in New York State and had no interest in moving to Green Bay. In all, the War Department counted 4,870 Indians living in New York in 1820.[52]

In the early years of the Statesburg settlement, law and order was maintained by the Stockbridges themselves. Congress established a federal territorial district court in 1823, covering the trans–Lake Michigan counties of Michilimackinac, Brown, and Crawford in the new Territory of Michigan, with James Duane Doty appointed the first district judge. That jurist, however, soon came to the conclusion that there was no U.S. jurisdiction in his three counties, since the land remained entirely Indian Country. He enforced this view in 1825, when he ordered the release of a bootlegger and whiskey seller held by the army at Fort Howard and went so far as to have the officers at the post indicted on kidnapping charges. The judge's ruling that the fort itself was illegally situated on Menominee land led to a political crisis. Similarly, Judge Doty ruled in 1826 that there was no federal jurisdiction over the Stockbridges at Statesburg. That October, Doty notified Secretary of State Henry Clay that he had no way to hold "a Stockbridge Indian, for the murder of a female of his tribe, at a place within the boundaries of the country owned by that tribe." Only a ratified treaty that ended Indian occupancy and secured U.S. title could bring U.S. jurisdiction to Green Bay.[53]

Visitors to Statesburg found a settlement with fenced land parcels, crops planted, livestock tended, a log church and school in operation, and the building of a grist mill and sawmill, using the falling water of the Fox at Grand Kakalin. The Statesburg settlement had the makings of a successful

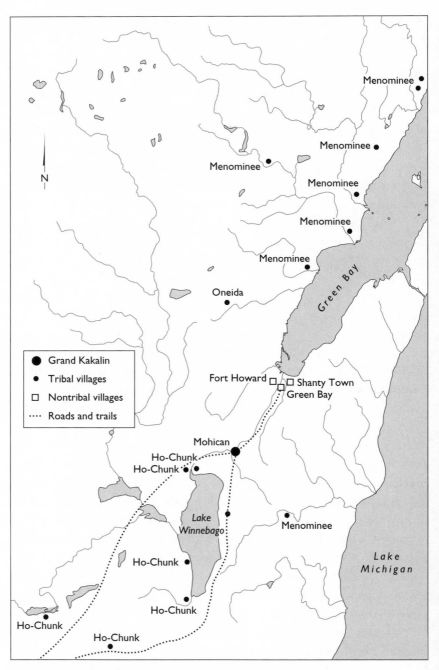

Map 3. The Mohicans' new environment: Wisconsin in 1825

venture for the Mohicans from New Stockbridge and the White River misadventure. But like the army garrison at Fort Howard, what was missing was clear title to the lands along the Fox River.[54]

At the beginning of the Adams administration in 1825, the head of the newly created Office of Indian Affairs (OIA) in the War Department reiterated the position of the Monroe administration in favor of the claims of the New York Indians under the 1821 and 1822 agreements. Thomas L. McKenney went so far in 1825 as to ask the secretary of war to direct the commander of the Fort Howard garrison to use "[m]ilitary force under his command" against the French-speaking Métis settlers at Green Bay who were urging the Menominees to void the intertribal treaties:

> The conduct of these settlers from the representation which has been made of it, is highly reprehensible & cannot be suffered by the Government with impunity. . . . It is very important to preserve peace between the Indians at Green Bay & the New York Indians who may join them the arrangements between them to this effect having been made with the Sanction of the Government, gives them a peculiar claim to protection against the arts of designing & intermeddling white men.[55]

The War Department in the Adams administration shifted its focus to mediating territorial claims between rival Indian groups in the trans–Lake Michigan region. In 1825 Supt. William Clark of the War Department and Gov. Lewis Cass of the Michigan Territory held a late-summer council at Prairie du Chien to which they invited all the Northwest tribes. The main task was to compel the Ojibwes and Dakotas to agree on territorial boundaries and to halt their longtime warfare in the upper Mississippi Valley. Three thousand Indians met the two U.S. commissioners that August 1825, but just as important, many other bands skipped the parley. Governor Cass returned to the Northwest the next summer, this time accompanied by the OIA head, Thomas McKenney. The Americans met some of the Ojibwes who had boycotted the Prairie du Chien gathering at Fond du Lac at the head of Lake Superior, up the St. Louis River a few miles from present-day Duluth, Minnesota. At the Fond du Lac meeting, the Ojibwes confirmed the 1825 understanding of their southwestern boundary with the Dakotas. A second task of establishing the eastern boundary between the Ojibwe and Menominee country got postponed to yet another summer, 1827, at Green Bay.[56]

By that time the southwestern part of the trans–Lake Michigan territory, known as Iowa County, was beset by violence between in-migrating white squatters looking for mineral wealth and the Ho-Chunk ("Winnebago") owners and occupants of the lands. Murder and retaliatory killing peaked with a small group of Ho-Chunks opening fire on a boat on the Mississippi, which resulted in additional deaths. The Ho-Chunk leader, Red Bird, was soon wanted by territorial officials, who reacted to the violence by labeling it the "Winnebago War" and calling out the Michigan Territorial Militia. This was a fateful decision by federal territorial officials in Detroit and War Department officials in Washington. They might have respected Ho-Chunk rights of occupancy to the "Lead District" in what today covers southwestern Wisconsin, northwestern Illinois, and northeastern Iowa. The War Department could have ordered the army to eject the white squatters. Instead the federal officials did nothing until blood was spilled between the invaders and the invaded, and then they used force against the Ho-Chunk Indians. From the perspective of the United States, any remaining chance that the land that became Wisconsin could yet be kept as intertribal territory ended with the Winnebago War.[57]

What were the Indians of Wisconsin going to do about the invasion of whites? Red Bird's band asked for help from the other Indian nations in Wisconsin. All faced the same choice: join Red Bird in what might develop as a grand intertribal Indian force to oppose the whites and drive them out of the territory or meet McKenney and Cass to talk about further boundary lines and concessions. Almost all chose the latter, including the Stockbridges and other New York Indians. On July 26, 1827, with Red Bird still at large and trying to gather a force, some 1,300 Indians met McKenney and Cass at Buttes des Morts (Hills of the Dead) forty miles upriver from Green Bay. The parties soon reached agreement on drawing the boundary line between the Ojibwe and Menominee countries. In addition, the Menominees agreed to support the claims of the Métis at Green Bay to the "French private claims." The United States then reached agreement with the Menominees to purchase the strip of land along the Fox River from the outlet at Green Bay upstream to Lake Winnebago, with the idea of confirming the "arpents" of the Métis that the U.S. commissioners had studied in 1820 and 1823.[58]

The one sticking point on which McKenney and Cass could not secure agreement among the participants was the status of the New York Indians in Menominee territory and the legality of the 1821 and 1822 treaties. The best the commissioners could do was to secure an agreement to let the president of the United States study the dispute and propose a resolution. On the conclusion of the treaty council at Buttes des Morts, McKenney and Cass called for Indian volunteers to join the Americans in the hunt for Red Bird. On August 23, 1827, a company of Menominees mustered into U.S. service, as did sixty-two Oneidas, Stockbridges, and Munsees as the New York Indian militia. Red Bird and one hundred of his followers surrendered to McKenney upstream at the Fox-Wisconsin portage on September 2, ending the Winnebago War. The Menominees and the New York Indians had made it clear they would side with the United States when called on.[59]

Some of the New York Indians were quite upset with the provision of the Buttes des Morts treaty that transferred some Fox River frontage lands from the Menominees to the United States. A group of New York Indians, including for the first time a subset identified as "Stockbridge and Munsee tribes," sent a petition to the U.S. Senate urging rejection of the Buttes des Morts treaty, precisely because it conflicted with the 1821 intertribal treaty:

> But how great was our surprise and sorrow, when at the late treaty held by his excellency Gov. L. Cass and Col. Thomas L. McKenny, at the Little Butte des Morts, our lands were purchased by them as commissioners of the United States, and thus our hopes of security in this last refuge destroyed. If treaties thus made by us with the approbation of public authority, and confirmed by the same, are to be thus disregarded and trampled on, on what can we rely, or where shall we ever rest? . . . We are not unwilling that our white brethren should have some land in this region, but we entreat you not to suffer our lands to be thus forcibly taken from us, contrary to solemn treaty, and without our consent.[60]

On the question of the status of the New York Indians, President Adams never issued a decision on validating or negating the 1821 and 1822 treaties. His slowness was a result in part of the Senate's failure to ratify the Buttes des Morts treaty until January 1829, near the end of Adams's term. However, the Senate considered the protests of the New York Indians that the Butte des Morts treaty violated their 1821 treaty with the Menominees and Ho-Chunks. In early 1829 the Senate gave its consent to the treaty. On the penultimate day of his presidential administration, March 2, 1829, Adams rather casually signed off on a War Department order setting aside lands at Green Bay for the Fort Howard garrison. No one at Green Bay knew of the presidential order for more than a decade, so stealthily was the decision made.[61]

By the time the Buttes des Morts council was held, Indian Affairs Commissioner Thomas McKenney had given up on the idea of the intertribal grouping in the Green Bay region under New York Indian tutelage. The transition to the Jackson administration in spring 1829 did nothing to cause McKenney to exert any effort on behalf of the grand intertribal region west of Lake Michigan. Instead he came to regard the problem as one of securing enough land from the Menominees to provide a separate homeland for the New York Indians. A letter to a New York land investor, Thomas Ogden, dated January 26, 1829, had McKenney expressing the following views:

> There can be no doubt but upon the judicious fixing of the limits at Green Bay for the New York Indians, in which as far as possible, their own views ought to be consulted, will depend on further emigration from New York. If that work is well, and satisfactorily done . . . I am clearly of the opinion a few years only need transpire to rid New York of its Indian population.[62]

From that point onward, a linkage was made between the size of the Indian population emigrating to Green Bay and the size of a new homeland in the trans–Lake Michigan region for the New York Indians. The final Mohican emigrant group left New Stockbridge, New York, in 1829, guided by John W. Quinney. Among the travelers were Hendrick Aupaumut and his wife. Estimates of the Stockbridge population at Statesburg ranged from a high of 350 to a low of 225.[63]

The new Great Father who took office in March 1829 had no interest in the idea of an Indian territory in the Green Bay region. President Jackson, instead, was more preoccupied with starting a grand Indian territory on the southern Great Plains as the final destination for the southern Indian nations in his Indian removal project. In September 1829 the newly arrived English-speaking inhabitants of Green Bay sent the first of a half-century's worth of petitions to Congress asking for federal spending on a series of canals to link Green Bay to the Atlantic and Gulf ports. Or, as the petitioners said in more sweeping terms, they wanted federal construction money to "form an uninterrupted communication by water from the city of New York to New Orleans, through the interior of the United States," that is, via Green Bay. Suddenly, according to the Green Bay boosters, the "salubrious climate and fertile soils" of the region soon to be known as Wisconsin would become home to a new set of immigrants from the eastern states. Aupaumut's view of an intertribal territory led wisely by the Stockbridges, on the road to Christianity and civilization, was clearly incompatible with the future envisioned by the Green Bay group.[64]

In spring 1830 the Jackson administration finally turned its attention to the Indian Question at Green Bay. Secretary of War John Henry Eaton appointed three treaty commissioners that spring to represent the president in carrying out his 1827 treaty mandate to solve the Menominee–New York Indian dispute. Eaton told his commissioners to gather all the parties at Green Bay in August 1830. Eaton set three goals for the commissioners to accomplish. The first goal was to have the Menominees make a land cession to the United States of their territory on the east side of the Fox River all the way south to the boundary with the Potawatomi territory at Milwaukee and all the way east to Lake Michigan, including the Door Peninsula. In effect, the Menominees were asked to cede and relinquish about three million acres of what in the next century became America's Dairyland. The second task for the commissioners was to get Menominee agreement to a small land cession for the benefit of the garrison at Fort Howard. The secretary made this directive apparently ignorant of the last-minute executive order initiated by President Adams on March 2, 1829. The third task for the three commissioners was to have the Menominees cede and relinquish to the United States a tract of land on the west side of the Fox River as a homeland for the New York Indians. Secretary Eaton gave an explicit formula for establishing the size of the homeland: 100 acres for each New York Indian who settled in the new territory. Based on the population estimates available to the War Department, Eaton thought that the New York Indians could be provided with a tract of about 136,000 acres to satisfy their needs. Under no condition, Eaton warned, was any type of land cession to be made for the New York Indian men that could in any way lead them to abandon agriculture for "the chase."[65]

The three U.S. commissioners, Erastus Root, James McCall, and John Mason, arrived at Green Bay in July 1830 and for several weeks studied maps and documents concerning the disputed region. Three thousand Indians arrived at Green Bay to take part in the treaty negotiations. Stockbridges, Brothertowners, Oneidas, Menominees, Ho-Chunks, and Ojibwes gathered at the "council house" not far from Fort Howard. That sizable a crowd inevitably led to conflicts, and soon enough a soldier from Fort Howard bayoneted a Menominee man. Peace was reestablished only when the "Great Captain" commanding at Fort Howard put his enlisted man in the stockade.[66]

The commissioners invited thirty men to make speeches and present positions for their tribes. The speakers were to use their native languages, and then the commissioners would supply translations into French, English, and Menominee. The Stockbridges selected John Metoxen as their spokesman. He made a lengthy speech in which he advanced three propositions about the history of the dispute. First, he recounted what he recalled as the invitation of the Menominees and Ho-Chunks to the Mohicans to come to Green Bay and live among them as tutors and guides to the new form of civilized life:

> We would all be one people. They promised to leave hunting and fishing, and raise corn like us, and that their women should spin like our women, and that we would become as good and great as white men.[67]

Second, Metoxen blamed the Adams and Jackson administrations for bungling and not supporting President Monroe's endorsement of the 1821 and 1822 treaties. He addressed the three commissioners with a statement and a request:

> Brothers, we did not think our great father, President Monroe would die so soon. We did not think that our great father had so many papers in his table-drawer, that he could not find the one, on which his agreement with us was written. . . . You say your instructions do not allow you to make the treaties [of 1821–22] a rule of settlement. We left our lands in the East country, and came here on the understanding of those treaties. We have trusted entirely to the faith they have pledged to us. If they cannot be depended on, we know not

what to trust. You offer to make a new treaty in the name of our great father. Make the old treaty good, brothers.[68]

The third charge was that the residents of Green Bay, both French-speaking Métis and newly arrived English-speaking Americans, conspired to alienate the affections of the Menominees and Ho-Chunks against the New York Indians. Mextoxen and other Stockbridges of Statesburg pointed especially to the role played by Judge Doty, the federal territorial district judge for the trans-Michigan territory. Doty served as legal adviser to the Menominees at the 1830 treaty council and the Stockbridges resented what they saw as his intrusions:

> We lived in peace with the Winnebagoes and Menominees, and with all the tribes of the North West. Our council fire burnt well, and did not go out. But . . . the white man came in, and threw a big stone against the fire, and scattered the brands among our feet, and knocked them upon our blankets.[69]

Metoxen and the Oneida and Brothertown representatives were adamant in holding fast to the treaties of 1821 and 1822. They advised the Menominees against making any land cession to the United States for such an action would spell the inevitable in-migration of white settlers. The trans–Lake Michigan country would become just another federal territory on the road to statehood. Ohio had been lost by intertribal confederacies this way in the 1790s and Indiana in the 1810s. Metoxen and his fellow Stockbridges held out in 1830 for a different fate and future for the Green Bay region.

The Menominees and their advisers in the Métis and American settlements at Green Bay were just as insistent on repudiating the 1821 and 1822 agreements and not granting a single acre to the New York Indians in the Menominee country. The treaty commissioners adjourned the council at the beginning of September and reported back to the War Department that no agreement could be reached. One of the features of the 1830 treaty council and associated negotiations was the prominent part played by white men who had settled at Green Bay in the 1820s. The historian Alice Smith wrote of "a few men . . . who formed a solid core around which the affairs of Wisconsin Territory revolved." In addition to dominating the political scene in Green Bay, and then Madison in the

1830s, the men Smith studied also had a profound impact on Stockbridge-Munsee affairs for fifty years after the arrival of the Mohicans and Munsees at Grand Kakalin.

Judge Doty was one of these men at the 1830 council, as was his cousin and fellow attorney Morgan L. Martin. The Irish immigrant Henry Baird was another attorney-lobbyist who played a part in treaty politics and New York Indian business. New York migrant Albert Ellis served as the surveyor–land looker for the treaty commissioners and passed up no opportunity to tout the economic advantages of the Menominee country. Finally, young Daniel Whitney was an agent of the American Fur Company in Green Bay and started the first bank west of Lake Michigan.[70]

That fall of 1830 President Jackson and Secretary Eaton decided to summon delegates from the failed Green Bay treaty council to Washington for direct talks at the War Department. The Stockbridges of Statesburg turned to Quinney to represent the nation at the negotiations, which began right after New Year's Day, 1831. For six weeks, the Menominees, Stockbridges, Oneidas, and Brothertowners met each day at the War Department for talks. The white adviser-lobbyist for the Brothertown Indians, Thomas Dean, kept a diary of his stay in Washington in which he noted the status of negotiations at the War Department each day. Some days the delegates met at the White House, where President Jackson took a direct part. For five weeks, the New York Indians held out for the 1821 and 1822 treaties, but despite support from the New York congressional delegation, there was no support forthcoming from the administration. Toward the end of January, Secretary Eaton tired of negotiating, and, according to Dean's diary entry for February 1: "The Secretary required an unconditional submition [sic] of the whole matter to him subject to the approval of the President of the United S." The New York Indians appealed to President Jackson on February 3, but he was determined to impose the settlement suggested by Eaton. That outcome happened on February 8, as Quinney and the other New York Indians "went to the President's house to see the execution of the Treaty between Col. Stambaugh & J. H. Eaton and the Menominees & the Instructions to set off 500,000 acres for the NY Indians."[71]

Samuel Stambaugh, the interim Indian agent at Green Bay, and Eaton, head of the War Department, signed a nation-to-nation treaty only with the Menominees. The terms of the treaty began with the cession of 2.5 million acres in east-central Wisconsin to the United States, for which the United States paid about ten cents an acre. The lands for the army garrison at Fort Howard were finally ceded by the Menominees to the United States in a separate article. Then the Menominees ceded an additional 500,000 acres west and north of the Fox River to the United States for benefit of the New York Indians. The terms of the cession limited ownership and occupancy of the proposed "New York Indian Tract" to 100 acres per Indian and gave the New York tribes just three years to move their five thousand members to Wisconsin. After three years the United States would gauge the numbers moved and, if below five thousand, cause a retrocession of the New York Indian Tract back to the United States in proportion to population. The New York Indian Tract included the main Oneida settlements along Duck Creek on the western side of the Fox River. The February 8, 1831, treaty also had an unusual clause giving the army garrison at Fort Howard off-reservation rights to forage for hay and gather wood for fuel outside the newly created Fort Howard Military Reservation and within the New York Indian Tract.[72]

The New York Indians did not accept the treaty signing on February 8 as a fait accompli. They knew that the Senate would have to ratify the agreement. On February 12 the Indians prepared a "remonstrance against the Treaty." On February 15, 1831, a week after the signing, Quinney submitted a separate petition to the president and to the Senate attacking the treaty's provisions for the New York Indians as "unjust, illegal and oppressive." He still held fast to the 1822 treaty between the New York Indians and the Menominees as the law of the land. On February 17 Secretary Eaton refused one last time to modify the treaty. Two days later the New York tribes submitted their remonstrance to the Senate and also printed it as a pamphlet for public distribution. Their lobbying paid off: the Senate Committee on Indian Affairs tabled the treaty of February 8, 1831, and, moreover, rejected the full-time appointment of Colonel Stambaugh as Indian agent at Green Bay. Quinney went home to report to his tribe on the stalemate.[73]

The February 8, 1831, treaty between the Menominees and the United States did nothing to recognize the Stockbridge and scattered intertribal Indian settlements at Statesburg and Little Kakalin on the east bank of the Fox. Before the treaty there were two ways of looking at the Stockbridge settlement at Statesburg: either it was within the grand comanaged Indian Country of the New York Indians and Menominees, according to

the 1821 and 1822 treaties; or it was a squatter village in Menominee
country, tolerated but just barely. Now, after the signing of the 1831 treaty,
the Stockbridge village at Statesburg was in danger of being just another
squatter village on the unsurveyed public domain of the United States with
no recognized rights of occupancy.

The Oneidas of Duck Creek could accept the New York Indian Tract as
the base for a future, sizable homeland. The Stockbridges could not, and
they told President Jackson directly that they would never live on the swampy
wastelands of the west bank of the Fox. They proudly told the president
and secretary that they were Christian, farming people and could not live
on lands "generally poor and altogether unsuited for agriculture."[74]

The Washington negotiations over the 1831 treaty show the young John
W. Quinney coming to the fore as the leader of the new generation of
Mohican statesmen. Quinney had only moved to Statesburg in summer
1829, but along with John Metoxen he quickly grasped the importance of
defending the new, if recently planted, Mohican outpost on the Fox River.
According to the new missionary minister at Statesburg, Rev. Cutting
Marsh, Quinney and the Mohicans said they feared a move to the New York
Indian Tract because, in addition to its swampy character, it was notorious
for its late spring and early autumn killing frosts.[75]

In November 1831 the tribe sent Quinney and Metoxen back to Washington to continue negotiations for a separate Stockbridge homeland.
Quinney and Metoxen had by now explored the half-million-acre reserve
set aside for the New York Indians and were determined not to have their
people relocated to the tract, despite the fact that "Gen'l Jackson represented it them as being almost one of the finest in the world." As Reverend
Marsh described the Mohicans that fall of 1831, "The National Affairs
seem to occupy their whole attention."[76]

The persistence of Quinney and the Stockbridges, together with their
allies in the New York congressional delegation, finally paid off in 1832.
The Senate took up the 1831 treaty again at the next session of Congress
and this time modified it to provide for the needs of the Stockbridges and
Brothertowners. There would be no move to the swampy New York Indian
Tract; instead, the Senate provided for the setting off of a retrocession of
three townships of land from the public domain back to Indian Country.
The retrocession came from the 2.5 million acres that the Menominees

had ceded and relinquished to the United States in Article 1 of the 1831 treaty. Now, in 1832, three of those townships were to be removed from the public domain for the exclusive future use of the Stockbridges (two townships) and the Brothertowners (one township). This was a remarkable political accomplishment by the Mohicans. It was very rare for land once ceded by an Indian tribe to the United States to be retroceded back to Indian Country.[77]

In summer 1833 the Mohicans prepared to relocate to their new home on Lake Winnebago. Reverend Marsh reported that it was a difficult twenty-mile trip by dirt path or an easy trip forty miles by water up the Fox and across the lake. Before the abandonment of Statesburg and the move to Lake Winnebago, the tribe hosted the Sac and Fox leader Black Hawk, the year after his band was defeated by the Americans in a war that bore his name. Mohican leaders reminded Black Hawk that their two peoples had exchanged gifts at least a century earlier, before the French war on the people called Les Renards drove them away from Lake Winnebago and Green Bay. The Mohicans were about to move to the site where the corn-planted rows of Sac and Fox agriculture were still visible more than a century after the French drove the tribe away.[78]

CHAPTER 3

John W. Quinney and the Mohican Republic, 1833–1855

The year 1830 marked a turning point in the political leadership of the Wisconsin Stockbridges. Captain Aupaumut made the move to Statesburg in 1829 but did not survive long in the new country. He died on September 9, 1830. The new Presbyterian missionary to the Stockbridges, Rev. Cutting Marsh, wrote, "[H]is sickness was of long duration and for two years past he was almost entirely helpless." John Metoxen spoke eloquently at the Green Bay treaty council just a few days before Aupaumut's death. Metoxen continued in a leadership role in the Mohican Nation, but it was John W. Quinney who emerged as the principal male leader. For the next twenty-five years, he dominated the conduct of Mohican politics.[1]

Quinney's first official visit to the White House on Mohican Nation business occurred when he was sent by the tribe to continue its fight to uphold the 1822 Menominee–New York Indian treaty. During his 1830 trip east, Quinney had performed ably for the tribe in a number of intertribal and internation dealings. Throughout the 1820s Quinney had divided his time between the new settlement at Green Bay and the old one at New Stockbridge. He was one of the Stockbridge delegates to the 1822 treaty with the Menominees at Green Bay. In 1825 he spent three months in Albany lobbying the New York legislature to pay full value for the New Stockbridge lands. In 1827 he returned to Wisconsin to take part in the fruitless negotiations at Buttes des Morts. The next year, Quinney was back in New York, trying to rally all the New York Indians "for the purpose of getting them to unite in a petition and appeal to Congress" for their rights under the 1821 and 1822 treaties. Next, in 1829, he "collected the poor of the Stockbridge nation, who were unable to remove themselves, to the number of thirty souls," and shepherded them west to Grand Kakalin. And then in September 1830 he set off on his first trip to Washington to lobby the secretary of war and the president of the United States. By his own account, Quinney made nine lobbying trips to Washington between the first one in 1830 and the last one in 1852, just a few years before his death. Quinney calculated that he had spent "63 months—or 5 years and 3 months" of his life "in an official or delegated capacity on important business of [his] tribe."[2]

The challenge for Quinney's generation of Mohican political leaders in Wisconsin was to build a new and successful Mohican community that could show to the world what a Christian and civilized Indian nation could do for itself. The location of the new homeland on the east shore of Lake Winnebago was promising:

> Winnebago Lake is an uncommonly beautiful sheet of water, somewhat of an oval form. . . . The country ceded to the United States, bordering on this Lake on the north, east, and south, is composed of the very best limestone land, and will be most likely to attract the attention of emigrants sooner than any other part of the ceded territory when the lands come into market. It holds an enviable position in the heart of a rich farming country.[3]

Colonel Stambaugh, Indian agent at Green Bay, reported this description well after the signing of the February 8, 1831, treaty but before the Senate had moved to retrocede three townships from the Menominee cession to the Stockbridge and Brothertown Indians. The problem for the Mohicans was that the Menominee land cession of 1831 led directly to a large addition of territory to the U.S. public domain. On June 26, 1834, Congress established a land office at Green Bay and a surrounding land district consisting of the Menominee cession. The General Land Office instructed the surveryor-general to begin surveying the Menominee cession, and by the end of 1834, much of the work had been done, with the chain-and-ax men counting off 114 townships for 2,624,103 acres. The survey work did not go unopposed by the Ho-Chunk Indians. The Ho-Chunks pulled up the surveyors's stone cairn markers or obliterated tree marks that denoted township corner lines. Still, such resistance to the new facts on the ground could not stop the surveyors from completing their work by the end of 1835.[4]

President Jackson promptly brought some of the newly surveyed lands to a public auction, and between 1835 and 1838 Presidents Jackson and Van Buren brought the rest of the Menominee cession to market. Those lands not bought at auction were available to purchasers at the private entry price of $1.25 an acre. Preemptors, known in the frontier vernacular as squatters, also began to move onto the newly surveyed lands of the Menominee cession. The three Indian-occupied townships on the east bank of Lake Winnebago were about to experience the backwash of an American land rush that built in size and intensity in the mid-1830s. In 1835 the Land Office at Green Bay registered 108,000 acres in land sales. The next year, the figure almost doubled, to 203,000 acres sold. Green Bay at the top of the land district and Milwaukee at the bottom began to boom.[5]

Federal officials, led by former Michigan Territory governor and now secretary of war, Lewis Cass, decided that the Menominee treaties of 1831 and 1832 were only short-term expedients. Cass wrote in early 1836: "From the nature of the country and the progress of settlements west of Lake Michigan, the Indians now holding lands in the vicinity of Green Bay can only be considered as temporary residents there."[6]

Stockbridge-on-the-Lake was starting to look like another New Stockbridge, New York. What began as a haven for Indians, isolated from white settlers, was soon overtaken by the next wave of white in-migrants. Congress severed the trans-Lake Michigan territory from the new state of Michigan in summer 1836 and recast it as the Wisconsin Territory.

One of the Indian-fighting veterans of the Winnebago War of 1827, Henry Dodge, became the first territorial governor. Dodge and his white contemporaries subscribed completely to Secretary Cass's 1836 statement that the Green Bay region should be cleared of Indians. The very icon of the new territory, the 1836 Wisconsin "great seal" is a visual fantasy of the benefits of Indian removal, all under the triumphal banner "Civilization Replaces Barbarism."[7]

What were the prospects for Mohican success in the midst of a large in-pouring of white settlers? The nation had to face the problem almost immediately on moving to Lake Winnebago. For the rest of the 1830s and again in the 1840s and 1850s, the members of the Mohican Nation debated among themselves the choices between persisting in Wisconsin or moving west of the Mississippi as so many other Indian tribes were doing in those decades. The visit of the celebrated Black Hawk to Grand Kakalin in 1833 briefly raised the possibility of an Aupaumut-style removal to the Sac and Fox country of Iowa. The Mohicans respectfully addressed Black Hawk as their grandson when they hosted him, and he invited them to visit the rest of their long-separated Sac and Fox grandchildren the next summer. From June 1834 to September 1834 a Stockbridge delegation led by John Metoxen and John N. Chicks visited the Sac and Fox country in Iowa. Metoxen and Chicks found a friendly reception among their Sac and Fox friends, but they were disturbed by the continuing low-intensity warfare between the Sac and Fox and the Dakota Indians. The two Stockbridge leaders reported back to the nation in fall 1834 that it was not feasible to relocate to Iowa to lead yet another intertribal confederacy. Not even a statesman as skilled as Metoxen could bring peace and an alliance between the warring nations on the Grand Prairie.[8]

Just as the Stockbridges were debating the move to their Sac and Fox grandchildren, the long-lost Munsee Indian brothers of the Mohicans showed up in great numbers, asking to be taken in. As many as two hundred Munsee refugees arrived at Stockbridge-on-the-Lake in 1835 from Munseetown and Moraviantown, Upper Canada (Ontario). They arrived impoverished and desperate for food, clothing, and housing. Despite some grumbling, the Stockbridges took the Munsees into their settlement at Stockbridge-on-the-Lake, and from 1836 onward the two nations have generally been allied in a permanent confederacy.[9]

Eighteen thirty-six proved another year of crisis for the Mohican nation. The great families split into disputing factions and then formed and split again and again into new rivalries. The four great families—the Hendricks, Quinneys, Chicks, and Metoxens—had agreed on the wisdom of the move from New York to Wisconsin. Now, in 1836, they split among themselves about the future. John Metoxen and Thomas Hendricks favored moving to a destination known in 1836 as "Southwest of the Missouri River" (near present-day Kansas City) and became the leaders of a set of families called the Emigrant Party. John W. Quinney, his cousin Austin E. Quinney, and John N. Chicks favored staying at Stockbridge-on-the-Lake and became known as the Wiskonsin Party. Of Chicks Reverend Marsh wrote, "He is in council, perhaps, the most powerful man in the Nation, and whatever cause or side of a question he takes up he pushes with all his powers of eloquence (which are certainly great)."[10]

The removal dispute of 1836, in retrospect, was a general crisis of the Mohican polity. The daunting problems began at the intertribal and internation levels but were played out most visibly at the intratribal level. The pronouncement of Secretary Cass in March 1836 that the Green Bay region could only be a "temporary" home for Indians set off the crisis. President Jackson repeated Cass's statement and called for Congress to appropriate money to conduct a series of treaty negotiations in summer 1836 with the Wisconsin tribes, all with an eye to Indian removal.[11] (See map 4.)

The external pressure of the United States and its officials came on top of a difficult year for the tribe at its new home. A whooping cough epidemic had hit Mohican children hard in 1835 and returned again in spring 1836. Then, in summer 1836, two intertribal conflicts erupted. The first and most immediate was the murder of a Brothertown Indian by two Stockbridge men in July 1836. According to Reverend Marsh, the two Stockbridges had been drinking heavily and used an ax and a club to kill the Brothertown man. The murder took place on the two-township Stockbridge Reservation, so U.S. officials at Green Bay said the incident was not under their jurisdiction. The identities of the two accused were well known throughout the community, and they were brought to public trial before a general council of all adults of the Stockbridges and Brothertowns, several hundred Indians in total. The council heard evidence about the crime and then deliberated as a body before both Indian nations voted the two accused guilty and sentenced them to die by hanging. Before the execution could take place, the two convicted murderers escaped confinement and disappeared from the reservation, according to some, fleeing to the new refuge "Southwest of the Missouri River." The joint tribal council's success in reaching a just verdict and punishment was overturned by the ease with which the condemned had escaped. Some Stockbridges drew one of two conclusions from the debacle: first, that close proximity to whites had once again made alcohol use rampant and that only removal to a faraway new Indian Country could solve the problem of alcohol-related violence; second, that the joint councils were incapable of ensuring law and order

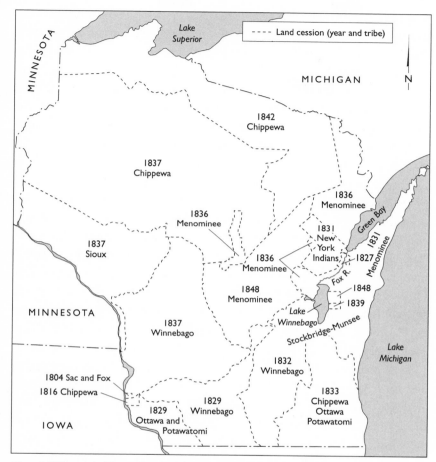

Map 4. Wisconsin Treaty land cessions, 1827–1848

and that the tribes should turn to the United States and seek citizenship as a way to secure the protection of the territorial criminal justice system. The two solutions were radically different, and adherents of each drew the appropriate conclusions when it came time to debate staying at Stockbridge-on-the-Lake or moving to the lands on the Great Plains west of the Missouri River.[12]

Another internal problem of the Stockbridges in 1836 was more subtle than criminal justice but nonetheless as important to the future of the tribe. This problem was the growing tendency of Stockbridge women to marry white men and black men and mixed-race native men from outside the nation. Five women made that decision in the first part of 1836, some marrying soldiers from Fort Howard. The sudden exogamous marriage of such a large number of women in sequence led to considerable recriminations within the nation. The nation was forced to decide if the new husbands and then the offspring would be welcomed into the tribe or treated as permanent outsiders. There were other problems associated with the choices by Mohican women to marry outside the Mohican nation.[13]

The 1836 tension over interracial marriage was the start of more than a century of racialized politics within and about the Mohican Nation. Interracial mixing was not new for the tribe. The Stockbridges had become accustomed to living in multiracial settings during their years in New York and New England, when many free blacks married Algonquian people. Belknap and Morse had noted the presence of free blacks at the Oneida-Stockbridge villages in their 1796 visit. Six years later, the mixed-race New Jersey Brotherton Indians came to live permanently among the Mohicans at New Stockbridge. Not to be confused with the New Jersey brethren, the Brothertown Indians were an amalgamation of seven New York and New England tribes. The first Wisconsin settlement of Mohicans at Grand Kakalin consisted primarily of Stockbridges, but after 1824 Brothertowners and some Oneidas lived nearby at Little Kakalin. "The majority of those settled near the Little Chute are half-negro," sniffed Colonel Stambaugh in 1830–31, a disturbing indication of how federal officials viewed the New York Indians. The climate of racial classification intensified at Green Bay in the 1830s, in part because of the growing importance of Yankee immigrants and southern army officers at Fort Howard. The relaxed acceptance of mixed-race people from the days of the Métis and the tolerant "Canadian" character of La Baye gave way to a more rigid racial hierarchy. The close relations between the Brothertowners and Stockbridges ensured that the Indian groups at the new Lake Winnebago reservations would be a triracial grouping of Indians, whites, and blacks and that the two nations could not stay immune from the larger racial attitudes of the expanding United States.[14]

While at Statesburg, the Stockbridges had lived ten miles upstream from Fort Howard. In 1828 the United States opened Fort Winnebago at the portage between the Fox and Wisconsin Rivers. When the Mohicans moved to Stockbridge-on-the-Lake after the 1832 treaty, they were directly astride the Military Road, built by enlisted men, connecting the two forts. This construction project led directly to fraternization between soldiers and Mohican women.[15]

With the creation of the Wisconsin Territory on July 4, 1836, the responsibility for local oversight of Indian affairs passed to the new territorial governor, Henry Dodge. For the next year, Governor Dodge embarked on a whirlwind of treaty negotiations with all the remaining Indian tribes in Wisconsin. For some of the tribes, such as the Ho-Chunks and Dakotas, the governor negotiated removal treaties under the terms of the Indian Removal Act of 1830. The governor also directed his attention to the three reservations in the Green Bay region that accommodated the tribes from New York: the Stockbridges on their two townships, the Brothertowners on their lone township, and the Oneidas on the almost twenty-two townships of the New York Indian Tract. Governor Dodge judged as a failure the project for removing the approximately five thousand Indians from New York to Wisconsin and instead thought that what was needed was a removal of all New York-descended Indians to the trans-Missouri region.[16]

Dodge could not attend every treaty council across the territory that summer of 1836. He concentrated his main efforts on negotiating a treaty with the Menominees that called on that tribe to cede and relinquish another four million acres to the United States. The War Department assigned a New Yorker, the Reverend John F. Schermerhorn, to negotiate treaties in the Wisconsin Territory with the Oneidas, the Stockbridges and Munsees, and the Brothertowners. The choice of Schermerhorn by the War Department was a strong signal of the policy objective of the Jackson administration in its last year in office. In 1835 Schermerhorn negotiated the controversial New Echota removal treaty with a rump faction of the Cherokees in Georgia, thereby setting in motion the infamous "Trail of Tears" of the Cherokee Nation. In 1836 Schermerhorn began his next task, the complete removal of all New York Indians to the trans-Missouri region, whether currently living in New York State or in the Wisconsin Territory. This plan required negotiations with the occupants of the three reservations in Wisconsin and the many tribes still on reserved land in New York.[17]

The historian Laurence Hauptman has recently characterized Schermerhorn in the severest terms: a "slimy supplicant" when it came to his own well-being and one who displayed "fanatical religiosity" in seeing the hand of the devil when it came to dealing with Indians who opposed him.

Hauptman discerns the New Echota treaty pattern in the way that Schermerhorn "secured agreements from the Oneida, Mohawk, Tuscarora,
Stockbridge, and Munsee by repeating his Cherokee formula, namely, by
promoting internal chaos." In 1836 Schermerhorn negotiated a removal
treaty with the Brothertowners that required them to cede and relinquish
their one township reservation and then remove to the trans-Missouri
region. With the Oneidas, he secured an agreement to cede and relinquish
90 percent of the New York Indian Tract north of Green Bay to the United
States and also to refuse to accept any more Six Nations emigrants from
New York State. This was the first step in getting the Wisconsin Oneidas
removed beyond the Missouri River.[18]

Reverend Schermerhorn then turned to the Mohicans and Munsees and
concluded a single treaty with the two tribes at Green Bay on September
17, 1836. The agreement required the Munsees to vacate Wisconsin and
move to the trans-Missouri region. For the Stockbridges, the treaty permitted
them to send a delegation to inspect the trans-Missouri lands and, if deemed
satisfactory, to remove as a tribe to the Great Plains. If the Stockbridges did
not like the trans-Missouri tract, they could stay on one-half of their two
townships but had to sell at least one-half of their reservation.[19]

The heads of the leading families of the Stockbridge Nation, including
the Metoxen, Quinney, and Chicks families, signed the treaty with Schermerhorn on September 17, 1836. Hendrick Aupaumut, Jr., also signed the
treaty. "Captain Porter," the Munsee leader in Wisconsin, signed the
agreement for that tribe, and then Schermerhorn appended a paragraph
stating that removal to the Great Plains was incumbent as well on the
remaining Munsees living in New York State. However, the draft treaty and
its U.S. commissioner soon came under fire, both in Washington and in the
Wisconsin Territory. In Washington, Schermerhorn's work was repudiated,
and he was sacked as a negotiator for the War Department in 1837, despite
worshiping at the same church in Albany as the new president, Martin Van
Buren. In Wisconsin, John W. Quinney, who had signed the September 17
treaty, found his voice and began a series of letters, petitions, and memorials
against the looming removal of the Mohicans.[20]

The New Echota pattern showed to Quinney the danger of having the
Mohican Nation organized by informal family chiefs and headmen. An
unscrupulous U.S. treaty commissioner, whether "slimy" or "fanatical"
like Reverend Schermerhorn, could negotiate a removal treaty with a part

of the tribe and have it applied to all. Quinney's solution to the problem of outside manipulation of the Mohican polity was radical: write a constitution and have the written document bind the Stockbridges into a new republic of laws and procedures. That is exactly what Quinney did in February 1837. The result was the the first written constitution of the Mohicans.[21]

The document that Quinney drafted bore the title "Declaration of Rights and Frame of Government of the Stockbridge Nation." In language and form, it borrowed liberally from the U.S. Declaration of Independence and the U.S Constitution and Bill of Rights. The adaptations to Mohican conditions, however, are noteworthy features for making sense of the Mohican polity at the time of the unratified Schermerhorn treaty. To begin, Quinney's 1837 constitution limited membership in the polity to Stockbridge Indians, not Munsees, Delawares, Brothertowners, Oneidas, or any of the other tribes allied with the Mohicans of Stockbridge, Massachusetts, and New Stockbridge, New York. Moreover, it did not allow women to vote or hold office. From the very first, then, the Quinney constitution proposed to shrink the polity in numbers.

The Constitution of 1837 began with the Declaration of Rights, the first of which was, "All hereditary titles and distinctions are annulled and abolished forever." This was a direct repudiation of the older rule of the patriarchs of the great families, annointed by the leading women of the tribe. Quinney made clear in the 1837 constitution that the Stockbridge Nation would be a republic:

> All power resides in the people and all officers and magistrates are their agents and substitutes. In order to prevent those who are vested with authority from becoming oppressors the people have a right to cause their public officers to return to private life in such manner as they shall appoint in their frame of government.

The Declaration of Rights also included recognition of the "force and validity of [Mohican] Treaties with the United States" and friendship with the United States. However, the Quinney document reaffirmed Stockbridge sovereignty with the statement, "we do not acknowledge allegiance to any power upon earth." Moreover, it contemplated a continuation of intertribal diplomacy. As Quinney wrote the clause, the new government of the Mohican Nation would enjoy the power to "regulate intercourse and Commerce with other Indian Nations."

The "Frame of Government" that followed the Declaration of Rights provided for executive, legislative, and judicial branches. The "First Supreme Magistrate" was to be known also by the older Mohican title sachem, and the minimum requirements for the three-year elected term were a profession of Christianity, $500 in owned property, the age of twenty-five, and at least three years' residence at Stockbridge-on-the-Lake. The legislature under the Quinney constitution was a five-man council, elected annually. It had the power to tax, to control the sale of lands, to borrow money, and to spend money on behalf of the nation. The council also made the civil and criminal laws. The judiciary consisted of a judge known as the "Peacemaker" who heard lesser civil suits. The Peacemaker also served as the nation's coroner, to investigate each death of a Stockbridge, and as the tax assessor. Criminal matters and appeals were heard by the "High Court," consisting of the sachem and the two councilors who received the highest vote totals. The three branches of government were assisted by a sheriff, who enforced legal orders, a secretary who maintained national records, and a treasurer who kept the nation's accounts.

The Quinney constitution of 1837 skillfully incorporated many Mohican traditions by retaining the names of some of the offices. It also borrowed from the Iroquois Confederacy and from the American Republic in separating the branches of government. Most significant, the Mohican constitution limited the polity to Stockbridge men and pointedly excluded the visiting Canadian Munsees at Stockbridge-on-the-Lake. The constitution of 1837 put an end to the practice of adopting outsiders into the tribe as full equals.

Quinney's male relatives accepted the new constitution, as did the men of the Chicks family. Men in the Hendricks and Konkapot families, however, refused to acknowledge the constitution or be governed by its framework. This set the stage for the continuing political crisis of the Mohican Nation in 1837, 1838, and 1839. Robert Konkapot and Thomas Hendricks sent letters, memorials, and petitions to U.S. officials in 1837 asking for the Senate to reconsider and approve the Schermerhorn treaty. (It was because of their wish to move to Kansas that the Konkapot and Hendricks families were known as the Emigrant Party.) They also made clear their opposition to Quinney, his new constitution, and his right to speak for the Stockbridges. Throughout 1837 and 1838 Konkapot and Hendricks insisted that their group formed the majority of the two nations, and they consistently included the Munsees as part of the polity.[22]

The U.S. Indian agent at Green Bay was largely sympathetic to the Emigrant Party. By contrast, the missionary at Stockbridge-on-the-Lake, Reverend Marsh, cast his support for the Quinney side, or the Wiskonsin Party, in part because he approved of the constitution and in part because he opposed removal to the trans-Missouri region. Starting in mid-1837, Marsh, in his correspondence with his superiors in Boston and Edinburgh, noted that the Konkapot-Hendricks faction was acting in a lawless manner. In the missionary's view, only the "wicked" in the tribe opposed the rule of law that the Quinney constitution promised, and each week in his English-language-only sermon, Marsh urged obedience to the new constitution and opposition to the Emigrant Party leaders. Soon enough, the church itself was split into two groups, with the minister solidly on one side. Reverend Marsh had Robert Konkapot excommunicated from the Presbyterian Mission church at Stockbridge-on-the-Lake in May 1838 for "slander, lying, and dishonesty." He also accused Konkapot of being an accessory to murder for his alleged part in helping the two Stockbridge killers of 1836 escape. Most heartless was Marsh's July 1838 opinion, "God has laid his hand of judgment upon the party chief . . . and cut down one of their leaders in the rebellion." This was a reference to the death of a Hendricks family member from smallpox.[23]

The Konkapot and Hendricks families did not forsake Christianity, despite their banishment from the church of their fathers. Instead, the two invited itinerant Baptist and Methodist circuit riders to come to Stockbridge-on-the-Lake and preach to the Emigrant Party. Marsh may have dismissed them as people "who were once members of the Church . . . but who now prefer the Pagan state," but the Konkapots and Hendricks found a new home among the Baptists, first in Wisconsin and later in the trans-Missouri River region.[24]

The Mohicans of Stockbridge-on-the-Lake spent 1837 and 1838 in dispute with one another about the direction of the nation. Nearby, their neighbors the Brothertowners and the Oneidas were themselves undertaking important changes. The Brothertowners turned their backs on their own unratified Schermerhorn treaty and decided that they did not want to move to the Great Plains to live with the other eastern tribes. Instead, they proposed a radically different idea. They would divide their lands at Brothertown into parcels for each family, dissolve their tribal connection, and become citizens of the United States and the Wisconsin Territory. In effect, they would go from red to white. This idea had some support from territorial officials, and in 1839 Congress granted the wish of the Brothertown Indians in a historic act whereby their lands were allotted in fee simple, the tribe was dissolved, and individual Indians were treated as citizens with access to the American legal and electoral system.[25]

In his 1836 negotiations Reverend Schermerhorn discouraged further emigration by New York Indians from the New York homelands to the Wisconsin Territory. Although not ratified, the wish of the United States in this regard coincided with the wish of the Indians still living in New York not to be moved, either to Wisconsin or to the Great Plains. An October 1834 population count by the U.S. Indian agent at Green Bay tallied 651 Oneidas along Duck Creek, just west of Green Bay, 320 Stockbridges on Lake Winnebago, and just 5 Senecas in all the trans-Lake Michigan territory. These numbers meant that the half-million-acre New York Indian Tract was too sizable for the Oneidas to occupy alone, so the United States approached that tribe and asked for yet another cession of most of the New York Indian Tract back to the United States. On February 3, 1838, the United States and the Oneida Nation signed a treaty in Washington that provided for a census to be taken of the Oneidas and then for a smaller Oneida reservation to be carved from the New York Indian Tract, in size proportional to one hundred acres for every Oneida. The census was finally taken in November 1838 and named 654 Oneidas living at Duck Creek. The surveyor from Green Bay laid out a new reservation of 65,400 acres, with the balance of 434,600 acres going back to the United States. Interestingly, the Oneidas in February 1838 received much less for the retrocession than Reverend Schermerhorn had offered; the 1836 proposal was seventy-five cents an acre for the retrocession of most of the tract. In 1838 the Oneidas received only $33,000 in U.S. payments to cover tribal debts, yet these payments were enough to smooth the negotiations at the treaty council.[26]

The Brothertown example exerted a powerful influence on territorial officials in Wisconsin, on the Stockbridges and Munsees, and on the Oneidas. Territorial officials, led by Governor Dodge, were determined to promote Indian removal in their territory. The Brothertown decision gave Wisconsin Indians a choice, as Governor Dodge saw it: they could move to the Great Plains as Indians or stay in Wisconsin as detribalized citizens, but they could not stay in Wisconsin as Indian tribes. Under Dodge,

Wisconsin would cease to be Indian Country. The territorial officials had their eyes on the two-township reservation at Stockbridge-on-the-Lake. In January 1838 the territorial legislature of Wisconsin sent a memorial to Congress asking "for the extension of the right of citizenship to the Stockbridge Indians." The memorial summarized how the territorial legislature viewed the Mohicans:

> The Stockbridge nation have arrived to a state of civilization; their pursuits are strictly agricultural; and they have entirely abandoned the chase. A large majority of them are persons of intelligence, possessing good moral habits, and a degree of industry seldom surpassed in the most civilized parts of our country.[27]

Here was a classic statement of the Enlightenment ideology of civilization. A civilized people made a living from the soil, not by hunting and gathering. "Persons of intelligence" was the mid-nineteenth-century way of describing applied literacy, that is, the ability to read and to learn from reading. "Intelligence" also described an individual's ability to defend his property, in court and at the ballot box if necessary. "Good moral habits" meant Christianity and temperance. And the comparison to the whites of the Wisconsin Territory of 1838 was earnestly meant. The Stockbridges, in the eyes of the whites ruling the territory, were ready to become white.

The Wisconsin legislators ended their 1838 memorial somewhat obliquely: "[We] deem it unnecessary to set forth any further reasons than have been stated, trusting to the liberality and wisdom of Congress." The measures of civilization needed explaining to Congress but not the benefits of citizenship. But what did Americans understand about citizenship in 1838? The historian Eric Foner has addressed the mid-nineteenth-century understanding of citizenship in a quite different context, the postbellum South for freed slaves. He wrote that citizenship was understood to begin with the right to one's own produce ("free labor") and then the ownership of property. A higher level of citizenship was the right to have access to the courts to protect one's property. And the highest level of citizenship was access to the ballot and the electoral slate, so as to go beyond individual property and to work on behalf of the larger community in the political arena.[28]

It took three constitutional amendments between 1865 and 1870 to establish these rights for the freed people of the South. Citizenship, as

Congress granted to the Brothertowners, and as some Stockbridges contemplated, involved the extension of individual rights at Foner's second,
third, and fourth levels. Citizen Indians would get their proportional individual share of the tribal property, to keep in fee simple ownership and do
with as they pleased. Citizen Indians would also be able to go to territorial,
state, or federal court and bring suit against anyone who damaged their
property. Citizen Indians could vote in local, territorial, state, and federal
elections. In effect, the Brothertown Indians in 1839 sought and achieved
the rights of man that the United States was not fully prepared to extend
to African Americans until 1870. But the cost was high: the abolition of the
Brothertown Indians as a recognized tribe.

In late fall 1838 Quinney embarked on yet another trip to Washington to
lobby U.S. officials for the Mohicans. He was accompanied by his cousin,
Austin. Together, they represented the constitutional party in the nation.
Thomas Hendricks and Robert Konkapot knew the date of the Quinneys'
departure and little else, but that was enough to cause Hendrick to write the
Commissioner of Indian Affairs, "Whatever Quinney proposes, we oppose."[29]

In March 1839 the House and Senate passed legislation providing for
money to underwrite a new treaty between the United States and, signifi-
cantly, the Stockbridge and Munsee tribes. The United States wanted to
deal with both tribes as one, the preference of Hendricks and Konkapot,
and not as two separate, unrelated tribes, as Quinney and Chicks preferred.
That summer, the Commissioner of Indian Affairs appointed another New
Yorker, Albert Gallup, to go to Stockbridge-on-the-Lake to negotiate a
new agreement that would satisfy the Emigrant and Wiskonsin Parties of
the Stockbridges and Munsees. Gallup was told by Commissioner T. Hartley
Crawford that the population of Stockbridges was about 250, "of whom it
is said 160 are anxious to emigrate," as well as 120 Munsees, all of whom
"are disposed to remove" to the territory southwest of the Missouri River.
Commissioner Crawford also repeated the desire expressed by the
Quinneys to remain in the Wisconsin Territory. There was no instruction
from the head of the Office of Indian Affairs that the upcoming treaty
include an either-or choice, emigration or detribalization. After all, the
Quinneys had simply expressed their opposition to being removed yet
again, for the third time in less than twenty years.[30]

Commissioner Gallup came to Stockbridge-on-the-Lake in late August
1839 to negotiate the treaty. He proposed that the Stockbridges cede one

of their two townships to the United States, have the township appraised and sold at auction, and split the proceeds between the Emigrant Party and the Wiskonsin Party. Gallup immediately met opposition from both parties, as they preferred to receive a known sum and counterproposed that the United States pay $1 an acre for the 23,040 acres it expected to acquire in the cession. That eventually became the basis for the treaty, and the next step was for Commissioner Gallup to draw up a roll of those choosing to emigrate. To his surprise, only eighty Stockbridges signed onto the Emigrant Party list, mainly members of the Hendricks and Konkapot families. "You may be somewhat disappointed that so few of the Stockbridges and Munsees proper, are inclined to emigrate," Gallup wrote to Commissioner Crawford. "The emigrating party have doubtless misrepresented their strength to the Indian Department and perhaps deceived themselves."[31] (See map 5.)

The Emigrants took the conclusion of the treaty on September 3 as their signal to embark for the land beyond the Missouri River, despite being warned by Gallup that the treaty was not in force until approved by the president and ratified by the Senate. Reverend Marsh crowed in triumph at the conclusion of the September treaty council, "The Hendrick Party was bought out entirely . . . and the Canadian Munsees and Delawares who have been here about two years annoying the Nation went with them." The Emigrants, including the Canadian Munsees, ignored the caution from Gallup and set out in late September for the Great Plains, well before the Senate had acted on the treaty or before the full Congress could appropriate money to fund its terms. Unfortunately, the Emigrants lacked enough money and supplies to reach their destination among the Delawares on the Missouri River, near Fort Leavenworth. At St. Louis they became public charity cases and had to be rescued by the U.S. Indian agent there.[32]

The separation of the Mohican Nation into a main Wisconsin stem and an offshoot Kansas branch was permanent but also permeable. The Mohicans of the trans-Missouri region merged their identity with their Munsee comigrants, and in turn, the Emigrants lived among a larger group of Delaware Indians who had left Ohio and Indiana for the Great Plains after the 1818 treaty. Noteworthy among the Emigrant Party was Mrs. Lydia Quinney Hendrick, widow of Hendrick Aupaumut, who was born in Massachusetts, lived in New York and Wisconsin, and died at Shawnee Mission, a year after the migration.[33]

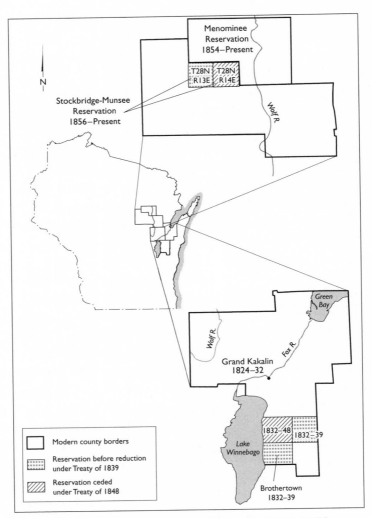

Map 5. Relocation of the Mohicans in Wisconsin, 1824–1856

Some of the Emigrants, however, drifted back to Stockbridge-on-the-Lake in the years after 1839. Reverend Marsh frequently noted, and took glee in, the apparent failure of the Mohican settlers to make a success of their western home. For example, he once stated that "murder and drunkenness" were rife at the Delaware Reserve near Fort Leavenworth. The Stockbridges and Munsees from Wisconsin began worshiping with the Baptist minister Ira Blanchard at Shawnee Mission in Kansas. Soon enough, in 1841, the Hendricks and Konkapot families renamed the church the Mohegan and Delaware Baptist Mission Church, at a place called "Stockbridge" on the Kansas River. By 1843 Thomas Hendricks got into a quarrel with Reverend Blanchard, and after failing to get the missionary fired, Hendrick and his wife were expelled from the church.[34]

Back in Stockbridge-on-the-Lake, the signing of the treaty and the departure of the Emigrant Party brought no peace. Marsh commented in October 1839, "It is well that the [Emigrant] Party has gone, still the devil has not yet gone. There are still elements of strife and perhaps of another division remaining."[35] The internal division that Marsh observed once again split along family and policy lines. The families among the Wiskonsin Party that quarreled and broke after 1839 were, on the one side, the Quinneys together with their old ally John Metoxen, and, on the other, the Chicks family, led by John N. Chicks and Jacob Chicks. The basic split between what soon became the Chicks Party and the Quinney Party was over the question of tribal disestablishment and citizenship. The Chicks Party favored following the route of the Brothertowners by dissolving the tribe, dividing the land into individual allotments, and taking American citizenship. This did not mean that the Chicks Party wanted to forgo a Stockbridge Indian identity. Far from it. But they reasoned that the only way the community could persist as a Mohican people, ironically, was to participate in the larger American polity of private property, courts, and elections. The Quinney Party opposed the citizenship proposal. Instead, the two leaders, John W. Quinney and Austin E. Quinney, held out a vision of prosperity as the Stockbridge Indian Nation if only the United States and the states of New York and Massachusetts paid damages for past wrongs. The economic development strategy of the Quinneys increasingly relied less on agriculture and more on what might be termed claims-farming.[36]

The amount of time devoted, the complexity of detail mastered, and sheer tenacity all marked Quinney's work as a tribal claims agent. He made his many trips to Washington primarily for the purpose of treaty making, or legislation influencing, but while at the capital he also lobbied OIA officials for payments to the Stockbridges for past wrongs. Between 1830 and 1848 Quinney pressed five claims on the United States that went back to New Stockbridge, New York, days and the time of the great migration to Green Bay. First, he sought to have the tribe share in the annuities in perpetuity paid the Six Nations under the treaty of 1794. Second, he attempted to have the Stockbridge Nation compensated for the value of the lands on the White River in Indiana that the Delawares sold in 1818 without asking permission of the Stockbridges. Third, after 1838 he asked for payment for part of the value of the New York Indian Tract that the Oneidas retroceded to the United States. He advanced the theory that Stockbridge money and gifts, in 1821 and 1822, allowed the New York Indians to settle among the Menominees in the first place, the necessary precursor to the 1831 treaty that established the New York Indian Tract. Fourth, Quinney wanted the United States to pay the costs of the removal of the nation from New York to Green Bay. Fifth and last, Quinney sought a part of the payments that the Delawares received for selling some of their Kansas lands after the Emigrant Party had moved in among them. To make matters more complicated, the Emigrant Party was counterlobbying Congress for a share of whatever money Quinney obtained.[37]

Another murder at Stockbridge in February 1840 only served to deepen divisions between the two factions. The Chicks Party pointed to the murder as evidence that lawlessness was rampant and could only be curbed by citizenship and the imposition of territorial law on the Stockbridges. The murderer was suspected to be a member of the Hendricks Party who had not yet left for Kansas in fall 1839. The suspect was caught, tried by the nation, and hanged, a process that sustained the Quinneys and Metoxen in their view that the Stockbridge polity was quite capable of maintaining law and order on the one-township reservation.[38]

The 1840 federal elections turned the Democrats out of the White House and the War Department and ended their control of Indian affairs in the Wisconsin Territory. As of 1840, the politics of the Stockbridge-Munsees overlapped with the politics of the Territory of Wisconsin; in short, both became highly contentious and confusing. At the territorial level, the Democratic Party of Jackson and Van Buren that had dominated politics throughout the 1830s fractured into several competing blocs. The group associated with former Governor Dodge stayed loyal to the Jackson–Van Buren wing of the Democratic Party. Another group, which included Daniel Whitney of Green Bay, coalesced behind the new Whig Party of Henry Clay and William Henry Harrison. Yet another group, led by Judge Doty, made common cause with the conservative Democrats helping President Tyler when he ascended to the presidency after the sudden death of President Harrison. The results in the Wisconsin Territory were split. In 1841 Judge Doty became the new territorial governor and superintendent of Wisconsin Indian affairs. The old Jacksonians mustered enough votes in the territorial elections to send Dodge to Washington to serve as the congressional delegate from Wisconsin.[39]

The Chicks Party observed that the Brothertown Indians gained citizenship through an act of Congress and not a bilateral treaty, so Jacob and John N. Chicks proposed citizenship to the new Tyler-appointed territorial governor, James Duane Doty and to Delegate Dodge. Here was a policy matter both white territorial rival politicians could agree on. In 1841 the Chicks Party told Dodge and Congress that law enforcement was weak at Stockbridge and that the Indians "can no longer enforce a proper government among themselves, unless they are backed and supported by the supreme law of the land." Governor Doty concurred with the citizenship plan, reciting the usual litany about the civilization of the Stockbridges:

> Their advances in civilization have gradually influenced them to abandon the hunter life. This had led them to adopt fixed places of abode, acquire individual property, cultivate the earth, and assume most of those habits and customs, amongst themselves, which go to distinguish the savage and nomadic life from that of educated and civilized man.[40]

The House of Representatives was more favorable to the idea than the Senate, passing a citizenship bill in the winter session of 1841–42, but the Senate did not take action on the bill. The next session of the 27th Congress saw both houses pass a Stockbridge citizenship bill nearly identical to the 1839 Brothertown Act, and President Tyler signed it into law on March 3, 1843.[41]

"An Act for the Relief of the Stockbridge tribe of Indians in the Territory of Wiskonsin" contained seven provisions. First, the one-township reservation would be allotted to individuals immediately in fee simple status. That meant that individual Stockbridges would have control over their own parcels. Second, the act superseded the 1837 constitutional government by setting up a board of five commissioners from the "head men of the tribe" to undertake the allotment of the reservation. The third provision set forth an election process for selecting the commissioners. The next three sections of the Act of 1843 instructed the commissioners on how to make the allotments and also to finish their work by July 1, 1843. At that point, the Stockbridge Indians would be "hereby declared to be, citizens of the United

States[,] . . . and the jurisdiction of the United States and said Territory [Wisconsin] shall be extended over the said township or reservation now held by them, in the same manner as over other parts of said Territory."[42]

Stockbridges and whites alike in the Wisconsin Territory began referring to the Chicks Party as the Citizens Party. The Quinney-Metoxen Party became known as the Indian Party because of its opposition to the Act of 1843. When news of the passage of the act reached Stockbridge-on-the-Lake, the Citizens Party, led by John N. Chicks, immediately moved to win the five slots on the Board of Commissioners. The Indian Party concentrated on lobbying federal officials to overturn the new law. Much as the polity divided in 1841–43 over the citizenship issue, so too did the church divide into rival groups. Reverend Marsh had earlier shown sympathy for the citizenship plan, but by 1843 he came out in strong opposition to the Citizens Party members in his congregation. For one thing, "the Indian Party ha[d] by far the most respectability in it." For another, the minister clashed personally with his onetime deacon, John N. Chicks, and excommunicated him from the church. Predictably, the Citizens Party members started to leave the church in large numbers and soon found worship services offered by Baptist and Methodist itinerant preachers. No doubt the weekly thundering of Reverend Marsh against Jacob Chicks and his "wicked, apostate sons" led the Citizens Party to seek religion six miles to the south among the Brothertowners and the Methodists meeting there, where Marsh doubted that "the cause of Christ" was served "amongst the ignorant."[43]

Marsh's contempt for the religious practices of the Methodists obscured for him what was an important spiritual development for the Mohicans and Brothertowners. A circuit-riding Methodist missionary named Wesson Miller observed the eighty-year-old Jacob Chicks preach in his own barn to hundreds of Stockbridges, Munsees, and Brothertowners. Chicks began preaching in English, "All me want now is to love him, Christ," but moved by the moment, he switched to the Mohican language the better to reach his listeners. Reverend Miller recalled thirty years later, "[F]or effectiveness, I never saw its equal." As for the impact of "Father Chicks" on the assembled Stockbridges and Brothertowners, Miller said, "Eternity alone can reveal the results of the day."[44]

The position of the Citizens Party was straightforward. It got its religion and its politics from the Brothertown community farther south along the

Lake Winnebago shoreline. Moreover, it viewed ethnic survival of the Mohican people as possible only through tribal dissolution. By contrast, the surviving documents written by the Indian Party leaders in the early 1840s show a belief that Mohican ethnic survival depended on maintaining the tribal polity. Especially noteworthy is the tone that John W. Quinney took in his written attacks on the Citizens Party. His opponents were "young men" and "foolish men" who ignored the advice of the "older and wiser" men of the nation. Quinney made no reference to the advice of women, whether young and foolish or older and wiser. His analysis of the Citizens Party was that it represented a revolt against patriarchal order and tradition.[45]

John W. and Austin E. Quinney asked President Tyler in June 1843 for a new treaty that would separate the two parties and let the Indian Party sell its Wisconsin property and move to the trans-Missouri region, just as the Emigrants had done four years earlier. The Tyler administration declined, noting that to hold a treaty with the Indian Party, or even the whole tribe, "would appear to contravene the Act of Congress relating to citizenship." That first setback did not stop John Quinney and the Indian Party from attempting to overturn the 1843 act. As Reverend Marsh noted in March 1844, the Indian Party is "determined not to come under the laws of the U.S." Quinney made yet another journey to Washington in June 1844 to lobby the Office of Indian Affairs and Congress on behalf of his Indian Party but without success.[46]

The Board of Commissioners finished the allotment selections on time in summer 1843, and according to Marsh, "The Citizens Party are selling their land fast as they can for anything which they can get." The lands of the one-township Stockbridge Reservation were soon encumbered with quitclaim deeds, power-of-attorney arrangements, promissory notes, and the like. Worse, relations between the Indian Party and the Citizens Party at Stockbridge-on-the-Lake went beyond policy disagreement or family enmity; a new split developed over racial identities. The Indian Party came to view its members as the true racial Indians and the Citizens Party as variously mixed, motley, mongrel, white, or African, especially the last-named category. In summer 1845 Reverend Marsh noted that the parties split over the practice of Stockbridge women marrying outside the tribe "to others having African blood." At a political meeting, one so-called African of the Citizens Party knocked out the teeth of an Indian allied with Quinney. The Indian Party began a process of self-segregation by refusing to have their children attend school with those of the Citizens Party: "They wish to defer from their School all Children who have any African blood."[47]

John Quinney went to Washington again in summer 1845. His petitions, letters, memorials, and briefs consistently stressed that the Act of 1843 was a breach of the Stockbridge Nation's constitution and sovereignty. He insisted with reference to rosters of members that only a minority of tribal members belonged to the Citizens Party. By Quinney's count, there were 149 Indian Party members and only 81 in the opposition. Speaking the language of Jacksonian America, Quinney insisted that no sovereign people could ever live under the tyranny of the minority. The will of the majority must prevail, he told Congress. The "General Census of the Stockbridge tribe" that Quinney took after passage of the Act of 1843 reveals both family and gender divisions. Quinney's tally of 149 in the Indian Party consisted of three sets of people: members of the Quinney, Mexoten, Pye, and Turkey families; widows with dependent children; and some scattered absentee families whose proxy Quinney claimed. The Citizens Party, by contrast, consisted of the Chicks, Jourdan, Davids, Gardner, Jacobs, Yoccum, and Moore families. According to Quinney, only two widows, both without dependent children, supported the Citizens Party.[48]

Quinney promised that if Congress overturned the 1843 act the Stockbridges would sign a new treaty with the United States agreeing to cede their one-township reservation and relocate to the Great Plains. Quinney's timing in 1845 and 1846 was more fortuitous, largely because of a shift in territorial officeholders. Henry Dodge departed the job of territorial delegate to Congress, and his replacement in 1845 and 1846 was a Green Bay attorney, Morgan L. Martin. Martin had long enjoyed close legal and business relations with the Quinney Party at Stockbridge-on-the-Lake, and he now worked on behalf of the repeal effort. Quinney and Martin found congressional backers to introduce the repeal bill. In the first session of the Twenty-ninth Congress, House Resolution (H.R.) 321, an act to repeal the Act of 1843, finally passed the House of Representatives and the Senate, a remarkable political triumph by the Indian Party, especially its, leader John W. Quinney.[49]

The Act of 1846 repealed that of 1843, "and the said Stockbridge tribe or nation of Indians [was] restored to their ancient form of government," which meant a return to the 1837 constitution polity. The act also directed the U.S. Indian agent at Green Bay to make an enrollment of those

Stockbridges (presumably members of the Citizens Party) who wished to remain U.S. citizens and not reenter tribal relations. The Indian agent was also to divide the township into two districts, an Indian District where the lands would be held in common, and a Citizens District where allotment in fee simple would apply. All this was to be done by the end of 1846. In addition, the the act nullified all prior sales of the 1843 allotments conveyed to non-Indians, a provision that caused legal difficulties for more than another decade. The final part of section 2 required that the Citizens Party members who wished to leave the tribe should forfeit any rights to a per capita share of tribal property.[50] The third and final section of the act capped eight years of hard lobbying by Quinney. The United States pledged to pay the Stockbridge Nation $5,000 for the gifts that the Stockbridges presented the Menominees and Ho-Chunks back at the treaty councils of 1821 and 1822. To be sure, the $5,000 payment was not the full amount that Quinney had sought as the Mohican share of the proceeds of the retrocession of the New York Indian Tract. Moreover, Congress conceded in the last paragraph that the $5,000 payment to the Stockbridge Nation was not to "impair any claim which said nation may have upon the Delaware nation to a share of the lands assigned to them west of the Missouri River," a reference to the aftermath of the 1818 treaty.[51]

With the passage of the Act of 1846, power in the Stockbridge Nation swung back to the Indian Party and Quinney. He was elected sachem and set about the task of driving away the opposition. Quinney was enraged that during the three-month enrollment period in fall 1846, not a single Citizens Party member stepped forward to separate from the tribe. Not one Citizens Party member wanted to become a citizen in 1846. In effect, Quinney was a victim of his own success as a lobbyist for tribal claims, since Citizens Party members had good reason to believe that they would receive a per capita share of any new funds that Quinney brought to the tribe. The act's provision denying tribal members who declared their citizenship again in 1846 was oddly counterproductive, since the Citizens Party saw no benefit in being denied a part of the tribal annuities that Quinney had brought and might yet bring to Wisconsin.[52]

During the Citizens Party interregnum of 1843–46, the territorial legislature extended civil government to the reservation. Newly formed Calumet County asked its sheriff and the county courts to maintain law enforcement on the reservation. More important, the territorial legislature created the town of Stockbridge, which promptly began assessing personal property and levying taxes. The Indian Party had bitterly protested this form of extension of citizenship between 1843 and 1846 and pointed to the case of Mrs. Hannah Marquis, "a sick and poor widow" who had a calf seized in lieu of $2.43 property tax payment. Others, including the former sachem Austin E. Quinney, also suffered the seizure of livestock for failure to pay property taxes to the town of Stockbridge and to Calumet County. The Indian Party called for relief from "the tax collector, the more unwelcome call of the bailiff, and the influence of designing and scheming whites," in asking Congress to repeal the Act of 1843.[53]

In fall 1846 the Citizens Party, with its hold on municipal government, refused to recognize the newly re-created polity of the Indian Party under the 1837 Quinney constitution. Two rival governments, one township and one tribal, claimed jurisdiction over the same area. This time the use of force, not just argument, was the result. The proximate cause was the township tax collector's attempt to enforce the assessment roll and collect tangible property from those he deemed in default. Reverend Marsh described what happened that Christmas of 1846:

> At length, the Collector with his "posse" went and took property. The Indian Party sent to the Oneidas and obtained some 30 or 40 to come and assist in retaking the property. They came and headed by the head men of the Indian Party together with their own party went around breaking open buildings and searching houses wherever they suspected the property was deposited & rescued a greater part. But it was a wonderful providence that no blood was shed in the affair. They were some two or three days collected in this manner, and a woman belonging to the Indian Party, when the Collector was seizing property, attempted to stab a Brothertown Indian, and a man of some distinction.[54]

What especially angered Marsh was that the founding father of the Stockbridge republic, John W. Quinney, was the leader of the mob that used force to oppose the tax collector. The Indian agent at Green Bay was summoned to suppress the riot, and he managed to get the Oneidas to return to Duck Creek. Henry Dodge, now back in office as territorial governor, wrote, "Stockbridge Affairs have become so complicated that the Govt. do not know what to do."[55]

An uneasy peace was restored after the New Year and into early 1847, but the Indian Party resolved to segregate itself from its opponents as much as possible. The Presbyterian Mission operated the one school in the northern part of the township, supposedly for all the tribe. However, in 1847 the Indian Party seized control of the school and declared it off-limits to the children of the Citizens Party because "they have a little African blood running in their veins." The parents in the Citizens Party tried to start a school in the southern half of the township, but the Indian Party dismissed it as "an African School" and sought to deny it funds from the mission. Indeed, the Indian Party called the southern half of the township bordering Brothertown "Guinea."[56]

In the midst of this intratribal conflict, there arrived a new missionary for the Presbyterian church. Rev. Jeremiah Slingerland claimed Mohican descent on his mother's side, and he moved to Stockbridge-on-the-Lake to serve his tribe after training for the ministry in New York. He preached the hardest line against the Citizens Party, both in and out of the pulpit. He saw no benefit to the Indian Party in cooperating with a racially mixed inferior people such as the Citizens Party. As he told Marsh, "Our people did all they could for those families in the State of New York and they enjoyed all the privileges which they did in schools and meetings." Slingerland then concluded that this attempt at racial uplift "did no good." Only four Citizens Party families remained in Slingerland's Presbyterian Mission Church, including "one man and his wife who is a mixture of African and Indian, and who was adopted by the Nation before leaving NY State."[57]

The situation at Stockbridge-on-the-Lake became intolerable for members of the Citizens Party, and also for the whites who had bought land through quitclaim deeds and other conveyances in good faith. The whites expected to get title to their lands after the Act of 1843 provided for allotment in fee simple. Instead, in the Act of 1846, Congress declared their claims null and void. The whites put pressure on territorial officials to find a way to enforce their contracts to obtain Indian land. One way was to influence delegates elected by the Wisconsin citizenry to write a new constitution. The document that was finally approved by voters in 1847, and by Congress thereafter, had a most unusual clause for a state constitution as to qualified voters: "Persons of Indian blood who have once been declared by law of congress to be citizens of the United States, any subsequent law of congress to the contrary notwithstanding."[58]

This clause showed the unhappiness of Wisconsin whites with the return of the Stockbridges to tribal status; whites could not sue tribal members for on-reservation actions in U.S. territorial or, after statehood, Wisconsin state courts. An unintended consequence of the constitutional clause was that tribal members got the right to vote in local, state, and national elections. Other Indian tribes had to wait until 1924 for a general granting of federal citizenship, by which time the Stockbridge-Munsees had been voting for more than seventy-five years.[59]

In summer 1847 the Commissioner of Indian Affairs asked Governor Dodge to compile a new census of the Stockbridges and Munsees in advance of making a treaty to resolve outstanding differences. The governor at first asked each side to prepare its own party census, but that effort soon went awry. The Citizens Party balked, and although the Indian Party cooperated with the project, it padded its roll with the names of Stockbridges and Munsees who had emigrated to the trans-Missouri region in 1839. Their self-reported total of 271 members was considerably inflated. Governor Dodge eventually compiled his own list of members of the two factions; he counted 116 Citizens Party members and 92 Indian Party members. The other 179 Indian Party members that he discounted were Canadian Munsees, Missouri River Emigrants, or someone like Jacob J. Maikua, "not here for many years; as likely to attach to one party as the other." Another would-be Indian Party member was George Bennett, "formerly of the Citizens Party; has sold out all his lands; expects to get it all back again under act of 1846." Governor Dodge was most upset at the listing of Eli Williams as a member of the Indian Party, of whom the governor noted, "This man went to Missouri, and returned, charged with murder."[60]

The more Governor Dodge investigated during that summer, the more he learned that the Citizens Party and the Indian Party lived and acted in similar ways, at least insofar as the sale of their lands was concerned. He compiled a long list of land parcels that had been allotted to members of both parties under the Act of 1843 and just as promptly sold to whites. The sellers included all the leaders of the Indian Party, including John W. Quinney, so it seems that members of both parties sold their parcels to whites when they had the chance. The biggest purchaser by far of Stockbridge lands in the one-township reservation was Daniel Whitney. This was not a man who was going to pay thousands of dollars in 1845 for prime lands along Lake Winnebago and then be rebuffed in 1846 by an act of Congress. Reverend Marsh, too, was upset by Quinney's and Slingerland's attitude that the Indian Party was under no obligation, thanks to the Act of 1846, to honor the quitclaim deeds to white buyers. What Governor Dodge reported of George Bennett was apparently true of others: the Act of 1846 put the tribe's members in a position to sell their lands a second time.[61]

The new state authorities in Wisconsin demanded a federal treaty to get the Stockbridges removed from the state. The Commissioner of Indian Affairs appointed two Green Bay residents, Morgan L. Martin, just returned from his service as territorial delegate to Congress, and Albert G. Ellis to negotiate a treaty. The Commissioner instructed Martin and Ellis to take a new census of the tribe and to organize a removal west of the Mississippi for those who chose to remain Stockbridge Indians. The census counted 177 Indians who made up the Stockbridge Nation. Others, notably in the Chicks and Davids families, were omitted altogether.[62]

John Quinney was once again appointed chief negotiator for the nation in the treaty talks with Martin and Ellis. He worked hard to achieve significant monetary payments. Quinney's opening demand in the treaty negotiations was a flat payment of $100,000 in cash, payable immediately for the cession of the one remaining township at Stockbridge-on-the-Lake. And "by payable immediately," Quinney told Commissioners Martin and Ellis, he meant that the funds be placed at the disposal of the sachem and councillors. There would be no trust account or annuity set up to be administered by the Indian agent at Green Bay or the Commissioner of Indian Affairs at Washington. Martin and Ellis balked at the demands. After fifteen days of hard bargaining, the two nations, the Stockbridge and the United States, finally reached an agreement. The Indian Party members were to receive $14,500 for the value of their improvements at Stockbridge-by-the-Lake, based on an inspection and appraisal by the two commissioners. The United States also agreed to pay the Stockbridges an annuity of $16,500 to provide education for their children, or, in the language of the treaty, "the rising generation." Yet another grant of $16,500 was to be paid to the Indian Party for relocation expenses. Article 11 committed the United States to pay an additional $3,000 to the sachem and council "in attending to the business of the tribe since the year 1843." In all, the Indian Party of 177 people came out of fifteen days of negotiation with Martin and Ellis with U.S. promises for $54,500. If that figure was not the $100,000 in cash that was the nation's negotiating demand, it was still far more money than the tribe had ever won before in dealings with the United States. The two commissioners also promised to recommend to their superiors in Washington that the administration append and the Senate approve a settlement of the long-standing Stockbridge claims for the value of the 400-square-mile tract of White River lands in Indiana.[63]

In return for the cash payments and annuity proceeds, the Stockbridge Nation agreed to leave Wisconsin in yet another removal and replant the fire of a new Moh-he-con-nuck somewhere west of the Mississippi in the newly established Minnesota Territory. At the same time, the United States made a renewed effort to remove the Menominees there too. The years 1848–50 were high tide for the Indian removal policy of Jacksonian America in Wisconsin. The Stockbridges and Munsees had helped begin the era for northern tribes after 1820 with their removal from New York to Green Bay. They had resisted removal in the second Jackson administration when the Schermerhorn treaty of 1836 went unratified. Now, in 1848, the nation's days in Wisconsin were numbered to 365, the exact length of time that the United States permitted them to wind up their affairs at Stockbridge-on-the-Lake before setting out for Minnesota.[64]

Outgoing Commissioner of Indian Affairs William Medill and Secretary of War William L. Marcy reviewed the treaty negotiating documents in January 1849. They recommended approval of the work of Martin and Ellis, and President James K. Polk sent the treaty to the Senate late in the session with a recommendation for its approval. In executive session on March 1, the Senate gave its consent to the treaty but inserted an amended article that generated even more controversy. The United States agreed to pay the Stockbridge Nation $25,000 for the loss of the White River lands in Indiana back in 1818, $5,000 immediately on acceptance by the nation and the balance of $20,000 payable in ten annual installments once the nation removed to Minnesota. Securing the payment of $25,000 was a remarkable personal triumph for Quinney. Thirty years after the disappointment of the White River episode, the nation finally achieved a measure of compensation. In addition, the appended article extended the time period to March 1851 for the nation's removal to Minnesota. But the conclusion of the White River claims came at a cost. The U.S. Senate and the president of the United States insisted that the Stockbridge Nation relinquish any further claims on the United States for compensation due from other previous negotiations with Miamis, Delawares, Menominees, or Winnebagos. The appended article was very much intended to put Quinney out of the claims business once and for all.[65]

The new Whig administration of President Taylor had the task of negotiating with the Stockbridge Nation approval of the treaty article appended by the Senate. In June 1849 William H. Bruce, the new Indian agent at Green Bay, journeyed to Stockbridge-on-the-Lake to secure the nation's agreement.

An admiring observer wrote that June of the Stockbridge "chiefs and head men [who are] . . . not to be distinguished in dress and manners from any collection of persons to be seen in our country towns." On June 6 the nation met in council and approved the $25,000 payment and the extended deadline to 1851 for removal. But the nation emphatically rejected the understanding that the Stockbridges could make no future claims on the United States for past unfair dealings. Instead, agent Bruce told the Commissioner of Indian Affairs:

> The said Stockbridges believe they do not thereby release the government of the United States from the payment, in future, of any annuities secured to the said Stockbridges by or under, former and subsisting treaties between them and said United States.[66]

It is fair to say that the United States signed the treaty of 1848 with the Indian Party. Just as in 1839, there is no mention of the Munsees or their rights to the tribal estate. The Citizens Party leaders were not to share in the proceeds from the treaty, although they and their parents had at least as good a claim as the Quinney Party to a share in the $25,000 for the White River claim. The unfinished business with the Citizens Party meant that the treaty of 1848 would not be the final action that the United States hoped would make the Stockbridge troubles disappear. And then there was the matter of removal to Minnesota, slated for no later than March 1851. The United States became quite active in Minnesota Indian diplomacy, negotiating land cession treaties with the Ojibwes, Ho-Chunks, and Dakotas between 1847 and 1851. These newly acquired tracts in the Minnesota Territory offered the possibility of homelands for Wisconsin Indian nations, including the Stockbridges and Menominees.[67]

Thanks to Quinney's skillful negotiating at the 1848 treaty council, the nation held a check on the power of the United States to select the site of their future home in Minnesota. The removal clause of the 1848 treaty read, "They will remove to the country set apart for them, or such other west of the Mississippi River as they may be able to secure." The Commissioners of Indian Affairs in the Taylor and Fillmore administrations interpreted this article of the 1848 treaty to mean that the United States would select the seventy-two sections of the new Stockbridge Indian Reservation, "the Indians to be consulted as to its location."[68]

Mere consultation was not what the Stockbridges thought they had agreed to in the 1848 treaty. Rather, they wanted to be the ones to do the selecting, and they would do the consulting with the United States after having made their selection. In summer 1849 a party of Mohicans set out from Stockbridge-on-the-Lake for Fort Snelling, Minnesota, where the Indian agent resided. The Stockbridges arrived unexpectedly and soon began looking at likely locations for their two-township reservation. The Stockbridges liked the area around Fort Snelling (the site of the present-day Minneapolis–St. Paul airport), and they told the Indian agent that they had made their selection. This news did not meet with the approval of the Commissioner of Indian Affairs, who saw in the selection a repeat of the history of the Grand Kakalin site, namely, an Indian reservation close to an army outpost, located on an important river thoroughfare, with all the possibilities for fraternization and trouble. The United States declined to endorse such a selection in the Minnesota Territory for a new Moh-he-con-nuck. The Stockbridges next turned their attention to a location on the Vermillion River in Minnesota, near present-day Hastings. That site, too, was disapproved by the United States. Instead, the United States had the idea of moving the Stockbridges onto lands ceded by the Dakotas in an 1851 treaty that resulted in the United States acquiring title to lands in the Minnesota River Valley. This area did not suit the Stockbridges, however, and the two sides remained at loggerheads on the topic of removal.[69]

The Stockbridges were just one of the Indian nations of Wisconsin that the United States attempted to remove to Minnesota. The Menominees had agreed in an 1848 treaty of their own to cede their remaining Wisconsin lands to the United States and remove to Minnesota. The United States expected the Oneidas to do the same, or to follow the example of the Brothertowners and divide their reservation into individually owned parcels, to become citizens, and to dissolve their tribe. The Wisconsin Ojibwes were forced in 1850 to seek their annuities in the Minnesota

Territory, in contravention of the established pattern of paying annuities at La Pointe on Lake Superior. In writing about the negotiations for Stockbridge removal in 1850, the Commissioner of Indian Affairs looked forward to the time when "Wisconsin, like most of the other States, will be relieved substantially of the evils of an Indian population."[70]

The Menominees and Ojibwes struggled after 1850 to remain in Wisconsin, and both tribes mobilized white sentiment in their favor. After the death of President Taylor and the accession of President Fillmore, the drive for a final Indian removal from Wisconsin eased and then halted. In the following Pierce administration, both the Menominees and the Ojibwes signed treaties with the United States securing new Wisconsin homelands as retrocessions from the public domain of the United States. The change of heart on the part of the United States also spared the Stockbridges and the Oneidas from renewed pressure to remove or to end tribal relations.[71]

As the Mohicans waited at Stockbridge-on-the-Lake for their future life in Minnesota, or wherever they might move, the intratribal strife continued. Quinney carried his search for claims payments too far as a result of the 1848 treaty, and his actions led the nation to repudiate him. Even before the 1848 treaty was ratified, Quinney had gone into business with Daniel Whitney to buy discounted shares of the anticipated treaty payments and annuities. For as little as twenty-five cents on the dollar, Quinney paid out Whitney's cash to Stockbridge members in 1848 and 1849 and in return secured the rights to the expected future stream of treaty-based payments from the United States. Desperately poor Stockbridges accepted the partial payments from their sachem, but he was little more than a front man for Whitney, who stood to reap a windfall when the payments from the United States finally arrived. Quinney's shady and likely illegal activities finally led the nation in 1852 to depose him as sachem and, in one of the saddest documents written in Stockbridge history, to instruct the Commissioner of Indian Affairs that John W. Quinney was no longer to be considered a representative of the nation. Even Austin, John's cousin, signed the declaration.[72]

Quinney did not cease lobbying after 1852, but from that point on he openly sought compensation for himself, first from the United States and later from New York State. Quinney petitioned Congress in 1852 for a personal payment of $15,456 out of the funds that the United States owed under the treaty of 1848 and also for a grant of 360 acres in the old Stockbridge Reservation on Lake Winnebago. Writing as "Wau-nau-con, the Muh-he-con-new," Quinney began his petition in a style that Hendrick Aupaumut would have recognized. He adopted a paternal tone in reminding Congress that his grandfather David Nau-nau-neek-nuk "was a warrior and . . . assisted your fathers in their struggle for liberty." In effect, he was placing himself a generation older than the men in Congress and called on them to grant his request as a mature and successful son would to an aging father. Quinney also made it plain that he would not remove with the nation to Minnesota or wherever it might go. Instead, he would live out his days at Stockbridge-on-the-Lake. An OIA employee sourly noted that the Stockbridges of both parties hoped to get their "hands into the pockets of 'Uncle Sam' through the hole made by John W. Quinney." Congress granted his petition for the 360 acres at Stockbridge-by-the-Lake but only $1,000 in cash payment.[73]

Rather than settle down in Stockbridge-by-the-Lake in quiet retirement, Quinney, at the age of fifty-six, made one last remove, this time back to Madison County, New York, where he began his final lobbying campaign to get additional compensation from New York State for the lands sold at New Stockbridge between 1815 and 1825. His Fourth of July address in 1854 is the last public document surviving from his pen. Again, in good Aupaumut style, Quinney attempted to forge a connection built on blood ties with his audience. He advanced the idea in his address that the Mohicans were the Lost Tribe of Israel, who washed up on the Pacific sometime during their exile and slowly made their way eastward to New York. Quinney recounted the history of the welcome that his "twenty-five thousand warrior" ancestors gave to Hendrik Hudson and the Europeans in the early seventeenth century. He was speaking to an audience in upstate New York that July that was in the midst of a political upheaval over the passage of the Kansas-Nebraska Act and the topic of the expansion of slavery in the American West. Quinney was not shy about commenting on the current state of race relations in the United States:

> The Indian is said to be the ward of the white man, and the negro his slave. Has it ever occurred to you, my friends, that while the slave is increasing, and increased by every appliance, the Indian is left to rot and die, before the humanities of this model *Republic!* You have your

tears, and groans, and mobs, and riots, for the individuals of the
former, while your indifference of purpose, and vacillation of policy
is hurrying to extinction, whole communities of the latter.[74]

As the children of God, now down on their luck, the Mohican John W.
Quinney, asked the New Yorkers not to forget the Lost Israelites. He did
not allude to his lobbying requests of the New York legislature, but he did
ask for justice for two hundred fifty years of Mohican generosity to the
Anglo-Saxons in the Americas.

After the Civil War, a Wisconsin cleric who knew the Stockbridges said
of Quinney that he was "a man of character, ability, and a Christian."
Furthermore, Quinney "was to his people what Clay and Webster were to
the whites." It is an interesting comparison, if not entirely apt. Quinney
probably had more in common with John C. Calhoun than the other two
members of the "Great Triumvirate." What is clear is that after Quinney's
death in 1855, the Mohican republic he helped to create died with him.[75]

CHAPTER 4

The Mohicans and the Pine Ring on the New Reservation, 1856–1871

The impetus for yet another treaty between the Mohican Nation and the United States began when the nation declined to remove to Minnesota by 1851, as stipulated in the amended treaty of 1848. The treaty committed the president to find the tribe a new home within two years of ratification, and when the United States failed to meet that deadline the Mohican leaders refused to move. Conflict over land titles escalated at Stockbridge-on-the-Lake between whites who wanted to take possession of parcels they bought in good faith and Mohicans who sold the lands but had nowhere to go. A renewed fight between the Indian Party and the Citizens Party broke out in 1853, and both factions inundated the Commissioner of Indian Affairs with requests for action. The tribe's leaders acknowledged the plenary power of Congress, but they preferred to deal with the United States on a nation-to-nation basis via the negotiated treaty. An 1854 petition from the Citizens Party faction noted:

> Congress has asserted the power (whether rightfully or not) to legislate for us at pleasure. It has given us civil and political privileges, and again deprived us of them without our consent, and in no instance of late years, by so doing, has it conferred favors upon us.[1]

The Pierce administration's Commissioner of Indian Affairs, George Manypenny, wrote in his 1854 and 1855 annual reports about the need to find a new Wisconsin location for the Stockbridge-Munsees. During the second session of the Thirty-third Congress (1854–55), an appropriation was made to underwrite yet another treaty negotiation with the Stockbridges. Because of reorganization of the Indian Office, the negotiations were undertaken by a new officer, the superintendent of northern Indian affairs, Francis Huebschman, who was based in Milwaukee. The Interior Department also dispatched to Stockbridge-on-the-Lake the commissioner of the General Land Office, John Wilson, because of his knowledge of the land title tangle in Calumet County. In June 1855 the United States and the nation reached a treaty agreement. The United States accomplished what Commissioner Manypenny wanted in the form of agreement by the Mohicans that all Stockbridges and Munsees were to be reunited without regard to political differences. The Mohicans got what they wanted also: the United States agreed to retrocede the one township of land in Calumet County that the nation had relinquished in the 1848 treaty. In addition, the Mohicans would have restored to them lands for which they had received individual payments from white buyers. Commissioner Wilson agreed that the United States would compensate the white deed holders in the amount of $20,000 but that they would have to leave the re-created reservation.[2]

When the signed treaty reached the Office of Indian Affairs for review, Commissioner Manypenny balked at the cost and at the idea of keeping the nation at Stockbridge-on-the-Lake. He refused to recommend ratification to the secretary of the interior and President Pierce. There matters remained for the rest of 1855. The Mohicans waited at Stockbridge-on-the-Lake for a new round of treaty making. Meanwhile, Commissioner Manypenny was reviewing the problems with land and title at the Calumet County reservation and concluded that the tribe would have to make a permanent move. On January 7, 1856, Manypenny wrote a letter to Northern Superintendent Huebschman that contained the following directive:

> Arrangements ought therefore be made at once to provide them [the Stockbridges] with a home, to which they could be induced to remove. The true interest and the happiness of the Indians will be promoted by a cheerful and ready acquiescence, and in the acceptance of such home wherever provided, and it should be a home alike for the Stockbridges, whether known as "citizens" or "Indians,"

and the Munsees, parties to the Treaty of September 8th, 1839, wherever they may now be. . . . [Y]ou are authorized to arrange with the Menominees for a portion of their reservation for a home for the Stockbridges and Munsees.[3]

Commissioner Manypenny also instructed Huebschman to include in the anticipated treaty a provision to allow tribal members to sever tribal relations and obtain individual landholdings at the town of Stockbridge, Wisconsin, that is, at the Calumet County site beside Lake Winnebago. In effect, this option repeated the article in the Act of 1846 allowing individual Stock-bridges to declare citizenship and obtain fee simple title to their parcels.

The treaty, signed on February 5, 1856, by Superintendent Huebsch-man, carried out the commissioner's instructions. The agreement gathered all the scattered Stockbridges and Munsees at a new unspecified site, where a roll was taken, and provided for them future allotments in trust. The last article, 16, provided for the severance from the nation of those who wished to remain at the town of Stockbridge. On February 23 Huebschman sent a report of his actions to Commissioner Manypenny. The Commissioner of Indian Affairs gave his approval to the treaty on March 3 and sent it to the Senate for its advice and consent. That body approved the treaty, with two amendments, on April 18, 1856.[4]

An important feature of the 1856 treaty was the provision that the new reservation be subdivided into individual allotments for tribal members. There was a sliding scale in the amount of acreage slated for the different Mohicans. Married men were to receive eighty-acre allotments; single men and women over the age of eighteen and children were to receive forty acres. The treaty stipulated that a sufficient amount of land was to be reserved for "the rising generation," a phrase taken verbatim from the 1848 treaty.

The 1856 treaty between the United States and the Stockbridge-Munsees anticipated in some ways the later policy of the United States promulgated in the General Allotment Act of 1887. Tribal or communal landowning was to end, with some exceptions, and individual ownership and proprie-torship of the lands was to begin. Control over the length of the trust period, during which individual allotments were inalienable, was in the hands of the tribal council, not the president of the United States.

Commissioner Manypenny oversaw the negotiation of other allotment treaties during the Pierce administration. There were, however, important differences between the 1856 treaty agreement on allotment and the 1887 congressional imposition of allotment. For example, according to the former, the tribal council controlled the length of the trust period on allotments during which the parcel remained inalienable. Certainly the 1856 treaty between the United States and the Stockbridge-Munsees did not call for an end to the nation. There was no provision leading to gradual citizenship, if only because the Mohicans had already been declared Wisconsin citizens in the new state's 1848 constitution.[5]

After learning of the April 18 Senate approval, the tribal council met to ratify the amended treaty and did so at the end of July 1856. By that time, tribal members had learned about Superintendent Huebschman's plans for locating them in Shawano County. In June Reverend Slingerland and other tribal members accompanied Huebschman to the Menominee Reservation and inspected the lands Huebschman had in mind for the tribe. In September 1856 Slingerland wrote to Commissioner Manypenny about his visit to the Menominee Reservation, saying that it was "rather doubtful of its meeting the agreement in the treaty of its being 'one-half arable land.'" He asked Manypenny to intervene with Huebschman and reserve all of "Township 28 North Range 14 East, thirty out of thirty-six sections in Township 29 North Range 14 East, and six sections from Township 29 North Range 15 East."[6]

Slingerland's comments indicate that the location of the new Stockbridge-Munsee Indian Reservation had not been definitively set in the 1856 treaty, for he made it clear that the tribe wanted what is now the town of Red Springs and the township to the north that includes the present settlement of Neopit, as well as a one-mile strip running east within T29N R15E to the Wolf River. His comments indicate that the tribe expected to receive a full two townships of land, the same amount the tribe had received under the 1832 treaty at Lake Winnebago and the same amount expected in Minnesota under the 1848 treaty.

Article 3 of the 1856 treaty directed that "sufficient land shall be reserved for the rising generation." The language is ambiguous; it is unclear if "rising generation" meant just the children alive at the time of the signing of the treaty or all children ever born to the signers of the treaty. The easiest way to measure the "rising generation" is simply to count the number of adults and children listed in the appendix to the treaty of February 5, 1856. Ninety-four adult men and 105 adult women signed the treaty and made the commitment to relocate from Stockbridge-on-the-Lake to Shawano County. That group also had 212 children. So one way to estimate the total extent of the tribe's political population and its rising generation is to call it the 199 adults plus the 212 children tabulated in the treaty of 1856. Article 3 also provided the formula for calculating how much land was to be allotted: "Each head of a family shall be entitled to eighty acres of land, and in case his or her family consists of more than four members, if thought expedient by the said council, eighty acres more may be allowed to him or her." The reference to families of more than four members is suggestive. If Stockbridge-Munsee families were occasionally, or commonly, more than four members, then perhaps a better definition of "rising generation" is childen ever born to signers of the 1856 treaty.

The federal census of 1900 offers some retrospective evidence about the number of children that women bore. That population count asked women about their marital status, the total number of live births they ever had, and the number of surviving children in 1900. The special "Census of Indian Population" for that year counted 86 women over the age of sixteen on the Stockbridge-Munsee Reservation and therefore who fit the category that historical demographers use when examining marriage and fertility. Nine of the 86 Stockbridge-Munsee women listed in the 1900 census were at least sixteen when the 1856 treaty was signed; that is, they were born no later than 1840. All 9 women were either married in 1900 or had once been married and were now widowed. Thus, in the language of the historical demographer, these 9 women had an "ever-married" ratio of 100 percent. All 9 bore children, 71 in all, making the average number of births just under 8 children per mother. The appendix to the 1856 treaty lists 105 adult women as members of the tribe, so if the 9 listed in the 1900 census are representative of their cohort, it is possible to project backward a fertility rate of 7.88 children ever born for an expected total of 827 total children. That is a much greater number, with quite different consequences for land and resources on the reservation, than just the 212 children listed in the treaty appendix. Taking care of the rising generation was an important political and economic challenge for the tribe.[7]

In addition to receiving complaints from Slingerland that fall of 1856, Commissioner Manypenny received a complaint that the land on the Menominee Reservation was ill suited for agriculture. Nonetheless, Superintendent Huebschman would not budge on his site selection. He

insisted that selections for allotments under the treaty be limited to the
south half of T28N R14E and in the "two southern tiers of Sections west
of Wolf River in T28 & R15."[8]

Commissioner Manypenny turned his attention to the boundaries of
the new Stockbridge-Munsee Indian Reservation. In a letter to Huebschman dated October 7, 1856, Manypenny wrote, "I apprehend the Menomonees [sic] will not consent that the Stockbridge and Munsees shall have
the land designated by Mr. Slingerland." Manypenny then turned the
matter back to Huebschman for further discussion and resolution. The
next month, the commissioner included in his annual report a short statement that the Stockbridge-Munsees were to receive a tract of land at the
"western edge of the Menominee reservation."[9]

Also in fall 1856, Superintendent Huebschman was busy fending off
charges of fraud and corruption made against him by Slingerland and
other Stockbridge-Munsees. In early 1857 Commissioner Manypenny
appointed a new OIA official, Amos Layman, to visit the old Calumet
County reservation and sort out the details of the Article 16 provisions
that allowed tribal members to leave the tribe and take up patents in the
town of Stockbridge.[10]

Congress established the two-township Stockbridge-Munsee Indian
Reservation in the 1857 Appropriation Bill for the OIA. Working with
Congress to establish the reservation was one of the last official acts that
Commissioner Manypenny undertook. Near the end of the third session
of the Thirty-fourth Congress (winter 1856–57), Congressman Charles
Billingshurst of Wisconsin wrote to Commissioner Manypenny, asking,
"Is any appropriation necessary to carry out the Treaty of Feb. 11 '56 with
the Menominees & if so how much?"[11] The answer was in the Appropriations Bill, which provided for a payment to the Menominees of a total
of $27,648, the product of multiplying sixty cents times 46,080, the
number of acres in the two townships. Congress thus explicitly endorsed
the two-township reservation in Shawano County as the new homeland
for the Stockbridge-Munsees.[12]

The move to Shawano County after the 1856 treaty forced a reunification
of the Mohican and Munsee Nations into a single polity. Commissioner
Manypenny held this as a prime goal in his treaty-making instructions, and
indeed scattered Stockbridges and Munsees from Wisconsin, Kansas, New
York, and British North America took the opportunity to start anew on the

Shawano County reservation. But forced political reunification did not bring a new era of tribal reconciliation.

The Mohican Nation had to devise a new economic base to feed and nurture the people. John W. Quinney had extracted as much money as possible from the United States in payment for the old claims to the White River lands, the Menominee-Winnebago treaties of 1821–22, the sale of the New York Indian Tract in 1838, and the cession of the Stockbridge Indian Reservation in 1839 and 1848. The Quinney era of basing a tribal economy on government claims payments and on quitclaim land sale revenue ended with the treaty of 1856. The new tribal economy, insofar as the United States planned it, was to be based on the individual agricultural efforts of Stockbridge and Munsee families. Unfortunately for the Mohican Indians, the poor soil of the site chosen by Superintendent Huebschman made such an economy almost impossible. The struggle to create a workable Stockbridge-Munsee economic base dominated the politics of the era of the nation's history from 1856 to 1893, even as the Citizens Party and the Indian Party continued to struggle for control of the Mohican polity.

The nation made another fresh start by scrapping the 1837 Quinney constitution and promulgating a new national charter in early 1857. Led by Citizens Party head John N. Chicks, the drafters of the new constitution began their preamble with an acknowledgment of the Great Spirit, who has "made His mighty arm bare in the preservation and establishment of a part of the Muh-he-con-neew." The constitution established a new, "united nation" of Mohicans and Delawares, Stockbridges and Munsees, whether living in Wisconsin, Kansas, or New York. All would be entitled to equal citizenship in the nation. Also, property qualifications and the religious test were abolished. The constitution of 1857 set forth rules for annual elections of a sachem, council, peacemaker, pathmaster, and sheriff. The constitution also included a Bill of Rights, which was limited to elements of the first, fifth, and eighth amendments to the U.S. Constitution. The main feature of the Chicks constitution of 1857 was that it reenfranchised the men whom Quinney had cast aside in the negotiations for the 1848 treaty. Under federal prodding, the nation once more consisted of the New York Munsees, the Kansas emigrants, and the Citizens and Indian Parties.[13]

An immediate political effect of the 1856 treaty was the loss of power by the Quinney family and its allies. Many in the family refused to recognize the legitimacy of the 1856 treaty and stayed as squatters at Stockbridge-on-the-Lake. In the political void of late 1856 and early 1857, the old Emigrant Party opponents of the Quinneys from the 1830s, the Hendricks family, reemerged to take power. Thomas P. Hendricks, Jr., grandson of Hendrick Aupaumut, became the new sachem under the 1857 constitution. The new council included members of the Chicks and Jacobs and Gardner families, members of the Citizens Party who had been shut out of political power since the Quinney resurgence in 1846. The ratification of the new constitution in 1857 did not lead to an era of political harmony. Instead, after a setback of a few years as political outsiders, the Indian Party faction worked to regain power and impose a final, irreversible defeat on their Citizens Party foes. The differences were not so much about policy or the direction of the nation but an all-out struggle for power by rival families. All the bitterness of the politics of the 1840s returned anew in the contest between the parties.[14]

At Stockbridge-on-the-Lake, the Mohican Nation's political leaders had retained control among themselves as much as possible. The U.S. Indian agent at Green Bay kept a respectable distance, and outside whites, such as Daniel Whitney, tried to intervene politically only when their investments were threatened by lawlessness on the reservation. At Moh-he-connuck on the Red River in Shawano County, by contrast, outside whites took a decided interest in the natural resources of the two-township reservation, none more than the longtime congressman for the Fifth District of Wisconsin, Philetus Sawyer. Where Hendrick Aupaumut and John W. Quinney dominated earlier periods of Mohican political history, the nation's history during the period 1856–93 was instead overshadowed by the machinations of Congressman and later Senator Sawyer. The proprietor of P. Sawyer & Sons Lumber Mills, president of the First National Bank of Oshkosh, and partner in numerous other businesses, Sawyer was aware of the need to secure ever more pine to feed the sawmills at Oshkosh, downstream on the Wolf River from the new Menominee and Stockbridge-Munsee Reservations.[15]

Superintendent Huebschman had made a bad decision to settle an agricultural people on land of such poor quality. He had at his disposal detailed information about the quality of the land that he selected to purchase from the Menominees for the benefit of the Stockbridge-Munsees. The two townships that formed the new Stockbridge-Munsee Reservation had been surveyed by the Interior Department's General Land Office in 1852 and 1853, that is, before the 1854 Menominee treaty established that tribe's reservation boundaries and well before Huebschman negotiated the 1856 treaty with the Stockbridge-Munsees. The surveyors first traced the exterior boundaries of the townships in 1852 and then returned the next year to fix the interior section lines. They recorded in their field notebooks their eyewitness observations that the two townships consisted mainly of second- and third-rate soil and swamplands that were marginal for farming. However, the surveyors noted that the townships contained a considerable white pine timber reserve.[16]

Huebschman and subsequent OIA officials lost interest in implementing the allotment terms of the treaty of 1856. Much of the OIA's attention in 1857, 1858, and 1859 was devoted to wrapping up affairs at Stockbridge-on-the-Lake and encouraging the scattered Stockbridges and Munsees to relocate to Shawano County. After the Civil War broke out in spring 1861, federal officials had neither the time nor the resources to devote to Stockbridge-Munsee affairs. Huebschman was to blame for not taking the first step in the allotment process, the survey of the two townships into 1,152 separate parcels of forty acres each. Instead, the Stockbridge-Munsees informally made preallotment selections of land parcels. The nation's minister, Jeremiah Slingerland, kept a record book of these selections, most of them in the easternmost of the two townships, T28N R14E. Most families lived around the combined church and school building at a hamlet known as Red Springs. Few tribal members lived on their parcel selections. Some families, notably the Touseys and Gardners, made selections on land in the adjoining Menominee Reservation in T28N R15E. The Tousey and Gardner families lived on their selections in a neighborhood that was known as the Two-Mile Strip.[17]

The tribe held elections at Red Springs on New Year's Day 1858 under the new constitution. John P. Hendricks was elected sachem, with John N. Chicks, Adam Davids, Peter Littleman, and Reverend Slingerland as councilors. The first order of business for the new council was to contemplate yet another removal of the Mohican Nation. The council appointed Hendricks, Slingerland, and Ziba Peters the task of "renewing [the nation's] Friendship with the Oneida Nation." The council had a proposal for the Oneidas and for the U.S. Indian agent at Green Bay: the Stockbridge-Munsees would sell their new reservation in Shawano County and use the proceeds to buy a township from the Oneidas, or about one-third of the land within the Oneida Reservation. The nation proposed an arrangement similar to the one that held between 1785 and 1825: the two nations would live adjacent to one another but on separate tracts. The Indian Office did not rule out the proposal, but the Oneida Nation did. Discussions on the proposed move to Oneida continued into 1859 and were revived again after the Civil War, but the Stockbridge-Munsees never received a welcome from the Oneidas.[18]

The unsuccessful proposal for a move to Oneida showed how little regard the Stockbridge-Munsees had for the economic geography of their new reservation. For the first several years of life in Shawano County, the tribe depended for food on emergency rations provided by the Indian Office. A payment in 1862 from the State of New York to the Stockbridges and Munsees for lands purchased decades earlier provided some desperately needed income.[19]

For the Stockbridge-Munsees on the new Shawano County reservation, the Civil War years were marked by disease, poverty, and hardship. Their children suffered through a measles epidemic in 1864, and in 1865 adults and young alike were stricken by a smallpox epidemic that killed five tribal members. Still, soon after the United States began recruiting Wisconsin Indians into service, forty-three men enlisted in Wisconsin volunteer regiments. Stockbridge-Munsee men saw some of the worst fighting of the war as their regiments deployed to the Virginia theater with the Army of the Potomac during its May and June 1864 offensive.[20]

Service in the U.S. Army brought back the issue of citizenship and sovereignty before the Mohican Nation. The specific issue was the jurisdiction of the Mohican Nation's High Court to hear a divorce case brought by Simeon Gardner against his wife, Eliza, on grounds of adultery. She fought the case and argued that the High Court lacked jurisdiction since Simeon had enlisted in the U.S. Army and therefore "has sworn himself citizen of U.S. and must look to that government for redress." The High Court rejected this argument with the statement that Simeon Gardner's enlistment papers "were nothing more than [an] oath of allegiance which makes him no more [a] citizen of the U.S. to deprive him of tribal privileges."[21] The Stockbridge-Munsee High Court worked out in this 1864 lawsuit an important political matter: a tribal member could serve the United States in one area of life and still retain tribal membership. Dual sovereignty was tried, and it worked in the Civil War. Like their American Indian neighbors, the Menominees and the Oneidas, the Stockbridge-Munsees volunteered for military service at a higher ratio than that of the general Wisconsin (or northern) population. This continued the tradition of the nation's military service to the United States that had started in the Revolutionary War, continued in the War of 1812, and subsequently in all the wars, conflicts, and police actions of the twentieth century.

In 1865 Congress finally addressed the economic problems caused by Huebschman's antebellum choice of location for the reservation. During the busy Thirty-eighth Congress, the House and Senate passed a bill permitting Stockbridge-Munsee tribal members to make land selections on the public domain under the provisions of the 1862 Homestead Act. Stockbridge-Munsees could select a quarter section (160 acres) on the public domain and receive patents from the General Land Office and then become citizens of the United States. Congress considered this a genuine boon to tribal members, since it was offering them the benefit of the public land laws unavailable to other Indian nations. There was no House or Senate hearing on the bill, no congressional report, and no discussion in the *Congressional Globe*. The results, however, of the Act of 1865, disappointed federal policy makers: few if any tribal members sought a citizen's life off the reservation on a new homestead.[22]

The Stockbridge-Munsee soldiers who mustered out of army service in summer 1865 returned to a reservation with little economic activity. That fall, forest fires swept through the northern part of the eastern township of the reservation and into the Menominee Reservation. The damage was so extensive that the affected area was soon dubbed the "Burnt District." The OIA's Green Bay agent asked for and received authority from the Commissioner of Indian Affairs to conduct logging operations in the Burnt District. The agent signed a five-year contract with lumberman Ransom Gillet. The start of logging operations on the reservation, even limited to the Burnt District, pointed the way to a productive economic future.[23]

The next federal effort to alleviate poverty among the Stockbridge-Munsees was a treaty negotiated by Acting Commissioner of Indian Affairs Lewis Bogy and signed in Washington on February 15, 1867. The treaty compelled the tribe to "cede and relinquish" its ownership of the two-township reservation. There was no ambiguity about the fact that the Shawano County reservation would end with implementation of the terms.

There was more to the treaty, however, than a land cession. It called for the Citizens Party to separate permanently from the tribe and the Indian Party to remove to an unspecified location. In return for ceding and relinquishing the reservation, the Citizens Party was to receive a payment of $32,829, along with another $10,259 for roads and public buildings on the reservation. The United States committed to paying the Indian Party's debts, up to $15,000, and to spending up to $30,000 in moving expenses for the Indian Party.[24]

The OIA dealt with the nation by treaty in 1867, despite the fact that the treaty of 1856 gave Congress the power to legislate the affairs of the Stockbridge-Munsees. On a matter of such importance as the ending of the reservation, and the second detribalization of the Citizens Party, the OIA felt it was important to negotiate a new treaty with the full consent of the tribe. The sum of just over $43,000 intended for the Citizens Party was only a fraction of the value of the standing timber in the two townships. This was understood at the time; John Hendricks, one of the Citizens Party leaders, wrote in a February 12, 1867, letter that the pine holdings were worth at least twice that amount alone. The Indian Party, remarkably, only insisted on receiving payment for the debts of the leaders doing tribal business (including lobbying the very treaty at issue) and for relocation expenses. This suggests that in 1867 neither the Indian Party nor the Indian Office had given much thought to the value of the reservation timber, nor had they thought about how to maximize its value for the benefit of the tribe. It is worth noting the presence in Washington of U.S. Indian agent and Green Bay resident Morgan L. Martin. He was the man who negotiated the 1848 treaty on behalf of the United States and had close ties to the Indian Party leaders.[25]

The treaty of February 15, 1867, moved quickly through the executive branch, receiving endorsements from the Commissioner of Indian Affairs on the 19th of that month, the secretary of the interior on the 25th, and President Johnson on March 13. The proposed treaty was read for the first time to the Senate the next day and referred to the Committee on Indian Affairs. That committee also gave its approval. However, the full Senate did not give its consent in executive session on April 13 and returned the treaty to the committee. As with several other treaties negotiated in 1867, the Stockbridge-Munsee treaty was held up because of wrangling between the Senate and the House over Indian treaty making. The Senate might approve treaties without the participation of the House, but without House support in the way of appropriations to meet treaty obligations the United States could not continue to deal with Indian nations via treaty. Senate consideration of the Stockbridge-Munsee treaty definitively ended in March 1869 when that body passed Resolution S30, which suspended treaty making between the United States and Indian nations.[26]

During fall 1867, Martin and his superiors in the OIA in Washington began to receive complaints about tribal member Jesse Wybro's logging operations in the north half of T28N R14E. The complainant, lumberman James Jenkins, protested at Christmas of that year that Stockbridge-Munsee Indians such as Wybro had no right to cut their own timber because they had signed it away in the February 1867 treaty. Jenkins also complained that Wybro's logs were likely to damage the wing dams and other navigation improvements on the West Branch of the Wolf River.[27]

The Senate's failure to ratify the treaty led Martin and his friends in the Indian Party to try once again in March 1868. Reverend Slingerland was driven to a frenzy by the failure of the 1867 treaty. He begged Martin to help rid the nation of the Citizens Party members, people like Jesse Wybro whom he disparagingly called "pine niggers" or sometimes "white men." That March, Martin drafted yet another treaty between the Stockbridge-Munsees and the United States. A review of the surviving letters in the Morgan Martin Papers shows that he was intimately involved in the negotiations for the 1867 treaty, the 1868 draft treaty, and congressional legislation in 1870 and 1871. He corresponded frequently with Indian Party leaders, and through him it is possible to retrace the workings of the combination of Indian Party men and lumbermen known to history as the "Pine Ring."[28]

Sachem Darius Charles and Reverend Slingerland (also an elected tribal councilor) urged Martin to return to Washington to get the OIA to negotiate directly with the Oneidas to relinquish a 10,000-acre portion of the Oneida Indian Reservation for the Indian Party of Stockbridges. At some point between January and March 1868, Martin and the Indian Party leaders abandoned the idea of moving to Oneida and instead hit on a new strategy. It involved yet another treaty, this one ceding to the United States all of the western township (T28N R13E) and the north half of the eastern township (T28N R14E) but keeping the south half for themselves. It is significant that the proposed treaty of 1868 contained no provision, as did the unratified one of 1867, for both Indian Party and Citizens Party to ratify the pact.[29]

Martin drafted such a treaty and had it signed by the Indian Party leaders. Next, the Commissioner of Indian Affairs gave his approval to the treaty, but his superior, the secretary of the interior did not, and once again the efforts of the Indian Party to separate its rivals from the tribe went for nothing. Unlike the unratified treaty of 1867, there is no evidence that Congress ever took any action on the draft treaty of 1868, or even that it was informed that the Commissioner of Indian Affairs had agreed to Martin's work to negotiate a new treaty.

In summer 1869 the Indian Party sachem, Darius Charles, and his councilors sent a petition to the Commonwealth of Massachusetts asking for compensation for the lands along the Housatonic River that the Mohicans vacated after the American Revolution. The Stockbridge-Munsee petitioners claimed that individual whites had cheated the Mohicans out of their land parcels for less than one cent per acre and that as a matter of law, the nation's "title ha[d] never been extinguished." Sachem Charles and his councilors sought to advance their argument with the Massachusetts legislature by borrowing liberally from John W. Quinney's 1854 Fourth of July address on the topic of whites, blacks, and Indians. In 1869 Charles and his party wrote that Massachusetts "petted and caressed the black man" but left the Indian "to rot." As the Stockbridge-Munsee petition read, the white man of 1869 called the black man "his brother" and the Indian "his ward." The Wisconsin Mohicans likely miscalculated the attitude toward race in Republican-dominated Reconstruction Massachusetts, as well as the different climate that prevailed in 1869. Although sentiment for African American political and civil rights was not popular with the Stockbridge Indian Party, it was an important article of political belief for Massachusetts Republicans. The Massachusetts House of Representatives denied the Mohicans' petition, noting that neither the Massachusetts Bay Colony nor the Commonwealth had countenanced fraud against the Stockbridges. Then the Massachusetts Republicans made a racist retort to the Mohican complaint about favored treatment of the freed slaves. Massachusetts chided the Mohicans for their "almost ineradicable national characteristics," which the Bay Staters said prevented the Stockbridges from having taken full advantage of the opportunities offered by several generations of New England tutelage.[30]

With the Massachusetts initiative a dead end, the leaders of the Indian Party turned their attention once again to Washington for a solution to their political and economic woes. The problems of poverty, disease, and unrest on the reservation were part of the background Congress understood when it took up legislation about the tribe in the Forty-first Congress (1870–71). However, the timing of the legislation had more to do with the increasing public recognition of the value of the tribe's timber holdings and the ongoing crisis in intratribal relations between the Indian Party and the Citizens Party. The economic relationships between the Stockbridge-Munsee people and their white neighbors in Shawano County and downstream on the Wolf River is crucial to explaining Congress's sweeping legislation affecting the Stockbridge-Munsees in 1871.

The Wolf River watershed was just one of the river networks stretching north into the pineries that enterprising Wisconsinites exploited in the Civil War era. Starting in the 1850s, Oshkosh emerged as the sawmilling capital of the Wolf River watershed, and the lumbermen of that city understandably took the measure of the pine resources upstream. Lumber prices surged during the Civil War years and stayed high even afterward, with good stumpage consistently bringing $5 per thousand board feet. Throughout the 1850s and into the 1860s, the Oshkosh market absorbed the cut pine of the Wolf. An 1870 publication, *Advantages and Productions of the Counties of Brown, Door, Oconto and Shawano*, proclaimed that Shawano County lumbermen were cutting 80 million to 125 million board feet of pine per year, at prices of $8 to $10 per thousand board feet. By the late 1860s the lumbermen had logged north on the river right up to the lands of the Stockbridge-Munsee and Menominee Reservations. In the mid-1850s those two reservations were viewed as fringe areas, away from the main path of white agricultural settlement. Now, after the Civil War, the two reservations, with their lands off-limits to lumbermen, thwarted the growth of Oshkosh and Shawano.[31]

According to the historian Richard N. Current, Congressman Sawyer and the Oshkosh lumbermen wanted to get at the twelve townships filled with white pine that constituted the Stockbridge-Munsee and Menominee Reservations, particularly the Menominee one, which contemporaries estimated held as much as 2 billion board feet of pine. Business success for the Oshkosh lumbermen depended on manipulation of the political process on the two reservations in Wisconsin, as well as in Washington, where the United States acted as trustee for the two tribes.[32]

The advent of the Grant administration in 1869 offered a new and better opportunity for the Indian Party and the Pine Ring to accomplish their separate goals as a combined package. New leadership in the OIA (including a new Green Bay agent) and the Interior Department meant that there was a better chance that a new initiative would win approval. The new Green Bay agent, J. A. Manly, had one idea about how to take best advantage of the reservation's timber, namely, to allow more logging in areas of the reservation, including by Indian loggers such as Citizens Party member Jesse Wybro. However, he was opposed by Congressman Sawyer. Sawyer wrote to the OIA commissioner in October 1869 that additional timber cutting would make future forest fires more likely and "injure ten times as much as is now injured." Sawyer reported that he had been on the Stockbridge-Munsee Reservation "and examined it [himself]." He then outlined his idea of appraising the value of the timber, auctioning the land to non-Indians, and establishing an annuity fund for the Mohicans. He concluded, "I should not feel that I had done my duty to see that fine Forest slaughtered without entering my protest against it."[33]

Sawyer's 1869 letter to the commissioner helps to clarify why merely selling Stockbridge-Munsee stumpage and leaving land title in the United States in trust for the tribe was not considered a viable policy option. Sawyer's view was that loggers would continue to abuse the terms of their contracts and commit extensive depredations on the stumpage. As Sawyer wrote, "If the pine is to be cut I do not know of but one way to do it and at the same time do the Indians justice"—and that involved selling the land itself, not just the stumpage rights. Of course, it was unthinkable for Sawyer to consider that the pine stay uncut on the reservation. The pine represented needed raw materials to keep his and other Oshkosh mills running. Sawyer could only see one way to realize the pine's value, namely, to sell it to men like himself and indeed as events transpired in 1871–72, men in league with himself. He could not envision a proposal to begin a tribal logging and lumber operation, nor could he support a December 1870 petition by tribal members to complete the allotment of the reservation under the 1856 treaty so that tribal members could log their own allotments. The white pine on the Menominee and Stockbridge-Munsee Reservations was simply too tempting to Wolf River lumbermen.

The tribe was in turmoil throughout 1869, with rival election slates and tribal government paralyzed. A January 1870 election clarified the lines of authority, at least as far as the Indian Office in Washington was concerned: Indian Party leaders Darius Charles and Jeremiah Slingerland were fully in charge. Sachem Charles promptly wrote to Morgan Martin, offering him a retainer to go to Washington and secure congressional passage of a bill that would once and for all terminate the Citizens Party:

> And now I want you should help me please then to throw those old Citizens of 1843 out of the tribe. I would rather pay you Two Thousand Dollars than to fail if we Should Succeed in our business we will pay you About that or maby more. Just what you think would be write. [34]

On March 2, 1870, Senator Timothy Howe of Wisconsin introduced two bills, S.B. 610 concerning the Stockbridge-Munsees and a parallel bill, S.B. 849, concerning the Menominees. The legislative bill files of the Senate show that Morgan L. Martin was the actual author of each. The earliest copy of S.B. 849 from March 1870 was penned in Martin's handwriting. And a letter from the Indian Party leaders dated March 16, 1870, claims authorship by Martin of S.B. 610. Martin had accompanied the Indian Party leaders Darius Charles and Jeremiah Slingerland to Washington that winter of 1870, and he was subsequently paid a lobbying fee of $1,600 by the Indian Party for securing ultimate passage of S.B. 610. [35]

Senate Bill 610, as authored by Martin, with assistance from Sachem Charles and Reverend Slingerland, accomplished what Congressman Sawyer's Pine Ring wanted, and what the Indian Party also wanted. The bill began with a provision for the appraisal of the entire two townships in distinct eighty-acre parcels, with special notice made of pine timber stands and with the work to be completed six months after the bill became law. Next the secretary of the interior was to conduct an auction at the Menasha Land Office of the parcels. This accomplished the goal of the Pine Ring—to get at the pine timber on the reservation. [36]

There was also a proviso in S.B. 610 that one-quarter of the lands (eighteen of the seventy-two sections) was to be reserved for the members of the Indian Party. The bill directed the Commissioner of Indian Affairs to conduct a new census of the Stockbridges and Munsees with members to be divided into two parties, Indian and Citizens. S.B. 610 also divided the proceeds of the sale of the fifty-four other sections within the reservation, along with the existing school annuity fund, into two funds, in proportion to the numbers on the tribal census rolls. The members of the Citizens Party were to receive a per capita distribution of the Citizens Party fund, and the United States would hold the Indian Party fund as an annuity and disburse to the "Stockbridge Tribe of Indians" an annual payment. To ensure that no political enemies from the Citizens Party declared themselves part of the Indian Party, the bill also had an unusual proviso that: "[No] person, or his or her descendants, be entered upon either said rolls who may have heretofore separated from said tribe and received allotment of lands under the [1843] act of Congress."

This clause was the Indian Party's revenge on the Citizens Party for having secured passage of the Act of 1843 and the negotiation and ratification of the treaty of 1856. In effect, the Indian Party was forcing the Citizens Party to separate permanently from the tribe and then also excluding almost all of the Citizens Party from making that choice, since the Citizens Party had engineered the old Act of 1843. Its reversal in 1846 by Quinney was not enough; now, in 1870, the Indian Party that Quinney had led wanted to vanquish its opponents. The party that Chicks had led that had sought to emulate the Brothertown example in the early 1840s was to be denied membership in either the Indian Party or the Citizens Party. Another effect of the bill's clause was to deny a per capita payment to Chicks Party members from the distribution of funds from the pinelands sales.

S.B. 610 had other provisions that satisfied the wishes of the Indian Party. The 1856 treaty allotment was scrapped in favor of a new allotment scheme solely for the benefit of its members. A further limitation that Morgan Martin wrote into the bill provided that "if any female shall marry out of said tribe she shall thereby forfeit all right to hold any of said lands as if deceased." The words "as if deceased" are striking: social and economic nullity was to be the fate of Mohican women who married white or black men and sought to include their husbands in the life of the nation, as tribal members had in New Stockbridge, Grand Kakalin, Stockbridge-on-the-Lake, and, more recently, Red Springs in Shawano County.[37]

S.B. 610 had no provision for approval by the entire nation, or even the elected tribal council. Nonetheless, the secretary of the interior, J. D. Cox,

wrote to Senator Howe on March 1, 1870, to reverse his 1868 predecessor's view about maintaining tribal protection for the Citizens Party,
this time giving the Interior Department's approval.[38]

Also on March 1, Senator Howe received a copy of the bill with a cover
letter signed by Sachem Charles and Councilor Slingerland, asking "if the
Senator will introduce the accompanying Bill as early as practicable." On
March 16 Charles and Slingerland sent a memorial to the Senate Committee on Indian Affairs asking approval of S.B. 610, sponsored by Senator
Howe. Charles and Slingerland signed their memorial as "Delegates" of the
Stockbridge-Munsee Nation, and both were in Washington at the time.
Their memorial informed the committee that S.B. 610 would accomplish
the sale of the Stockbridge-Munsee pinelands. Charles and Slingerland
wrote that "much the larger portion of these lands [on the reservation] are
unfit for cultivation, and are only valuable for the pine timber growing
thereon. None of them can be called first rate farming lands." The two
delegates pledged that the monies received would be fairly distributed.
They also called for the termination of tribal status for those who wanted
to become citizens and promised a "final settlement of [their] affairs, and
that too without any charge to the government." Finally, they asked Congress to approve payment of up to $11,000 "to pay just debts contracted
by the Sachem and Counselors on behalf of the Tribe."[39]

S.B. 610 was referred to the Committee on Indian Affairs. In the first
(March 2) draft of the bill there was a blank space left for the amount of
tribal debt that the Indian Party asked in reimbursement. When the draft
was reworked in committee, three amendments were attached. The first
was to insert the figure $11,000 for the tribal debts per the March 16,
1870, request from Charles and Slingerland. The second was to limit the
Indian Party's ability to adopt persons not of Indian descent. And the third
was to clarify how the rolls of the two parties were to be drawn.[40]

Over on the House side of the Capitol, Congressman Sawyer
introduced two parallel bills of his own. H.R. 1457, "A bill for the Relief
of the Stockbridge and Munsee Tribes," was introduced on March 7, 1870,
and H.R. 1547, "A Bill to Authorize the Sale of Certain Lands Reserved
for the Use of the Menominee Tribe of Indians," was introduced ten days
later. S.B. 610 was brought out of the Indian Affairs Committee with a
positive vote and soon passed the full Senate, but when it went over to the
House side, it died in June, before the end of the session. The Menominee

bill, S.B. 849, had the same fate—passage in the Senate but failure in the House.[41]

News about the possible opportunity to buy Stockbridge-Munsee timber spread quickly to the lumbermen of the district. For example, in late March 1870 a lumberman named S. E. Gilbert, operating out of Shawano, wrote to the Commissioner of Indian Affairs, "I see by the papers that there has been a bill Introduced to sell the pine timber on this Reserve and I understand that the Stockbridge Indians wish to sell their pine Timber on their Reserve." Gilbert offered $2.20 per thousand board feet for the exclusive right to Indian stumpage.[42]

That spring of 1870, the reservation was in turmoil over logging issues, tribal governance, and OIA personnel. Jesse Wybro went on trial for illegal lumbering, in federal court in Green Bay on May 2. Specifically, Wybro was charged with logging in the west half of the northeast quarter of Section 15, Township 28 North Range 14 East. The prosecution called its principal witness, Green Bay Indian agent Manly, who testified that he observed Wybro running a logging camp with fourteen other Indians and two white teamsters.

Wybro's defense attorney chose to rely on his client's claimed right to cut timber on his own 1856 treaty allotment selection. The defense introduced Jeremiah Slingerland's allotment selection entry book, which the councilor had begun back in fall 1856 at the direction of Superintendent Huebschman. Jesse Wybro made his selection on the parcel in question within the Burnt District in October 1866, and one of his fellow loggers had selected the adjoining east half of the quarter section earlier in 1859. The defense introduced additional testimony about Wybro's ownership claim of the parcel in the Burnt District, where Sachem Charles had also made a selection. Wybro claimed to have a permit from the sachem giving him permission to log his own parcel. In addition to the documentary evidence, the defense chose to put on the stand Sachem Charles, Wybro's political rival. Charles started uncooperatively for the defense, but when pressed by Wybro's attorney, he gave testimony contrary to the official OIA line:

Q: Are any of your people farmers?
A: They are all farmers. I believe so far as I know.
Q: All farmers?

A: Yes Sir.

Q: They do not lead a roving wild life?

A: No Sir. They go somewheres where they can get work for a living.
There aint half of them up there. I guess there is only one third
up there on the reservation on account of the poor country. Some
of them have land down in Calumet County for two or three
years because they can't get a living on these lands.

Q: Wouldn't it be an advantage to your people if they could be
allowed to go and sell their timber and get money by which to buy
flour and food and clothing?

A: I don't know. I guess it would not. It would be better advantage
if they could sell the whole of it and get some other land.

Q: Well if you have got to have land and get your living out of that
land it would be an advantage to you to get money and clothing
for your timber, better than it would be to starve?

A: Yes Sir in the winter time.

Q: In the winter time your people have nothing to do?

A: Yes Sir there is a good many places to work in the winter time.
There is lumbering going on all around our country.

Q: Now if they can work on their own reservation and get pay for it
it benefits them?

A: Yes Sir it would be.

Q: Now besides getting pay for their work if they could get pay for
their lumber it would be a greater benefit still?

A: Yes Sir.

Q: Now when you gave this license to Wybro to cut this timber you
thought it would be a good thing for your people didn't you?

A: Yes Sir. I thought it would be a good thing for our people that
wanted to work close by home.

Q: Is that good farming land on that reservation?

A: No Sir not very good.[43]

The colloquy in Judge Drummond's courtroom showed the two possible avenues of economic development for the tribe. On the one hand,
the federal government, led by the Office of Indian Affairs and the U.S.
Attorney were determined that the Stockbridge-Munsees would be farmers,
and initially this is how Sachem Charles characterized his people. On the

other hand, the land was suited to lumbering, and this is what tribal members like Wybro did for a living, at least in the winter. The tribe itself, under Sachem Charles, began issuing permits to log, although without OIA approval.

In February 1870 Congressman Sawyer managed to get the OIA to sack its Green Bay agent, J. A. Manly, and replace him with W. R. Bourne.[44] Agent Bourne almost immediately encountered problems trying to help the tribe do its business. In April 1870 Darius Charles wrote to Morgan Martin to protest Bourne's inquiry into the tribal split:

> [Agent Bourne] would not let any of the old Indian Party say anything only me and he tryed to pump me to tell everything what we had done at Washington. I toald him that he would know this summer. . . . [H]e wanted to know how much we pade you to go with us. . . . [H]e wanted to call for a new Election to have new head men I toald him I wanted to see his authority that coold him down but he toald them that he would send for authority and then he would have a new Election and have just the head men he wanted.[45]

This was a remarkable turn of events. The Indian Party, with help from Martin, was busy launching its own private lobbying of Congress for a bill that would radically alter the course of the nation. Yet the U.S. Indian agent whose job was to act in the field as the direct trustee of the United States for the nation, knew nothing about the lobbying. This became a pattern throughout the history of the drafting and ultimate passage of S.B. 610. The bill was initiated by the combined forces of the Pine Ring of lumbermen and the Indian Party of Stockbridges. The Grant administration was largely a passive spectator to this new making of federal Indian policy.[46]

In fall 1870 the Pine Ring, composed of Sawyer, Howe, Martin, and others, became too impatient to wait for Congress to act. Congressman Sawyer exerted pressure on the Interior Department in two ways. First, at Sawyer's insistence, the OIA dismissed the new Green Bay agent, Bourne, from his post. The editor of the *Oshkosh Times*, a Democratic newspaper opposed to Sawyer, wrote on October 12, 1870, that Sawyer's "Pine Land Ring" had taken over the Interior Department. The editor ridiculed the congressman's protestations of innocence with the observation, "Of course P. SAWYER didn't know anything about it. Of course not; he's so innocent pine pitch won't stick to his hands."[47]

The second action by the Interior Department in fall 1870 was shocking in its audacity. On September 27 the department placed an advertisement in a Chicago newspaper for the sale of Menominee pinelands in tracts of township size (23,040 acres, or 36 square miles), by sealed bid, at Washington, D.C. The news soon reached Wisconsin, in the midst of Sawyer's reelection campaign. The reaction was so unfavorable to such an open land grab by Sawyer and his associates that the congressman and Senator Howe had to repudiate the sale plan and ask for its reversal. The story put out by Sawyer and Howe was that a clerk in the Interior Department devised the plan on his own, without the knowledge of the secretary or anyone in Congress. The secretary of the interior, Jacob Cox, resigned amid the scandal, and the sale was canceled. The Democratic press of Wisconsin held up the attempted pine grab as emblematic of the set of scandals that had emerged from the "Big Barbecue" Republican Grant administration. The *Marquette Express* editorialized on October 22 that "Esquire Sawyer stands convicted" of "fraud" in an underhanded effort to "gobble the whole tract."[48]

The Fifth District Republicans weathered the scandal, and after the November elections, with their leader, Sawyer, safely returned to the House, the Pine Ring returned to the task of passing S.B. 610 and 849. In December 1870 Citizens Party members provided Congress with an estimate of the timber holdings of the Stockbridge-Munsees's two-township reservation. The House Committee on Indian Affairs and its Senate counterpart received a petition from "Members of the Stockbridge and Munsee Tribes of Indians." Seventy-three men and women signed a document that read, in part:

[T]he said two townships of land now have upon them, One hundred and fifty million feet of pine timber merchantable, and worth some five dollars per thousand feet as it now stands, and were the right given us to cut, and take the said timber to the Oshkosh market in said State of Wisconsin, under the Superintendence of a proper man, we would realize after paying expenses, double the above named sum per thousand for said timber, and this would give employment to a large class of the said Indians for a number of seasons.[49]

The Indian Party was confident that Citizens Party opposition would be overcome by Congressman Sawyer and that S.B. 610 would be passed.

Councilor Slingerland attributed partisan reasons for the antagonism between the Citizens Party and Sawyer. Slingerland also connected the politics of the Stockbridge-Munsee Nation and the politics of Wisconsin when he wrote, "[D]uring the last election they [the Citizens Party] voted against Sawyer & he knows it & has promised that nothing from them shall meet with any attention by him at Washington."[50]

Slingerland's letter about Sawyer's intransigence puts a new face on the subsequent history of the Citizens Party petition against S.B. 610, received by the Senate Committee on Indian Affairs on January 5, 1871. Sen. James Harlan, chair of the Indian Affairs Committee, worked with Howe and Sawyer to get the bill through as quickly as possible, and without regard for the objections of the Citizens Party. At the start of the third session of the Forty-first Congress, on December 13, Senator Howe reintroduced S.B. 610 "for the relief of the Stockbridge and Munsee Tribe of Indians." This time, the bill easily passed the Senate. However, there was considerable debate on the floor of the House. S.B. 610 came to the House on January 13, 1871, and was referred to the Committee on Indian Affairs. The committee chair, Rep. William Armstrong (R-Pa.) moved the bill through committee, despite the opposition voiced in the petition from the Citizens Party, and returned the bill with the committee's approval to the full House. On January 18 the bill came up for a final reading in the House. The House amended the bill so that the General Land Office would conduct land sales at the Menasha, Wisconsin, Land Office.[51]

The full House debate on S.B. 610 showed a congressional interest in three particulars of the legislation: the consent of the Stockbridge-Munsee Tribe to the proposal; the role of Congress in selling land outside the public domain; and the manner in which the land was to be sold. The discussion on the floor by representatives who questioned the legislation, and by its backers, sheds light on the intent of the House in passing the bill. Rep. Halbert Paine (R-Wis.) began the floor debate with the simple question of whether the bill was in accordance with the wishes of the tribe. Representative Armstrong answered, "It is; at least so the committee is informed," omitting mention of the Citizens Party opposition. He continued that the Stockbridge-Munsees "cannot make this sale without the aid of an act of Congress. . . . It is in the interest of the Indians that the lands shall be sold, and they very much desire it."[52]

This statement on the floor of the House furnished members of Congress with the rationale for the bill—to sell pinelands. Representative Armstrong had an additional debate with William Lawrence of Ohio and John Hawley of Illinois on the question of congressional authority to sell land reserved from the public domain for an Indian tribe:

Lawrence: Can the Government by treaty vest the title to the public lands in Indians?

Armstrong: I have no doubt of it.

Lawrence: Can the Senate, then, vest the title of all the public lands of the United States?

Armstrong: So long as the Government of the United States in its political capacity recognizes the Indian tribes and treats with them as independent Powers, so long are we bound by our contracts with them and we cannot repudiate them.

Hawley: If these are not public lands, by what authority does Congress assume to dispose of them?

Armstrong: Congress does not assume authority to sell these lands except by consent of the Indians. They ask that these lands may be sold. The bill provides that the lands shall not be sold for less than their appraised value. If open to settlement, men would come in as preemptors and take up the lands at $1.25 per acre. They are worth more, and ought to realize to these Indians their full value.[53]

The above exchange is instructive about how Congress understood the difference between public lands and Indian lands. At the time the Constitution was ratified, it was expected that the proceeds from public land sales would pay off the federal debt. When the Jackson administration paid the public debt, Congress decided on many new uses for the public lands. In the decades before the Civil War, Congress passed a host of laws that were intended to promote rapid settlement and development of the public lands into productive farmer-homesteads. By contrast, the federal government treated Indian lands as different and under the various "Non-Intercourse Acts" had long sought to keep whites off Indian lands. The same nonintercourse policy had made it plain that only the United States could extinguish

Indian title and end Indian occupancy—not states, not individual whites, and not even an Indian tribe itself.[54]

In the House floor debate, Lawrence wanted to know the extent of the government's power to administer the public lands. Armstrong responded with the answer that Congress even had the power to take land out of the public domain and make it Indian land. Lawrence pushed even harder: could the Senate alone take public land and make it Indian land? This was certainly not an issue in the bill being considered; however, it got to a portion of the House's complaint about the reach of the Senate's treaty-making powers. And that very session the Senate Committee on the Judiciary had issued an opinion that the recently ratified Fourteenth Amendment to the Constitution did not apply to Indian tribes and that their existing treaties remained in force. Nonetheless, Armstrong answered the question and included a strong defense of previously signed treaties. The House had to respect existing treaties, including the 1856 treaty with the Stockbridge-Munsees. Congressman Hawley brought the discussion back to ground by asking how Congress could sell land not in the public domain. Armstrong's answer made it clear that the lands were not part of the public domain. The interest of Congress was not to promote the rapid settlement of farmer-homesteaders but rather to maximize revenue to the tribe for selling the pinelands.[55]

The final point of contention in the House debate was over the terms of purchase by non-Indians of the land for sale. Congressman Hawley wanted to limit purchasers to a maximum of 160 acres, so as not to lead to a monopolization of the lands by speculators and capitalists. However, the House declined to support this provision in the bill. Congressman Sawyer spoke in the floor debate against the proposal to limit purchasers to a quarter-section by pointing out that the lands were valuable precisely for their timber and not as farmlands and that lumbermen wanted access to large quantities of pinelands for their operations.[56]

All the discussion in the *Congressional Globe* for both S.B. 610 and S.B. 849 was on the House side. The very questions aimed at backers of S.B. 610 and 849 echo the problems of well-publicized fraudulent theft of Indian lands in Kansas: Were the lands intended to go into the public domain? Would insiders dominate the auction process? Would the process actually benefit the Indians, or would it be fraudulent? In discussing the Menominee bill, S.B. 849, Congressman Beck stated on January 18, 1871, "There is hardly a case, where lands have been sold or money has been paid . . . that there have not been men from Washington and elsewhere following the payments . . . to the utter ruin of the Indians and the injury of all the interests involved." Beck continued that "the result is that Congress is being disgraced and the country is being disgraced by a swarm of supernumeraries stealing from the Indians all or nearly all they get."[57]

An understanding of the Kansas frauds is important for making sense of Hawley's objection to S.B. 849 and 610 and how the House viewed the past and future of the Stockbridge-Munsee lands. Hawley had sought to amend both bills so as to limit an individual purchaser to no more than 160 acres of land. This would have prevented large buyers (like Sawyer) from aggrandizing themselves with the purchase of Indian lands, as had been the problem in post–Civil War Kansas. The Hawley Amendment would also have effectively killed the bill for the lumbermen, as both Armstrong and Sawyer objected. The House heard Hawley's impassioned plea on behalf of the farmer-settler and against the big purchaser and speculator but nevertheless rejected it.[58]

In 1871 Congress never expected the Stockbridge-Munsee pinelands to be taken up by settlers, either at the auction or even after the pinelands were logged. The House knew the problems with fraud in Kansas Indian lands but went ahead with approval of S.B. 610 and S.B. 849 with the expectation that no would-be settlers faced denial of homes, because the land was unfit for farming. Congress expected the lumbermen to buy the land, through competitive bidding; Congress had no interest in what became of the land after the trees were cut. There is no evidence that either chamber thought the fifty-four sections put up for sale under S.B. 610 would be repopulated by white farmer-homesteaders, thereby changing the character of the two-township reservation.

S.B. 610 passed the House on January 18. The Senate concurred the next day in the House amendment to hold land sales at the Menasha Land Office. The bill was enrolled by both houses on January 24 and then went to the White House for the president's consideration. The next day, President Grant's executive secretary queried the secretary of the interior for his opinion. Four days later, Secretary Columbus Delano responded equivocally: "I have the honor to return herewith, Senate Bill No. 610. . . . While I cannot advise that the Executive approval be withheld from the

Bill, some of its provisions do not fully accord with the views of the Department." President Grant allowed ten days to elapse after the bill's receipt. His inaction allowed the bill to become law on February 6, 1871.[59]

News of the passage of S.B. 610 in both houses quickly reached the Indian Party leaders in Shawano County. On January 24 the sachem and councilors wrote to Congressman Sawyer about the "pleasing news . . . that the Stockbridge Indian Bill has passed and become a law." The balance of the letter was a plea to Sawyer to have Morgan L. Martin named "as the one whom we wish to be appointed by the Secretary of Interior to make the two Rolls of Indians & Citizens as contemplated in Section Six of said Bill." What counted to Sachem Charles, Councilor Slingerland, and the others was prompt enrollment of the two factions and speedy expulsion of the Citizens Party from the tribe.[60]

The rest of Shawano County, including the Citizens Party, soon learned about the passage of S.B. 610 from their local newspaper, the *Shawano Journal*. The editor, Myron McCord, covered the story in the January 26, 1871, issue as a triumph for Congressman Sawyer and repudiation of Democratic Party charges that the congressman was leading a "Pine Ring" theft of Indian timber. "This timber (not the land) will now be offered for sale in accordance with the terms of the law," McCord wrote, and then he dismissed the editor of the *Oshkosh Times* and "other unscrupulous blatherskites" for having their efforts "gotten up on the eve of election to defeat Hon. Philetus Sawyer."[61]

McCord was closely allied with Congressman Sawyer, and it is significant that he too understood S.B. 610 as a timber stumpage sale bill, not a land sale bill or a bill that diminished the reservation. The new Indian agent at Green Bay, W. T. Richardson, was ignorant of the passage of the bill, nor had he known of Sachem Charles and Councilor Slingerland's lobbying trips to Washington. He knew nothing of the internation and intratribal politics concerning S.B. 610 in the third session of the Forty-first Congress, much as his predecessor, Agent Bourne, had been bypassed in the second session. In mid-February Richardson wrote to the Commissioner of Indian Affairs asking for a "copy of the bill recently passed by Congress in reference to the sale of pine land belonging to the Stockbridge and Munsee and Menomonee reservations." He too, on learning of S.B. 610 and 849, understood them to be sales of pineland.[62]

Although not written into the statute, the next step in the process was for the Stockbridge-Munsees to express their consent to the legislation affecting their tribe. Congressman Sawyer explained this to Councilor Slingerland in a February 16, 1871, letter:

> I have been waiting for the land bill to be printed to send you a copy. It has come today from the printers, and I send you some copies herewith. It was delayed at the Presidents, I suppose for further consideration, and as you will see has become a law without his signature, but it goes into force and operation all the same, being now a law of the U.S. I have seen the Secretary of the Interior, about this law and he says it will now be necessary for you to call a council of the tribes and lay this bill or Act before them, and have them sanction it in every part, and when they have done so, have it signed by the head men and appended to one of the copies of the law I now send, and then mail it to me and I will lay it before the Secretary of the Interior, who cannot take any steps in regard to it until he gets the sanction of the tribes.[63]

The "sanction of the tribes" proved a controversial matter, among both the Stockbridge-Munsees and the Menominees. The bitterness of the dispute between the Indian Party and the Citizens Party intensified amid the fight over the passage of S.B. 610. The tribe's constitution called for annual elections on New Year's Day, but in the 1871 contest the two factions called rival elections at separate polling places. Sachem Charles and the Indian Party designated the sachem's private house as the polling place, a decision not calculated to increase voter turnout.[64]

The correspondence of the Indian Party leaders showed that their motivation was primarily to expel their Citizens Party rivals from the tribe and secondarily to collect on past claims against the United States. By contrast, when the Citizens Party learned of the passage of S.B. 610, its leaders protested their imminent separation from the tribe and the loss of tribal lands. The sachem and councilors of the tribe (Citizens Party branch) wrote to President Grant at the end of March protesting the Act of 1871 as a violation of the treaty of 1856. The Citizens Party told the president that the new law was "distasteful" and pleaded, "Now our only hope is that our Great Father the President of the U.S. raise a helping hand in defense of the Oppressed in order that no unjust Laws be enforced on us."[65]

The United States was soon enough presented with rival claims to Mohican constitutional legitimacy, and also rival actions taken on S.B. 610. Agent W. T. Richardson duly forwarded the matter to H. R. McClure, Acting Commissioner of Indian Affairs. Members of each party resorted to the local newspapers to air their grievances. An unsigned letter from a member of the Citizens Party (likely Jesse Wybro), appearing in the April 26, 1871, *Oshkosh Times*, presented this summary of the power play that led to the Act of 1871:

> The Indian Party got up a power of attorney to send two delegates to Washington, to dispose of the whole of our interest. This instrument being distasteful, many (more than one half) would not sign their names to the same. The delegates went anyway, with a friend, or so we have lately learned, employed a resident of Green Bay, taking the sum of $750 and with the cooperation of the Member of Congress of this district. But when the delegates returned, in 1870, they would not report what they had done, keeping silent and making no public report whatever to the whole tribe. Of course, we who opposed their going to Washington did not know what bill they consented to, in the Senate in 1870, until lately. . . . The law as passed will throw out more than one half of the tribe. . . . This is done by those who are willing to throw away our whole pine timber for a mere song—timber which we claim to be worth at least $5 per M stumpage.[66]

The Indian Party had a correspondent answer the *Times* letter in the rival, Republican *Oshkosh Northwestern* a week later. The unnamed author provided a lengthy history of the Acts of 1843 and 1846 and the treaty of 1856, which he considered a swindle by the Citizens Party in league with Superintendent Huebschman:

> As to the contemptible fling of this capitalist about our Member of Congress, I have only to say that whatever else Mr. Sawyer may have done he has certainly done his whole duty by the Indians in keeping trespassers off of the Indian lands (both Stockbridge and Menominee) and aided them to get just and fair laws passed to enable them to sell their timber.[67]

On April 18, 1871, Acting Commissioner McClure brought some of this information to the attention of the secretary of the interior. McClure forwarded a dossier "containing the signatures of sixty members of the Stockbridge and Munsee Tribes of Indians, indicating their concurrence in, and approval of the [Act of 1871]." McClure also forwarded in the same dossier a counterpetition signed by fifty-four Citizens Party members protesting the Act of 1871. The perplexed commissioner added, "It is proper to state that several of the names signed to this petition also appear upon the first named document, but it is stated in the petition that they were placed there without authority."[68]

In a remarkable ten-day period in late April and early May 1871, the Acting Commissioner intervened decisively on the side of the Indian Party, despite receiving the disturbing information about possible fraud in the tribal sanction to the Act of 1871. First, on April 24 McClure decided to recognize Darius Charles and the Indian Party as the legitimately elected government of the Stockbridge-Munsees. Then, on May 4, he appointed the *Shawano Journal* editor, Myron McCord, to head a three-man team to oversee the appraisal and sale of the fifty-four sections of the reservation.[69] The appointment of McCord to begin the appraisal of tribal pinelands effectively ended any inquiry into the dispute over the "sanction of the tribes" to the Act of 1871.

When leaders of the Citizens Party complained about the impending appraisal and sale of tribal pinelands in March to Wisconsin congressman Jeremiah Rusk, they learned a hard lesson in congressional privilege. Rusk wrote back, "Yours of March 21st in regard to lands situated in Shawano County is received. I stated the case to Mr. Sawyer, he said he had the law passed and it was right and it being wholly within his district I could not interfere in the matter."[70]

There was no follow-up investigation into the matter of the "sanction of the tribes," not by either house of Congress or by the OIA. The Act of 1871 ended the democratic polity of the Citizens Party and restored the Indian Party to control. By contrast, S.B. 849 had a provision calling for the Menominees to give their assent to the law calling for the appraisal and sale of multiple townships of land on that nation's reservation. The Menominees met in council with the Green Bay Indian agent soon after passage of S.B. 849. They quickly rendered their unanimous opposition to the legislation. The Green Bay agent reported this news to the Commissioner of Indian Affairs, and that was sufficient for the OIA to refuse to stipulate the provisions of the act. Congressman Sawyer suffered an unusual political defeat at the hands of the Menominees in 1871, and he redoubled his efforts to acquire access to Menominee timber in the following years. He also sought to get at the timber on the Lake Superior Chippewa reservations at Lac Courte Oreilles, Lac du Flambeau, and Fond du Lac in 1872 legislation. That law, too, was foiled by the unanimous disapproval of the affected Chippewa bands. Only the Stockbridge-Munsee Nation, as a direct result of its bitter internal political disputes, was opened to Sawyer-led outside logging in the 1870s.[71]

In 1879, more than twenty years after leaving the OIA, former Superintendent Huebschman wrote to the secretary of the interior about the ways in which the Act of 1871 violated the treaty of 1856:

> The treaty of 1856 was being carried out until under the influence of Pine Land Speculators forwarded by Hon. P. Sawyer & T. O. Howe in the year 1871 a law was got through Congress, without the knowledge of the parties interested in the treaty of 1856, which contemplated arrangements conflicting with the treaty mentioned and under the construction put upon it deprived numerous parties to the treaty of their rights.[72]

The main political question facing the Stockbridge-Munsees was how the Citizens Party would accept the Indian Party–Pine Ring violation of the treaty of 1856.

CHAPTER 5

The Restoration Polity of the Indian Party, 1871–1893

A story about Philetus Sawyer's encounters with the Stockbridge-Munsees and the Act of 1871 surfaced in the early 1930s, more than three decades after the old lumberman's passing from the scene. According to tribal member Benjamin Jourdan, Congressman Sawyer made a secret journey to the reservation in fall 1870 to plot strategy with Councilor Jeremiah Slingerland and Sachem Darius Charles. It was at this meeting, according to Jourdan, that the Mohican leaders explained their terms for disfranchising and expelling their opponents in the Citizens Party. On leaving the all-night meeting, Sawyer muttered, "This is not a nation of Indians. This is a nation of lawyers." This was a bit of unintended prophecy and a more than accurate contemporary description, because it would take a nation of lawyers to understand and implement the Act of 1871. To make sense of the law, its interpreters needed to begin with an understanding of previous treaties.[1]

The treaty of February 5, 1856, was the longest, most detailed, and most complicated of all the treaties that the Mohicans and Munsees signed with the United States, starting in 1794. It was so detailed that the U.S. Superintendent for Northern Indian Affairs forgot to order the necessary land survey that would implement the allotment provisions of the treaty. And Supt. Francis Huebschman was hardly alone in his neglect. Treaty making, with its fundamental characteristic of mutual agreement, was one matter. What happened after treaty ratification by both sides was another, and in the nineteenth century the implementation of treaties by both parties was called treaty "stipulation." The frequent failure by the United States to stipulate the terms of treaties became a sore point in U.S.-Indian relations and a central grievance of the Red Power movement of the 1970s. A demand of the protest known as the "Trail of Broken Treaties" in 1972 was to enforce the stipulations of the nineteenth-century treaties.[2]

Congress passed the Act of 1871 "for the Relief of the Stockbridge-Munsees" in the same session that it ended formal treaty making between the United States and American Indian nations. However, as historian Francis Paul Prucha has observed, the United States continued after 1871 to engage in treaty-like negotiations with tribes. During the floor debate in the House, representatives were assured that S.B. 610 was desired by the Stockbridge-Munsees. And although the legislation did not require tribal assent, Congressman Sawyer acted in a February 16, 1871, letter to Sachem Charles and Councilor Slingerland as if it were a treaty that needed the approval of the Mohican's tribal council and all the voters of the Mohican Nation. The Act of 1871 was every bit as complicated as the treaty of 1856, and in writing the legislation, Morgan L. Martin placed the responsibility for its stipulation on both the Commissioner of Indian Affairs and his superior, the secretary of the interior.[3]

It is no exaggeration to state that Mohican politics in the years 1871 through 1893 revolved around the stipulation of the terms of the Act of 1871. Table 5.1 provides a summary of the sections of the Act of 1871 and their subsequent stipulation.

After resolving the intratribal political dispute in favor of Sachem Charles and his Indian Party, the OIA moved in May to stipulate Section 1's provision for an appraisal of all 72 sections, in 80-acre parcels. The OIA appointed Congressman Sawyer's political supporter Myron McCord of Shawano to lead the appraisal team with directions to fix a value for the pine in each 80-acre parcel of the 46,080-acre reservation. He was offered the appointment on May 4, 1871, and was acutely aware that he had to complete the appraisal by July 25 to fulfill the statutory requirement of completion within six months of passage of the act. The appraisal work got off to a slow start. A surviving letter, datelined "In Camp, Township 28N Range No. 13E," that McCord wrote on June 8 to the Commissioner of Indian Affairs gives a picture of the difficulties his team faced:

TABLE 5.1
Stipulation of the Act of 1871

SECTION	PROVISION	ACTION TAKEN	DATE
Sec. 1	Appointment of appraisers	by commissioner of Indian affairs	May 4, 1871
Sec. 1	Appraisal completed	by McCord team	July 25, 1871
Sec. 2	Advertised land parcels for logging	in local newspapers	Sept. 30, 1871
Sec. 2	Auction	at Menasha	Jan. 8. 1872
Sec. 2	1-year time limit	by Indian Party to commissioner of Indian affairs	Jan. 8, 1873
Sec. 2	Proviso for 18 reserved sections		July 24, 1871
Sec. 3	$11,000 tribal debt	suspended by commissioner of Indian affairs	Sept. 18, 1872
Sec. 4	Last public sale and resulting schedule	by secretary of the interior	Act of June 22, 1874
Sec. 5	Money division	by Commissioner of Indian Affairs	after 1874 Wells Roll
Sec. 6	Indian Party and Citizen Party rolls	started by Agent Richardson and halted restarted by Inspector Wells revised by Act of 1893 and done in 1894	Sept. 1871 1874
Sec. 7	Consent of tribe	Citizens Party consent never given	Mar. 25, 1871
		Indian Party sachem and councilors to Commissioner of Indian Affairs	Oct. 25, 1872
Sec. 8	Allotment selections	by secretary of the interior	started Oct. 1874, suspended 1876, restarted 1894
Sec. 8	Survey of allotments	secretary of the interior	(not done until 1907)
Sec. 9	Allotments in trust	secretary of the interior	1894-1910 (but in fee simple after 1910)

SOURCE: "An Act for the Relief of the Stockbridge and Munsee Tribe of Indians in Wisconsin," 16, *Statutes at Large*, 404 (1871).

May 14th we went onto said lands and have been in camp since that time. We find much difficulty in prosecuting our work. It is almost impossible to obtain experienced men to go into the woods in this season of the year . . . mosquitoes and flies are so terribly annoying this season.[4]

Section 2 specified the ways in which at least 54 and as many as 72 sections would be auctioned to the public. In late July 1871 the Indian Party met to discuss the part of the Act of 1871 that called on them to reserve 18 sections from the upcoming auction. Sachem Charles and his councilors wrote the Commissioner of Indian Affairs to this effect on July 24, 1871. The notation on the file from the OIA clerk is that the sachem and councilors sent in a "plat of land they desire to have set apart as a selection." The Indian Party had to take this action before the land auction, if only to preserve its right to stay on the reservation. More than a year later, in October 1872, the Indian Party decided to stay on the reservation and accompanied their letter of notice with a crudely drawn map showing the bisected sections 13, 14, and 15 and 19, 30, and 31, together with all of sections 20–29 and 32–36. This fulfilled the terms set forth in Section 7 of the Act of 1871. The Indian Party made it quite clear that they wanted their new home to be known as the Stockbridge Indian Reservation and had no use or space for the Munsees.[5]

After receipt of the McCord appraisal, the OIA turned the auction matter over to its fellow bureau in the Interior Department, the General Land Office (GLO). On September 30 the GLO began advertising in Wisconsin and Chicago newspapers about the upcoming auction, set for January 8, 1872, at its Menasha Land Office. Republican papers, including the *Shawano Journal* and the *Oshkosh Northwestern*, printed Myron McCord's appraisal of the parcels in the 54 sections at auction. On auction day lumbermen bid on about 12,000 acres, mainly rich pineland parcels along the Red River and other driving streams on the reservation. The biggest bidder was Laban Beecher, a Boston capitalist, who used money borrowed from Philetus Sawyer's Oshkosh bank to underwrite his bids. The second biggest bidder was Congressman Sawyer's son.[6]

The auction process and the Act of 1871 soon wound up before the U.S. Supreme Court, the first of many Stockbridge-Munsee issues to come before it. The issue at law was a conflict between two rival white claimants to the same logs on an 80-acre parcel on the reservation. Laban Beecher had acquired a parcel in section 16 of T28N R13E at the 1872 auction. Earlier, the state of Wisconsin had claimed the same section 16 as school lands subject to state jurisdiction under the Northwest Ordinance of 1787 and the statehood enabling act of 1848. The state's Commissioners of Public Lands had put the section 16 parcel up for sale in 1865 and a lumberman named Daniel Wetherby had purchased it. The Interior Department had blocked Wetherby from logging the parcel before 1871, and even after passage of the Act of 1871 the department contended that the Indian Country nature of the section 16 parcel was a superior claim to that of the state to its school lands. The federal district court in Wisconsin agreed with the United States, but the Supreme Court reversed in 1877 and awarded title to the land, and the logs, to Wetherby. This was the first in a series of conflicts between the state of Wisconsin, on the one hand, and the United States and the Mohican Nation, on the other, over jurisdiction on the reservation.[7]

Section 4 of the act followed logically after Section 2 in the sense that it addressed the aftermath of the land sales. It provided that the United States would pay the tribe for parcels not sold at the auction, but at the low rate of sixty cents an acre, the same figure that the United States paid the Menominees back in 1856 for the entire two townships. After the close of the auction, the United States placed the remainder of unsold land parcels up for private entry at $1.25 an acre. For two years after the auction, lumbermen gradually bought these parcels. The conclusion to the Act of 1871 appraisal and auction process was the purchase by the United States of the unsold tribal lands in 1874, about 11,800 acres. And in an act of Congress passed on June 22, 1874, the United States made good on Section 4 and paid the Stockbridge-Munsees $11,813 for the remaining unsold parcels. At that point, the Stockbridge-Munsee Indian Reservation consisted of 18 sections of land closed to non-Indians and 54 sections opened to non-Indians.[8]

Section 3 of the act proved more troublesome to stipulate than the first two and the fourth. Charles and Slingerland had supplied Congressman Sawyer and Senator Howe with a figure of $11,000 as the amount due from the proceeds of the auction sales for "tribal debts." But when the two tribal leaders asked for payment of $11,000 based on Section 3, Indian agent Richardson began his own investigation into the tribal accounts. Charles and Slingerland could produce no records to support their claim that the council had expended $11,000 on the tribe's business, despite the requirement in the nation's constitution of 1857 that "the Sachem and Council take care to safeguard the archives of the Nation." With support from the Commissioner of Indian Affairs, Richardson moved to suspend tribal government, and he dissolved the Indian Party tribal council. Slingerland had other problems that fall: unknown parties set fire to his barn and outbuildings one night in what the *Shawano Journal* saw, with some hyperbole, as an unholy alliance of the Citizens Party and advance forces of the Paris Commune.[9]

The polity of the Mohican Nation broke down in the years surrounding the passage of the Act of 1871, just as it had in the fight over Indian removal in the late 1830s and over the Act of 1843 and its repeal in 1846. One tribal member wrote of the almost nonstop "counciling night after night." The Indian Party acted quickly in 1871 to suspend the 1857 constitution and soon was operating under the older 1837 Quinney constitution. And in June 1872 the tribal council moved to expand the membership of the tribe by adopting six white women who had married Indian Party men, including Sarah Slingerland, wife of the tribe's missionary. Here was further evidence of the change in political gender roles in the Indian Party. The Quinney Party had forbidden membership to non-Stockbridge husbands and expelled their Stockbridge wives before 1848. Now, in 1872, the Indian Party welcomed white wives of tribal men. Outside the council deliberations, vigilante actions characterized by threats and counterthreats replaced debate. Unlike the late 1840s, the United States intervened directly during winter 1871–72 by suspending tribal government and all the parts of the Act of 1871, except, of course, for the sale at auction of the pineland parcels to the Oshkosh lumbermen.[10]

Not until May 1874 did the OIA initiate the work of stipulating the remaining sections of the Act of 1871. Section 5 provided for a money division of the tribal estate, but that presupposed a basis for making the division. The basis was set forth in Section 6, the most complex part of the overall legislation. It required a national census to determine the members of the Citizens Party and the Indian Party, with the proviso that any tribal member who had taken an allotment based on the Act of 1843 was deemed ineligible for membership in either party.[11]

The OIA appointed Henry Wells special commissioner to take the census. Unofficially, he was aided in his work by Myron McCord and Morgan

L. Martin. Even more unofficially, Wells spent his time in Wisconsin dead drunk in a Shawano saloon, while McCord and Martin actually conducted the tribal tally seven miles away at the Menominee Reservation agency town of Keshena. The two operatives of the Pine Ring went about the task of creating three groups of Stockbridge-Munsees. The first was the Indian Party, which kept control of the reservation. This group numbered 112 souls and was dominated by Quinney and Miller descendants. The second group, consisting of 142 members, constituted the Citizens Party, which was to be severed from the nation and to take its share of the national wealth as a per capita distribution. Membership in the Citizens Party was hardly by choice: to be counted in this second group, according to one eyewitness, required a notarized assignment to McCord and Martin of anywhere from one-fourth to one-half of the expected per capita payment. The third and largest group of tribal members consisted of about 200 people whom McCord and Martin labeled as beneficiaries under the old Act of 1843 and therefore ineligible to be enrolled in either the Indian Party or the Citizens Party. Some wound up in this third group in limbo because they refused to pay the bribe demanded by the two Sawyer cronies. Martin, moreover, placed others in this third category as punishment for their previous political opposition to Congressman Sawyer. To distinguish themselves from the second category, the excluded Stockbridge-Munsees started calling themselves the Old Citizens Party, in contrast to those who cashed out under the Wells-McCord-Martin census as the New Citizens Party. The leader of those in the Old Citizens Party protesting the 1874 census was a Quinney descendant named John C. Adams, a young college-trained Mohican who spent the remainder of his life fighting the Act of 1871 and its implementation.[12]

The combination of the auction, the private entry sales, and the U.S. purchase of the remainder yielded a sum of more than $179,000 in proceeds for the nation. After subtracting the costs of the McCord land appraisal of 1871, the balance due to the Stockbridge-Munsees in 1874 was more than $169,000. And according to the so-called Wells tribal census of that year, the New Citizens Party was entitled to $94,000 of that amount, or $675 per capita. The Indian Party kept $75,000 in a U.S. trust fund, with interest payable semiannually. The approximately $40 that each Indian Party member received per year after 1874 became a mainstay of the tribal economy for the rest of the nineteenth century. The Old Citizens Party, a creation of McCord and Martin through their interpretation of Section 6, got nothing.[13]

In fall 1874 the Green Bay Indian agent started to stipulate Sections 8 and 9 about allotting the eighteen sections kept separate for the Indian Party. His actions were suspended by the Commissioner of Indian Affairs in 1876, not to be resumed until the 1890s. And just as the OIA had bungled the job of making a new survey after the Treaty of 1856, so too did it skip the important task of surveying the reservation after 1871. In fact, no land survey was done until 1907. In the absence of a survey, the distinction, or dividing line, between reserved Indian lands and land opened on the reservation to loggers was almost certain to be exploited by lumbermen.[14]

John C. Adams began collecting documents and writing to Congress and the Interior Department to protest the Wells roll and the way the Act of 1871 was being stipulated. He also drafted bills to overturn portions of the act and as early as 1876 had one introduced by a friendly Democratic congressman. The Office of Indian Affairs received a steady stream of protests and memoranda from Adams about the problems of the Stockbridge-Munsees. Finally, in 1877, the OIA sent Inspector Edward Kemble to the reservation to make an inquiry. Kemble interviewed members of both the Indian Party and the Old Citizens Party. His report to the commissioner confirmed most of Adams's charges about the corrupt way in which Wells, McCord, and Martin had taken the national census in 1874. Kemble went further and recommended that Congress pass a follow-up law to the Act of 1871 that would appraise and sell the remaining eighteen sections of Indian Party land parcels and then make the Indian Party members in effect into New Citizens Party members who would walk away with a per capita payment. The Mohican Nation would then end. The Commissioner of Indian Affairs accepted the Kemble Report but declined to recommend its legislative solution to Congress.[15]

After the suspension of tribal government under Sachem Charles, the Indian Party was led by Reverend Slingerland until his death in 1884. Even before his 1877 visit to the reservation, OIA Inspector Kemble journeyed to the Stockbridge-Munsee Indian Reservation in summer 1874 to inquire into the state of political affairs after the Wells census and stipulation of Section 6. Kemble was shocked that the Indian Party leaders had ignored the commissioner's suspension order of 1872 and reinstituted tribal government under their own authority:

From an interview I had with a member of the Stockbridge Council
elected in defiance of the orders of the Department, I should judge
that they already considered themselves released from respect and
obedience to the authority of the agent and were quite an independent power on the Reservation.[16]

Clearly outraged at the independence shown by the Stockbridge council,
Kemble continued:

I think it necessary for the welfare of the Tribe, from the best information that I can obtain on the Reservation, that their council should
be dissolved, and that the secret bargaining contract-makers and
politicians of the Tribe be informed that their government is not
"independent" of the Department at Washington, represented in the
office of the Agent. The leading politicians of this conclave informed
me that they didn't want their rights as an independent people
"interfered" by the Department.[17]

Reverend Slingerland led the Mohicans on the Stockbridge council who
refused to relinquish their sovereignty to Inspector Kemble or the new
Green Bay Indian agent, Thomas Chase. Slingerland served continually
on the post-1871 tribal council and was occasionally elected sachem.
Slingerland and his wife, Sarah, also served as the teachers at the two tribal
day schools on the Stockbridge Indian Reservation throughout the 1870s;
and after his death, the two schools were consolidated under Mrs. Slingerland's supervision. The Slingerlands maintained a degree of independence
from the Office of Indian Affairs in the operation of their schools too, as
the funds came from the annuity known formally as the Stockbridge Consolidated Fund, and, in turn, Slingerland's control over tribal government
and his connections to Congressman Sawyer ensured that the annuity
funds flowed without interruption. But at least in the opinion of the various
men who served as Green Bay Indian agent, the education offered by the
Slingerlands was substandard. One agent complained that school attendance by Mohican children was so poor that the "rising generation" would
be the first in which the sons were worse educated than the fathers. Another
complained in the late 1880s that Mrs. Slingerland had lost parental
support for the school and that "the better class send their children to
boarding schools."[18] Finally, politics entered education just as it had at

Stockbridge-on-the-Lake. So long as Reverend Slingerland was headmaster of the Stockbridge schools, no child of parents belonging to the New or the Old Citizens Party was allowed to attend school. Slingerland insisted that this was only fair since the schools were funded by the Indian Party's own annuity funds; the Citizens Party families had no business living on the reservation, in Slingerland's opinion, and if they wanted education for their children, they should seek it elsewhere. The losers, of course, were the children of the many outcast families living on the reservation.

Slingerland continued to preside at worship services in the Presbyterian church, as he had done since the departure of Rev. Cutting Marsh in 1847. The Presbyterians were the only denomination allowed on the reservation, but Reverend Slingerland was not subject to the supervision of the Foreign Mission Board in Edinburgh as was Marsh. Instead, the tribe paid his salary as its established religious leader. The various Green Bay Indian agents estimated that one-third to one-half of Stockbridges attended services in the 1870s. The agents often complained of intemperance among the Stockbridges (and of the Oneidas and Menominees in the Green Bay Agency), and they blamed Slingerland for not showing more diligence in sponsoring temperance work. But the most disturbing charge that the agents raised about the Stockbridges under Slingerland was that many had become addicted to opium, including, rumor had it, Reverend Slingerland. Another OIA inspector reported to the Commissioner of Indian Affairs in 1880 that "their instructor is an old man, though a minister of religion, he is said to be an opium-eater—at any rate he is superannuated and worthless as a teacher."[19]

Along with Slingerland, Albert Miller took the lead as spokesman for the Indian Party. He was the son of Samuel Miller, an adopted Stockbridge from New York State who had sided with the Indian Party in the political battles of the 1840s and 1850s. Albert Miller's influence in the Indian Party was so pronounced that outsiders came to call his group the "Miller Party" rather than the Indian Party. Political conflict between the Millers and their opponents in the Indian Party became so severe that in 1878 Albert Miller led a successful impeachment effort against the then-sachem, Dennis Turkey, charging him with "maladministration, and for illegal discharge of his official duties as Sachem, and for violating the laws, and constitution." Turkey's response was to boycott his trial date, several times, until finally the council, sitting as the High Court of the Nation, voted to remove him from office. Slingerland succeeded him for a term as sachem, followed by Albert Miller, who maintained a leadership position on the council for the remainder of the 1880s.[20]

Sovereignty issues dominated the deliberations of the Stockbridge Nation's council during the 1880s. There were three matters especially that took up many of the meetings of the council and often the "General Council" of the nation, that is, the men in the tribe age twenty-one and over. One of these involved membership in the tribe. In 1881 the former sachem under the 1857 constitution, John P. Hendricks of the Old Citizens Party, asked the OIA to re-enroll him as a member of the tribe. The Commissioner of Indian Affairs directed his Green Bay agent to ask the tribal council its opinion. Not surprisingly, the council went on record "protesting against the enrollment of said Hendricks and family." That action ended Hendricks's bid to regain his tribal membership via an administrative decision of the United States, overruling the 1874 Wells enrollment census. Later in 1881 the tribal council warned the Green Bay agent against attempting to meddle in the appointment of an executor of an estate for a deceased tribal member. The council quoted its 1837 constitution to the agent and made it clear that only the Stockbridge Nation High Court could hear matters of probate and that the United States had no authority in a "purely national matter." Another matter of sovereignty arose in 1883 when the council took up the issue of women's suffrage, at least for widows with children. Advocates on the council pointed out that women who headed families needed to have a formal voice in national matters. The tribal council decided the question was so important that the General Council needed to make the decision. The latter (consisting only of men) heard the two sides of the question and voted 14 to 6 against widows' suffrage.[21]

The sovereignty issue that occupied the most time in the 1880s was the Old Citizens Party's effort to reverse the Act of 1871, or at least the Wells census of 1874 that had detribalized them. Between 1876 and 1893 members of the House and Senate considered a bill favored by John C. Adams and the Old Citizens Party that would reaffirm the Treaty of 1856, add the Old Citizens Party members back to the tribal rolls, and grant them allotments. Also, between 1882 and 1893 the House and Senate considered an alternate bill favored by Albert Miller and the Stockbridge Tribal Council that would extend the Act of 1871. The terms of the Miller bill called for the OIA to appraise and sell the eighteen reserved sections on the reservation, combine the proceeds with the Stockbridge Consolidated Fund, and then divide the whole on a per capita basis among tribal members, that is, tribal members listed on the Indian Party roll of 1874. Table 5.2 presents the history of the rival bills from 1876 through 1893.

The bills shepherded by John C. Adams had the same text for seventeen years running. After starting with a preamble concerning the treaty of 1856, the bill continued:

Whereas by the interpretation placed by Government officials on the act of February sixth, eighteen hundred and seventy-one, an act for the relief of said Indians, a large part of said Indians (and their descendants) who signed said treaty of eighteen hundred and fifty-six, and have continued with said tribe from the making of said treaty to the present time, are excluded from participating in tribal funds and the right to occupy said reservation.

The bill then reincorporated the Old Citizens Party into the tribe and ordered the secretary of the interior to take a roll. There was no effort made in the bill to recover the lost land parcels sold to the lumbermen under the Act of 1871, but the all-important Section 6 was, in effect, nullified. Adams and the Old Citizens Party gained an ally in Wisconsin senator Angus Cameron, who introduced the bill in the Forty-sixth Congress.[22]

The Stockbridge Tribal Council was slow to react to the bill in the Forty-fourth Congress but became alarmed when Senator Cameron took up the cause of the Old Citizens Party. Led by Albert Miller, the tribal council petitioned Congress against the Cameron bill "contemplating the incorporation into the Stockbridge Tribe of certain parties who have heretofore separated their relation with said tribe." It was also during that Congress that the Indian Party's tribal council came to embrace the idea suggested by Inspector Kemble back in 1877, namely, the dissolution of the tribe and the division of the eighteen sections of land and the tribal fund. In January 1881 the council petitioned Congress "to become citizens of the republic and to have the money which was placed to their credit . . . paid to them per capita."[23]

The 1880 federal census takers who combed Shawano County trying to count everyone as directed by the U.S. Constitution, except "Indians not taxed," ran into a perplexing problem. The census marshal who enumerated

TABLE 5.2

The Struggle in Congress
between the Old Citizens Party and the Indian Party

YEAR	CONGRESS	SESSION	OLD CITIZEN'S PARTY BILL	INDIAN PARTY BILL	BILL'S FATE
1876	44th	1st	H.R. 3245		Not enacted
1876	44th	1st	H.R. 4086		Not enacted
1880	46th	3d	S.B. 1163		Not enacted
1880	46th	3d	H.R.3678		Not enacted
1881	47th	1st	S.B. 611		Not enacted
1881	47th	1st		H.R. 6666	Not enacted
1883	47th	2d	H.R. 7175		Not enacted
1884	48th	1st	H.R. 2889		Not enacted
1886	49th	1st	H.R. 3749		Not enacted
1888	50th	1st	H.R. 5043		Not enacted
1888	50th	1st		S.B. 1881	Not enacted
1890	51st	1st		H.R. 4227	Not enacted
1890	51st	1st		S.B. 712	Passage by both houses, but pocket veto by Pres. Harrison
1892	52d	1st		S.B. 2873	Not enacted
1892	52d	1st	S.B. 2977		Not enacted
1892	52d	1st	H.R. 3594		Not enacted
1892-93	52d	2d	H.R. 3594		Passed by both houses and signed into law by Pres. Harrison

SOURCE: *Congressional Record*, 44th Cong., lst sess., pp. 1876, 5698; 44th Cong., 2d sess., p. 1391; 46th Cong., 3d sess., pp. 717, 747, 1581, 1942, 2062; 47th Cong., lst sess., pp. 186, 2315, 4813, 5347, 5667, 5977, 6185; 48th Cong., lst sess., pp. 291, 2171, 5823; 48th Cong., 2d sess., pp. 2278–79; 51st Cong., lst sess., pp. 10401–02, 10643; 51st Cong., 2d sess., pp. 2892, 2933–37, 3087, 3105; 52d Cong., lst sess., pp. 302, 1833, 3077, 7004; 52d Cong., 2d sess., pp. 1056, 1175, 2088; "An Act for the Relief of the Stockbridge and Munsee Tribe of Indians, in the State of Wisconsin," 27, *Statutes at Large*, 744 (1893).

the town of Herman kept encountering people whom he regarded as "citizens" but who protested that they were really Indians. The marshal devised his own compromise tally for that year and recorded 278 "civilized Indians" in Shawano County, who were a mix of Indian Party and Citizens Party individuals.[24]

The Indian Party control of tribal government was greatly aided after the 1880 elections when the Wisconsin legislature sent Philetus Sawyer back to Washington as a U.S. senator. Now the tribe's legally recognized government had a powerful ally to safeguard its interests against J. C. Adams and his Old Citizens Party. Nonetheless, in 1883, during the Forty-seventh Congress, the tribal council became so alarmed at the prospect of success by Adams and his faction that it voted national funds to send Albert Miller to Washington, D.C., to lobby against the Old Citizens Party bill and in favor of its own. At a tumultuous 1884 Senate hearing on H.R. 2889, Miller set forth the case for the Indian Party's interpretation of recent Mohican history. He took Congress through the complicated history of termination and restoration in 1843 and 1846 and then highlighted the importance of the treaty of 1848. As to the treaty of 1856, Miller dismissed it as a fraud imposed on the tribe by Superintendent Huebschman in league with dishonest "white men and negroes." As far as Miller was concerned, the Act of 1871 fixed the injustice of the 1856 treaty. Miller downplayed the importance of enacting the rival Indian Party bill that called for tribal termination and distribution of the tribe's property. He focused much more on defeating the proposal of Adams and H.R. 2889.[25]

Back at home, Miller worked to have the Department of the Interior expel the Old Citizens Party members still residing on the reservation. He began this campaign in 1882, and in spring 1883 he managed to convince the Commissioner of Indian Affairs to issue an order to the Green Bay agent to eject the unwanted opponents. But then, in fall 1883, the secretary of the interior overruled his commissioner and suspended the order. Still Miller persisted, and for the rest of the decade, he sent frequent requests to the Interior Department to have the 1883 order enforced.[26]

Adams, who had relocated to Washington to work full-time on Old Citizens Party business, testified in 1884 in favor of H.R. 2889. His history of the Mohican Nation differed from that of Miller. His account of the 1840s had both Citizens Party and Indian Party members taking allotments under the Act of 1843, and therefore both factions were indistinguishable on policy matters. Indeed, the very name of the Citizens Party was misleading four decades later because Adams's faction wanted to be restored to tribal status, in effect, to become Indians again. Unlike Miller, Adams saw the treaty of 1856 as the definitive arrangement of Mohican affairs. He insisted that Congress had been duped in 1871 by the Indian Party and the Pine Ring and that the Wells enrollment census of 1874 represented the real injustice.[27]

In the Forty-seventh and Forty-eighth Congresses, Miller's termination proposal was backed by the ironically named Sen. Francis Stockbridge (R-Mich.) and by Philetus Sawyer (R-Wis.). The alternative bill favoring the rights of the Old Citizens Party and reaffirming the 1856 treaty was backed by Wisconsin's other senator, William Vilas. The Vilas bill (S.B. 2873 and H.R. 3594) repeated the Adams formulation that Citizens Party members who signed the treaty of 1856, or their descendants, who kept up their tribal connection should be restored to the tribal rolls. Moreover, the Vilas bill confirmed the allotment selections of 1856, such as that of Jesse Wybro, that Reverend Slingerland had registered and ordered federal officials to issue patents to the rightful Indian owners, whether of the Indian Party or the Citizens Party.[28]

The Old Citizens Party protest did not receive a fair hearing in Washington so long as Senator Sawyer held sway with the Republican-controlled Interior Department about affairs in his state. But with the election of Democrat Grover Cleveland in November 1884, party control over the Department of the Interior and the OIA shifted. The partisan alignment of 1870–71 still held where the Indian Party allied itself with Philetus Sawyer and the Republicans, and the Citizens Party with the Democratic opposition.

In 1886 a Senate subcommittee held hearings at Keshena, Wisconsin, on the Menominee Indian Reservation about Stockbridge affairs. At that hearing state officials testified in favor of restoring the Old Citizens Party to the tribe. But members of the Miller family were not ready to yield to the reversal of political fortunes. In August 1886 Zacharias Miller wrote to his brother Albert Miller that J. C. Adams had been visiting the reservation settlement at Red Springs and "had told some good stories to his friends . . . that A. Miller could not do a thing in the Department [of Interior] because the new administration did not like A. Miller." But, Zacharias Miller continued, a member of the Metoxen family stood up to

Adams's smooth talk and stated that Albert Miller deserved praise for trying to "get those dam nigers off the reservation."[29]

The secretary of the interior in the first Cleveland administration was William Vilas, the influential Wisconsin Democrat. It was under his leadership that the department and the OIA launched a major investigation of Stockbridge-Munsee affairs. The OIA sent veteran Indian inspector William Parsons to Wisconsin to investigate. The resulting Parsons Report was a devastating exposé of the fraudulent nature of the passage of the Act of 1871 and especially the 1874 enrollment provisions carried out by OIA Inspector Wells. Now the Old Citizens Party had its fair hearing in Congress—indeed, a whole set of hearings with hundreds of pages of testimony about the collusion of the lumbermen and the Indian Party at the time the Act of 1871 was proposed and passed.[30] The state of Wisconsin sent its own official legislative memorial to Congress reaffirming the 1856 treaty and repudiating the Act of 1871. For the first time, the administration in the Interior Department and Office of Indian Affairs supported the bill favoring the restoration of the Citizens Party to the tribe. But the Senate balked at passage in the Fiftieth Congress, thanks to the blocking efforts of senators Sawyer and Stockbridge.

The two factions of Mohicans had a great deal at stake in the elections of 1888. A Democratic victory would keep the Interior Department and the OIA sympathetic to the Old Citizens Party. Perhaps a Democratic victory in Wisconsin and Michigan state legislative elections would result in the replacement of Sawyer and Stockbridge in the U.S. Senate. A Republican victory nationwide, by contrast, would put the recognized Indian Party tribal government in a stronger position to deny the Adams party its goals, and perhaps to get its own legislation enacted. In a very close election in 1888, the Republicans carried the White House, and also gained control of both houses of Congress. This was the most opportune time for the Indian Party to get its way in Washington, a fact recognized by Albert Miller and by the tribe's hired attorneys, Joseph McDonald of Indianapolis, former Congressman Halbert Paine of Milwaukee, and William A. Cook of Washington, D.C.[31]

The Old Citizens Party, under Adams's leadership, however, made one key alliance outside of government during the first Cleveland administration: Adams had won the support of the Indian Rights Association (I.R.A.), a private group based in Philadelphia that actively worked to influence federal Indian policy. The I.R.A. was one of the self-styled "friend of the Indians" assimilationist groups that believed strongly in the reform power of the Dawes Allotment Act. All things being equal, the I.R.A. ideology in the 1880s might have had it siding with the Indian Party in advocating the dissolution of the tribe and the division of its property. But the I.R.A. was also heir to the Mugwump tradition of Republicanism and abhorred the type of corrupt lumberman politics represented by Philetus Sawyer. As William Hagan, the historian of the I.R.A., wrote, "The IRA normally was happy to expedite the transformation of reservation Indians into allotted citizens; nevertheless it would not do so simply to gratify the greed of white men." At the same time that the I.R.A. moved in 1889 to help the Old Citizens Party, it was engaged in a struggle on the Menominee Reservation to oppose yet another grab by Senator Sawyer of that reservation's timber.[32]

With the Republicans restored to power in the 1888 elections, Sawyer managed to advance his own bill during the first session of the Fifty-first Congress in spring 1890, first by having it favorably reported from the Senate Indian Affairs Committee and then obtaining the same from the House. The language in the Sawyer bill was blunt: enactment into law meant the "extinction of the tribe." It is a measure of how desperate the Miller-led opposition was to the Old Citizens Party that the ruling tribal government was willing to contemplate the end of the Mohican Nation rather than see its opponents readmitted. The Sawyer-sponsored bills passed both houses of Congress on February 23, 1891, near the end of the long first session, and were sent to President Harrison for his presumed signature. At this point, the I.R.A. intervened decisively to secure a presidential veto. The principal lobbyist for the I.R.A., Charles C. Painter, secured a meeting with President Harrison in which he explained his group's opposition to the bill. Painter spared no words; he accused the Republican chair of the Senate Indian Affairs Committee, Henry L. Dawes of Massachusetts, of conduct that was "dishonest and disreputable" on the Stockbridge-Munsee bill. The president also asked the Interior Department for an opinion, and on February 27, the Commissioner of Indian Affairs, in quieter terms, recommended a presidential veto rather than see the Sawyer bill become law. Harrison simply withheld his signature from the bill, and when the congressional session adjourned on March 3, 1891, the bill died as a result of his pocket veto.[33]

At the same time Senator Sawyer pursued his bill in Congress, the Indian Party renewed its efforts to have the Old Citizens Party expelled from the reservation. In 1890 the Indian Party managed to get the Commissioner of Indian Affairs to issue a new expulsion order with directions to the Green Bay agent to use federal marshals to do the work. One family in particular drew the ire of the Indian Party and the OIA, the family of Stephen Gardner. The Indian Party considered the Gardner family African American, not Stockbridge, but could not peacefully persuade Stephen Gardner to leave his house and farm plot on the reservation. In response to the commissioner's order, Gardner worked out an arrangement with officials in the U.S. Attorney's office in Milwaukee to have his status tested in court. Abandoned, in effect, by the U.S. Attorney and the marshals under him, the Commissioner of Indian Affairs suspended the expulsion order once again and in 1892 permanently canceled it.[34]

During the last year of the Harrison administration, 1892, the Congress once again took up Stockbridge-Munsee affairs. The Senate Indian Affairs Committee held another hearing on the rival bills and took testimony. Painter of the I.R.A. was the star witness, and he immediately launched into a denunciation of the passage of the Act of 1871 as "covertly secured." The committee next heard at length from Adams, who presented a memorial from the Wisconsin legislature and the "principal men" of Shawano in favor of "relief for the Old Citizens Party." Making the case for the Indian Party were Albert Miller and J. C. McGowan, their Washington, D.C., attorney. McGowan repeated the Indian Party charge that the treaty of 1856 was illegitimate because Huebschman had signed it with the "Citizens Party and others, who were neither citizens nor Indians, but negroes and white men." The testimony and supporting documents from both sides were extensive. Adams alone prepared hundreds of pages of documents that he introduced as exhibits.[35]

Sentiment in the House of Representatives favored the Old Citizens Party bill and was led by the Democratic congressman who represented Shawano County, Thomas Lynch. However, Senators Stockbridge and Sawyer managed to block the Old Citizens Party bill in the first session of the Fifty-second Congress, and they continued to delay its passage in the second session. It was not until after the defeat of President Harrison and the Republicans in the fall 1892 elections, with William Vilas now sent to the U.S. Senate and Philetus Sawyer weakened in Republican circles by the insurgent challenge of Congressman Robert M. LaFollette, that H.R. 3594 finally got through both houses of Congress. The bill came up for Senate passage on February 13, 1893, a day when almost half of the eighty-seven senators were absent. Senator Sawyer and his allies again sought to have the bill sent back to the Indian Affairs Committee. This produced outrage from Senator Jones (D-Ark.):

> I wish to say that the subject matter proposed to be disposed of by House bill 3594 has been before Congress for twenty years. The Stockbridge Indians are living on lands where they were put in 1856 and persistent efforts have been made to deprive them of their homes. . . . The delay is not creditable to the Government of the United States, and is an outrage on these Indians.[36]

Senator Vilas also reaffirmed the treaty of 1856:

> The simple, plain measure of justice, which the Committee on Indian Affairs had no difficulty determining, lies merely in awarding to certain Indians their title to lands which they have occupied for thirty-six years, which was made perfect to them by a treaty of the United States, and for which they have been entitled to a patent under the terms of that treaty for a quarter of a century.[37]

Senator Jones brought the bill up again on February 24, and this time Senator Sawyer relented. "I am not going to object," he stated, but he added, "I do not think the bill ought to pass, but still I am not going to make any opposition except to vote against it."[38] The bill quickly passed the Senate and President Harrison signed it into law before his term ended.

The archival records of the House and Senate are quite clear that in passing the Act of 1893, Congress was rejecting the Act of 1871 and upholding the 1856 treaty. Again, an understanding of the partisan lineup is essential to making sense of how the two sides viewed the 1856 agreement. The Democrats, led by Vilas as secretary of the interior and later as senator, saw the main function of the 1856 treaty as a gathering of the disparate parts of the tribe at the new Shawano County location. The Senate bill file in the National Archives makes this clear because the senators in 1893 had at hand a copy of Commissioner Manypenny's January 7, 1856, instructions to Superintendent Huebschman. The Senate

Indian Affairs Committee relied on that document, along with the text of the treaty, to interpret the government's intentions in the treaty of 1856. By contrast, the Republican faction led by Senator Sawyer called for an appraisal and sale of the tribe's eighteen sections, followed by a severing of federal relations with the tribe. Senator Sawyer envisioned this policy as the logical extension of the Act of 1871. However, in the end, Congress rejected Sawyer's Indian Party bill and in 1893 passed the rival Vilas bill with its explicit repudiation of parts of the Act of 1871.[39]

No action of Congress in relation to the Stockbridge-Munsee Nation ever generated more hearings, testimony, affidavits, documents, correspondence, and legislative reports than the Act of 1893, a full seventeen years in the making. No single Mohican worked harder on the nation's behalf on a single piece of congressional legislation than John C. Adams. At no time before or after did the two House and Senate Indian Affairs Committees spend so much time investigating the history and current claims of the tribe and its factions. Never was Congress so well informed about the tribe. The Act of 1893 looked backward to restore the tribe as a whole as much as possible under the Treaty of 1856 and overturn to the extent possible the Act of 1871.

The Act of 1893 reaffirmed the 1856 treaty as the basis for membership in the tribe and pointedly renamed it the Stockbridge-Munsee Tribe of Indians. Congress also reconfirmed the allotment selections made in good faith after the 1856 treaty, as was the tribe's occupancy of its 1856 reservation. Nineteen years after the corrupt census of Wells, McCord, and Martin, the tribe was to get an honest enrollment. The only flaw in the legislation is that Congress failed to appropriate any money to conduct the new roll. So Charles Painter, or "Professor Painter" as he was known because of his onetime faculty status at the freedmen's Fisk University, volunteered to take the census at no charge to the tribe or to the United States. Painter proceeded to travel to Wisconsin, Canada, and New York in search of disfranchised Mohicans and Munsees who deserved to be on the Stockbridge-Munsee tribal roll. For six months Painter labored patiently to make sense of the genealogy of the Stockbridge and Munsee Indians. Once again, Adams proved indispensable; he helped Painter to navigate the history of marriages, births, deaths, and adoptions of the people, or what the professor (also an ordained Congregational minister) called "the bitter factional strifes of twenty-three years, and fearfully mixed marriages, and great liberty of divorce." It was Adams's final service to his people before his death in early 1895.[40]

The leaders of the Indian Party refused to participate in the census, calling the Act of 1893 the "most unjust, outrageous and unconstitutional legislation" ever passed by Congress in regard to the internal matters of an Indian tribe. In numerous letters and petitions to the secretary of the interior, Zacharias Miller and others in the Indian Party protested Painter's census, at one time calling it an "illegal enrollment of unauthorized persons and their descendants under Act of March 3rd, 1893 of mixed Races of whites & Negroes." Miller also ignored J. C. Adams's participation as an assistant to Professor Painter and complained to Secretary of the Interior Hoke Smith that the true guiding force behind the census was "one Simeon Gardner, a notorious negro bigamist and profligate." In an echo of the accusations leveled at the 1874 Wells census, Miller charged that Painter's September 1893 work took place in Gardner's "private residence."[41]

Whatever the circumstances of the enrollment location, Painter's census carefully delineated individuals by membership in the Indian Party, the Old Citizens Party, New York Munsees, "Outsiders," and a special category, the "Tousey Family." He made a genuine effort to be inclusive, and there were no subsequent charges of bribery or corruption as there had been directed against Wells. Table 5.3 shows the numbers of Mohicans and Munsees in the different categories.[42]

Painter's numbers are instructive when compared to the tally that Wells had produced in 1874: 112 members of the Indian Party and 137 members of the New Citizens Party. On the face of it, the tribe had doubled in population in just twenty years. Even if the excluded Old Citizens were included in 1874 and Adams consistently estimated their numbers at about 150, the tribe still showed impressive growth in the late nineteenth century.

An OIA inspector who had visited the reservation in 1880 had commented about the Stockbridge-Munsees and their disagreements that the "factions [are] as fierce and vindictive as through they represented great interests."[43] Perhaps in 1880 there was not very much at stake materially. If the Stockbridge Consolidated Fund was divided on a per capita basis within the Indian Party only, each tribal member would receive about $500. If the Citizens Party was included, the per capita payment might decline by one-half to two-thirds. Perhaps the intratribal dispute between the Citizens Party and Indian Party illustrates the principle that the intensity

TABLE 5.3
C. C. Painter's 1894 Tally of the Stockbridge-Munsees

PAINTER'S CATEGORY BY PARTY	PAINTER'S 1894 TABULATION	PAINTER'S COMMENTS
Indian Party	143	"All are persons to the enrollment of whom there is no opposition."
Citizens Party	84	"Old Citizens Party and women of the tribe of 1856 who married outside the tribe and their children"
"Out in 1856 and now again enrolled"	10	"Persons who went out in 1856 and are back upon the present enrollment"
New Citizens Party	12	"Persons of the New Citizens Party who are related to such as separated under the Act of 1871 and are enrolled owing to the absence of any recognition of the established custom or law of the tribe"
New York Munsees	50	"residing on the Cattaraugus, Onondaga, or Seneca reservations in New York"
"Outsiders," not including the Tousey family	152	"such persons as are not of either of the other classes. . . . [T]he relationship is so complex that any sub-classification is only partially satisfactory."
Tousey Family	52	"The Tousey Family—a special class"
Total	503	

SOURCE: "Stockbridge Indians" (1894), Special Case 42, Box 5, Records of the Bureau of Indian Affairs, Record Group 75, National Archives.

of a conflict is inversely related to the stakes of its outcome. But by 1893 the stakes were quite a bit higher. By that date, the tribal council of the Stockbridge Indians (i.e., the Indian Party) had joined other New York, Wisconsin, and Indian Territory (present-day Oklahoma) tribes in a combined lawsuit against the United States. *New York Indians v. United States* required an enabling act of Congress to allow the plaintiff tribes to seek redress before the U.S. Court of Claims for wrongs done the tribes by the United States in the 1838 Buffalo Creek Treaty in New York State. Launched in 1883, the lawsuit was nearing decision a decade later. And not only was the Stockbridge tribe represented as a plaintiff, but the lead counsel on the case, J. C. McGowan, served as the tribe's principal counsel at the 1892 congressional hearings. McGowan asked the Court of Claims for $400,000 in damages for wrongs done his Stockbridge clients in 1838. Although Congress forbade a claim of interest on the amount, the possible award was enough incentive to keep the Indian Party battling to exclude the Citizens Party from a share. The payments finally reached individual Stockbridges and Munsees in 1905 and 1906, with each of 425 tribal members receiving $175. The local newspaper wrote, "This will be a nice sum and will help the Indians purchase the articles which they have long needed. The merchants of Shawano will no doubt be well patronized."[44]

The Act of 1893, the death of J. C. Adams, and the overthrow of the Indian Party polity marked another turning point in the history of the Mohicans. Instead of a small, dwindling band of barely one hundred Indians, the new roll prepared by Professor Painter showed more than five hundred members. Here, suddenly, was the rising generation that was foreseen in the treaty of 1856. Indeed, from the viewpoint of the newly restored members of the tribe, it seemed as if, with the implementation of the treaty of 1856, history had resumed after almost four decades. In the next period of Stockbridge-Munsee history, the tribe and the United States would have to face the consequences of a growing population on a small landholding.

CHAPTER 6

The Politics of Allotment and Land Claims, 1893–1934

When the Office of Indian Affairs sent Inspector Parsons to visit the Stockbridge Reservation in 1886, he expressed a reaction similar to that of Inspector Kemble in 1874 and 1877 and, for that matter, Congressman Sawyer in 1870. Parsons viewed the Stockbridge-Munsees as a thoroughly political people in the sense that they took politics seriously and participated actively in the political life of their nation. Outsiders like Kemble and Parsons saw the split between the Indian Party and the Citizens Party as evidence of a dysfunctional tribe obsessed with factional fighting. Indeed, the reaction of Congress and the executive branch under both Democrats and Republicans was that the tribe was too focused on politics and not focused enough on agricultural development. In 1895 the Interior Department accepted Parsons's 1886 recommendation that the Stockbridge-Munsee tribal government be dissolved. On December 6, 1895, the secretary of the interior directed the "abolition of any so called local government, constitution or laws of the Stockbridge Tribe of Indians of Wisconsin, and that all of the government business with said tribe, to be hereafter transacted, be through a Business Committee." The secretary then appointed a new Tribal Business Committee, headed by John P. Hendricks, a descendant of the old Emigrant Party and an opponent of Samuel Miller, leader of the Indian Party. Secretary of the Interior Hoke Smith's 1895 directive represented a usurpation of the sovereignty of the Stockbridge-Munsee tribe (no longer recognized as a nation) and its 1856 treaty rights that Congress had just reaffirmed in the Act of 1893. Smith also breached the separation of federal powers and flouted Article 11 of the 1856 treaty when he acted without congressional directive or Senate approval in his abolition order.[1]

The United States was determined to remove politics from Stockbridge-Munsee affairs. The historian can only say, however, that politics was part of the culture of the Stockbridge-Munsees and any abolition of the tribal council and tribal constitution simply meant that the political arena in which tribal members participated would move elsewhere. The other venues included a local school board and township government, the state legislature and Wisconsin Department of Justice, the federal courts, the federal Interior and Justice Departments, Congress, and even the League of Nations.

Politics in the 1895 to 1934 period revolved around righting the many wrongs done the tribe in the nineteenth century. What is striking about the political history of the Stockbridge-Munsees after the Act of 1893 is how the old divisions started by Indian removal in the 1820s and 1830s began to heal, even if incompletely. The healing came slowly and was more pronounced by the early 1930s than the later 1890s, but it was unmistakable. The race-baiting eased and then largely disappeared; there was no more debate about who had African American parentage between and among the Indian Party and the Citizens Party. Marriages between descendants of the Indian Party and the Citizens Party became common. And over time, white consciousness of racial differences with the Stockbridge-Munsees intensified in Shawano County and throughout Wisconsin, which had the paradoxical effect of bringing the parties of the tribe closer together.

Above all, the period was dominated by the process of land allotment to individual members of the Stockbridge-Munsee tribe. The 1856 treaty had set forth land allotment on the new Shawano County reservation with the provision that the individual allotments would remain in trust for at least ten years. This provision made the land inalienable by Stockbridge-Munsees to non-Indian purchasers. The trust period, under the 1856 treaty, would only end when the tribal council said so. The Act of 1893 sought to implement the treaty of 1856. The administrative responsibility for allotment, in the absence of a sovereign Stockbridge-Munsee tribal council, rested on the secretary of the interior and the Commissioner of Indian Affairs.

The Office of Indian Affairs soon recognized the problem of making additional allotments to the Citizens Party members. In the words of the commissioner, "The office was forced to the conclusion that allotments could not be made under the treaty of 1856, because of an insufficiency of land, and if made under the General Allotment Act of February 8, 1887 (24 Stat. 388), each Indian would receive only about 18 to 20 acres." The OIA calculated that only 8,920 acres remained in common lands of the tribe, yet 24,800 would be needed to satisfy the demand for allotments that was anticipated by the Act of 1893. The OIA sent an inspector to the Stockbridge-Munsee Reservation to investigate and resolve the situation in fall 1900.[2]

Inspector Cyrus Beede received his appointment from the Interior Department on October 8, 1900, and instructions from the Commissioner of Indian Affairs in a letter on October 27. The commissioner's charge to Beede came in the first paragraph: "conferring with the Indians with the view of formulating a plan for the allotment of the common land of said reservation in severalty." The instructions continued with a lengthy recitation of the history of the Treaty of 1856, the Acts of 1871 and 1893, and various other documents. All the instructions concerned the issues of allotment and the tribal trust funds. The commissioner recognized the problem of too many allottees and too little land: "You will have observed that, to use a somewhat vulgar expression, this [is] a case of trying to make a small shoe fit a large foot, so far as the land is concerned."[3]

Inspector Beede read the background material and journeyed to the Stockbridge-Munsee Reservation in late November and held what he called open councils on November 24 and 29. He also had additional meetings with individuals and small groups of tribal members, and he asked each faction to appoint subcommittees to submit a written plan to be considered by all in open council. The "Miller Party" (as Beede called the Indian Party) subcommittee's plan called for a new tribal roll to be made and, predictably, for removing Citizens Party members from the rolls. The Citizens Party subcommittee's first draft, submitted on November 30, called for (1) allotment of tribal lands; (2) provision of land "elsewhere in like ratio" if not enough tribal land existed to satisfy all allottees; (3) division of the tribal trust fund on a per capita basis; and (4) "That the tribal relationship shall be dissolved and citizenship be declared for the entire membership on consummation of settlement." The discussion in the open council of November 29 about tribal dissolution makes clear that the context was one of law enforcement and liquor violations, with one Citizens Party leader stating the desirability of having Wisconsin state law enforcement as a public safety matter.[4]

Inspector Beede called for second drafts of the plans on December 1 and worked to draw up a composite plan. The second draft of the Citizens Party contained just two proposals: (1) allotment of the remaining tribal lands; and (2) acquisition of additional lands as needed, or the payment in money at a rate of $2 an acre to allottees who preferred cash to land. None of the second-draft plans included any language or reference to tribal dissolution, or about the law enforcement question.

The inspector called the tribe together for a council on December 8 to ratify a third draft, which became the "Proposed Plan of Settlement." This plan called for the allotment of the remaining tribal lands, the acquisition of additional lands as needed; a money–not land option at $2 an acre, with the funds to be supplied by the U.S. Treasury; and a distribution of the tribal trust fund on a per capita basis. There was no language in this plan about tribal dissolution or the law enforcement problem. The plan received seventy-four adult male votes in support, and Inspector Beede proclaimed it adopted by a majority vote.[5]

The secretary of the interior soon supplied Congress with the "Proposed Plan of Settlement" and associated documents and urged passage. The House Committee on Indian Affairs received the secretary's submission, but no bill was introduced that session before congressional adjournment. When the new Fifty-seventh Congress began its work in 1902, Senator John Spooner of Wisconsin introduced Senate Bill 3620, which would make the "Proposed Plan of Settlement" law. The title of that initial bill is instructive: "A bill adjusting matters pertaining to the affairs of the Stockbridge and Munsee Tribe of Indians." S.B. 3620 was referred on February 6 to the Senate Committee on Indian Affairs, and there it remained for the session. It was reintroduced as S.B. 335 at the January 1903 start of the Fifty-eighth Congress but again made no progress. In the second session, in 1904, S.B. 335 passed the Senate but failed in the House. It disappeared from view in the first session of the Fifty-ninth Congress. Both the Indian Party and the Citizens Party hired attorney-lobbyists to attempt to sway Congress one way or the other. The Indian Party had never consented to the plan that Beede devised and tried to stymie the new legislation and then repeal the Act of 1893.[6]

The long delay in the passage of S.B. 3620 resulted in part from opposition in the House over the issue of who would pay for the "money–no land" provision. Inspector Beede and the tribe had asked Congress to appropriate up to $35,000 from the Treasury for this purpose. Between 1903 and 1906 the House and Senate differed on the matter of who would pay the qualified allottees who chose money instead of acreage, as well as on the need for a new enrollment of tribal members, a policy urged by the minority Indian Party. Finally, in 1906, the bill passed according to the House preference that the funds for "money–no land" allottees be paid out of the tribal trust fund, not out of a congressional appropriation from the Treasury. The Act of 1906 recapitulated many of the provisions of the December 8, 1900, "Proposed Plan of Settlement," but the tribe neither asked for nor received a "final dissolution."[7]

The problems with timber cutting, railroads, and allotments finally sped the different factions and Congress to cooperate. The rider to the Indian Office appropriations bill that passed Congress in summer 1906 had some important differences from the Beede plan of 1900. The most important was that the tribe's own fund—derived from the Indian Party's share of the sale of fifty-four sections between 1872 and 1874—was to be used to pay for the acquisition of additional lands and to pay for money–no land disbursements. This was bitterly opposed by the Indian Party, which regarded the legislation as a raid by its undeserving opponents on tribal funds. To soften the blow a bit, there was a ceiling price of $2 an acre for new land purchases and for money–no land payments. As the House learned at a 1904 hearing, few sellers in the north half of T28N R14E (present-day Red Springs Township) or in T28N R13E (present-day Bartelme Township) would sell their land at that low price, meaning that most tribal members under the Act of 1906 were bound to receive a money–no land payment, even if they preferred land.[8]

Paragraph 7 of the Act of 1906 provided for money–no land payments to tribal members. The administration of this OIA responsibility took a lengthy period to implement. The first step, antedating even the Act of 1906 itself, had been the establishment of a roll of those tribal members who did not receive an allotment and patent under the treaty of 1856 and the Acts of 1871 and 1893. Since only 42 tribal members had actually received patents by 1897, after the implementation of the Act of 1893 a large backlog of tribal members awaited their allotments. This backlog, of course, was understood by the OIA after 1897 and explains Inspector Beede's "big foot, small shoe" task at the reservation in 1900. By 1904 OIA Inspector James McLaughlin came to Stockbridge-Munsee and prepared a roll that totaled 552 tribal members entitled to an allotment. After Congress passed the Act of 1906, McLaughlin returned to the reservation and inquired first of the Menominees and then of private landowners if either would be willing to sell land to the United States to provide allotments for Stockbridge-Munsees. The answer in each case was no, certainly not at $2 an acre. McLaughlin's report in September 1906 triggered a new round of census taking, recriminations, and delays. A minority of tribal members received land allotments, which, as a subsequent legal case showed, could be worth $15 an acre. The majority of the tribal members, on the other hand, stood to receive the lesser money–no land payment of $2 an acre.[9]

OIA inspector Robert Waugh came to the Stockbridge-Munsee Indian Reservation in September 1907 and took yet another roll that provided allotments for enough tribal members to take up the remaining 7,500 acres of the eighteen sections. The county surveyor, J. Melendy, was hired to survey these sections, a task he completed in November 1907. In 1909 the allotment selections of the approximately 100 fortunate tribal members were sent to the OIA. In January 1910 the secretary of the interior approved the allotments and in April issued the patents. For the next three years, the other 400-plus tribal members who had been counted in 1904 had to wait for the money–no land payments. Not until April 1913 did the OIA get itself organized to determine yet another roll of eligible members and prepare their payments. In August 1913 a new roll was prepared showing 545 tribal members entitled to the payments. Ultimately, $32,000 of the Stockbridge Consolidated Fund, received from the Menasha auction sales of 1872 and subsequent land sales of the fifty-four sections, was disbursed in 1915 as money–no land payments to the long-waiting tribal members.[10]

The Tribal Business Committee carried on government-to-government relations between the tribe and the United States. In addition to overseeing the Court of Claims lawsuit against the United States, the committee worked with OIA personnel to carry out the terms of the Act of 1906. The pattern

TABLE 6.1
Party Distribution of Allotments and
Money–No Land Payments, 1907–1915

TALLY	NUMBER OF INDIAN PARTY MEMBERS (PERCENT OF TOTAL)	NUMBER OF CITIZENS PARTY MEMBERS (PERCENT OF TOTAL)
1894 Painter roll	143 (30%)	335 (70%)
1907 allotments	33 (30%)	76 (70%)
1915 money–no land payments	83 (33%)	148 (67%)

SOURCE: From Census of Stockbridge-Munsees, 1910 and 1916, Tribal Censuses, National Archives Microfilm M-595, Records of the Bureau of Indian Affairs.

of making allotments and no land–money allocations, under the Act of 1906, suggests that the Tribal Business Committee in cooperation with Waugh rewarded tribal members based on their family status rather than their family's party. Tables 6.1 and 6.2 display the pattern of allotments and money–no land payments.

Table 6.1 shows that the more valuable land allotments, worth as much as $10 an acre, and the less valuable money–no land payments, at the rate of $2 per acre, were made in almost exact proportion to the expected percentages of the members of the Indian Party and the Citizens Party, based on Painter's 1894 roll. The data suggest that there was no bias for or against tribal members based on their family's affiliation with one party or the other. That was an act of tribal cooperation that had not been seen since the years after the 1856 treaty, the period when the tribe established a new home on the Shawano County reservation.

Table 6.2 shows that the allocation of more valuable allotments was biased toward older persons, married persons, men, and unmarried parents, both male and female. The Tribal Business Committee, working with Inspector Waugh, came up with their own solution to the big foot, small shoe problem.

In the years after Beede unveiled the "Proposed Plan of Settlement," the Stockbridge-Munsees once again became a main concern of federal Indian policy on logging and lumbering. This time the outcome reversed federal policy as set in the post–Civil War years. In 1870, in *U.S. v. Wybro*, the Office

TABLE 6.2
Social Distribution of Allotments and Money–No Land Payments

CATEGORY	1907 ALLOTTEES	1915 MONEY–NO LAND PAYEES
Median age	33.5 yrs	18.5 yrs
Married male heads of household	28 (26%)	5 (2%)
Married women	15 (14%)	5 (2%)
Single men	37 (34%)	70 (30%)
Single women	9 (8%)	37 (16%)
Unmarried fathers	7 (6%)	6 (3%)
Unmarried mothers	11 (10%)	15 (7%)
Minor boys	2 (2%)	46 (20%)
Minor girls	0 (0%)	47 (20%)
Totals	109 (100%)	231 (100%)
All males	74 (70%)	128 (55%)
All females	35 (30%)	103 (45%)
Totals	109 (100%)	231 (100%)

SOURCE: From Census of Stockbridge-Munsees, 1910 and 1916, Tribal Censuses, National Archives Microfilm M-595, Records of the Bureau of Indian Affairs.

of Indian Affairs tried to argue before Judge Drummond that Jesse Wybro had no individual right to cut pine on land within an Indian reservation still held in common. The judge reluctantly agreed only because Superintendent Huebschman had botched the job of getting the selections turned into actual allotments. The 1870 *U.S. v. Foster* case also failed to sustain the OIA principle that the trees were part of a federal trust in land that no individual Oneida Indian could touch. But in *U.S. v. Cook*, also from the 1870 spring term at Green Bay, the OIA finally found a winning case at the U.S. Supreme Court. The Court reasoned that the treaty of 1838 only guaranteed the Oneida Nation a right of "occupancy" of their reservation, not a right of ownership. Ownership, at least for Indian lands, could only be practiced by individual Indians on allotments or by the United States on common lands held in trust. The right of occupancy did not give individual Oneidas the right to cut timber on unallotted lands.[11]

After 1900, when individual Stockbridge-Munsees began to sign contracts with Shawano lumbermen to log the trees on the eighteen sections reserved for Indian occupancy, they ran afoul of the *Cook* ruling. The pine and hardwoods on the eighteen sections had largely gone unlogged, unlike the timber on the fifty-four sections of the opened portion of the reservation. The OIA insisted that the Green Bay agent work with the U.S. Attorney and the U.S. marshal for the Eastern District of Wisconsin to seize logs and prosecute the lumbermen. A number of prominent lumbermen found themselves charged in U.S. District Court with illegal lumbering on the Stockbridge-Munsee Indian Reservation. Two cases made their way to federal court in Milwaukee and became combined into one ruling: *U.S. v. Torrey Cedar Company* and *U.S. v. Paine Lumber Company*, both initiated in 1903 and decided in 1904. In effect, these cases were the relitigation of *Wybro*. Judge William H. Seaman, presiding over the district court, surprised the OIA by ruling against the United States and for the defendant lumber companies. Judge Seaman reasoned that the Treaty of 1856 with the Stockbridge-Munsees differed from that of the Oneidas' 1838 treaty because the former directly contemplated allotment of the reservation. Therefore, even if an individual Stockbridge-Munsee member did not have a trust or fee patented allotment, he or she still had the necessary property stake in a future allotment-to-be, and, by contrast, the United States had no trust interest. The United States appealed the *Torrey Cedar* and *Paine Lumber* decisions to the Seventh Circuit, which affirmed Judge Seaman, and on to the U.S. Supreme Court, which in 1906 also affirmed the district court. Stockbridge-Munsees who made an allotment selection, even if they had no allotment certificate from the OIA, could now legally sell the timber on their lands to lumbermen.[12]

A follow-up case, *U.S. v. Gardner* of 1909, extended the right to individual Stockbridge-Munsees to make timber sales, including the right to be thoroughly fleeced by white timber buyers. In the *Gardner* case, a lumberman signed a contract to buy an allotment parcel from a tribal member. Payment was to be in two parts, the first on cutting the timber from the parcel and the second after the allottee received fee simple title. The problem was that Gardner had no interest in owning the parcel after he stripped it of its timber. The United States sued to recover the value of the timber, but the judge in the case ruled that the passing of title in the form of a fee simple patent was merely a "ministerial" function of the Interior Department and therefore should not stay the right of Gardner to have cut the timber in the first place, notwithstanding his failure to live up to the rest of his bargain.[13]

One more factor complicated the division of reservation lands into allotments. The Wisconsin Northern Railway sought a right-of-way across the Stockbridge-Munsee Reservation in early 1905 for the purpose of building a railroad that connected Gresham at its southern end and the Soo Line Railroad thirty-seven miles to the north. In addition to bisecting the eastern part of the Stockbridge-Munsee Reservation, the contemplated rail line cut through the Menominee Indian Reservation at the site of the planned new sawmill at the Menominee village of Neopit. The railroad received its right-of-way permission from the secretary of the interior in 1906. The secretary made no reference to the 1856 treaty with the tribe, or the 1856 treaty with the Menominees as the legal basis for granting the right-of-way and instead relied on a more recent 1899 congressional act. Under the terms of that act, the secretary approved the map of the planned route of the right-of-way and also the proposed compensation due to individual Indians and to tribes.[14]

The terms of the payments to individual tribal members possessing allotments along the right-of-way covered both damages to property and what appears to have been a flat payment of $7.50 per mile. The Wisconsin Northern only made the one compensation payment; the secretary of the interior chose not to insist on an annual rental payment for the right-of-way, as he sometimes did with other rights-of-way. The individual tribal members received what the secretary considered fair compensation, presumably for having their contemplated allotments bisected by a railroad. However, the tribe received no compensation for a railroad right-of-way that actually traversed tribal lands when first granted.[15]

From the start of its operations, the Wisconsin Northern planned a small station and log-loading operation on the Stockbridge-Munsee Reservation. The station came to be known as Morgan Siding after tribal members David and Maria Morgan, whose allotment selections encompassed the station. Morgan Siding was roughly halfway between Neopit and Gresham. Unbeknownst to the secretary of the interior when he approved the right-of-way for the Wisconsin Northern, the hamlet of Morgan Siding was destined to be a center of notoriety on the reservation for decades to come.[16]

With allotment completed in 1910 and Judge Seaman's ruling in the *Gardner* case the year before, the Stockbridge-Munsees who had land parcels were free to dispose of their property. However, the passage of the Act of 1906 did not settle the affairs of the Stockbridge-Munsees, as Congress might have hoped. In fact, there was continuing business of the tribe with Congress dating back to the unresolved problems of the Acts of 1871 and 1893. The specific problem involved the Stockbridge Consolidated Fund, which had a balance of $75,988 in 1906. This fund was set up by the Act of 1871 as the trust account for the Indian Party's portion of the receipts from the sale of the fifty-four sections. In 1908 Daniel Davids, a Civil War veteran and a tribal member restored to the rolls by the Act of 1893, asked the OIA for back annuity payments from 1874 to 1894, the years he had wrongfully been excluded from the tribe. Davids and other Old Citizens Party members had shared in neither the portion of the $169,000 in land sales receipts paid to the New Citizens Party who separated from the tribe in 1874 nor the annuity payments for the first twenty years of the Stockbridge Consolidated Fund. Now Davids and his fellow claimants wanted the thirty-seven annuity payments they had missed, totaling $567 per capita.[17]

The Davids claim arrived at the OIA as a petition in 1908, and it was initially approved by the agency. However, the auditor of the Department of the Interior disallowed the claim. That decision was then referred to the Treasury Department, which overruled Interior's auditor, and Davids got his money in 1911. The Treasury Department wrote in 1911 of the Davids case:

> The disallowance of the claimant's interest in tribal funds from 1874 to 1894 would very materially defeat the purpose of the Act of 1893, and be a travesty upon the justice intended by that act. The present allowance of their claims would appear but a tardy and incomplete correction of the wrong long endured by the claimants.[18]

Davids's children and other claimants soon filed their own claims for their just share of the Stockbridge Consolidated Fund. This new set of claims happened at the same time that the fund was hypothecated to pay for the possible purchase of lands in the two townships or from the Menominee Reservation, and to pay for money–no land claims. Suddenly, the fund of only $75,988 was in jeopardy of being overwhelmed, what with 343 claims for tribal members asking up to $146,000 on the same grounds as Davids. So the Interior Department froze new claims after Davids and asked Congress for help. In 1913 Congress took up the matter for the first time, but the proposed amendment providing general revenue funds to pay the claimants failed to win inclusion in the Indian Appropriation Bill. The next year, 1914, Congressman Thomas Konop introduced H.R. 12297 authorizing the use of general Treasury funds to pay the claims. His bill failed, but with the backing of Wisconsin's Ninth District congressman, Edward Browne, the bill (now H.R. 10385) passed in the winter 1916 session.[19]

Claims for payment under the Act of 1916 continued to arrive at the OIA, even as late as 1938. Inevitably, the administration of the Act of 1916 produced conflicts and disappointments. At first the Interior Department limited payments to tribal members alive during the period 1874–94. Later, their direct descendants were included. The Interior Department solicitor wrote in 1917 that the fund was limited to tribal members and off-limits to heirs of deceased tribal members who were themselves not tribal members. This opinion was a strong affirmation of the continuity of the tribe and the U.S. responsibility to administer its funds for the benefit of the tribe.[20]

The ramifications of the Act of 1893 and its resulting restoration to the tribe of the Old Citizens Party continued to live on after the passage of the Act of 1916. Once Congress admitted an injustice had been perpetrated by the Act of 1871, it could not very well stop the grievances with the Davids claim and the Act of 1916. After the Act of 1916, the very formula for distribution between Citizens Party and Indian Party in Section 5 of the Act of 1871 came under fire as flawed and in need of remedy.

In 1921 the tribe hired Dennison Wheelock to pursue additional Act of 1871 claims. Wheelock was also hired to regain for the tribe from the state the parcels of swamplands in the two townships. His main effort, however, was to pursue a payment to the Old Citizens Party members based on what would have been their share of the money received for the sale of the fifty-four sections. Wheelock and the tribe, with the aid of Congressman Browne, got Congress to begin considering the tribe's claim. In the Sixty-seventh Congress, H.R. 8493 and S.B. 3111 were introduced but failed to pass. In the next Congress, the Senate version of the bill passed both houses, and it was signed into law on June 7, 1924. The act provided for the U.S. Court of Claims to hear the case of the tribe, rather than to have Congress determine the validity of the claims. Attorney Wheelock prepared and presented his case in 1925. In all, he asked for $102,000 to be paid to tribal members wrongfully denied enrollment in the Indian Party in 1874 by Commissioner Wells. The result of Wells's crooked work, Wheelock charged, was that the Stockbridge Consolidated Fund was too low and the payout to the New Citizens Party of 1874 too high. The Court of Claims heard and rejected the tribe's suit, mainly on the grounds that Congress had never specifically promised the back payment, either in 1893 or in 1906 or in 1916 (the Court of Claims viewed the three statutes as a troika). A resubmission by Wheelock of the case in 1927 was also rejected by the Court of Claims.[21]

After defeat in the Court of Claims, the tribe pursued a two-pronged strategy. The first part was to ask the Wisconsin attorney general to help them press the same claim against the United States. The second was to return to Congress and seek additional legislative relief. The Wisconsin attorney aeneral proved unsuccessful. As for the second part of the strategy, it finally met with success during the Seventy-third Congress (1933–34), the most famous Congress in U.S. history, the one that passed the "100 Days" New Deal legislation in its first session and the Indian Reorganization Act in its second session. Also in the second session, the Congress passed a bill to reauthorize the Court of Claims to hear all the Stockbridge-Munsee outstanding complaints, including a rehearing of the 1921–27 cases. However, President Franklin Roosevelt vetoed that bill on the grounds that the Interior Department, not the Court of Claims, should hear individual Indian claims for unpaid timber money and that the Court of Claims should not have to rehear the 1924–27 case. The next Congress, the Seventy-fourth, separated the Stockbridge-Munsee legislation into two bills, one for the Court of Claims hearing of tribal claims and the second for an Interior Department hearing of individual claims. President Roosevelt vetoed each bill, the first because he said the Court of Claims had definitively ruled and the second for the following reason:

> The only individual claims which have been brought forward are those of persons who claimed to be members of the Stockbridge and Munsee Tribe of Indians but whose claims were disallowed when the rolls of the tribe were prepared. It would require great expense to investigate the merits of any and all claims which might be asserted by an individual Indian, with little prospect of any benefits to be derived.[22]

It also seems that both Commissioner of Indian Affairs John Collier and Secretary of the Interior Harold Ickes opposed the two bills in 1935, in part because they were already busy planning their own assistance to the tribe, the Stockbridge Purchase Project, which they hoped would be a showpiece of their Indian New Deal.

After allotment was completed and the fee patents distributed to the individual Indian allottees, the state of Wisconsin moved to extend local government over the Stockbridge-Munsee Indian Reservation. In rural Wisconsin that meant the establishment of township governments that provided roads, schools, and civil law enforcement. By 1910 township government was extended over the other allotted Indian reservations in the state, in fact, for all the other reservations except the Menominee Reservation, which remained unallotted. The enabling act in the Wisconsin legislature that established the town of Red Springs (T28N R14E on the public lands survey) and the town of Bartelme (T28N R14E) passed the legislature after the 1910 census was taken. Township government, especially in Red Springs, became a locus of political activity among the Stockbridge-Munsees, not least in the ten elected offices that provided employment income to Mohican men, and, as important, political leadership opportunities. In 1915 the OIA closed the government day schools it had overseen. The Mohican children in Red Springs began attending state-supported local public schools, under the supervision of a Mohican-led school board.[23]

Town government and school board administration in Red Springs and Bartelme dealt with increasing populations but populations that were skewed by age and gender. Table 6.3 summarizes the age and gender distribution of the Stockbridge-Munsee Indian population on the reservation for the census years 1900 and 1910 and, for 1920 and 1930, the two townships of Red Springs and Bartelme that were contiguous with the reservation.

The summary numbers show a slight imbalance of the sex ratio, with more men than women during the thirty-year period. The median age for both genders dropped by six years for both men and women, indicating a growing population of children. The number of families rose and then fell by 1930. The sharp rise in the household size for that year suggests some reaction to the economic difficulties felt in rural Shawano County. The changes in the median age are the most suggestive of an important

TABLE 6.3

Demography of the Stockbridge-Munsee Indian Population, 1900–1930

	1900	1910	1920	1930
LOCATION	STOCKBRIDGE-MUNSEE INDIAN RESERVATION	STOCKBRIDGE-MUNSEE INDIAN RESERVATION	TOWNSHIPS OF RED SPRINGS AND BARTELME	TOWNSHIPS OF RED SPRINGS AND BARTELME
Males (percent of total)	189 (52%)	230 (54%)	286 (53%)	280 (52%)
Females (percent of total)	172 (48%)	195 (46%)	255 (47%)	257 (48%)
Totals	361 (100%)	425 (100%)	541 (100%)	537 (100%)
Median age of males	25.0	20.5	22.0	19.0
Median age of females	22.0	24.0	18.0	16.0
Number of households	85	116	117	94
Median household size	4.4	4.3	4.7	5.7

SOURCE: Population Census Schedules, Stockbridge-Munsee Indian Reservation, 1900 and 1910, and Towns of Bartelme and Red Springs, 1920 and 1930.

demographic change occurring on the reservation. When the summary age and gender figures are disaggregated into five-year birth cohorts, as shown in figures 6.1 and 6.2, a different pattern emerges. In the 1900 census, the population was balanced by gender through the age cohort of those born between 1841 and 1845 (55-to-59-year-olds). Only among the elders was there a consistent imbalance of more men than women, and the overall number of elders was small.

By 1930 two changes were evident in the population profile of the Stockbridge-Munsees living in the reservation townships of Red Springs and Bartelme. First, the people were collectively quite a bit younger than they had been in 1900. More than half (55.3%) of the tribe's population was under the age of twenty (figure 6.2). In 1900 the tribe had many young people, but they constituted 43.3 percent of the total reservation population. Moreover, the youthful part of the population in 1930 was concentrated in the two youngest age cohorts, 0 to 4 and 5 to 9 years old.

FIGURE 6.1

Age Distribution of the Stockbridge-Munsee Indians, 1900

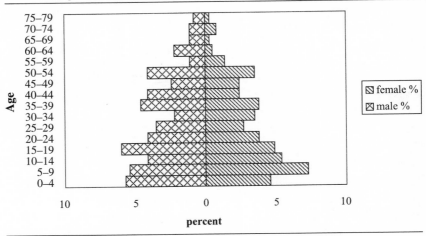

SOURCE: Population Census Schedules for Stockbridge-Munsee Indian Reservation, 1900

FIGURE 6.2

Age Distribution of the Stockbridge-Munsee Indians, 1930

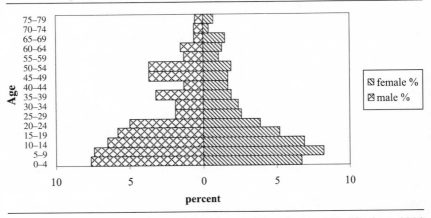

SOURCE: Population Census Schedules, Towns of Bartelme and Red Springs, 1930

The other significant change in the tribe's population structure consisted of the gender imbalance among the adults. The age cohorts of 20-to-24-year-olds, 35-to-39-year-olds, and 45-to-54-year-olds were heavily weighted to men. A pattern developed on the reservation after 1900 whereby more women than men left the tribe's homeland. For example, this pattern is evident in 1915, when the OIA made its money–no land payments. Of those who received money–no land payments, 101 persons lived off the Stockbridge-Munsee Reservation. The OIA kept records of the names and addresses of the recipients, and from that tally it is possible to reconstruct the out-migration of Mohican adult women. Of the total of 101 recipients, 52 were adults and 49 were children. Of the adults, 33 were women and 19 were men. Of the children, 39 lived with their mothers and 10 lived with their fathers. The Mohican women who lived off the reservation were concentrated in three places: Chicago primarily, with fewer in the small cities of the Fox Valley and in Calumet County, near the old (pre-1848) Stockbridge Reservation. Well before the post-1945 federal relocation policy, the Stockbridge-Munsee women were leaving the reservation in search of other homes.

Adult women were not the only Mohicans leaving the reservation between 1900 and 1930. Overall, there was a high level of out-migration among both genders for each ten-year period between census counts. Table 6.4 displays a count of on-reservation Stockbridge-Munsees tabulated in one census who were also tabulated as living on the reservation in the succeeding census. The calculations in this table undoubtedly understate persistence by not capturing women who married and changed their surnames while continuing to live on the reservation. The calculations also do not include deaths and therefore overstate the low levels of persistence. Nonetheless, the numbers reported in table 6.4 are comparable to those reported in studies of nineteenth- and early-twentieth-century American cities.[24]

One source of population growth in the newly organized township of Red Springs was the establishment of a new Christian mission and surrounding village. The Mohicans had their first experiences with missionaries in the mid-eighteenth century. The idea of a mission village, with church, missionary's residence, and surrounding hamlet, was quite well known to them. The Mohicans had lived among missions at Stockbridge, Massachusetts, Pine Plains, New York, Picqua, Ohio, New Stockbridge,

TABLE 6.4

Geographic Persistence of the Stockbridge-Munsees, 1900–1930

YEAR/ CATEGORY	MEN (% PERSISTING)	WOMEN (% PERSISTING)	TOTALS (% PERSISTING)
1900 reservation-dwellers still on the reservation in 1910	89 (52%)	49 (28%)	138 (40%)
1910 reservation-dwellers still on the reservastion in 1920	99 (43%)	74 (38%)	173 (41%)
1920 reservation-dwellers still on the reservation in 1930	111 (39%)	72 (28%)	183 (34%)

SOURCE: Population Census Schedules, Stockbridge-Munsee Indian Reservation, 1900 and 1910, and Towns of Bartelme and Red Springs, 1920 and 1930.

New York, Statesburg, Wisconsin, and Stockbridge-on-the-Lake, Wisconsin. But the Shawano County reservation was not a mission in this sense. At the end of the nineteenth century, German-speaking Missouri Synod Lutherans picked the Stockbridge-Munsees of Shawano County as a people in need of a new Christian mission. Starting in 1897, that is what happened. The Lutherans built a church and a school, sent a missionary and a school-teacher, and encouraged the growth of a hamlet around the mission. The mission school was particularly successful with the parents and children on the reservation. The Lutherans soon expanded the day school into a residential boarding facility. At its peak in the 1910s, the school attracted up to seventy-five Indian children, mainly Stockbridge-Munsees but with a few Menominees, Oneidas, and Ho-Chunks (Winnebagos) as well. The Lutheran mission to the Stockbridge-Munsees at the beginning of the twentieth century marked the third and the most successful effort to bring Christianity to the Mohicans.[25]

A striking feature of the decades after the Act of 1893 was the spread of many new Christian denominations among the Stockbridge-Munsees. The Lutherans figured most prominently because of the mission. In addition, a Roman Catholic church was established at Red Springs in 1893 and flourished until the mid-1920s. After Morgan Siding began its population growth with the arrival of the Wisconsin Northern Railway, the Lutherans soon followed. The pastor at the mission also began conducting worship services at the Government Day School in 1907 at Morgan Siding, a practice that continued until the 1930s. Also, the Presbyterians made a comeback among the Mohicans and sent visiting clergy to conduct services on the reservation. William F. Brown, one such Presbyterian minister, conducted services for "15 communicants" during an August 1895 visit. The Presbyterians established the John Sergeant Memorial Presbyterian Church in Red Springs in 1911. Alas, the "early congregation consisted mainly of elderly people, consequently it became a dying church," according to the historian Thelma Putnam.[26]

The Presbyterians held a centennial observation in November 1922 on the anniversary of the arrival of the Stockbridges into Wisconsin. The church had three Sunday services on Centennial Sunday at Red Springs, at nearby Gresham, and at Morgan Siding. Even more than the arrival of the Mohicans in Wisconsin, the church remembered a century of adherence by the faithful in the tribe to Presbyterianism.[27]

As a result of the issuance in spring 1910 by the secretary of the interior of fee patents to the 109 allottees on the Stockbridge-Munsee Reservation and the extension by the state legislature of civil government to the reservation, there was a miniature land rush of non-Indians onto the reservation. The 1920 census showed that the population of the reservation had nearly tripled, from 478 in the 1910 count to 1,208 in 1920. The population density increased from 6.6 to 16.7 persons per square mile. Moreover, the majority of the total population in the combined two towns were non-Indians: 644 whites, 544 Indians, and 18 blacks.

The 1920 census asked the enumerators to list the place of birth and the parents' place of birth for each person counted. The returns for 1920 for both Bartelme and Red Springs show that many of the new non-Indians living on the Stockbridge-Munsee Indian Reservation were German born

TABLE 6.5

Place of Birth of Non-Indian White Immigrants in Bartelme, 1920

	Wis.	Other U.S.	"Ger- many"	Pomer- ania	Prussia	Other East Elbe Provinces	Other Foreign Born	Total
Place of birth of enumerant	253	13	14	10	9	6	2	307
Place of birth of enumerant's father	166	18	78	14	12	10	9	307
Place of birth of enumerant's mother	163	16	71	24	13	11	9	307

SOURCE: Population Census Schedules, Towns of Bartelme and Red Springs, 1920.

or descended. For some persons, the Bartelme and Red Springs census enumerators gave a specific German province or, pre-1919, principality. For others, the listing was simply "Germany." For those with a specific listing in pre-1914 Germany, the largest number came from the East Elbian provinces of the German Empire, especially Prussia and Pomerania. Table 6.5 displays this pattern for the town of Bartelme.

The foreign born were asked to list the year they emigrated to the United States, and with a few exceptions, most arrived before 1893, nearly two decades before the reservation was opened to non-Indians. Thus the migration of the East Elbians was not direct but was preceded by an earlier, long-term stay in the United States, especially Wisconsin. But for the years after 1910, the rush to take up Indian lands in Shawano County was part of a larger migration of immigrants and second-generation Americans to farm the lands of northern Wisconsin.[28]

The Stockbridge-Munsee leader Carl Miller wrote to Commissioner of Indian Affairs John Collier in 1933 that the tribe had about 100 families living on the reservation, but due to the allotment policy, the tribal members were almost entirely landless. Miller mentioned five tribal members who owned land but noted that all held heavily mortgaged properties. In

TABLE 6.6

Land Tenure of Families in Red Springs and Bartelme, 1920–1930

YEAR AND RACE	FAMILIES RENTING	FAMILIES OWNING WITHOUT MORTGAGE	FAMILIES OWNING WITH MORTGAGE	FAMILIES OWNING (NO MORTGAGE INFORMATION)
1920 whites	42	38	63	—
1920 Indians	43	21	48	—
1920 blacks	2	2	1	—
1930 whites	39	—	—	100
1930 Indians	36	—	—	61
1930 blacks	2	—	—	0

SOURCE: Population Census Schedules, Towns of Bartelme and Red Springs, 1920 and 1930.

April 1910, by contrast, 109 tribal members received fee simple title to their lands. Miller had also complained to the OIA in 1923 that the German newcomers were a "grasping" kind of people who took advantage of Indians and, once in possession of land, would not let go. Yet the census returns do not fully bear out Miller's laments. Table 6.6 shows information about land tenure by race from the 1920 and 1930 censuses.

There is no statistically significant difference in the land tenure arrangements of Indians and whites for 1920. In the 1930 census whites were somewhat overrepresented among landowners, but the important number is that twenty years after allotment, some sixty-one Stockbridge-Munsee Indian families still owned land within the reservation. If Miller was correct that there were only five landowning families in 1933, then the effects of the deepest part of the Great Depression must indeed have been fearsome on those sixty-one families.

The population growth on the reservation was expressed in the expansion of hamlets beyond Red Springs and even the Lutheran mission. The fate of one of these, Morgan Siding, was tied to the railroad and to the numerous taverns that flourished in the hamlet. In 1897 Congress passed a general statute prohibiting alcohol manufacture and sale throughout Indian Country, that is, on federally recognized American Indian reservations. The OIA enforced this legislative mandate aggressively. Each year, local agents and superintendents were required to file reports specifying the actions taken to stamp out liquor sale and use on their reservations. This change in federal Indian policy in the early 1900s coincided with the emergence of Morgan Siding as a center of alcohol sales and consumption. The result was an ongoing struggle between the United States and individual Stockbridge-Munsees over alcohol.

The undisputed king of Morgan Siding was a Stockbridge-Munsee named Dan Tousey. Born in 1881 and one of ten children borne by Hannah Tousey, Dan grew up in Red Springs. He figured out sooner than any other proprietor that the allotment of the reservation in fee simple title made him a "Citizen Indian" outside the reach of the OIA and its agents. His career may be followed in the annual reports of the Keshena superintendent and in the court papers of state and federal jurisdictions. His first serious brush with the law at Morgan Siding occurred in 1913, when he was indicted for reckless homicide. Dan and a friend were target shooting at empty beer bottles set on a log outside the Tousey Tavern when a drunken patron, a German immigrant named Rheinhold "Whitey" Sidletz, woke up from his slumber on the far side of the log. Unfortunately for Sidletz, he stuck his head up right behind the next target. Dan's bull's-eye shattered both the bottle and Sidletz's head. Charged with reckless homicide, Tousey hired the outside counsel for the tribe in Shawano County to represent him, and after a series of motions filed by his lawyer, the judge dismissed the indictment and set Dan free. By 1915 Dan Tousey became a regular subject of complaint of the Keshena Indian agent to the U.S. Attorney in Milwaukee and the Commissioner of Indian Affairs in Washington, and for the next two decades the OIA struggled mightily to put him behind bars.[29]

The liquor laws regulating American Indians were strengthened in 1916 when the Supreme Court interpreted the Act of 1897 to cover Indians who had received their fee simple allotment patents and were otherwise not subject to OIA supervision. This made Dan Tousey and other Stockbridge-Munsee tavern keepers at Morgan Siding more vulnerable to prosecution. But what really made Tousey a figure of notoriety, at least among OIA personnel, was the advent of Prohibition. Tousey went from being a legitimate saloonkeeper to a bootlegger–speakeasy operator. So long as drinking was legal in Shawano County but not on the Menominee Reservation, the superintendent satisfied himself with trying to keep alcohol outside Menominee and putting up with illegal drinking by individual Indians at Morgan

Siding. But after the passage of the Eighteenth Amendment and the Volstead Act, the Keshena agent made it a personal crusade to shut down Dan Tousey.[30]

All through the 1920s, the Keshena superintendent's reports vilified Tousey as "the worse offender against law and decency." Keshena Superintendent Edgar A. Allen wrote in 1923 that the village of Morgan Siding "is noted as the most iniquitous little community in the whole country round" and that while the "Stockbridge mixed blood" Tousey was the worst, other white men also ran speakeasies, "some of whom are quite prominent in local politics." In 1924 the OIA sent a special police agent from Duluth to raid Dan Tousey's speakeasy. Tousey, described as a "mixed blood Stockbridge and Negro," pleaded guilty and paid his $100 fine. The disgusted superintendent considered Tousey's liquor selling "guilty under God's law of murder" and despaired that the fine "doubtless was made back in a couple days of good business." The next year, 1925, the Keshena superintendent complained: "On a good Saturday night enough can be made . . . to pay the amount of the fine imposed." Tousey's tavern was where "women and men congregate . . . and the most vicious and obscene practices are indulged in." Superintendent Allen posted a notice at the Neopit sawmill: "Any man found in this town [Morgan Siding] under any pretense whatever will be discharged from our service."[31]

By 1926 one senses a note of surrender in the superintendent's annual report. He made his observations about conditions on the Stockbridge and Oneida reservations and found "situation as to law and order . . . much worse on the Stockbridge reservation in the vicinity of Morgan's siding." Then in an exasperated pronouncement, Superintendent Allen continued, "The Oneidas are very much superior to the Stockbridges and especially the larger portion of the Stockbridges who contain a considerable portion of Negro blood." By 1930 the superintendent had pretty much given up; the winner of the contest was Dan Tousey:

> The State of Wisconsin has recently passed what is known as the Severson Act, the purpose of which was in reality to renounce the National Prohibition Law. Since the passage of this act we can expect very little cooperation from State and County officials in enforcing the Eighteenth Amendment. . . . It is impossible to improve law and order conditions on the [Menominee] reservation until this Stockbridge country can be thoroughly cleaned up of saloons and bootleggers.[32]

In the end, the G-men got their man, Dan Tousey, but not until after the repeal of Prohibition. In 1938 Tousey was convicted in federal district court in Milwaukee of liquor sales violations to underage Indians and received a two-year sentence in the federal penitentiary at Leavenworth, Kansas. After his release, Tousey lived a quiet life, stayed out of trouble, and died on the reservation in 1950.[33]

The great unfulfilled land claim hope of the 1920s was that the Stockbridge-Munsees would reclaim eighteen million acres of New York State as part of a greater League of Six Nations. The New York claim was the brainchild of a Wisconsin Oneida woman, Laura Cornelius Kellogg, perhaps the foremost American Indian woman leader of the early twentieth century. Kellogg had been active in the Society of American Indians from its 1913 inception but dropped out of that organization because of differences with people she regarded as "pumpkin-heads." She next turned her attention to taking over the Oneida Indian School and converting it into a rural industrial village, on the Aurora, New York, model. When that failed, she devised the idea of pressing a lawsuit against the state of New York for illegal occupation of Iroquois lands in violation of various federal laws that prohibited states from acquiring Indian land cessions. The suit cost money, Kellogg told her followers at Oneida, Wisconsin, throughout the scattered Iroquois settlements in New York, and soon enough at the Stockbridge-Munsee Reservation and among the Indian-descended inhabitants at the old Stockbridge-on-the-Lake and neighboring Brothertown-on-the-Lake. Kellogg created the League of Six Nations, to which Mohicans and Brothertowners were invited. Membership cost both an initiation fee and ongoing monthly dues. The prize was that members of the League could share in the billions of dollars anticipated when the great lawsuit was won. Unfortunately, the lawsuit was dismissed from federal court in New York, and Kellogg was unable to pursue the claim, despite talk of taking the case to Geneva before the League of Nations.[34]

No full accounting was ever made of how much money Kellogg and her husband raised from Wisconsin Oneidas, Stockbridge-Munsees, and Brothertowners, but it was likely in the tens of thousands of dollars, if not more. Some money went to attorney fees, but quite a bit more went into the wardrobe and living expenses of the Kelloggs. By all accounts, Kellogg was a dynamic speaker and leader, with a great vision of restoring the land base of the Iroquois confederacy. The OIA and its agents did all that they could to dissuade Wisconsin Indians from supporting her, but, one agent wrote, "advice of the Government not to contribute to these people [the Kelloggs] has been very largely disregarded." Even the OIA agent at Keshena recognized that the Oneidas and Stockbridge-Munsees had their own views of their history and that whatever the OIA said, the tribes believed that New York illegally took their lands. As the agent wrote, "Unfortunately, the Indian has more confidence in these people [the Kelloggs] than they have in the government." Clearly, Laura Cornelius Kellogg's message resonated among many Stockbridge-Munsees. Oral history indicates that she recruited members to her League of Six Nations at the taverns and juke joints of Morgan Siding on her trips to the Stockbridge-Munsee Reservation. Whatever may be made of her financial dealings, there can be little doubt that she inspired tribal and racial pride in many Wisconsin Indians at Oneida and Stockbridge-Munsee, and, moreover, she inspired a treaty consciousness among Wisconsin and New York Indian people in the 1920s. The old treaties did matter, Kellogg said, and they were still good law. Although unsuccessful in her 1927 case, her cause was taken up again after World War II and eventually won a favorable U.S. Supreme Court decision.[35]

In addition to the Kellogg initiative, or perhaps as an alternative, Stockbridge-Munsees in the 1920s organized a fraternal organization known as the Society of Mohicans, also known colloquially as the Mohican Club. The Society of Mohicans required members to pay a fifty-cent initiation fee and monthly dues of twenty-five cents. The benefits included discounts of 10 percent on purchases at the general store in Gresham and at another store in Shawano. The Mohican Club met monthly in Red Springs to discuss history and politics and social matters. About thirty Stockbridge-Munsees were members. The Mohican Club also began to sell life insurance, or more precisely, death benefits, to cover the funeral expenses of its members. The officers and directors of the Mohican Club were descendants of both nineteenth-century tribal parties. Carl Miller and Myron Miller, Cornelius Aaron, and Elmer Putman were born into families once prominent in the Indian Party. Elmer Davids, Harry Chicks, and MacMullen (Mac) Tousey came from Citizens Party families restored to tribal membership by the Act of 1893.

The tribe had a significant population surge in the decade between 1910 and 1920, which had a related outcome for land use: tribal members began

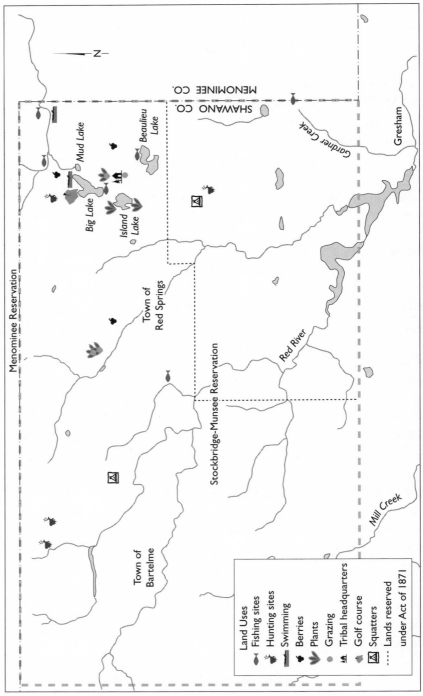

Map 6. The Elders Remember: A GPS Study of Stockbridge-Munsee historical land use, 1900–1930

moving out of the south half and into the north half in the town of Red Springs. The migration to North Half coincided with greater use of the water, fish and game, and vegetation resources of the two townships by tribal members. In June 1999 and June 2000 the Stockbridge-Munsee Legal Department organized interviews of elder women and men who recalled their youthful hunting, fishing, swimming, trapping, and gathering habits throughout the two townships. The six elders (Bernice Miller Pigeon, Priscilla Church, Virginia Johnson, Walter Jacobs, Clarence Chicks, and Virgil Murphy) all grew up and lived in the town of Red Springs until the late 1930s move to the Moh-he-con-nuck settlement on new lands in the town of Bartelme. (See map 6.)

Tribal members made use of the lands and waters throughout the north half of Red Springs and up the Red River into Bartelme. These activities took place from the 1910s through the 1930s. A poignant detail told by one of the elders was the loss in the late 1920s and early 1930s of access to several of the lakes in North Half. That was the time when outside white people began buying lakefront property for summer cabins. According to the elder, the whites quickly posted Private Property—No Trespassing signs around the circumference of the lakes and shut off Indian access to old and favored fishing spots.

At the same time today's elders were growing up as young girls and boys, their parents and grandparents were rapidly losing ownership of their forty- and eighty-acre allotment parcels. The tribe's people were living for the most part as tenants or as squatters on abandoned lands. Almost all the timber was gone from the entire seventy-two section reservation. A Woodland Indian people lived for the most part landless on a treeless reservation.[36]

CHAPTER 7

The Indian New Deal Polity of the Stockbridge-Munsees, 1934–1948

The Stockbridge-Munsees took advantage of the Indian New Deal to remake their polity and regain a measure of local self-government, tribal sovereignty, and tribal economic enterprise. The events of the 1930s and 1940s demonstrated that the tribe possessed a leadership cadre capable of working in the larger national political world to seek and secure the larger goals of the tribe.[1]

The preeminent political leader of the tribe was Carl Miller, former Red Springs official, sometime chair of the Tribal Business Committee, and officer of the Mohican Club. In the early 1930s Miller gave his version of the history of the Act of 1871:

> In 1871 through the efforts and manipulation of Timothy O. Howe and Phil. Sawyer who had great influence with the dep. at Washington a majority of the members of the Tribe were stricken from the rools and shoved thro out where by the largest and most valuable portion of our reservation was sold to this same Ph. Sawyer and his Lumbering Interest for the sum of $169,000. We claim treaty violation. 1st Because the Fed. Gov. allowed a portion of the tribe to sell what belonged to the whole tribe. 2nd They allowed a small portion of the tribe to sell what belonged to the rising generation.[2]

Although Miller was the grand-nephew of Indian Party leader Albert Miller, he had developed a broad bipartisan understanding of the past. He considered the Act of 1871 unjust because it terminated the Citizens Party members. And he believed that it was a swindle, even a treaty violation.

The year 1934 was one of the most significant in the history of the Stockbridge-Munsee Mohicans. In the first week of the year, six hundred men, including all the Stockbridge-Munsees, lost their emergency relief jobs in Shawano County. Some Stockbridge-Munsee men picked up part-time work with the Civil Works Administration (CWA) for $3.75 a day, but the tribe's families needed more in the way of assistance.

The Tribal Business Committee closely followed the change within the Office of Indian Affairs and the 1933 appointment of John Collier to the commissioner's post. Carl Miller wrote to Collier at the beginning of 1934: "We are still intact as a Tribe altho we are practically home less having lost our homes and land through mortgages and foreclosures and sales." Miller asked the commissioner directly for help in the form of "a few thousand acres of new land . . . so that [they] could plant and raise good gardens and feed a cow or two." But the "title to this land," Miller felt, "should remain in the Government so that it could not be mortgaged or sold again." Miller closed with a practical question that demonstrated his understanding of the American political system: "Shall we make a request by petition signed by the whole tribe? Shall we petition our Senators and Congressmen?"[3]

Miller had the core of an idea in his 1934 letter, namely, that the United States would acquire land parcels inside the reservation in trust for the tribe and help them to rebuild the tribal economy. That idea was also part of the national legislation that Collier and the OIA had in preparation for the Congress during its second session of 1934. By that date, if not earlier, most observers agreed that the allotment policy of the Dawes Act had failed American Indians. The OIA had in mind legislation that would halt further sales or loss of individual allotments and an effort to reacquire communal lands within reservations for tribes.[4]

On April 3, 1934, the town of Red Springs held its elections. Carl Miller won the contest for town chairman, and Mac Tousey won one of the supervisor slots. Myron Miller and Nelson Gardner, two of the few Stockbridge-Munsees who owned working automobiles in 1934, used their vehicles to drive around Red Springs and deliver Indians to the polls. With the election returns tallied, Carl's son Occum Miller noted that the Stockbridge-Munsees went to the town hall "at once so as to shut off the old board from activity." Control of town government offered at least a little in the way of employment on township road repairs.[5]

Carl Miller and the Tribal Business Committee did everything they could to keep the Stockbridge-Munsees before the OIA as the tribe most deserving of federal help in this new venture. Seven weeks after Miller's January 1934 letter to Collier, the Tribal Business Committee followed up with a "Joint and Several Resolution." Committeemen Carl Miller, Fred L. Robinson, Clark Cuish, Louis La Roy, and Adrian Yoccum told Collier that they had a problem and a solution for him to implement. Their document included the following statement:

> Whereas, such system of allotments has proved to be principally an instrument whereby the Stockbridge Indians were deprived of their former holdings of land, and has wrought great disaster, hardship and suffering upon the Stockbridge Tribe of Indians, as a whole and as individuals. . . . Resolved, that John Collier, commissioner of Indian Affairs . . . be apprised of the fact that 18 Sections of land in the aforementioned Town of Red Springs, and all Sections of land in the Town of Bartelme . . . consisting largely of cut-over land, is available for purchase.[6]

This was the first written specification of the idea that Miller and other Stockbridge-Munsees had been discussing in 1933 and 1934—a renovated homeland for the tribe within its historic 1856 reservation boundaries. Miller reasoned that the next step was to meet directly with Collier to press the plan. That opportunity arose in April when the OIA held one of its series of Indian Congresses across the country to gauge support for the proposed Indian Reorganization bill, also known as the Wheeler-Howard bill for its two sponsors. Collier himself was unable to attend the April congress at Hayward, Wisconsin, but his deputy commissioner, William Zimmerman, attended and met with Carl Miller and Cornelius Aaron to discuss the tribe's future. The key question that Miller and Aaron asked Zimmerman was if the pending Wheeler-Howard bill covered the Stockbridge-Munsees. Zimmerman received similar questions from the Saginaw Chippewas, another landless tribe. Zimmerman answered that the Wheeler-Howard bill recognized tribes that include descendants of formerly recognized tribes within a present Indian reservation or those with "1/4 Indian blood." Another big question that Miller and Aaron posed to Zimmerman concerned the status of tribal claims against the United States. Would the Indian Reorganization bill halt those claims? They were reassured to learn that the proposed bill did not affect ongoing claims, such as the Kellogg claim in New York State.

Miller returned to the Stockbridge-Munsee Reservation ready to support the Wheeler-Howard bill. Aaron, a Stockbridge-Munsee, returned to his pulpit at the Lutheran church on the nearby Oneida Indian Reservation. Aaron was a graduate of the Lutheran Mission on the Stockbridge-Munsee Reservation and then went on to pastoral studies at the Concordia Theological Seminary in St. Louis. That Aaron and Miller could cooperate on tribal business in 1934 was itself noteworthy. Fifty years earlier, Miller's great-uncle Albert had worked to remove Aaron's namesake and grandfather, Cornelius, as sachem. Now, in 1934, the two had patched up an intratribal dispute to work together on behalf of the tribe.[7]

While visiting Wisconsin, Zimmerman talked with OIA officials in the Keshena Superintendency about Carl Miller's idea. In May Commissioner Collier pursued the idea further. He directed the Keshena superintendent to draw up a plan for rebuilding the land base of the Stockbridge-Munsee Indian Reservation. In June Congress passed the Wheeler-Howard bill many of whose provisions were directly applicable to the Stockbridge-Munsees, especially Section 16, which empowered the commissioner to acquire lands deemed "sub-marginal" for the benefit of tribes. The promise of help from the OIA and Congress in the form of the Indian Reorganization Act gave hope to the Stockbridge-Munsees that May and June, and just at the right time. After surviving a difficult winter, the tribe and its neighbors in Shawano County suffered daily temperatures of 105 degrees in May and a dust storm that made visibility difficult.[8]

In retrospect, it is clear that the complexity of the Indian Reorganization Act resulted in subsequent confusion for the OIA and the Stockbridge-Munsees, as two separate issues came together in the wake of congressional passage of the Wheeler-Howard bill in June 1934. The first was a new governing structure for Indian tribes, including the Stockbridge-Munsees, and the second was federal relief in the form of land acquisition for landless tribes or tribes that had suffered greatly from the implementation of the allotment policy. The two issues were separate in 1934: the tribe sought to gain OIA approval of a constitution submitted in September of that year, and the OIA began to implement Carl Miller's vision of a restored land base in the form of an initiative called the Stockbridge Purchase Project. The two issues of governance and lands were still separate in 1935. They became linked only after the Interior Department solicitor rejected the second draft of a tribal constitution by insisting that the tribe have a current land base. This interpretation of the IRA is different from that Assistant Commissioner Zimmerman gave Miller and Aaron at the Hayward Indian Congress in 1934: Zimmerman had said that the IRA was an offer to those tribes within present reservations or those having a one-fourth blood quantum. The blood quantum issue disappeared from consideration, as the tribe decided to base membership on descent from the allotment roll of 1910. From February 1936 onward, there was a connection between acquiring land under the IRA and getting Interior Department approval of the new tribal government. This change stemmed not from any new analysis of Stockbridge-Munsee history by the OIA but from a different reading of the Indian Reorganization Act.[9]

Members of the Stockbridge-Munsee business committee met on June 11, 1934, with representatives of the Brooks-Ross Lumber Company, the principal corporate landowner in the two townships, and with the OIA's Keshena school superintendent, W. A. Beyer. The group reviewed the elements needed to make the Miller plan a reality. Carl Miller estimated that the tribe's on-reservation population was about five hundred and that they would require at least 8,000 acres to support a subsistence economy of small farming, gardening, and forestry. The lumbermen estimated that there were more than enough parcels for sale in the town of Bartelme alone to satisfy the tribe's needs, probably at prices of $5 to $10 an acre. Superintendent Beyer expressed the hope that the OIA could make the purchases and establish "a satisfactory permanent community Home for the Stockbridges."[10]

During summer and fall 1934, whites and Indians alike in Shawano County gave their support to the Stockbridge Purchase Project. The county's director of outdoor relief, Mary Koonz, wrote that the "Stockbridge Indians could become a self-sustaining group and thus relieve the county, state and nation of the huge financial burden which they are placing on them at the present time."[11] Other whites besides Mrs. Koonz welcomed the prospect that the United States would take responsibility for the economic support of the Stockbridge-Munsees.

It is noteworthy that the Stockbridge Purchase Project evolved from Miller's straightforward request for a land-in-trust purchase into a bigger New Deal social reform project. The planners began by defining the two towns of Red Springs and Bartelme as "the problem area." And the problem people were not just the Stockbridge-Munsees on relief. Nearly half of the white families depended on county relief for survival. And the settlers, many of them of German and Scandinavian descent, failed "to develop productive farms." The planners also decried the costs of providing roads and schools. A photograph taken in 1934 of a settler's cut-over farmstead had the caption "Thrift and industry mis-spent" and the annotation, "This settler's children require transportation over ten miles of forest trail to nearest school." Moreover, the planners expressed disapproval of the "unsanitary living conditions" of the poor whites. It was no wonder that local officials welcomed a federal takeover of "the problem area."[12]

The Indian Reorganization Act gave the Commissioner of Indian Affairs the power to purchase lands for tribes, but Congress chose not to appropriate funds for that task. Commissioner Collier showed his bureaucratic skills in late 1934 by asking Harry Hopkins, administrator of the Federal Emergency Relief Administration (FERA), to buy some initial parcels in the "problem area" to start the Stockbridge Purchase Project. Hopkins authorized spending $12,000 in FERA funds to buy submarginal lands, which allowed the OIA to purchase up to 1,250 acres in the town of Bartelme. This was a start in implementing Carl Miller's vision of the Mohicans restored to their lands.[13]

Throughout the remainder of 1934, the Mohicans and the Tribal Business Committee worked on the two tasks of establishing self-government under the IRA and planning for life as part of the Stockbridge Purchase Project. In late August it appointed an ad hoc committee composed of Reverend Aaron as chair, Carl Miller, Earl "Dud" Davids, Myron Miller, and Harry Chicks to draft a new tribal constitution. These men represented a wide spectrum of the families of the tribe. The Millers and Aarons had led the Indian Party in the years after the Act of 1871, and the Chicks and Davids families were prominent leaders of the Citizens Party. Now they were working together to build a common future. The drafting committee produced a remarkable document that blended part of the old Quinney 1837 and Citizens 1857 constitutions with the ideas of the Indian New Deal. The draft document started with thanks to the "Great Spirit [who] has made his might[y] arm bare in the preservation and establishment of a part of the Moh-he-con-neew on the western part of the Wolf River."

Article 1 provided for universal suffrage among Mohicans over the age of twenty-one but restricted membership on the tribal council to men. Article 2 provided for a tribal council headed by a chief, a subchief, and three councilors. "Sub-ordinate" officers included a secretary, a treasurer, two pathmasters, a conservation warden, a forester, and a sheriff. The council had the power to acquire and protect tribal property and to levy a poll tax on tribal members. The council also was charged with the responsibility "to cultivate arts, crafts, and culture" of the Mohican people. In the draft bylaws, membership was further defined as any currently enrolled "member of the Mohican Tribe and their descendants of one fourth or more Indian blood." The politics of race had not disappeared from Mohican life, however, as membership was in fact abolished for "any member of said Stockbridge or Munsee Tribe who hereafter contracts marriage with a member of the Oriental or Negro race." The penalty for such a marriage was that the tribal member would "be banished from the Tribe and thereby forfeit all rights in said Tribe."[14]

On September 18, 1934, the Tribal Business Committee approved the new Mohican constitution. The committee sent the document to Secretary of the Interior Harold Ickes for review and called on him to schedule a ratification vote on the reservation. The draft Mohican constitution died in the files of the Interior Department, however, because Ickes and the Commissioner of Indian Affairs deemed that the Mohicans had jumped the gun. The plan that Commissioner Collier wanted to follow was to have each tribe across the United States have an initial election on the question of support or rejection of the Indian Reorganization Act. Those tribes that indicated their support could then proceed to the stage of drafting a constitution for the secretary's review. The Mohicans of Red Springs and Bartelme had skipped that stage and gone directly to writing their own constitution.[15] After being chastised by the OIA, the tribe gave its near-unanimous support for the IRA in a December vote (166–1), but the September draft constitution was not then promulgated. Nonetheless, Commissioner Collier wrote to the "Indians of the Stockbridge Reservation" after learning of the overwhelming vote for the IRA, "The eyes of the Nation have been upon you to see what the Indians would do with an opportunity such as have been afforded them."[16]

While waiting on the Interior Department for approval of the new constitution, the Tribal Business Committee also attended carefully to the details
of the Stockbridge Purchase Project. In October 1934 the committee held
a general council of the tribe to discuss the project. The general council voted
unanimously in favor of the project.[17]

During summer 1935, Commissioner Collier kept a close watch on the
Stockbridge Purchase Project. He understood the Indian Reorganization
Act to include both political reform and economic reform. He wrote to
one Wisconsin OIA official and offered the opinion that "[t]he Stockbridge
Tribe would probably be the band which could be organized and rehabili-
tated most effectively and most speedily." Collier also expressed the hope
that once again the "Hopkins organization" might provide new funds to
purchase housing for the Stockbridge-Munsees.[18]

That fall, the Keshena Agency worked on the final details of the Stockbridge Purchase Project. The superintendent identified more than 21,000
acres of submarginal land for federal acquisition out of the total of 46,000
acres in the two townships. Acquisition of land for the greater Stockbridge
Purchase Project depended on the assistance of a federal agency with much
greater resources than the Office of Indian Affairs. The statutory authority
for the FERA expired at the end of 1935, so Commissioner Collier needed
to find another ally in the New Deal executive branch. That ally turned out
to be Rexford Tugwell, head of the newly formed Resettlement Administration (RA), established by executive order in April 1935 as part of the
Department of Agriculture. The mission of the RA, in Tugwell's words,
was to address the problem of the more than one million impoverished
farm families "dependent at one time or another on local, State, or Federal
Governments." The causes of this dependency, according to Tugwell, were
threefold: the farming of submarginal land; reckless exploitation of forests;
and "over-farming." The first two causes certainly applied to the townships
of Red Springs and Bartelme. The RA offered the remedy of large-scale
acquisition of submarginal lands and support for reforestation projects.
When necessary, the RA could spend money to relocate the families from
failed rural settlements. Here was a New Deal federal agency with a
mission that fit perfectly the evolving Stockbridge Purchase Project. And
between 1935 and 1938 the RA (and in its subsequent reorganized form,
the Farm Security Administration, or FSA) acquired almost 14,000 acres
in Bartelme and Red Springs for the use of the Stockbridge-Munsees. The

FSA acquired all the lands from corporate owners. It did not remove and relocate the poor whites from the two townships as occurred at other Wisconsin projects.[19] In 1938 President Roosevelt issued an executive order transferring administrative jurisdiction over federally acquired submarginal lands on Indian reservations from the FSA to the Interior Department. Roosevelt's executive order limited the title transfer, however:

> The title to these lands is taken in the name of the United States, and they will not become the property of the Indian tribe, for whose use they were purchased, until Congressional action is obtained specifically transferring such title.[20]

After the general council of the Mohicans voted its support of the IRA, the tribe could return to the matter of a new constitution and some measure of self-government. But bureaucratic problems in the OIA delayed the move. One such problem in 1935 involved the transfer of the Stockbridge-Munsees from the Keshena to the Tomah Superintendency. A new superintendent had to learn the complexities of Mohican issues. But the bigger obstacle was the OIA plan to draft tribal constitutions from its Washington headquarters. The result was a delay for most of the year until a second draft constitution was prepared for the Mohicans by a special constitutional unit at the OIA's Washington headquarters.[21]

The second draft constitution of 1935 was rejected in December by no less an authority on federal Indian law than Felix Cohen, at that time an assistant solicitor in the OIA. After reading the second Mohican constitution, Cohen commented:

> This document has all the earmarks of something offered to the Indian committee and swallowed without thinking. Its phrases conform almost entirely with several other constitutions that have been submitted, and the document bears no resemblance to a draft constitution which these Indians submitted to the Indian Office for approval about a year ago and which this Office agreed to consider in working out further organization plans. I think it is putting a good deal of strain on the idea of self-government to expect something of this sort, without any roots, to flourish.[22]

Cohen also wondered why the second draft constitution used the OIA census of 1916 as the basis for determining tribal membership:

I do not understand why this census roll is selected. There may be some good reason for it, but the only excuse for making a census roll that I have been able to discover is that it is up to date. If we are going back into history, why not use an official membership roll? Attention is called in this respect to the act of March 3, 1893.[23]

Cohen refused to give his approval to the second draft constitution because its first article referred to the jurisdiction of the tribe as defined in the 1856 treaty. He read his copy of the treaty and realized it did not specify the boundaries of the reservation as Township 28 North, Ranges 13 and 14 East. Cohen's December 1935 objections led to Assistant Commissioner Zimmerman's January 1936 suggestion that the draft constitution refer to "the present confines," and when the Department of the Interior's solicitor discovered that the tribe was landless, the second draft constitution was stymied.[24]

In 1936 the tribe's desire to organize self-government under the IRA became dependent on the Stockbridge Purchase Project. Once the OIA finished the purchase and title work on the first 1,250 acres of submarginal land in the town of Bartelme, the tribe could be said to have a land base, a task not completed until early 1937. In April 1937 Assistant Commissioner F. H. Daiker wrote to Harry Chicks of the Tribal Business Committee informing him, "The tribe can now complete work on its tentative constitution and by-laws, and before very long, we hope, submit it to tribal vote."[25]

In 1937 the Stockbridge-Munsees read a third draft constitution, prepared for them in Washington. There were at least two versions of this constitution. A summer 1937 draft referred to "all lands purchased, now or hereafter," as the basis of the reservation. In a November 1937 draft that language was altered to lands "heretofore" purchased. The secretary of the interior then organized a ratification vote on the constitution, which passed easily by a vote of 112 in favor to 13 opposed.[26]

The Stockbridge-Munsee constitution reads very much like other tribal constitutions approved after passage of the IRA.[27] Article 1 began with a new name for the tribe, "Stockbridge Munsee Community." Article 2 determined membership on the basis of "all persons whose names appear on the Stockbridge allotment roll of 1910 and who are residing within the original confines of the Stockbridge Reservation." The drafters ignored

Felix Cohen's suggestion to base membership on the Painter roll of 1894. Instead, the drafters in Washington chose the 1910 allotment roll.[28] Gone too were the elements that continued Mohican political forms highlighted in the first 1934 draft.

During spring 1937, the first twenty families, led by Carl Miller, moved from Red Springs at one end of the reservation to Moh-he-con-nuck at the other end. The first settlers made use of the abandoned headquarters building of the Brooks & Ross Lumber Company building for their new community center. The housing for the twenty families consisted of scattered buildings and shacks also left by the lumber company.[29] (See map 7.) For the school year 1937–38, Stockbridge-Munsee children were scattered among five elementary schools, three public schools in Red Springs, one public school in Bartelme, and the Lutheran Indian Mission School in Red Springs.

The majority of tribal members continued to live in Red Springs, awaiting housing and employment opportunities at Moh-he-con-nuck. Again, the Stockbridge-Munsees took advantage of the Indian Reorganization Act; under Section 17, the community organized itself as a federally chartered corporation. One hundred forty-nine community members signed a petition to the secretary of the interior in February 1938 asking for a federal corporate charter. The effect of the incorporation of the Stockbridge-Munsee Community was that the tribal government could operate businesses, and, most important, borrow money from the United States. The importance of having access to credit was crucial for the Stockbridge-Munsees and represented a third leg for the emerging tribal economy. Land purchases by the FERA and RA-FSA was the first leg. Employment by federal work relief agencies was the second. But lands and jobs did not help tribal members living in shacks and chicken coops on the reservation. They needed a source of funds to construct new housing. However, after the wave of mortgage foreclosures and lien attachments in the early 1930s, few if any tribal members could borrow from private lenders. The corporate charter of the Stockbridge-Munsee Community solved the problem by giving the tribal council the authority to borrow funds from the United States and then use those funds to make subsidiary loans to tribal members for housing. The Stockbridge-Munsee Community quickly borrowed $27,000 from the Interior Department and set about helping tribal members to build thirty new houses.[30]

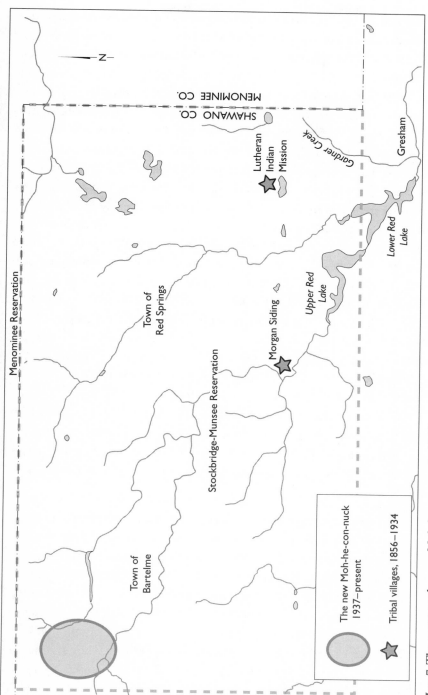

N

MENOMINEE CO.

SHAWANO CO.

Lutheran
Indian
Mission

Gardner Creek

Gresham

Lower Red
Lake

Upper Red
Lake

Menominee Reservation

Town of
Red Springs

Morgan Siding

Stockbridge-Munsee Reservation

Town of
Bartelme

The new Moh-he-con-nuck
1937–present

Tribal villages, 1856–1934

Map 7. The move to the new Moh-he-con-nuck, 1937

The dispersed pattern of settlement across the reservation soon presented a political problem for the tribe and the Department of the Interior. The problem was the tension between the ambiguous jurisdictional boundaries and the clear 1856 reservation boundaries for voting and elections. In 1938 Carl Miller came under attack by several dissident members. Miller's response to this criticism was to attempt to narrow tribal office-holding to those who lived on the newly acquired IRA lands in the town of Bartelme. In anticipation of the November 1938 council elections, Miller sought support from Washington. He bypassed the Tomah agent, as well as Commissioner Collier and his staff in the OIA, and went directly to the secretary of the interior for a ruling. Miller quickly got the answer he wanted from the assistant secretary of the interior, which confirmed that only those who lived on the new lands were eligible to stand for office in tribal elections. There was an immediate backlash from tribal members living in the town of Red Springs and from concerned officials in the OIA. Together, those opposed to the assistant secretary's decision appealed for a reversal. When the assistant secretary learned the geography of the Stockbridge-Munsees, he quickly reversed his decision and reaffirmed the tribal constitution article that extended the opportunity to run for elected tribal office to all tribal members living within the 1856 reservation boundaries, that is, in the towns of Bartelme and Red Springs.[31]

The Interior Department correction of January 17, 1939, closed with an incisive summary of the tension within the tribe's constitution about the spatial meaning of the Stockbridge-Munsee Community. Assistant Secretary Oscar Chapman's conclusion in his letter to Carl Miller bears close study:

> This is especially true since it happens that the constitution appears to foster two ideas in its use of the word "community." First of all, there is the actual physical area over which the organized group shall have jurisdiction, and in this case the word "community" is clearly linked to "all lands purchased, heretofore, or hereafter, by the United States for the benefit of said Community." At the same time, a larger meaning is intended in defining membership in the Community; in the latter case the term comprehends "all persons whose names appear on the Stockbridge Allotment Roll of 1910 and who are residing within the original confines of the Stockbridge Reservation,

TABLE 7.1

U.S. Land Purchases and Transfers on the
Stockbridge-Munsee Reservation, 1934–1972

Year Purchased	Acreage	Purchasing Agency	Year Put into Trust
1935	1,050	FERA	1937
1936	1,200	FERA	1948
1937	13,077	FSA	1972

SOURCE: Stockbridge Purchase Project, Stockbridge-Munsee Historical Library
and Museum.

in Shawano County, State of Wisconsin, on the date of the adoption
of this Constitution and By-Laws." As I see it, the Department has
no interest in either restricting or broadening the term, except as the
Indians themselves may indicate their wishes in the matter.

It now appears that the meaning intended by the Stockbridge
Munsee Indians is that the word "community," when used to define
eligibility for holding office within the Community, shall refer to all
residents within the area of the original Stockbridge Reservation. I
see no reason why this meaning should not be accepted by the
Department, and you should inform the Stockbridge Munsee elec-
torate to that effect.[32]

The key point is that the Interior Department recognized the tribe's understanding that its community—its homelands—extended to the full two
townships.

Table 7.1 shows the pattern of federal land purchases for the Stockbridge-
Munsees in the 1930s. The very first purchases by the FERA for Commissioner Collier were situated in the north half of Bartelme, several miles
from the village of Bowler. This site became the new village for the Mohicans, a new and promptly named Moh-he-con-nuck. The Mohicans who
moved to Bartelme in the mid-1930s proved themselves pioneers, in a very
self-conscious way. They constructed a road to link their village to Bowler
and later to Red Springs and Gresham. They built stone cottages as the
first permanent houses of the village. They cleared cut-over brush, dug
gardens, and established a Lutheran church. The church in Red Springs

was the Mission Church. The new church in Bartelme took on the name Church of the Wilderness to indicate the faith of the Mohican pioneers.[33]

The Great Depression proved a fertile time for the propagation of the gospel among the Stockbridge-Munsees, both at the new settlement of Moh-he-con-nuck and at the older settlements, Red Springs, the Lutheran Mission, and Morgan Siding. The Lutherans of Morgan Siding, who had been meeting for decades in a schoolhouse, built their new Our Saviour's Lutheran Church in 1932. The Lutheran Mission had to close the boarding part of the school in 1933 because of a funding shortage, but the day school continued, as did the Immanuel Lutheran Church, the heart of the mission. The two most striking manifestations of resurgent Christianity among the Stockbridge-Munsees in the 1930s were the Presbyterian and the Assembly of God denominations. The Presbyterians of the John Sergeant Memorial Church in Red Springs had dwindled to just a handful of members in the 1930s, when a crisis over personnel assignments in the presbytery prompted a walkout from the Presbyterian Church, U.S.A. Led by members of the Shepherd and Tousey families, the protesters established the Old Stockbridge Orthodox Presbyterian Church in Morgan Siding. At first the group was without a building, so they met in the saloon of Dan's brother, Mac Tousey, until after World War II. The Tousey tavern had a second life in the 1930s; it also hosted services of the new Assembly of God church in Morgan Siding. The Pentecostal worshipers of the Assembly of God stayed in the Tousey tavern until 1940, when they built a church.[34]

The planners for the Stockbridge Purchase Project in 1934 and 1935 had established a set of goals for the new Mohican homeland. The word "development" appeared frequently in the plans. The Stockbridge-Munsees, under OIA supervision, intended to develop fire protection facilities, new forest trails and roads, fish and game "resources," and even new water power sites.[35] The Stockbridge-Munsees would have to develop housing for the hundred or so families expected to live at the new Moh-he-con-nuck. The project planners estimated that one hundred three- or four-room houses could be built for $156,000 and that the construction could employ up to three hundred individuals. Another two hundred outbuildings and outdoor structures needed to be built. The project planners also budgeted for livestock and basic agricultural tools. However, they did not budget for tractors. Neither did they budget or plan for electricity for the new Moh-he-con-nuck.

Purchasing the cut-over land from the lumber companies was just one task the project planners faced. They also had to devise some way to hire Stockbridge-Munsees to perform the labor on the project. Kenneth Abert, a Menominee and OIA employee, became the project director. Abert faced an immediate crisis, in that Shawano County and Wisconsin state officials in the WPA suspended work plans for fire prevention and road building in the two townships. Tribal members who had held WPA jobs found themselves unemployed yet again. Commissioner Collier, Tomah Superintendent Frank Christy, and Director Abert sought funds from two federal work relief programs, the Emergency Conservation Work (ECW) and the Civilian Conservation Corps (CCC). It is a measure of the racial segregation in New Deal programs that the OIA administered the ECW and the CCC separately from their larger national organizations. This actually worked to the advantage of the Stockbridge-Munsees since the CCC–Indian Division (CCC-ID) did not have an upper age limit for workers. Thus Mohican men over twenty-five gained employment on CCC-ID conservation projects on the reservation until after the United States entered World War II.[36]

The reestablishment of a tribal land base within the reservation, along with its development by the CCC-ID during the 1930s, led the Stockbridge-Munsees into a new set of conflicts with their white neighbors and with the state of Wisconsin. Even before the United States completed purchase of the initial 1,050 acres by FERA, the tribe had alerted the OIA about unauthorized trespassers on federal lands. In October 1935 the Tribal Business Committee asked Commissioner Collier to "take the necessary steps to frustrate such offense." And if the United States was unwilling to do so, the Mohicans volunteered to "take this matter in hand."[37]

By fall 1937 the Stockbridge-Munsees did take matters in hand. The newly elected tribal council invited the Shawano area state game warden, O. K. Johnson, to discuss the situation. By the end of their meeting, the council hired Johnson as a "Deputy Special Officer" of the Stockbridge-Munsee Community. His charge from the council was to "enforce game laws on the Stockbridge Reservation with the understanding non-Indians would be excluded." Johnson, of course, knew the lands of the reservation well from his regular state work and knew where "non-members of the tribe had previously killed game in that area . . . regardless of closed deer seasons."[38]

Deputy Special Officer Johnson and the Stockbridge-Munsees did not have to wait long for a challenge to their authority. The white hunters of Shawano County were informed on November 24 that they could not hunt deer on federal lands. They grumbled but took the notice peacefully that day. Two days later, another group of white hunters received the same verbal notice, but they responded with threats of violence against Johnson and his Mohican deputies.

The issue of white access to on-reservation hunting did not go away after the 1937 season. Indeed, it became a near-perennial dispute for the remainder of the twentieth century. The tribe demonstrated its newly won sovereign control of its resources by posting federal lands as off-limits to non-Indians and by confronting white hunters who trespassed on the reservation. To the white hunters, especially those of the reservation border town of Gresham, the actions of the tribe smacked of special rights for one race over another. In 1939 a group known as the Gresham Sportsman Club complained to the State Conservation Commission that Stockbridge-Munsee Indians stopped club members from hunting. Further: "The Indians demanded to see our licenses, which the club feels they have no right to do." The Gresham Sportsman Club also offered the legal opinion that as "the land was sold to the Federal Government, the state still governs the land and therefore the Indians have no right to stop whites from hunting there."[39]

The state conservation director, H. W. MacKenzie, at first insisted the federal government was a mere "proprietor" and therefore subject to "state criminal laws and hunting and fishing laws . . . as such laws are enforced on lands owned by individuals." But on further reflection, MacKenzie decided to write to Commissioner Collier for clarification. Collier's answer contradicted the legal analysis of both the Gresham Sportsman Club and the Wisconsin Conservation Commission. Collier stressed that the status of the federal lands, those purchased with FERA funds as well as those purchased with FSA funds, was "entirely different" from "open and unclaimed public lands owned by the Federal Government." In short, non-Indians had no guaranteed hunting rights on lands reserved for the use of an Indian tribe.[40]

The Gresham Sportsman Club did not give up its fight to regain access to hunting and fishing sites on the Stockbridge-Munsee Indian Reservation. In 1943 the club's president, Mike Fischer, wrote to the State Conservation Commission again, this time acknowledging that "the Government has a right to post these lands," but he reasoned, "that would leave it open to no one not even the Indians." Fischer registered his strong disapproval of Indians posting the federal lands: "We want to know what right they have?" Toward the end of his complaint, Fischer made clear his underlying objection: "Most of the so-called Indians which they call them selfs are of the part negro class. There claims are in South Africa [*sic*]."[41]

By 1943 the United States, the state, the tribe, and the Gresham Sportsman Club had resolved three issues. Whites could not hunt on federally owned lands on the reservation. The state claimed that its fish and game laws applied to tribal members on the 13,000 acres of FSA lands. And the tribe claimed that the state could not regulate fishing and hunting on the 2,250 acres purchased by the FERA under the IRA and put in trust by the United States for the Stockbridge-Munsee Community. But this meant that the larger collection of FSA lands would be a focus of future politics. The tribe's intention to get those FSA lands put into trust, the same status as the IRA lands, led to a long-term battle with the Gresham Sportsman Club. It was not until 1972 that the tribe finally prevailed.

During World War II, the Stockbridge-Munsees served in the armed forces and in the civilian wartime industry. One hundred forty-three Stockbridge-Munsee men and women were in uniform, and many others relocated in 1942–43 to Sturgeon Bay, Manitowoc, and Milwaukee to work in the naval shipyards and other war-related plants. A sizable number of Mohican men and women chose not to return to the reservation after the war. For the first time in their lives, these tribal members were enjoying prosperity and did not wish to return to a life of poverty. They did not cut ties to their older friends and relatives at home, and in Milwaukee especially they kept their Stockbridge identity within a larger community of other Wisconsin Indians.[42]

CHAPTER 8

The Fulfillment of Mohican History

Securing the Stockbridge-Munsee Homeland, 1948–1974

The Stockbridge-Munsees entered the post–World War II period facing difficult challenges. In fact, in one form or another, almost all the political issues from the previous century confronted the tribe. The Mohicans had endured and persisted through Indian removal. They had survived termination legislation by Congress in 1843 and again in 1891. They had sought and lost and gained homelands in various states and territories. And they had pursued intertribal agreements and understandings in both politics and religion. All those historical experiences served the tribe well when it confronted the era that the historian Donald Fixico calls "termination and relocation."[1]

A striking feature of Mohican history in the Termination Era was the ways in which the tribe's leaders reached out to support and lead other Indian tribes, in Wisconsin and across the United States. For example, in 1944 Tribal Chairman Arvid E. Miller attended the founding meeting in Denver of the National Congress of American Indians (NCAI). In 1961 the tribe sent several delegates to the American Indian Conference at the University of Chicago that produced an upsurge of pan-tribal feeling. Finally, in 1966, the Stockbridge-Munsee tribal council took the lead in organizing other Wisconsin tribes in the Great Lakes Inter-Tribal Council, and Miller served as the first chairman of the first formal gathering of the Wisconsin tribes since the 1820s.

The political groundwork to build intertribal organizations was combined with new thinking about the role of American Indians in the American polity and creative thinking about the role of the Stockbridge-Munsees. This intellectual ferment caught the eye of a visiting anthropologist, Marion Johnson Mochon, who called what she observed the Stockbridge ideology, a set of political beliefs that revolved around the historical memory of the special place of the Mohican people. The Stockbridge ideology can be glimpsed in various publications and speeches given by tribal leaders at the intertribal gatherings. For example, in conjunction with the 1961 Chicago conference and another intertribal conference in Milwaukee, Elmer Davids of the Stockbridge-Munsees wrote a document for the tribe titled "Our People—Past, Present and Future." Davids began:

> Even though our people have been in close contact with European civilization for more than 300 years, we still remain as an identifiable group. It appears that this is true because of the fact that our philosophy of life differs in many respects from that of the Europeans. The concept of money or the profit motive was entirely foreign to our ancestors.[2]

Davids continued with a recitation of the postwar problems the tribe faced and ended with a three-point plan for the future: to secure a permanent homeland for the Stockbridge-Munsees; to educate all schoolchildren about American Indians and to ensure "that the white public [is] educated to look upon a reservation in the true meaning of the word: something the Indian Tribes have reserved for themselves out of the vast territory of this country"; and to ensure that "any act of Congress or Bureau dealing in Indian affairs should first consult with the Indians themselves, that they should sit in their councils, not just once, but repeatedly, before taking any action concerning their welfare." Davids's manifesto summarized what he had learned "from . . . family circles and corroborated in recorded history." His principles were central to the Stockbridge ideology, especially the securing of a Mohican homeland "for all time."[3]

The political history of the tribe in the thirty years after World War II once again centered on a set of federal, state, intertribal, and intratribal issues. Securing the Mohican homeland meant placing enough land into federal trust to sustain a growing population of Stockbridge-Munsees in the two townships of Red Springs and Bartelme. Here was the intersection of township and reservation and state and federal politics in the postwar years. The desire of the Mohicans to expand the land base within the reservation boundaries conflicted with the wishes of the non-Indians of Shawano County. Politics began with the census count of the relative populations of Stockbridge-Munsees and non-Indians in Red Springs and Bartelme. Table 8.1 shows the aggregate population of whites and non-whites (the Census Bureau's most consistent category) over the course of the twentieth century.

The total population of the two towns almost certainly increased considerably between 1910 and 1920, after they were organized politically. The trend was slightly downward in the 1920s, with a population loss of about 5 percent, but then a rebound occurred during the depression decade, with 1940 as the peak year for population. There was a severe depopulation of the two townships between 1940 and 1960, with population falling almost 40 percent to just 844 individuals. Since 1960 the population of the two townships rebounded to 1920 levels. A separate examination of the population of the two townships shows that Bartelme has increased its relative share of the total population within the 1856 reservation boundaries from one-third of the total in 1920 to more than one-half by 1980 and 1990. Bartelme's population nadir was in 1930, and the all-time high was in 2000. By contrast, Red Springs had one peak population in 1940, hit its low point in 1970, and only surpassed the 1940 level in 2000. The most interesting finding from the table is the relative change over time in the composition of the population of the two townships. The 1990 relative percentages are the opposite of the distribution for 1920; in that year, Bartelme was 80 percent white, and Red Springs was 61 percent Indian.

At the federal level, at the same time Stockbridge-Munsees faced termination of their status as a recognized tribe they were attempting to win significant payments from the United States before the Indian Claims Commission. At the state level, the tribe continued to contest its hunting and fishing rights within the reservation against the assertion of Wisconsin state regulation. The tribe faced an even more daunting task than in the wartime years, because in 1953 Congress delegated law enforcement powers in Indian Country to the state of Wisconsin under Public Law 280. At the intertribal level, the tribe attempted to build pan-Indian alliances in the 1960s, notably within the National Congress of American Indians and the newly formed Great Lakes Inter-Tribal Council (GLITC). And at the

TABLE 8.1

White and Nonwhite Populations of Bartelme and
Red Springs Townships, 1920–2000

CATEGORY	1920	1930	1940	1950	1960	1970	1980	1990	2000[a]
				Town of Bartelme					
Whites	302	229	254	no data	150	143	177	163	164
Nonwhites	77	31	256	by race	188	256	406	455	536
Total population	379	260	510	470	338	399	583	618	700
				Town of Red Springs					
Whites	322	376	471	no data	336	303	383	388	450
Nonwhites	507	513	435	by race	170	171	141	216	531
Total population	829	889	906	707	506	474	524	604	981
				Two townships combined					
Whites	624	605	725	no data	486	446	560	551	614
Nonwhites	584	544	691	by race	358	427	547	671	1,067
Total population	1,208	1,149	1,416	1,177	844	873	1,107	1,222	1,681
Percent of nonwhites	48	47	49	Unknown	42	49	49	55	63

SOURCE: U.S. Census of Population, 1920-2000

[a]2000 nonwhite population includes 276 American Indians living in the Menominee-Stockbridge-Munsee joint area.

intratribal level, the leadership of the Mohican Nation struggled to foster economic development on the reservation to provide housing and employment for tribal members as an alternative to out-migration and relocation.[4]

Many American Indian tribes faced the Termination Era challenges still divided over the new IRA tribal governments. Not so the Mohicans at the Stockbridge-Munsee Reservation. Few tribes had benefited so directly from tribal reorganization as the Mohicans had under Cornelius Aaron and Carl Miller. Unlike other tribes in the 1940s and 1950s, there was no faction at Stockbridge-Munsee that wanted to see tribal government abolished. This was one advantage that the tribe enjoyed. Another was stability in tribal leadership, notably that of Arvid E. Miller, the fourth child born to Carl and Dolly Miller. Arvid was first elected tribal chair in 1939 and served as either chair or council member continuously until his death in 1969.[5]

In the postwar years Congress turned decisively away from the reforms of the Indian New Deal and back toward the idea of terminating federal supervision of American Indian tribes. The historians of termination point to the wartime actions of Congress, especially the Select Senate Committee on the Investigation of Indian Conditions and its 1944 report advocating the abolition of the Office of Indian Affairs and the ending of government-to-government relations with tribes. But before the United States could sever its government-to-government relations with tribes, it acknowledged that there was still work to do to right the wrongs of the past. The old process of U.S. payment for past wrongs involved special enabling congressional legislation followed by litigation in the U.S. Court of Claims. The Stockbridge-Munsees had more than a decade's worth of experience between 1921 and 1935 with the old procedures and did not win a dollar in awards in the two decisions rendered by the U.S. Court of Claims.

The Stockbridge-Munsees were not the only tribe to have such a history. As early as 1935 Congress considered means of delivering speedier justice by adding an administrative level and subtracting the legislative one. Under the new Indian Claims Commission (ICC) authorized in 1946, tribes had up to five years to present their claims for past injustices and seek monetary compensation. No special act of Congress was needed. The ICC would hear the claim and, if confirmed, make a recommendation to the Court of Claims and to Congress for payment.[6]

In the immediate aftermath of World War II, the ICC idea seemed a remarkable expression by the victorious United States that it recognized its own sometimes bloody and ignoble past and wanted to make amends. The most important language in the Indian Claims Commission Act of 1946 was the clause that set a standard of "less than fair and honorable" dealings by the United States as a ground for a tribe to win compensation. But

Congress set important limits on American generosity. Lands unfairly taken could not be recovered, only their value in money. Moreover, the money was to be largely in nineteenth-century dollars. Thus the artificially low price of $1.25 an acre, set in 1820 for the American public lands, worked as a ceiling on how much Indian lands were valued in 1946 and after. Finally, the Congress carefully limited the paying of interest on damage awards from ICC cases.[7]

Perhaps no tribe in the United States in 1946 felt it had more experience with "less than fair and honorable" dealings with the United States during the nineteenth century than the Stockbridge-Munsees. The tribe filed two claims with the ICC in 1951, one as part of an alliance of some of the same tribes that had pressed the old 1883 *New York Indians v. United States* suit and one as the sole plaintiff against the United States. One claim proved successful and remunerative; the other was successful but empty of significant compensation.[8] If the ghost of John W. Quinney did not sit at the plaintiff's table before the ICC, at least his written set of documents from the 1820s through the 1850s were available for use by his descendants in the tribe and their attorneys.

The more successful of the two claims won by the Tribe was the case *Emigrant New York Indians v. United States*. The "Emigrant New York Indians" included the Stockbridge-Munsees, the Wisconsin Oneidas, and the individual descendants of the Brothertown Tribe of Wisconsin, since that tribe had officially dissolved in 1839. The tribes filed their claim on August 10, 1951, and then spent more than four years preparing their case contending that the United States had shown "less than fair and honorable" dealings in upholding the 1821 treaty that the New York tribes had signed with the Menominees and Ho-Chunks and the 1822 treaty signed with the Menominees. At trial in 1956, the Emigrant New York Indians, led by Stockbridge-Munsee tribal chair Arvid Miller, insisted that the 1821 and 1822 treaties had received support from President Monroe and that President Jackson's own commissioners to the 1830–31 treaty negotiations had also acknowledged the validity of the intertribal treaties. Therefore, the Emigrant New York Indians argued, the 1821 treaty that ceded more than 800,000 acres to the New York tribes and the 1822 treaty that provided for joint New York Indian–Menominee occupancy of more than 7 million acres should still be seen as good law. The French-speaking Métis of Green Bay and the Menominees had resisted that understanding of the two agreements, first at the 1827 Butte des Morts treaty negotiations and then again at the 1830 Green Bay negotiations. The compromise worked out in the February 1831 Washington treaty negotiations was that the Oneidas and other expected New York Indian migrants would receive, not the combined 8 million acres, but 500,000 acres in the so-called New York Indian Tract. The supplemental 1832 treaty awarded the Stockbridge-Munsees their own 46,060-acre reservation on Lake Winnebago and the Brothertowners an adjoining 23,030-acre reservation. This was the crux of the suit brought by Arvid Miller and others in 1956: 569,060 acres in 1831–32 was not the same as 8 million acres from 1821–22, or even 4 million acres if joint occupancy with the Menominees was acknowledged, as stated in the 1822 treaty. The United States, Miller asserted in 1956, had shown less than fair and honorable dealings with the New York tribes in 1827 and 1831–32.[9]

The United States, in the person of Assistant Attorney General Ramsey Clark, argued to the contrary that the Emigrant New York Indians had already had a chance to press this claim in the lawsuit they filed in 1883, *New York Indians v. United States*. And since the tribes had prevailed in that litigation and been compensated, there was no need to pay them again for their move from New York.[10]

The Indian Claims Commission made its decision in February 1957. Their key finding was that the agreement of the New York Indians to the 1831 and 1832 treaties "was not given of their own free will" and that they had wrongly been denied occupancy of and payment for the full 8 million acres they had acquired in 1821–22. The ICC agreed that the land should be halved to 4 million acres to take into account the joint occupancy anticipated with the Menominees.

The ICC next took the step of securing expert testimony from historian-land appraisers that the 8 million acres had contained an estimated 14 billion board feet of white pine in 1832 and also that by 1832 prices, a fair estimate of the value of the lands was eighty cents an acre. After hearing the experts, the ICC ruled in 1962 that the United States owed the plaintiffs almost $1.5 million as compensation for the less than fair and honorable dealings of the Adams and Jackson administrations. The United States attempted to reduce this amount by introducing as evidence what the ICC termed "offsets," or expenditures by the United States for the benefit of the Emigrant New York tribes. Among the expenditures that the

ICC did accept as an offset was the $22,000 spent by the OIA using FERA money in 1934 to acquire lands in the town of Bartelme for the Stockbridge-Munsees. In 1964, after totaling the value of the offsets, the ICC reduced the award to the Emigrant New York Tribes to $1,313,472.65.[11] It took additional years for this award to reach tribal members at Oneida and Stockbridge-Munsee. Not until 1980 did Stockbridge-Munsee members receive what was simply termed "Indian Money" payments for the successful pursuit of the 1951 ICC claim.

Arvid Miller also pursued another claim before the ICC in August 1951, this one for past unfair and less than honorable dealings by the United States with the Stockbridge-Munsees alone. The tribe made two claims in the filing *Stockbridge-Munsee Community v. United States*, one about dealings that New York State had with the tribe in the first half of the nineteenth century and the second about dealings that the United States had with the tribe at the treaties of 1827, 1839, 1848, and 1856. The Indian Claims Commission assigned the Stockbridge-Munsee filing one overall docket number, 300, but placed the New York claims in a subdocket, 300A, and the Wisconsin treaty claims from 1827 through 1856 in the regular "300" docket.

Docket 300A represented a claim by the Stockbridge-Munsees that they had been underpaid for the value of their lands adjacent to the Oneida lands in the period after the 1785 Mohican removal from Massachusetts. The attorneys for the tribe patiently reviewed for the ICC the 1788 New York State law that recognized a thirty-six-square-mile township. New York State confirmed that landholding in an 1811 law. Yet starting in 1817 and continuing through 1847, the state of New York purchased in thirteen separate treaties all of the lands in the township. The Stockbridge-Munsees claimed that they had not been paid the full value by New York State and asked the United States, via the ICC, to make right this past wrong. The ICC, however, did not recognize any responsibility on the part of the United States to rectify what it saw as a private disagreement between a state and a tribe and denied the Stockbridge-Munsee claim in Docket 300A.[12]

The Wisconsin part of Docket 300 involved a claim by Chairman Miller and the tribe that the United States had failed to live up to treaty promises in the 1827, 1839, 1848, and 1856 treaties to make payments to the tribe. The attorneys for the tribe calculated that the United States had failed to make payment of $22,335 in treaty promises. In effect, the lawsuit was about a set of failed treaty stipulations. Once again, Clark argued for the defendant, the United States. He tallied a list of payments to the Stockbridge-Munsees during the starving times at the Shawano County reservation between 1858 and 1870 when the United States had furnished food and fodder without charge. Now, Clark replied, it was only fair to subtract the cost of those provisions from the unpaid treaty stipulations. When the Assistant Attorney General had finished his arithmetic, he calculated that the United States only owed the Stockbridge-Munsees $4,203 for unfair and less than honorable treaty dealings.[13] The ICC did not actually make that recommendation for an award until 1973.

The other side of the coin about the Indian Claims Commission was the termination of tribal relations. The reasoning of Congress was that once tribes received compensation for past wrongs, the United States could proceed to sever present-day relations. The termination policy move gained strength with the Republican sweep of the 1946 congressional elections and with the Hoover Commission's reorganization of the federal government and the OIA into the new Bureau of Indian Affairs (BIA). The BIA's role, Congress made clear, was to put itself out of business. To that end, one of the first tasks Congress asked of the BIA was to survey the readiness of American Indian tribes for termination. The BIA had classified the Stockbridge-Munsees as ready for termination of federal supervision and government-to-government relations. This was not an idle bit of bookkeeping. The neighboring Menominee tribe was also classified as ready for termination, and in 1954 Congress passed and the president signed the Menominee Termination Act. As a nation of firsts, Stockbridge-Munsee could easily have been next up on the block in Wisconsin.[14]

The House of Representatives' Committee on Indian Affairs followed up on the Senate's work regarding the readiness of tribes for termination. The House asked the BIA to produce a detailed accounting of each tribe's status. The document, published in 1952, is filled with the language of freedom and liberty and responsibility. The House asked the BIA directly, "What still remains to be done to completely free the Stockbridge-Munsee group?" The BIA reported that for the Stockbridge-Munsees to be free of federal supervision and responsible for themselves, three things had to happen. First, the tribal members would have to divide up the 2,250 acres of land-in-trust. Remarkably, the House report suggested dividing the land among the members in a new round of land allotments. Nothing could be a sharper rebuke of the Wheeler-Howard Act than a return to the allotment policy. The BIA listed the status of the Farm Security Administration's 13,077 acres within the reservation as a second issue to be resolved. The House report noted that the land could be returned to the public domain. This too was a repudiation of the 1934 Taylor Act, which closed sales of the public lands. In spirit, this part of the House proposal was akin to the surplus land acts that Congress passed in the 1890s and early 1900s in taking land once reserved for tribes but then deemed more valuable for non-Indian homesteaders. The House did in fact make the caveat that returning the lands to the public domain would seem to violate the spirit of the 1938 transfer of the lands from the Department of Agriculture to the Department of the Interior for the exclusive benefit of the tribe. And third, the secretary of the interior would have to hold an election among the tribe's eligible voters asking them to abolish their tribal government and corporate charter and liquidate their assets.[15]

Arvid Miller made a shrewd political decision. He did nothing to encourage termination sentiment among the tribe as a way to curry favor with the new regime in Washington. There would be no volunteering to be first for termination, as Aaron and Carl Miller had volunteered to go first with tribal reorganization and rehabilitation in 1934 under the IRA. Nor would Arvid Miller request the division and allotment of the 2,250 acres of IRA-FERA acquired land-in-trust for the tribe. Instead, Miller decided to focus his political efforts on opposing the BIA's second recommendation that the 13,077 acres in FSA lands be returned to the public domain. For the rest of his life, Miller devoted himself to having those 13,077 acres put into trust for the tribe the same as the 2,250 acres already in trust. In short, Miller decided to buck the termination policy trend by having the federal government expand its supervision of the Stockbridge-Munsees by more than a fivefold increase in the area of lands-in-trust.

Miller's legislative efforts rivaled and perhaps even surpassed those of John W. Quinney in the 1840s or of J. C. Adams in the 1870s, 1880s, and 1890s. The tribe had not tried to win congressional approval of legislation since the unsuccessful 1935 attempt to have the U.S. Court of Claims reconsider yet again the claim for back payments due from the application of the Act of 1871. Miller waited until after the secretary of the interior proclaimed the remaining 1,200 acres of IRA land-in-trust for the Stockbridge-Munsees in December 1948. He then worked with Wisconsin Congressman Reid Murray to introduce legislation placing the RA-FSA 13,077 acres in trust for the tribe. Murray introduced H.R. 3843 in the first session of the Eighty-first Congress (1948). The bill went to the House Committee on Interior and Insular Affairs, the successor to the old House Committee on Indian Affairs, but did not emerge from committee. Murray reintroduced the bill during the next session of Congress and successfully maneuvered it through the committee and full House passage. But the bill died in the Senate Indian Affairs Committee. Congressman William Van Pelt introduced the bill to put the FSA lands into trust in the first session of the Eighty-second Congress. The bill went nowhere that session, but during the next session, Van Pelt was able to get the bill passed through the House; once again, however, it languished in the Senate.[16]

The voters of Wisconsin's Seventh Congressional District, which included the Stockbridge-Munsee Indian Reservation, elected Republican candidate Melvin Laird of Stevens Point to represent them in the 1952 election. For the next sixteen years, Arvid Miller worked to convince Laird to support the Murray and Van Pelt bills calling for placing the FSA lands into trust for the tribe. And for many of those years, Congressman Laird heard from many Shawano County whites opposing the bill. And also over those years, Congressman Laird devoted himself to supporting and overseeing the details of the termination of the Menominee Tribe whose reservation was also located in his district.[17] Arvid Miller worked hard to interest Laird in supporting the land-into-trust bill. In April 1953 he wrote to Laird:

> [The success of the bill] will mean the difference of many of our people being only partially self-supporting as the land status is today—or complete economic stability which will occur with this additional land. . . . Your every effort in securing this land transfer will never be forgotten and will be in the interest of democratic government in fulfilling a promise and a great need to a minority people.[18]

On April 21, during the 1953 congressional session, Laird agreed to introduce the bill in the House. That day, he wrote to the secretary of the interior requesting the position of the department on the topic. The secretary responded that the department continued to support placing the lands into trust for the benefit of the tribe:

In view of the fact that these urgently needed lands are within the boundaries of the reservation and adjoin tribal lands, that they were acquired for the use and benefit of the Indians, and that proper utilization cannot be made of these lands until the Indians' right to occupy and use the lands is confirmed, I believe that [the bill] should be enacted to carry out their understanding had at the time the purchase project was initiated.[19]

The bill also received support from the Izaak Walton League, an environmental organization. But a different outdoors group, the renamed Gresham Sportsmens Club bitterly opposed the bill, as it had also opposed it in the Eighty-first and Eighty-second Congresses. Led by members Ken Traeger, Mike Fischer, and Clarence Otto, the Gresham Sportsmens Club wrote to Laird and to Wisconsin senators Alexander Wiley and Joseph McCarthy on May 6, 1953:

This land should remain under Federal control and be open to the public for hunting and fishing according to the regulations of the Wisconsin Fish and Game Laws. If the Indians keep these 13,000 acres, they no doubt will log the little timber there and then it will go back to the government anyway. Furthermore, there isn't very many true blood Indians left on the government allotted land. There is only one family on the Munsee Indian land capable of making a living and they are Negro and White combination. Why should they live on tax free land at the expense of the taxpayers? . . . We as Sportsmen know that the three best trout streams and some of our best hunting is on this land which is stocked by the State and also the Federal Government.[20]

In the view of the Gresham Sportsmens Club, the bill deserved defeat. It would deny club members access to prime hunting and fishing areas. It would not succeed as an economic development plan because of the tribe's incompetence. And besides, the Stockbridge-Munsee Indians were not really Indians but something other than "true blood."

The disposition of the lands-into-trust bill for the Stockbridge-Munsees once again suffered the same fate. It passed the House of Representatives but failed to win passage in the Senate. Tribal member Annie Besaw and Izaak Walton League member Mrs. Edward LaBudde of Milwaukee pinned the blame for the defeat of the bill on the junior senator from Wisconsin, Joseph McCarthy. A onetime county judge in Shawano County, Senator McCarthy had close ties to the men in the Gresham Sportsmens Club, and according to Mrs. LaBudde, McCarthy had vowed that he would never let the lands-to-trust bill become law. Moreover, McCarthy apparently promised Ken Traeger, Mike Fischer, and Clarence Otto in Gresham that he would move to secure the 13,077 acres of FSA land in the towns of Bartelme and Red Springs for the state of Wisconsin as future hunting and fishing grounds. Without the support of a key U.S. senator, the Senate Committee on Indian Affairs refused to report the bill to the full Senate.[21]

Arvid Miller attributed the failure to pass the bill in the Senate in 1953 to a combination of "the sense of the congress in termination policies" and also to the efforts of the Gresham Sportsmens Club, whose president, Miller claimed, "is capable of saying or doing anything in an attempt to gain his own way, right or wrong."[22] As long as the sentiment in Congress was for more tribes to be terminated, it would be difficult to get lands placed into trust, which had the effect of increasing the federal role in tribal affairs.

Miller and the Stockbridge-Munsees lived through the rest of the 1950s on their reservation with its mix of IRA lands, FSA lands, and non-Indian lands. The tribal council decided to encourage home building on FSA lands with funds advanced from the council's line of credit. In this regard, the council made use of its powers under the 1938 Corporate Charter to borrow funds and distribute the money to individual tribal members for authorized uses, such as housing construction and repair. The initial 1937 settlement at Moh-he-con-nuck in the town of Bartelme expanded in the 1950s as tribal members built new homes on FSA lands. The council felt it had the needed authority to build housing on FSA lands, based on a 1952 opinion from the BIA. That opinion had drawn on an older U.S. Supreme Court decision that held federally owned lands for the exclusive use of Indians to be "Indian Country." Thus, the BIA decided, the FSA lands on the Stockbridge-Munsee Indian Reservation constituted "Indian Country." That opinion remained the guiding one until 1960, when the superintendent of the Great Lakes Agency (successor to the Tomah Superintendency) decided that the tribe had no authority to make any use of the 13,077 acres of FSA lands. The superintendent did not order the outright dismantling of existing housing, but he made it clear that no new houses could be built, or for that matter, any other economic development attempted. This BIA decision provoked a crisis and a renewed effort by Arvid Miller to effect a congressional solution to the problem.[23]

With the advent of the Kennedy administration and its turn away from additional tribal terminations, there was new support in the White House and in Congress for placing lands into trust. Miller characterized the new administration as one that favored "development, not termination." In 1961 Senator Frank Church of Idaho introduced a bill in the first session of the Eighty-seventh Congress to place submarginal lands into trust for twenty-three separate tribes, including the Stockbridge-Munsees. Miller feared, however, that the Church approach would not "meet with the approval of the Congress, simply because there would be problems that would involve leases, oil, grazing and many other basic factors." Furthermore, the wholesale character of the Church bill might "influence eventual termination." Miller would have none of that, telling his congressman, "Termination we would not consider at this time as our neighbors, the Menominees, aren't going to make a go of it with their vast timber potential."[24]

Arvid Miller did not neglect to notify the new Commissioner of Indian Affairs about his tribal council's opinion on termination. In a remarkable 1961 document, the tribal council made the following statement about the historic role of the Stockbridge-Munsee Mohicans and their place in the larger national polity. The Miller-written document read:

> The most significant clue to achieving full Indian democracy, within and as a part of the American democracy, is the continued survival through all historical change and disaster, of the Indian tribal group, both as a real entity and as a legal entity. . . . The reason [is] that nearly three hundred years of deeply rooted distrust, and an attitude toward life which does not regard the piling up of material means as a first consideration, or of bulwarks against the future as a major significance.[25]

With this statement of political philosophy, the tribal council submitted an economic development plan for the reservation tied to passage of the FSA lands-into-trust bill. The council's plan began with another statement about Mohican history and practice:

> And we know that if history means anything, it means both a struggle for freedom and a struggle to preserve achieved values against the

disintegrating forces of time and change. We believe, in short, that we can maintain our old proved values while selectively absorbing new values from the modern world.[26]

The plan itself involved some specific projects and some general aims. The council anticipated "development of a maple syrup industry," the construction of a fish hatchery for the upper Red River, and the development of a rural scenic parkway to run along the Red River in the town of Bartelme. More generally, the "consolidation of the land base" would make available more land to build "good homes" and also a "unit to be used as a home for the aged." A modern sanitation system could be built. Industry could be attracted to the reservation. All of these development ideas required the transfer of the 13,077 acres of RA-FSA land into trust so that the tribe could depend on the new land base.[27]

Miller did all he could to muster allies inside and outside of Shawano County and Wisconsin to support the latest version of the Laird bill. He secured support from the Bowler Advancement Association, from the Izaak Walton League again, from the Town Board of Bartelme (where Miller served as one of the supervisors), from the Shawano County Welfare Department, from the National Congress of American Indians, from various church congregations and synods, and from a petititon signed by the tribe's members. Opposing the Laird bill, once again, was the Gresham Sportsmens Club, led by Mike Fischer. Fischer did not recognize any land rights of the Stockbridge-Munsees, at least in Wisconsin. "If they rightfully own any land," he wrote to Congressman Laird, "I would say it must be in the East around New York for thats where they originated." And Fischer struggled to understand the new move away from termination: "From the way the Menominee tribe ended up it indicates to me that the government is trying to have these Indian tribes to be self supporting. By setting up a new reservation for the Stockbridge Munsee Indians is not my idea of being self supporting."[28]

The Laird bill failed in the Eighty-seventh Congress. As Laird explained to Miller, the House Interior and Insular Affairs Committee "is entirely controlled by the Democratic Party and any failure to act on this legislation is the responsibility of the Committee since it must be reported to the Floor of the House before I will have an opportunity to vote on it."[29] When Laird tried once again in the next Congress, he encountered opposition from Wisconsin's junior senator, Gaylord Nelson. The senator wanted to take a portion of the 13,077 acres and give the parcels to the state of Wisconsin for conservation purposes. The Laird bill was going nowhere. Laird's bills met the same fate in the Eighty-ninth and Ninetieth Congresses (1965–67 and 1967–69). With the election of Richard Nixon to the presidency in 1968, Congressman Laird accepted the president-elect's invitation to join the cabinet as secretary of defense. Sixteen years of Melvin Laird's work for the tribe went unrewarded, or at least that work did not meet with legislative success.

Melvin Laird's successor as representative of Wisconsin's Seventh Congressional District was David Obey, a Democrat from Wausau. Obey convinced Senator Nelson to work with him to place the entire 13,077 acres of FSA land into trust for the tribe and not to divert any timberlands to a state forest or recreation area. The duo was unsuccessful in the Ninety-first Congress (1969–71), but they finally secured a hearing on their bill before the Senate Sub-Committee on Indian Affairs during the first session of the Ninety-second Congress (1971–72). Senators William Proxmire and Nelson testified for the bill, as did Congressman Obey and Louis Bruce, Commissioner of Indian Affairs.[30]

The leadership of the tribe also appeared at the Senate hearing, including Aught Coyhis, chair, Felix Bruette, Land Committee chair, Bernice Miller, widow of Arvid Miller and chair of the Arts and Crafts Committee, Roland ("Bud") Davids of the tribal council, and Thelma Putnam, formerly on the council. All five testified to the importance of securing the FSA lands in trust to the tribe. Senator Quentin Burdick of North Dakota asked the tribal leaders if the value of the FSA lands, whether in 1938 or 1971, should not be subtracted from any forthcoming award from the Indian Claims Commission. After all, Burdick reasoned, "all during these years . . . you have just been using them [the FSA lands]." Why should not the $69,000 the FSA spent in the 1930s be counted as an offset when the ICC did its arithmetic? Felix Bruette had a simple answer: "Well, sir, I would put it this way: I would say that we were more or less taking care of the land, as caretakers."[31]

Finally, Harold Gross of the National Council on Indian Opportunity testified. He told the Senate hearing that an important change in the status of the FSA lands had occurred in the mid-1960s. The second-growth scrub woods had matured into harvestable timber, and it was now the United

States that was letting contracts to local loggers for cutting the timber. Between 1964 and 1971 the United States, not the Stockbridge-Munsees, had earned more than $93,000 in stumpage fees. "If the United States retains this money," Gross testified, "it will mark one of the few times in history where the United States made a profit on emergency relief administration."[32]

In the next session of Congress, the Senate passed the Nelson bill (S.B. 722) first and then the House passed it. President Nixon signed it in June 1972 to the great satisfaction of his defense secretary. As Table 8.2 shows, the struggle to pass legislation placing the FSA lands in trust was comparable in length and difficulty to that waged by John C. Adams to get Congress to reverse the Act of 1871.[33]

With the passage of Senate Bill 722 by Congress in 1972, the followers of Arvid Miller had secured in perpetuity title in trust for the tribe. This was a significant achievement but by itself did not secure the homeland. The original Shawano County reservation established by the twin treaties of 1856 had counted two townships, or 46,060 acres, in size. As of 1972, only a bit more than one-third of that acreage was in trust for the tribe. The remaining two-thirds was owned largely by non-Indians. The question that the tribe's leaders now asked was this: did the Stockbridge-Munsee Indian Reservation extend to the boundaries of the towns of Bartelme and Red Springs, in the way that the 1856 treaties envisioned, or was the Stockbridge-Munsee Reservation something smaller, merely the 15,327 acres in trust? Put another way, was the full 46,060 acres of the two townships "Indian Country," even if not in trust, or only the 15,327 acres? The answer to this question had important significance for Stockbridge-Munsee tribal members to hunt and fish within the two townships without being subject to state of Wisconsin fish and game regulations.

On the question of reservations and "Indian Country," it must be said that the Stockbridge-Munsees were not the first nation to wrangle with the state of Wisconsin. Indeed, for almost all the twentieth century, the state had sought to reduce and eliminate any special treaty-guaranteed rights of Indians to hunt and fish without being subject to state regulations. Most of these state dealings were with the Lake Superior Chippewas of northern Wisconsin. The state of Wisconsin had successfully won a 1908 judgment in its supreme court that the Chippewas did not have a right to fish outside their reservations despite such guarantees in separate 1837

TABLE 8.2

The Struggle in Congress to Place the FSA Lands in Trust, 1949–1972

YEAR	CONGRESS	SESSION	BILL NO.	SPONSOR(S)
1949	81st	1st	H.R. 3843	Murray
1950	81st	2d	H.R. 3843	Murray
1951	82d	1st	H.R. 5577	Van Pelt
1952	82d	2d	H.R. 5577	Van Pelt
1953	83d	1st	S.B. 1013	Laird
1960	86th	2d	H.R. 8115, S.B. 2543	Proxmire
1961	87th	1st	H.R. 3534, H.R. 9275, S.B. 2183	Laird
1963	88th	1st	H.R. 999	Laird
1965	89th	1st	H.R. 7565	Laird
1967	90th	2d	H.R. 789	Laird
1969	91st	2d	H.R. 18016, S.B. 4438	Obey and Nelson
1971	92d	1st	H.R. 4865, S.B. 722	Obey and Nelson
1972	92d	2d	H.R. 9865, S.B. 722	Obey and Nelson

SOURCE: *Congressional Record,* 81st Cong., lst sess., p. 3320; 81st Cong., 2d sess., pp. 1827, 2858, 2901; 82d Cong., lst sess., p. 12572; 82d Cong., 2d sess., pp. 2412, 3189, 3225; 88th Cong., 1st sess., p. 52; 89th Cong., lst sess., p. 8229; 91st Cong., 2d sess., pp. 19289, 35094; 92d Cong., lst sess., pp. 2407, 3657, 6314; 92d Cong., 2d sess., pp. 19264, 20268-69, 20275, 20428, 33180, 33401, 34788; "To declare that certain federally owned lands shall be held by the United States in trust for the Stockbridge-Munsee Indian Community, Wisconsin," 86, *Statutes at Large,* 795 (1972).

and 1842 treaties. Further than that, the state was stymied by the OIA and later the BIA that state regulation did not apply on Indian reservations. But as at the Stockbridge-Munsee Indian Reservation, the four Chippewa reservations established by an 1854 treaty had lost significant parts of their land base to allotments and foreclosures.[34]

The Termination Era only emboldened the state's Conservation Commission to do away with any exemption of any Indians from state fish and game laws. Matters became so bad in 1959 that the Bad River Band of Lake Superior Chippewas declared that a "State of Cold War" existed between the tribe and the state. The Bad River Chippewas charged that state game wardens shadowed tribal deer hunters and waited to make an arrest until a deer bounded from a land parcel in trust to a land parcel in fee simple, at which exact point the legal status of the animal changed from an "Indian deer" to a "state deer." And in the 1960s, after the Menominee tribe was terminated, the state made one final move to stop recognition of on-reservation Indian fishing and hunting rights. In 1964 Attorney General John Reynolds (son of the failed state litigator-friend of the Stockbridge-Munsees in 1931) issued an opinion that tribal members could no longer hunt and fish anywhere in the state, including on tribal trust land, without being subject to state law. The Reynolds opinion helped to unite all the tribes in Wisconsin to oppose this newest power grab by the state. Led by Arvid Miller, the eleven federally recognized tribes in Wisconsin formed the Great Lakes Inter-Tribal Council in 1966 as a research and lobbying group to advocate for the tribes on matters of common interest. Miller secured the outside counsel of the leading federal Indian law practice law firm in the country, Wilkinson, Cragun, and Wilkinson. Miller asked the firm on behalf of the GLITC to contest the attorney general's opinion. Unlike in 1908, when the Lake Superior Chippewas were unable to defend their treaty rights, the tribes would be able to fight against the state without having to rely on the BIA as an intervening power.[35] Faced with widespread opposition to the Reynolds opinion, the state in 1968 renounced it and admitted that it did not have fish and game enforcement powers in Indian Country. That 1968 defeat began a comeback for the Lake Superior Chippewas in their efforts to regain on- and off-reservation hunting, fishing, and gathering rights, a process that was only finally secured by a 1999 U.S. Supreme Court decision.[36]

The term "Indian Country" extended back in American history to at least 1763 when George III issued a proclamation that drew a line down the Appalachian Mountains separating English from native lands, with the native lands termed "Indian Country." The United States picked up the term, even if the line that George III drew had long since been breached. In 1834 Congress formally defined the term "Indian Country," and that definition held for the rest of the century and into the twentieth. After defining the trans-Mississippi West as Indian Country (except for the new states of Missouri and Louisiana and the Territory of Arkansas), Congress more specifically stated that the lands "to which the Indian title has not been extinguished . . . be taken and deemed to be the Indian country."[37]

The problem with the 1834 definition in the mid-twentieth century is that it could not accommodate the reality on the ground of post-allotment reservations with their so-called checkerboard patterns of landownership.

Here was a parcel in trust, and there was one owned by a non-Indian, and over there was one owned by allottees in fee simple. This was the checkerboard pattern of landholdings that resulted in the situation on the Bad River Reservation where an animal was variously an Indian deer or a state deer. In 1948 Congress redefined Indian Country as follows:

> The term "Indian Country" . . . means . . . all lands within the limits of any Indian reservation under the jurisdiction of the United States government, notwithstanding the issuance of any patent, and including rights-of-way running through the reservation.[38]

Now, in 1948, Congress said that all the lands within a reservation's boundaries constituted Indian Country, even if owned by non-Indians or as rights-of-way, such as the one granted the Wisconsin Northern Railway in 1906.

The question of what constituted Indian Country on the Stockbridge-Munsee's Shawano County reservation came up in two legal cases, one before the 1948 recodification of the federal law and one after. In 1945 tribal member Perry Bowman was indicted for attempted murder after he was accused of having slashed his wife's throat on Moh-he-con-nuck Road. Brought to trial in Shawano County before Judge Joseph McCarthy, Bowman's lawyers tried to get the case dismissed from state court on the grounds that the slaying took place on the reservation and therefore in "Indian Country." Bowman's assault on his wife took place on land purchased by the RA-FSA, and although in federal ownership, in 1945 it was not in trust for the tribe. Judge McCarthy would have none of the defense that his court did not hold jurisdiction, and after conviction, he sent Bowman to the state prison at Waupun.[39]

Judge McCarthy's ruling took place before the 1948 recodification of the federal law regarding crimes in Indian Country, and also before the 1953 congressional devolution of criminal law enforcement from the United States to certain states, including Wisconsin. Known as Public Law 280, the 1953 statute extended state criminal law enforcement to Indian reservations in several states, Wisconsin among them.[40]

The other state judge to rule on the question of Indian Country and the Stockbridge-Munsee Indian Reservation was an even more unfortunate choice from the viewpoint of the tribe than Judge "Tailgunner Joe" McCarthy. In 1968 tribal member Vincent Malone found himself in

Shawano County Court before Judge Ken Traeger, onetime president of the Gresham Sportsmens Club. And the charge was possessing trout out of season. Judge Traeger not only found defendant Malone guilty of fishing for trout out of season, but used his opinion as a way of settling a number of old scores, both with former President Roosevelt and with the Stockbridge-Munsee tribe. Of President Roosevelt's actions, Judge Traeger wrote:

> After this land was purchased by the Resettlement Administration and Farm Security Administration, and I believe one other of the countless governmental agencies, the then President of the United States, Franklin Delano Roosevelt, attempted by executive order to create a new reservation of some thousand acres by executive order but this was never passed. This court is compelled to hold that the President of the United States was without constitutional authority to create an Indian reservation and make less than full citizens out of full citizens of this nation.[41]

Having disposed of the New Deal's IRA, Judge Traeger then turned his attention to the tribe and its claim to live on an Indian reservation:

> 1. That the Stockbridge-Munsee Indians have obtained their papers of competency and are full citizens of the United States of America.
> 2. That the land is only called a reservation, but it is not legally created reservation.
> 3. That this is not Indian lands or Indian Country, but is patented lands under the jurisdiction of the State of Wisconsin and the State of Wisconsin not having relinquished its rights to the jurisdiction of this land has full and complete authority to enforce the laws of the State of Wisconsin, be they conservation, hunting, fishing, motor vehicle, civil or criminal, and has the full rights and jurisdiction over this area as it has over any other portion of the State of Wisconsin.[42]

With that ruling, Judge Traeger promptly found Vincent Malone guilty. Tribal Chair Leonard Miller wrote to Congressman Laird, alarmed at the ruling in the Malone case. Laird asked the BIA for a legal opinion on Traeger's ruling. The BIA asked its Minneapolis area field solicitor to review the case, and that office fell back on the ruling in the Bowman case of 1945 that the key empirical question was the status of the FSA lands. The BIA attorney wrote, "There is no authority which supports a claim of Indian hunting and fishing rights on such lands. If as it appears, the fishing was on FSA lands, the decision of Judge Traeger was correct."[43]

Although the BIA did not necessarily agree with the radical view expressed by Judge Traeger that no Stockbridge-Munsee Indian Reservation existed, its 1968 position was that the "Indian Country" portion was merely the 2,250 acres of IRA land acquired back in 1935–36, not the FSA 13,077 acres, and not the entire two townships of 46,060 acres that were within the boundaries established pursuant to the two treaties of February 5 and February 11, 1856. The tribal council did not accept Judge Traeger's ruling and made a formal request to the BIA for a determination of the status of the Stockbridge-Munsee Indian Reservation. Not until 1974 did the BIA respond with a formal opinion, but when it did, the answer was highly satisfying to the Tribe. Acting Commissioner of Indian Affairs Kenneth Payton wrote to Tribal Chair Leonard Miller in 1974 with his recitation of the history of U.S.-Mohican relations. He reviewed the 1856 treaty and the congressional legislation, especially of 1871 and 1906, and found no explicit action by Congress to disestablish the reservation or to terminate federal supervision of the tribe. Payton further pointed out: "Had Congress intended to terminate the Stockbridge and Munsee Indians, reorganization of the tribe under the Act of June 18, 1934 would not have occurred in the absence of restoration legislation."[44] Payton concluded with an affirmation that the two-township Shawano County reservation that emerged from the two 1856 treaties was never diminished or disestablished by any "clearly expressed intent" of Congress. Payton concluded, "Therefore, it is our opinion that the exterior boundaries of the present reservation continue to encompass T. 28 N., R. 13 E., and T. 28 N., R. 14 E."[45]

The 1970s were good for the tribe. The ICC cases came to conclusion, and Congress finally acted to place the FSA lands in trust. With the 1974 BIA opinion that the two townships of Bartelme and Red Springs constituted the Stockbridge-Munsee Indian Reservation, it is fair to say that the Mohican homeland in Wisconsin was secure. The tribe had avoided termination. It had won some measure of justice from the ICC regarding failure to uphold the 1821 and 1822 treaties. The placement of the FSA lands in trust allowed the Mohicans to build more housing secure in the knowledge that the lands could not be disturbed. And the BIA opinion that the reservation was the full two townships of 46,060 acres constituted a clarification that the Act of 1871 had merely sold land parcels within the reservation and had not effected any sort of diminishment. The heirs of Hendrick Aupaumut, John W. Quinney, John P. Hendricks, John C. Adams, Carl Miller, and Arvid E. Miller had a permanent and secure homeland in Wisconsin.

Tribal Constitutions of the Stockbridge-Munsees, 1837–1937

DECLARATION OF RIGHTS & FRAME OF GOVERNMENT (1837)

We the Chiefs and Warriors of the Stockbridge Nation acknowledging the goodness of the Great Spirit in affording us an opportunity of forming a new Constitution for ourselves and posterity and devoutly invoking his guidance and assistance Do Agree Upon and Ordain and Establish the following declaration of Rights & Frame of Government as the Constitution of our Nation.

DECLARATION OF RIGHTS

Art. 1st. All hereditary titles and distinctions are annulled and abolished forever.

Art. 2nd. All men are born free and equal and under the protection of Laws. They have the right to defend life and liberty—Acquire and hold property—Seek & enjoy happiness.

Art. 3rd. It is the right of every man to worship God in his own manner and time and to be free from molestation in so doing provided he does not break the public peace in so doing or disturb others in their worship.

Art. 4th. It is our unalienable right to institute such modes and forms of Government & to enact from time to time such laws & regulations as we may deem most proper and conducive to the order & welfare of our community at large and to do all such other acts and deeds as a free people of right may do within their own country and in regard to their own interests.

Art. 5th. We recognize the force and validity of our Treaties with the United States in the full sense and meaning of their terms and admit the necessity and propriety of the protection intended to us and of the alliance and friendship on which we stand to that Government. But we do not acknowledge allegiance to any power upon earth.

Art. 6th. All power resides in the people and all officers and magistrates are their agents and substitutes.

Art. 7th. In order to prevent those who are vested with authority from becoming oppressors the people have a right to cause their public officers to return to private life in such manner as they shall appoint in their frame of Government.

Art. 8th. All Elections shall be by ballot.

Art. 9th. Every individual of the Nation shall have the right of legal redress for injuries committed upon his property character and person. But no person shall be compelled to furnish evidence against himself. All trials shall be fair.

Art. 10th. No offence shall be punished under any law enacted after the offence was committed. No person shall be tried twice for the same offence. Excessive fines shall not be imposed nor shall private property be taken for public use unless paid for justly.

FRAME OF GOVERNMENT

Art. 1   Sec. 1st. The Government of this Nation shall be entrusted to and administered by a Supreme First Magistrate and a Council Composed of five members.

Art. 2   Sec. 1st. The term of service of the First Magistrate Shall be three years. An Election Shall be held on the First Tuesday of January in every third year by which the Individual receiving a majority of all the votes present Shall be declared the First Magistrate for the three years next ensuing. The title of the First Magistrate shall be Sachem.

Sec. 2. No person shall be eligible to this office unless at the time of his election he shall have been a resident in the Nation for three years next preceeding—and unless he shall declare himself a Believer in the Christian Religion and unless he be possessed of property of the value of Five hundred dollars—and unless he shall be of the age of twenty five years.

Sec. 3. The First Magistrate Shall be the Supreme executive officer— There shall be annually elected by the legal voters of this Nation five persons to be members of the Council for the year next ensuing who shall be called Counsellors. No person Shall be eligible to the office of a Counsellor unless at the time of his Election he shall have been a resident in the Nation for two years next preceeding— and unless he Shall declare himself a believer in the Christian Religion—and unless he Shall be of the age of twenty two years.

Art. 3   Sec. 1. The First Magistrate and the Council Shall decide up on the validity of elections to their own body.

Sec. 2. All vacancies in the Council by death resignation or removal from the Nation shall be filled by immediate election so soon as such vacancies shall occur. In case of the death resignation or removal from the Tribe of the First

Magistrate the Member of the Council who Shall have received at the Election the highest number of votes shall become the First Magistrate and execute all the duties of that office for the remainder of the term of three years.

Sec. 3. The First Magistrate and the Council of five being thus Constituted and appointed shall adopt such laws both criminal and civil as may be necessary from time to time, and best suited to the Circumstances and condition of the Nation. They shall have power to constitute other needful officers than those specified in this Constitution to regulate the disposition of the lands belonging to the Nation and all appropriations to be made out of the same for public and private purposes—to levy and collect taxes—to pay National debts—to borrow money on the faith and credit of the Nation—to establish a Rule by which members from other Nations may be received into this Nation—to regulate Intercourse & Commerce with other Indian Nations—and to encourage and promote by wholesome regulations the progress of Civilization and Knowledge and the useful arts.

Sec. 4. The First Magistrate Shall preside over the deliberations of the Council—In all laws for the appropriation of money for any object—and in the imposition of taxes the First Magistrate shall not be entitled to vote except in the equal division of the Council he shall in such a case give the casting vote.

Sec. 5. The First Magistrate and three members of the Council Shall constitute a quorum to proceed to business. In case of the temporary absence of the First Magistrate from Sickness or any other Cause the Council Shall elect a President pro tem.

Sec. 6. The sessions of Council shall be Semi-annual or once in six months.

Art. 4   Sec. 1. The First Magistrate and those two members of the Council who shall at election have received the highest of votes shall constitute the high court of the Nation.

Sec. 2. The sessions of this Court Shall be Quarterly or once in three months unless there shall be an attendance of one of the judges within three days after the commencement of the term. The Secretary of the Court shall proclaim it adjourned until the next term.

Sec. 3. All last wills and testaments shall be proved before this Court. Letters of administration upon the estate of persons dying without will shall be granted by this Court. The settlement of Account of Guardians and the general charge of orphan children shall be held and done by the Court. All Civil Suits when the amount exceeds the sum of Fifty dollars—Actions of Slander—of Divorce either for a dissolution of the marriage contract or for a temporary Separation of the Parties—All the suits against the Sureties of the Treasurer or any public officer—All actions against the Treasurer or any officer for embezzlement of the public money—All actions for illegal and improper and oppressive Conduct by the Peace Makers and Sheriff—All actions for resistance of the Sheriff in the legal discharge of his duty Shall be originated and tried in this Court.

Sec. 4. All actions and trials for murder and manslaughter—for Larceny where the amount exceeds thirty five dollars for resistance of a Sheriff or any other officer in the legal discharge of his duty.

Sec. 5. All civil actions where the title to the land to be tried.

Sec. 6. In all cases where the Peace Makers are interested trial shall be held in this Court.

Sec. 7. All writs and process from the high Court shall run in the name of the Stockbridge Nation and bear a test in the name of the Chief Judge if not interested in the suit. If interested, they shall bear test in the name of one of the other Judges.

Sec. 8. An appeal Shall be had and taken from the Court of the Peace Makers by either plaintiff or defendant to the high Court in all cases where the judgment and cost shall exceed the sum of fifty dollars Provided the party appealing shall enter Security with the Peace Makers that he will prosecute his appeal to trial and pay the Amount with interest and costs in case the judgment is affirmed in the high Court. And all judgments passed by this Court upon any of the afore mentioned cases shall be final.

Art. 5   Sec. 1. The council shall appoint one individual from their number to fill the office of a Secretary.

Sec. 2. The Records of the Nation Shall be kept by the Secretary.

Sec. 3. He Shall keep a Record of the Council when sitting as a Legislature, and also when sitting as a Court. The judgment and decisions of the Court Shall be kept in one Book and its amendments and proceedings when Sitting as a Legislature in another Book.

Sec. 4. It shall be the duty of the Secretary to read aloud in the hearing of the people every regular session of the Council this Constitution and the laws which have been passed at that session.

Sec. 5. He shall place in the most conspicuous place written notice of the time of the annual Elections at least five days before the Election takes place and also written notices of the time when the quarterly sessions of the Court and the sessions of the Legislature will each take place. He shall also be present at the annual Elections and take down a list of the names of all the voters as their ballots are deposited in the Box.

Art. 6   Sec. 1. There shall be at the annual Election one person elected to fill the office of a Treasurer to the Nation.

Sec. 2. Before entering upon the duties of his office the Treasurer shall give security to be approved of by the Council in the sum of [blank space] for the faithful & upright discharge of his duties.

Sec. 3. All monies and funds belonging to the Nation shall be paid over to him and all demands upon him from the Council in pursuance of Law shall be paid he giving and receiving acquittances for the same. All taxes shall when collected be paid to him and receipt shall be a proper voucher to the officer collecting the same.

Sec. 4. He shall keep a regular account and statement of the affairs of the office and shall be required to make regular returns to the Council as often as it is convened of the State of the funds of the affairs of his office.

Sec. 5. No person shall be elected Treasurer unless he shall have resided three years in the Nation and unless he is possessed of property of the balance of [left blank]

Art. 7   Sec. 1. There shall be chosen at the annual election two persons to fill the office of Peace Makers.

Sec. 2. It shall be the duty of the Peace Makers to hear & try all offences under any law which may be made by the Council, and to sit & hear & try all civil actions the amount of which does not exceed the sum of Fifty dollars. Such cases both criminal and civil as are herein provided for and referred to the high Court being excepted.

1857 CONSTITUTION

THE CONSTITUTIONAL CONVENTION

A council was called and held by the males of the Moh-he-con-news (commonly called the Stockbridge and Munsee tribe) at Aaron Konkaput's house at our new homes near the southern boundary of the Menomonee Reservation, in the State of Wisconsin, this 30th day of December, A.D., 1856.

Resolved. That John N. Chicks, Timothy Jourdan and Ziba T. Peters be a committee to form a Constitution similar to that heretofore adopted by the tribe to present the same week from to-day for adoption.

Resolved. That the tract of land granted to the united nation of the Stockbridge and Munsee Indians and is located in the State of Wisconsin, near on the north side of the southern boundary line of the Menomonee Reservation and west from Wolf River, shall hereafter be called or named, Moh-he-con-nuck, and by this name the place aforesaid shall ever hereafter be designated in all public acts and documents whereinsoever it may be named.

Resolved. That the council now adjourn until one week from to-day, when there shall be an election of national officers, and that Ziba T. Peters, the Sachem, be authorized to provide victuals for the people on the expense of the nation.

Entered of record by Pon-poon-hout, alias

JOHN N. CHICKS.

Pursuant to adjournment the males of said tribe held a general council at the dwelling house of John Yoccum, this 6th day of January, A.D. 1857. The committee reported the following articles of Constitution, which were read and adopted and are in the following words, to-wit:

The Constitution

Whereas, The Great Spirit has made His mighty arm bare in the preservation and establishment of a part of the Moh-he-con-neew (known as the Stockbridge and Munsee tribe), on the western part of the Wolf River, on the north side of the southern boundary line of the Menomonee Reservation, in the State of Wisconsin.

Therefore, We, the Chiefs, Braves and Warriors of the Stockbridge and Munsee tribe, being assembled at our new fire place at Moh-he-con-nuck, in the State of Wisconsin, this 6th day of January, a.d. 1857, having considered that our peculiar situation highly demands combined efforts in order the more efficiently to execute our best intentions and purposes hereinafter enumerated, do hereby voluntarily make, ordain and declare, that the following articles of our union and confederation, which shall remain unalterable unless by common consent.

Article I.

There shall be no distinction made of the united tribe of Stockbridge and Munsee Indians on account of descent or birth (saving where character and qualification shall render any person ineligible for any post of trust or honor), but all shall alike be entitled to enjoy the rights, privileges and advantages of the nation.

Article II.

That all such of the Stockbridge and Munsees, whether they are now residing in the State of New York or Wisconsin, or any where in the United States, who were not provided for either in land or money, shall at least have the privilege of coming and taking up lots of land on the tract given to the Stockbridges and Munsees, by the treaty of February 5th, 1856.

Article III.

Every male of the age of twenty-one years or upwards (or under twenty-one years if legally married, in which case he shall be admitted on an equal footing with those of the age aforesaid), shall be entitled to vote for national officers herein elective.

Article IV.

Schools and the means of education shall ever be encouraged.

Article V.

No person or any assembly of people, met for the worship of God on the Lord's day or at any other time, shall be disturbed.

Article VI.

There shall be a Sachem elected for the term of three years, and five Counsellors for the term of one year. One of the Counsellors shall be chosen by the Sachem and Counsellors a Secretary, whose duty it shall be to keep all the acts and proceedings of the Councils, and generally do such writing of a public nature as be required by the Sachem and Counsellors; and in consequence of the death, resignation or necessary absence of the Sachem, one of the Counsellors who received the highest number of votes, shall execute all the power and perform all the duties of the

Sachem, during the vacancy occasioned by the resignation, death or necessary absence of the said Sachem. And in case of the death or resignation of a Counsellor, the Sachem shall by notice, either in writing or otherwise, appoint a time and place to elect another in his stead to serve for the residue of the term. The Sachem and the two others who had received the highest number of votes for Counsellors, shall constitute the high court of the nation.

Article VII.

A Treasurer, two Peace Makers, two Path Masters and one Sheriff, shall be elected annually on the day of election, and their powers and duties shall be prescribed by law.

Article VIII.

The general election shall be held on the first Tuesday of January annually, and it shall be the duty of the Secretary to give notice of the day of election, by posting up notices in two or three of the most public places of the town at least six days before the day of election.

Article IX.

The election shall be by ballot.

Article X.

The election shall be opened between the hours of nine and ten o'clock in the forenoon and shall be kept open until four o'clock in the afternoon.

Article XI.

The Legislative Council and High Court of the Nation shall be held at such time as shall be provided by law.

Article XII.

The Sachem and the five Counsellors or a majority of them, shall adopt such of their original laws, criminal and civil, as may be necessary and best suited to the circumstances of the tribe. They also shall have the authority to make other laws in all cases for the good government of the tribe, not repugnant to any of the articles herein enumerated.

Article XIII.

Bill of Rights

SECTION 1. All men are born equally free and independent. All power is inherent in, and all government of right originates with the people, is founded in their authority and instituted for their peace, safety and happiness.

SECTION 2. The people shall at all times have the right in a peaceable manner to assemble together to consult for the common good.

SECTION 3. Excessive bail shall not be required. Excessive fines shall not be imposed and cruel and unjust punishment shall not be inflicted.

SECTION 4. No person shall be deprived of his liberty or property, but by the judgment of his part or the law of the Nation; should the public exigencies make it necessary for the common preservation, to take any person's property or to demand his particular services, full compensation shall be made for the same.

Article XIV.

The Sachem, Counsellors, Treasurer, Peace Makers, Path Masters and Sheriff shall, before they enter upon the duties of their respective offices, take and subscribe the following affirmation: I do solemnly affirm that I will faithfully discharge the duties of the office of _____ according to the best of my ability.

Article XV.

Immediately after the signing of the articles herein enumerated, the Council will proceed to elect two or three inspectors for the election of such officers as are required in the foregoing articles by ballot, and who shall act in that capacity to all intents and purposes therein, during the term in which they are elected.

As witness our names and marks, the day and year above written

Jeremiah Slingerland
John W. Quinney, Jr.

Ziba T. Peters
John (X) Yoccum
Humble Jourden
Cornelius M. Anthony
Daniel (X) Gardner
Jacob (X) Konkapot
Eli Williams
Harvey (X) Johnson
John P. Hendricks
Jacob Jacobs
Jeremiah Slingerland
Cornelius Littleman
Cornelius (X) Yoccum
Aaron Konkapot
George T. Bennett
Alexander (X) Wilber
Daniel Toucey
John W. Quinney, Jr.
Moses (X) Smith
Jasper (X) Bennett

Stephen Gardner
Benjamin (X) Pye, Third
Paul W. Quinney
Levi S. (X) Konkapot
Levi (X) Half Town
Jefferson (X) Half Town
Doc. (X) Big Deer
Jesse M. Jourdon
Joseph L. Chicks
John N. Chicks
Adam Davids
Cornelius Aaron
William Gardner
Jedediah Wilber
Edward (X) Waterman
P. D. Littleman
Dennis T. Turkey
John (X) Lewis
William (X) High Fly

CONSTITUTION AND BY-LAWS OF THE MOHICAN TRIBE OF RED SPRINGS, WIS. (1934)

PREAMBLE

Whereas: The Great Spirit has made his mighty arm bare in the preservation and establishment of a part of the Moh-he-con-neew (known as the Stockbridge and Munsee Tribe) on the western part of the Wolf River bordering the southwest corner of the Menominee Reservation in the State of Wisconsin. Therefore, we the Chiefs, Braves and Warriors of the aforesaid Mohican Tribe being assembled at one new fireplace, at Moh-he-con-neew, now known as Red Springs in the State of Wisconsin, this 13th day of September, 1934, a.d. Having considered that our peculiar situation highly demands combined efforts, in order to more efficiently execute our best intentions and purposes hereinafter enumerated, do hereby voluntarily make, ordain and declare that the following articles shall be considered as articles of our union which shall remain unalterable unless amended by a majority vote.

CONSTITUTION

Article I. Membership:

Section 1. [dropped line in original] where character and qualifications as designated in our by-laws shall render any person ineligible for any membership post of trust or honor, but shall alike be entitled to enjoy the rights, privileges and advantages of the nation.

Section 2. Every member of the age of twenty-one years shall be entitled to vote for national officers herein elective, with the understanding that no female shall be eligible for office such as chief, sub-chief or councilmen, but such may be eligible to hold subordinate offices.

Article II. Offices:

Section 1. The governing body under this Constitution shall be the Tribal Council which shall be composed of, one Chief, one Sub-Chief and three Councilmen, who shall be chosen by ballot by the Mohicans, qualified to vote and twenty-one years of age or over. Sub-ordinate officers shall consist of the following— Secretary and Treasurer, two path-masters, conservation warden, forester and sheriff and any other office that may be created.

Article III. Tribal Council:

Section 1. The powers and duties of the Tribal Council shall include all the purposes expressed in the Preamble to and in this Constitution; all powers now vested in the present Tribal Council by the Act of June 18, 1934 (Pub. 383, 73d. Congress), and acts amendatory thereof or supplemental thereto. In addition to the aforementioned powers, the Tribal Council shall have power

a) To adopt resolutions to effectuate all the purposes of this Constitution.

b) To promulgate the uses and disposition of Tribal property, to protect and to cultivate arts, crafts and culture, to administer charity and to protect the health, security and general welfare of the community.

c) To provide for the appointment of guardians for orphan minor members of the Tribe, to administer tribal or other funds or property which may be transferred or entrusted to the Tribe or Tribal Council by the Federal Government.

d) To create and maintain a Tribal Council Fund by accepting grants or donations from any persons, State or the United States and or by levying assessment of not to exceed one dollar ($1.00) per year per capita on the qualified voters of this Reservation; provided the payment of such per capita levy shall be made before any person shall vote in any election held more than six months after the date of said levy. Any money so collected shall be disposed of as provided in Section 4 of this Article.

Article IV. Meetings:

The annual meeting shall be held on the second Monday in June each year. Special meetings shall be held at any time, at the request of the Tribal Council.

BY-LAWS

Article I. Membership:

1) Any person who is now an enrolled member of the Mohican Tribe and their descendants of one fourth (1/4) or more Indian blood.

2) Any Indian of Stockbridge or Munsee blood who qualifies under the term—Indian—under the Wheeler-Howard bill.

3) Any member of said Stockbridge or Munsee Tribe who hereafter contracts marriage with a member of the Oriental or Negro race will be banished from the Tribe and thereby forfeit all rights in said Tribe.

Article II. Nomination and Election of Officers:

1) A caucus shall be held thirty days before the annual Tribal meeting, the place and time to be designated by the Caucus Committee.

2) The Caucus Committee to be appointed at this time by the Chairman of the Indian Business Committee but hereafter and anon by the Chief of said organized Tribe. All elections are to be held by ballot.

Duties of Officers:

1) Each member of the Tribal Council and each officer, or subordinate officer, elected or appointed hereunder shall take an oath of office prior to assuming the duties thereof, by which oath he shall pledge himself to support and defend the Constitution of the United States and this Constitution and By-Laws.

2) It shall be the duty of the Tribal Council and each member thereof to promote the general welfare of the Mohicans of this Reservation and to carry out the provisions and purposes of this Constitution.

3) It shall be the duty of the Chief to preside over all meetings of the Tribal Council and to carry out all orders of the Tribal Council. All members of the Tribal Council and all subordinate officers shall assist the Chief in all proper ways in carrying out the orders of the Tribal Council. The Chief shall be regarded by the Mohicans of this Reservation in the same manner as were the Chiefs of the Tribe under our old Tribal life and government.

4) The Tribal Secretary shall keep a full record of all proceedings of each regular and special meeting of the Tribal Council and shall perform such other duties of like nature as the Tribal Council shall from time to time by resolution provide. Copies of the minutes of each meeting shall be transmitted by the Secretary to the Tribal Chief, to the Tribal Secretary and to the Tribal Council.

5) The Tribal Treasurer shall be the custodian of all money which comes under the jurisdiction and/or control of the Tribal Council. He shall keep accounts of all receipts and disbursements and shall report the same to the Tribal Council at each regular meeting of the Tribal Council. He shall perform such other similar duties as the Tribal Council shall by resolution from time to time provide. He shall be bonded in such an amount as the Tribal Council shall by resolution provide. The books of the Tribal Treasurer shall be open, at all times, to all of the qualified voters of this Reservation.

6) The subordinate officers of the Tribal Council shall perform such duties as the Tribal Council shall, by resolution from time to time provide.

7) The individuals qualified to vote from and after the ratification and approval of this Constitution and By-Laws shall be as follows: At the first election a qualified voter shall be any Mohican twenty-one years or over, enrolled at Red Springs. At the second and subsequent elections held herein qualified voters shall be the aforesaid class increased by such persons of $1/4$ or more Indian blood, which the Tribal Council, shall have admitted to membership, and such combined classifications shall be diminished by those persons who have failed to pay the levy as provided for by Article III, Section 1, Subsection D.

We, the following adult members of the Mohican Tribe of Red Springs Reservation, in the State of Wisconsin, Shawano County, do hereby propose the within and foregoing as the Constitution and By-Laws of the Mohican Tribe of Red Springs, Wis. We respectfully request the Honorable Secretary of the Interior to call a special election at which the question of ratification of the within and foregoing Constitution and By-Laws shall be submitted to the adult members of this Tribe.

CONSTITUTION AND BY-LAWS OF THE STOCKBRIDGE-MUNSEE COMMUNITY (1937)

CONSTITUTION

Preamble

We, the people of the Stockbridge and Munsee Band of Mohican Indians, grateful to the Great Spirit for his fostering care, in order to reestablish our tribal organization, to conserve and develop our common resources and to promote the welfare of ourselves and our descendants, do ordain and establish this Constitution and By-laws.

Article I—Name

The name of this Community shall be "The Stockbridge-Munsee Community."

Article II—Territory

The jurisdiction of the Stockbridge-Munsee Community shall extend to all lands purchased, heretofore or hereafter, by the United States for the benefit of said Community.

Article III—Membership

SECTION 1. The membership of the Stockbridge-Munsee Community shall be composed of all persons whose names appear on the Stockbridge Allotment Roll of 1910 and who are residing within the original confines of the Stockbridge Reservation, in Shawano County, State of Wisconsin, on the date of the adoption of this Constitution and By-laws.

SEC. 2. Descendants of members of the Community, as provided for in section 1 of this Article, shall be members provided such descendants are of one-fourth or more Stockbridge-Munsee Indian blood and are residing within the original confines of the Stockbridge Reservation on the date of the adoption of this Constitution and By-laws.

SEC. 3. All children of one-fourth or more Indian blood born to members of the Community shall be members; *Provided,* That the parents are residents of the Community on the date of the birth of said child.

SEC. 4. The Tribal Council shall have authority to promulgate ordinances, subject to the approval of the Secretary of the Interior, governing the adoption of new members and loss of membership in the Community.

Article IV—Governing Body

SECTION 1. The governing body of the Stockbridge-Munsee Community shall be a Tribal Council, composed of a President, a Vice-President, a Treasurer and four councilmen, to be elected by popular referendum.

SEC. 2. The officers and councilmen shall be elected as follows: the President and Treasurer shall be elected for a term of two years, the Vice-President and four councilmen shall be elected for a term of one year.

SEC. 3. The Tribal Council shall have authority to appoint a Secretary and such boards and committees as may be deemed necessary.

SEC. 4. Any member of the Stockbridge-Munsee Community is eligible to be elected to the Tribal Council; *Provided,* That he is 25 years of age or over and has maintained a continuous residence in the Community for at least one year immediately preceding his election.

SEC. 5. Any member of the Community who is 21 years of age or over shall be entitled to vote in any election at which he presents himself at the polls on election day during the official voting hours.

SEC. 6. The present Business Committee shall call, hold, and supervise the first Tribal Council election within 60 days after the adoption and approval of this Constitution and By-laws under such rules and regulations as the committee may provide. The Tribal Council shall provide by ordinance, rules and regulations governing the date and manner of holding future elections.

Article V—Removal

SECTION 1. The Tribal Council may, by an affirmative vote of five, expel any member of the Council for neglect of duty or gross misconduct; *Provided,* That the accused shall be given an opportunity to answer any and all charges at a designated Council meeting. The decision of the Tribal Council shall be final.

SEC. 2. The Tribal Council shall fill vacancies in the Council caused by death, removal, resignation, or otherwise, such appointment to be in force and effect until the next annual election.

Article VI—Referendum

Upon a petition of at least 30 per cent of the eligible voters of the Community, any enacted or proposed ordinance, resolution or other regulative act of the Tribal Council shall be submitted to a referendum of the qualified voters of the Community.

Article VII—Powers

SECTION 1. *Enumerated Powers.*-The Tribal Council of the Stockbridge-Munsee Community shall exercise the following powers, subject to any limitations imposed bv the Constitution and laws of the United States and this Constitution and By-laws:

(*a*) To negotiate with the Federal, State, and local governments;

(*b*) To employ legal counsel, the choice of counsel and fixing of fees to be subject to the approval of the Secretary of the Interior;

(*c*) To veto any sale, disposition, lease, or encumbrance of Community lands, interests in lands, or other Community assets;

(*d*) To advise with the Secretary of the Interior with regard to all appropriation estimates or Federal projects for the benefit of the Community prior to the submission of such estimates to the Bureau of the Budget and to Congress;

(*e*) To manage all economic affairs and enterprises of the Community in accordance with the terms of a charter that may be issued to the Community by the Secretary of the Interior;

(*f*) To promulgate and enforce ordinances, subject to the approval of the Secretary of the Interior, governing the conduct of members of the Community; providing for the manner of making, holding, and revoking assignments of land or interests therein; providing for the levying of assessments on members of the Community and the appropriation of available Community funds for public purposes; providing for the licensing of nonmembers coming upon the reservation for purposes of hunting, fishing, trading, or other business, and for the exclusion from the territory of the Community of persons not licensed; and establishing proper agencies for law enforcement in the Community; *Provided,* That no assessments made on the members of the Community shall be effective until ratified by a majority vote in an election called for that purpose in which at least 30 per cent of the qualified voters shall vote.

(*g*) To charter subordinate organizations, subject to the approval of the Secretary of the Interior, for economic purposes and to delegate to such organizations, or to any subordinate boards or officials of the Community any of the foregoing powers, reserving the right to review any action taken by virtue of such delegated power;

(*h*) To adopt resolutions not inconsistent with this Constitution and By-laws, regulating the procedure of the Tribal Council itself and of other agencies; officials, and organizations of the Community.

SEC. 2. *Future Powers.* The Tribal Council may exercise such further powers as may in the future be delegated to the Council by members of the Community, or by the Secretary of the Interior, or any other duly authorized official or agency of the State or Federal Government.

SEC. 3. *Reserved Powers.* Any rights and powers heretofore vested in the Stockbridge and Munsee Band of Mohican Indians, but not expressly referred to in this Constitution, shall not be abridged by this Article, but may be exercised by the Community through the adoption of appropriate by-laws and constitutional amendments.

SEC. 4. Any resolution or ordinance which by the terms of this Constitution, is subject to review by the Secretary of the Interior, shall be presented to the Superintendent of the reservation who shall, within ten days thereafter, approve or disapprove the same.

If the Superintendent shall approve any ordinance or resolution it shall thereupon become effective, but the Superintendent shall transmit a copy of the same, bearing his endorsement, to the Secretary of the Interior, who may, within 90 days from the date of enactment, rescind the said ordinance or resolution for any cause by notifying the tribal council of such rescission.

If the Superintendent shall refuse to approve any ordinance or resolution submitted to him, within ten days after its enactment, he shall advise the Council of his reasons therefore. If these reasons appear to the Council insufficient, it may, by a majority vote, refer the ordinance or resolution to the Secretary of the Interior, who may, within 90 days from the date of its enactment, approve the same in writing, whereupon the said ordinance or resolution shall become effective.

Article VIII—Amendments

This Constitution and By-laws may be amended by a majority vote of the qualified voters of the Community at an election called for that purpose by the Secretary of the Interior; *Provided,* That at least 30 per cent of those entitled to vote shall vote in such election; but no amendment shall become effective until it shall have been approved by the Secretary of the Interior.

It shall be the duty of the Secretary of the Interior to call an election on any proposed amendment upon the receipt of a petition submitted by the Tribal Council, signed by not less than one-third of the qualified voters of the Stockbridge Munsee Community.

BY-LAWS OF THE STOCKBRIDGE-MUNSEE COMMUNITY

Article I—Duties of Officers

SECTION 1. *Duties of the President.*-It shall be the duty of the President to preside over all meetings of the Council and to carry out the orders of the Tribal Council. It shall be the duty of the President to countersign all checks drawn against the funds of the Community by the Treasurer .

SEC. 2. *Duties of the Vice-President.*-The Vice-President shall assist the President when called upon to do so and in the absence of the President, he shall preside.

When so presiding he shall have all the rights, privileges and duties as well as the responsibilities of the President.

SEC. 3. The Secretary shall conduct all correspondence for the Council and shall keep an accurate record of all matters transacted at Council meetings. It shall be his duty to submit promptly to the Superintendent of the jurisdiction copies of all minutes of regular and special meetings of the Council and to perform such other duties as the Council may direct.

SEC. 4. The Treasurer shall accept, receive, receipt for, preserve and safeguard all funds in the custody of the Council, whether they be Community funds or special funds for which the Council is acting as trustee or custodian. He shall deposit all funds in such depository as the Council shall direct and shall make and preserve a faithful record of such funds and shall report on all receipts and expenditures and the amount and nature of all funds in his possession and custody, at each regular meeting of the Tribal Council, and at such other times as requested.

He shall not pay out or otherwise disburse any funds in his possession or custody, except in accordance with a resolution duly passed by the Tribal Council.

The Treasurer shall be required to give a bond satisfactory to the Tribal Council and to the Commissioner of Indian Affairs.

SEC. 5. The duties of all appointive boards or officers shall be clearly defined by resolution at the time of their creation or appointment and such boards and officers shall report to the Tribal Council from time to time as required.

Article II—Meetings

The Tribal Council shall meet semi-annually with members of the Community on the first Saturday of May and November, and at such other times as the Tribal Council may provide by resolution. The Tribal Council is further authorized to hold such other meetings as may be provided by resolution, at which members of the Community may be auditors. The Tribal Council may hold executive sessions but no final decisions on matters before the Council shall be made except at open regular or special meetings.

Article III—Oath Of Office

Each member of the Tribal Council and each officer, or subordinate officer, elected or appointed hereunder, shall take an oath of office prior to assuming the duties thereof, by which oath he shall pledge himself to support and defend the Constitution of the United States and this Constitution and By-laws.

Article IV—Ratification

This Constitution and By-laws, when adopted by a majority vote of the qualified voters of the Stockbridge and Munsee Band of Mohican Indians, voting at a special election called by the Secretary of the Interior, in which at least 30 per cent of those entitled to vote shall vote, shall be submitted to the Secretary of the Interior for his approval, and shall be effective from the date of such approval.

Certification of Adoption

Pursuant to an order, approved October 4, 1937 by the Assistant Secretary of the Interior, the attached Constitution and By-laws was submitted for ratification to the qualified voters of the Stockbridge and Munsee Band of Mohican Indians of Wisconsin, and was on October 30, 1937 duly ratified by a vote of 119 for, and 13 against in an election in which over 30 per cent of those entitled to vote cast their ballots, in accordance with section 16 of the Indian Reorganization Act of June 18, 1934 (48 Stat. 984), as amended by the Act of June 15, 1935 (49 Stat. 378).

Ratified and Unratified Treaties of the Stockbridge-Munsees, 1794–1867

TREATY OF 1794

A treaty between the United States and the Oneida, Tuscorora and Stockbridge Indians, dwelling in the Country of the Oneidas.

WHEREAS, in the late war between Great-Britain and the United States of America, a body of the Oneida and Tuscorora and the Stockbridge Indians, adhered faithfully to the United States, and assisted them with their warriors; and in consequence of this adherence and assistance, the Oneidas and Tuscororas, at an unfortunate period of the war, were driven from their homes, and their houses were burnt and their property destroyed: And as the United States in the time of their distress, acknowledged their obligations to these faithful friends, and promised to reward them: and the United States being now in a condition to fulfil the promises then made: the following articles are stipulated by the respective parties for that purpose; to be in force when ratified by the President and Senate.

ARTICLE I.

The United States will pay the sum of five thousand dollars, to be distributed among individuals of the Oneida and Tuscorora nations, as a compensation for their individual losses and services during the late war between Great-Britain and the United States. The only man of the Kaughnawaugas now remaining in the Oneida country, as well as some few very meritorious persons of the Stockbridge Indians, will be considered in the distribution.

ARTICLE II.

For the general accommodation of these Indian nations, residing in the country of the Oneidas, the United States will cause to be erected a complete grist-mill and saw-mill, in a situation to serve the present principal settlements of these nations. Or if such one convenient situation cannot be found, then the United States will cause to be erected two such grist-mills and saw-mills, in places where it is now known the proposed accommodation may be effected. Of this the United States will judge.

ARTICLE III.

The United States will provide, during three years after the mills shall be completed, for the expense of employing one or two suitable persons to manage the mills, to keep them in repair, to instruct some young men of the three nations in the arts of the miller and sawyer, and to provide teams and utensils for carrying on the work of the mills.

ARTICLE IV.

The United States will pay one thousand dollars, to be applied in building a convenient church at Oneida, in the place of the one which was there burnt by the enemy, in the late war.

ARTICLE V.

In consideration of the above stipulations to be performed on the part of the United States, the Oneida, Tuscorora and Stockbridge Indians afore-mentioned, now acknowledge themselves satisfied, and relinquish all other claims of compensation and rewards for their losses and services in the late war. Excepting only the unsatisfied claims of such men of the said nations as bore commissions under the United States, for any arrears which may be due to them as officers. In witness whereof, the chiefs of those nations, residing in the country of the Oneidas, and Timothy Pickering, agent for the United States, have hereto set their hands and seals, at Oneida, the second day of December, in the year one thousand seven hundred and ninety-four.

Timothy Pickering, [L. S.]

Wolf Tribe:
Odotsaihte, his x mark, [L. S.]
Konnoquenyau, his x mark, [L. S.]
    Head sachems of the Oneidas.
John Skenendo, eldest war chief, his x mark, [L. S.]
    Bear Tribe:
Lodowik Kohsauwetau, his x mark, [L. S.]

Cornelius Kauhiktoton, his x mark, [L. S.]
Thos. Osauhataugaunlot, his x mark, [L. S.]
    War chiefs.

    Turtle Tribe:
Shonohleyo, war chief, his x mark, [L. S.]
Peter Konnauterlook, sachem, his x mark. [L. S.]
Daniel Teouneslees, son of Skenendo, war chief, his x mark, [L. S.]
    Tuscaroras:
Thaulondauwaugon, sachem, his x mark, [L. S.]
Kanatjogh, or Nicholas Cusick, war chief, his x mark, [L. S.]

Witnesses to the signing and sealing of the agent of the United States, and of the
chiefs of the Oneida and Tuscarora nations:
    S. Kirkland,
    James Dean, Interpreter.

Witnesses to the signing and sealing of the four chiefs of the Stockbridge Indians,
whose names are below:
    Saml. Kirkland,
    John Sergeant.
    Stockbridge Indians:
Hendrick Aupaumut, [L. S.]
Joseph Quonney, [L. S.]
John Konkapot, [L. S.]
Jacob Konkapot, [L. S.]

TREATY OF 1821

Articles of a Treaty made and concluded at Green Bay, in the Territory of Michigan,
between Tayhyutaknen, alias John Antony, Tahnonsongotha, alias John Skenadore,
Ononqwatago, alias Cornelius Bread, Iganawty, alias Thomas Christian, of the
Oneida Nation; Yawentanawen, alias Abraham LaFort of the Onondaga Nation;
Dagaoyoseh, alias Jacob James, Harsaongowin, alias George Jamison of the Seneca
Nation; Deputies authorized and empowered to represent an association of the Six
Nations or Tribes of Indians of the State of New York; Eleazer Williams, alias
Onwarenhiaki, a deputy authorized and empowered to represent the St. Regis
Indians of the State of New York; Uhlaunnowaunowaua, alias Solomon U.
Hendricks, Wausaunah, alias Jacob Konkapot; Wenowwaundug, alias Abner
Hendrick, Cheeksoken, alias Jacob Chicks, Naukawate, alias Robert Konkapot,
deputies authorized and empowered to represent the Stockbridge Nation or tribe
of Indians of the State of New York; Rufus Turkey, alias Katakosakont, a deputy

authorized and empowered to represent the Munsee Nation or tribe of Indians; and Chiefs, head men of the Menomini and Winnebago Nations of Indians, residing within the vicinity of Green Bay aforesaid, this Eighteenth day of August in the year One Thousand Eight hundred and twentyone.

Article First. The Menomini and Winnebago Nations of Indians, in consideration of the stipulations herein made on the part of the Six Nations and the St. Regis, Stockbridge and Munsee nations of Indians, do hereby cede release and quit claim, to the people of the said Six Nations and the said St. Regis, Stockbridge and Munsee nations, forever, all the right, title, interest and claim of them, the Menomini and Winnebago nations of Indians to the Lands described by and comprehended within the following boundaries; Viz. Beginning at the foot of the rapids usually called the Grand Kaccalin, on the Fox River; thence running up the said river to the rapids at the Winnebago Lake; and from the river extending back in this width on each side, to the Northwest and to the South East, equidistant with the claims of the said Menomini and Winnebago nations of Indians.

Article Second. The Six Nations and the St. Regis, Stockbridge and Munsee nations of Indians, do promise and agree to and with the Menomini and Winnebago nations of Indians, that they, the Menominis and Winnebagoes shall reserve to themselves, the right to use and occupy a necessary proportion of the Lands herein ceded, for the purpose of hunting, and also the right of fishing: Provided nevertheless, that they the Menominis and Winnebagoes in such use and occupation shall commit no waste or depredation on such Lands as may be under actual improvement by either of the Six Nations or the St. Regis, Stockbridge or Munsee nations.

Article Third. In consideration of the cession aforesaid, the Six Nations, and the St. Regis, Stockbridge and Munsee nations aforesaid do agree to pay to the Menomini and Winnebago nations aforesaid within one year from the date hereof, the sum of fifteen hundred dollars in goods; and they have also given to the said Winnebago and Menomini nations this day, Five Hundred Dollars; the receipt whereof is hereby acknowledged by the said Menomini and Winnebago Nations.

In Testimony Whereof, the said Deputies and the said Chiefs and head Men have hereunto set their hands and seals, at the place & on the day and year aforesaid.

WINNEBAGO CHIEFS

Serachon, his X mark,	or The Smoker
Shokkapon, his X mark,	or Dog's Head
Ochopkan, his X mark,	or Four Legs
Karandull, his X mark,	or The Elk
Hompensnick, his X mark,	or Day Walker
Shonkskonksup, his X mark,	or Black Wolf
Cheaukoo, his X mark,	or Crooked Tail

Chansekp, his X mark,   or Black Deer
Kauhauk, his X mark,   or The Dove

MENOMINI CHIEFS

Eskenanin, his X mark,   or The Young Man
Asekutaw, his X mark,   or The Pine Shooter
Josette Tomas
Weekau, his X mark
Muckoometa, his X mark,   or Bears Fat
The Spaniard, his X mark
Kishcunakenon, his X mark

DEPUTIES

Tahyentakeken, his X mark,   alias John Antony
Tahnonsongotha, his X mark,   alias John Skenadore
Onongwatgo, his X mark,   alias Cornelius Bread
Sganawaaty,   alias Thomas Christian
Yawentanwen, his X mark,   alias Abram LaFort
Dagayoset, his X mark,   alias Jacob Jameson
Hanasongwas, his X mark,   alias George Jameson
Solomon U. Hendricks   alias Ulhaunowausont
Jacob Konkapot   alias Wausaunah
Abner Hendrick, his X mark   alias Wenowonong
Jacob Chicks, his X mark,   alias Cheeksoken
Naukakwan, his X mark,   alias Robert Konkapot
Rufus Turkey, his X mark   alias Katakoskont

Signed, Sealed & Delivered In Presence of

N. Pinkney, Col. 3rd Reg Infy
W. Whistler, Capt, 3rd Reg Infy
Jno Garland, Capt.
S. Cowan, Lt.
M. Irwin, U.S. Factor
Jno W. Johnson, U.S. Factor
Lewis Rouse
J.B.J. Russell, Lt., USA
Charles Trowbridge, Agent of the Deputation

TREATY OF 1822

*Articles of a treaty between the Menomonee Nation of Indians, and the Stockbridge,
Oneida, Tuscarora, St. Regis, and Munsee nations, done at Green Bay in the Michigan
Territory, September 23, 1822.*

ARTICLE I.

The Menomonee nation of Indians, in consideration of the stipulations herein made on the part of the Muhheconnuk or Stockbridge, and the first Christian party of the Oneida, and the Tuscarora, and the St. Regis, and the Munsee nations, do hereby cede, release and quit claim to them, the people of the said Stockbridge, Oneida, Tuscarora, St. Regis, and Munsee nations, forever, all the right, title, interest, and claim of them, the Menomonee nation of Indians, to all the lands and islands comprehended within and described by the following boundaries, viz:

Beginning at the foot of the rapids on Fox river, usually called the Grand Kakalin; thence southeast (or on the lower line for the lands last season ceded by the Menomonee and Winnebago nations of Indians, to the Six Nations, St. Regis, Stockbridge, and Munsee nations) to or equidistant with the Manawahkiah river, emptying into Lake Michigan; thence on an easterly course to and down said river to its mouth; thence northerly, on the boarders of Lake Michigan, to and across the mouth of Green Bay, so as to include all the islands of the Grand Traverse; thence from the mouth of Green Bay, aforesaid, northwesterly course, to a place on the northwest shore of Lake Michigan, generally known and distinguished by the name of Weyohquatonk by the Indians, and Bay de Noque by the French; thence a westerly course, on the height of land separating the waters running unto Lake Superior and those running into Lake Michigan, to the head of the Menomonee river; thence continuing nearly the same course, until it strikes the northeastern boundary line of the lands ceded as aforesaid by the Menomonee and Winnebago nations to the Six Nations, St. Regis, Stockbridge, and Munsee nations of Indians in eighteen hundred and twenty-one; thence southerly to the place of beginning.

ARTICLE II.

The Stockbridge, Oneida, Tuscarora, St. Regis, and Munsee nations aforesaid, do promise and agree to and with the said Menomonees, that they, the said Menomonees, shall have the free permission and privilege of occupying and residing upon the lands herein ceded, in common with them the Stockbridge, Oneida, Tuscarora, St. Regis, and Munsee nations; provided, nevertheless, that they, the Menomonee nation, shall not in any manner infringe upon any settlements or improvements whatever, which may be in any manner made by the said Stockbridge, Oneida, Tuscarora, St. Regis, and Munsee Nations.

ARTICLE III.

The Stockbridge, Oneida, Tuscarora, St. Regis, and Munsee nations, do further promise and agree to and with the said Menomonees, that, according to their request, all the French and other inhabitants who have just and lawful claims to, and are now settled and living upon, any lands herein ceded, shall remain unmolested by them the said Stockbridges, Oneidas, Tuscaroras, St. Regis, or Munsees. It is also expressly understood by the Stockbridge, Oneida, Tuscarora, St. Regis, and Munsee nations, that the Menomonees do not herein cede to them, the Stockbridge, Oneida, Tuscarora, St. Regis, and Munsee nations, any lands in the vicinity of Fort Howard, or near the mouth of Fox River, the title of which may have been heretofore extinguished by the American Government.

ARTICLE IV.

In consideration of the cession herein made by the Menomonees, the Stockbridge and Munsee nations of Indians aforesaid have, by the hands of their deputies, paid to the chiefs and head men of the Menomonee nation, this day, the sum of one thousand dollars in goods, in full of all demands in this treaty on their part, the receipt whereof is hereby acknowledged by the Menomonee nation. And the Oneida, Tuscarora, and St. Regis nations of Indians do promise and agree to and with the Menomonee nation, to pay to them, the Menomonees, the sum of one thousand dollars in one year from the date hereof, and also one thousand dollars in two years from the date hereof—the whole to be paid in goods; which respective sums are to be a full and complete recompense and compensation for the lands hereby ceded, released, and quit claimed to the Stockbridge, Oneida, Tuscarora, St. Regis, and Munsee nations.

In testimony whereof, the said deputies, and the said chiefs and head men, have hereunto set their hands and seals, at the place and on the day and year above written.

TREATY OF 1827

Articles of a treaty made and concluded at the Butte des Morts, on Fox river, in the Territory of Michigan, between Lewis Cass and Thomas L. M'Kenney, Commissioners on the part of the United States, and the Chippewa, Menomonie, and Winebago tribes of Indians.

ARTICLE 1.

Whereas, the southern boundary of the Chippewa country, from the Plover Portage of the Ouisconsin easterly, was left undefined by the treaty concluded at Prairie du Chien, August 19, 1825, in consequence of the non-attendance of some of the principal Menomonie chiefs; and, whereas it was provided by the said treaty, that, whenever the President of the United States might think proper, such of the tribes, parties to the said treaty, as might be interested in any particular line, should be convened, in order to agree upon its establishment; Therefore, in pursuance of the said provision, it is agreed between the Chippewas, Menomonies and Winebagoes, that the southern boundary of the Chippeway country shall run as follows, namely: From the Plover Portage of the Ouisconsin, on a northeasterly course, to a point on Wolf river, equidistant from the Ashawano and Post lakes of said river, thence to the falls of the Pashaytig river of Green Bay; thence to the junction of the Neesau Kootag or Burnt-wood river, with the Menomonie; thence to the big island of the Shoskinaubic or Smooth rock river; thence following the channel of the said river to Green Bay, which it strikes between the little and the great Bay de Noquet.

ARTICLE 2.

Much difficulty having arisen from negotiations between the Menomonie and Winebago tribes and the various tribes and portions of tribes of Indians of the State of New York, and the claims of the respective parties being much contested, as well with relation to the tenure and boundaries of the two tracts, claimed by the said New York Indians, west of Lake Michigan, as to the authority of the persons who signed the agreement on the part of the Menomonies, and the whole subject having been fully examined at the Council this day concluded, and the allegations, proofs, and statements, of the respective parties having been entered upon the Journal of the Commissioners, so that the same can be decided by the President of the United States; it is agreed by the Menomonies and Winebagoes, that so far as respects their interest in the premises, the whole matter shall be referred to the President of the United States, whose decision shall be final. And the President is authorized, on their parts, to establish such boundaries between them and the New York Indians as he may consider equitable and just.

ARTICLE. 3.

It being important to the settlement of Green Bay that definite boundaries should be established between the tract claimed by the former French and British governments, and the lands of the Indians, as well to avoid future disputes as to settle the question of jurisdiction—It is therefore agreed between the Menomonie tribe and the United States, that the boundaries of the said tracts, the jurisdiction and title of which are hereby acknowledged to be in the United States, shall be as follows, namely:—Beginning on the shore of Green Bay, six miles due north from the parallel of the mouth of Fox river, and running thence in a straight line, but with the general course of the said river, and six miles therefrom to the intersection of the continuation of the westerly boundary of the tract at the Grand Kaukaulin, claimed by Augustin Grignion; thence on a line with the said boundary to the same; thence with the same to Fox river; thence on the same course, six miles; thence in a direct line to the southwestern boundary of the tract, marked on the plan of the claims at Green Bay, as the settlement at the bottom of the Bay; thence with the southerly boundary of the said tract to the southeasterly corner thereof; and thence with the easterly boundary of the said tract to Green Bay. Provided, that if the President of the United States should be of opinion that the boundaries thus established interfere with any just claims of the New York Indians, the President may then change the said boundaries in any manner he may think proper, so that the quantity of land contained in the said tract be not greater than by the boundaries herein defined. And provided also, that nothing herein contained shall be construed to have any effect upon the land claims at Green Bay; but the same shall remain as though this treaty had not been formed.

ARTICLE. 4.

In consideration of the liberal establishment of the boundaries as herein provided for, the Commissioners of the United States have this day caused to be distributed among the Indians, goods to the amount of fifteen thousand six hundred and eighty-two dollars, payment for which shall be made by the United States.

ARTICLE. 5.

The sum of one thousand dollars shall be annually appropriated for the term of three years; and the sum of fifteen hundred dollars shall be annually thereafter appropriated as long as Congress think proper, for the education of the children of the tribes, parties hereto, and of the New York Indians, to be expended under the direction of the President of the United States.

ARTICLE. 6.

The United States shall be at liberty, notwithstanding the Winebagoes are parties to this treaty, to pursue such measures as they may think proper for the punishment of the perpetrators of the recent outrages at Prairie du Chien, and upon the Mississippi, and for the prevention of such acts hereafter.

ARTICLE. 7.

This treaty shall be obligatory after its ratification by the President and Senate of the United States.

Done at the Butte des Morts, on Fox river, in the Territory of Michigan, this eleventh day of August, 1827.

TREATY OF 1831

WHEREAS certain articles of agreement were entered into and concluded at the city of Washington, on the 8th day of February instant, between the undersigned, Commissioners on behalf of the United States, and the chiefs and warriors, representing the Menomonee tribe of Indians, whereby a portion of the Menomonee country, on the northwest side of Fox river and Green bay, was ceded to the United States, for the benefit of the New York Indians, upon certain conditions and restrictions therein expressed: And whereas it has been represented to the parties to that agreement, who are parties hereto, that it would be more desirable and satisfactory to some of those interested that one or two immaterial changes be made in the *first* and *sixth* articles, so as not to limit the number of acres to one hundred for each soul who may be settled upon the land when the President apportions it, as also to make unlimited the time of removal and settlement upon these lands by the New York Indians, but to leave both these matters discretionary with the President of the United States.

Now, therefore, as a proof of the sincerity of the professions made by the Menomonee Indians, when they declared themselves anxious to terminate in an amicable manner, their disputes with the New York Indians, and also as a further proof of their love and veneration for their great father, the President of the United States, the undersigned, representatives of the Menomonee tribe of Indians, unite and agree with the Commissioners aforesaid, in making and acknowledging the following supplementary articles a part of their former aforesaid agreement.

First. It is agreed between the undersigned, commissioners on behalf of the United States, and the chiefs and warriors representing the Menomonee tribe of Indians, that, for the reasons above expressed, such parts of the *first* article of the agreement, entered into between the parties hereto, on the eighth instant, as limits the removal and settlement of the New York Indians upon the lands therein provided for their future homes, to three years, shall be altered and amended, so as to read as follows: That the President of the United States shall prescribe the time for the removal and settlement of the New York Indians upon the lands thus provided for them; and, at the expiration of such reasonable time, he shall apportion the land among the actual settlers, in such manner as he shall deem equitable and just. And if, within such reasonable time, as the President of the United States shall prescribe for that purpose, the New York Indians, shall refuse to accept the provisions made for their benefit, or having agreed, shall neglect or refuse to remove from New York, and settle on the said lands, within the time prescribed for that purpose, that then, and in either of these events, the lands aforesaid shall be, and remain the property of the United States, according to said *first* article, excepting so much thereof, as the President shall deem justly due to such of the New York Indians, as shall actually have removed to, and settled on the said lands.

Second. It is further agreed that the part of the sixth article of the agreement aforesaid, which requires the removal of those of the New York Indians, who may not be settled on the lands at the end of three years, shall be so amended as to leave such removal discretionary with the President of the United States. The Menomonee Indians having full confidence, that, in making his decision, he will take into consideration the welfare and prosperity of their nation.

Done and signed at Washington, this 17th of February, 1831.

John H. Eaton, [L. S.]
S. C. Stambaugh, [L. S.]
Kaush-kau-no-naive, his x mark, [L. S.]
A-ya-mah-taw, his x mark, [L. S.]
Ko-ma-ni-kin, his x mark, [L. S.]

Ko-ma-ni-kee-no-shah, his x mark, [L. S.]
O-ho-pa-shah, his x mark, [L. S.]
Ah-ke-ne-pa-weh, his x mark, [L. S.]
Shaw-wan-noh, his x mark, [L. S.]
Mash-ke-wet, his x mark, [L. S.]
Pah-she-nah-sheu, his x mark, [L. S.]
Chi-mi-na-na-quet, his x mark, [L. S.]
A-na-quet-to-a-peh, his x mark, [L. S.]
Sha-ka-cho-ka-mo, his x mark, [L. S.]

Signed in presence of—

R. A. Forsyth,
C. A. Grignon,
Law. L. V. Kleeck,
John T. Mason,
P. G. Randolph,
A. G. Ellis.

[NOTE.—"This treaty was ratified with the following Proviso contained in the Resolution of the Senate:
Provided, That for the purpose of establishing the rights of the New York Indians, on a permanent and just footing, the said treaty shall be ratified with the express understanding that two townships of land on the east side of the Winnebago lake, equal to forty-six thousand and eighty acres shall be laid off, (to commence at some point to be agreed on,) for the use of the Stockbridge and Munsee tribes; and that the improvements made on the lands now in the possession of the said tribes, on the east side of the Fox river, which said lands are to be relinquished, shall, after being valued by a commissioner to be appointed by the President of the United States, be paid for by the Government: *Provided*, however, that the valuation of such improvements shall not exceed the sum of twenty-five thousand dollars; and that there shall be one township of land, adjoining the foregoing, equal to twenty-three thousand and forty acres, laid off and granted for the use of the Brothertown Indians, who are to be paid, by the Government the sum of one thousand six hundred dollars for the improvements on the lands now in their possession, on the east side of Fox river, and which lands are to be relinquished by said Indians: Also, that a new line shall be run, parallel to the southwestern boundary line, or course of the tract of five hundred thousand acres described in the first article of this treaty, and set apart for the New York Indians, to commence at a point on the west side of the Fox river, and one mile above the Grand Shute on Fox river, and at a sufficient distance from the said boundary line as established by the said first article, as shall comprehend the additional quantity of two hundred thousand acres of land, on and along the west side of Fox river, without including any of the

confirmed private land claims on the Fox river, and which two hundred thousand acres shall be a part of the five hundred thousand acres intended to be set apart for the Six Nations of the New York Indians and the St. Regis tribe; and that an equal quantity to that which is added on the southwestern side shall be taken off from the northeastern side of the said tract, described in that article, on the Oconto Creek, to be determined by a Commissioner, to be appointed by the President of the United States; so that the whole number of acres to be granted to the Six Nations, and St. Regis tribe of Indians, shall not exceed the quantity originally stipulated by the treaty."]

WHEREAS articles of agreement between the United States of America, and the Menominee Indians, were made and concluded at the city of Washington, on the eighth day of February A. D. one thousand eight hundred and thirty-one, by John H. Eaton, and Samuel C. Stambaugh, Commissioners on the part of the United States, and certain Chiefs and Headmen of the Menominee Nation, on the part of said nation; to which articles, an addition or supplemental article was afterwards made, on the seventeenth day of February in the same year, by which the said Menominee Nation agree to cede to the United States certain parts of their land; and that a tract of country therein defined shall be set apart for the New York Indians. All which with the many other stipulations therein contained will more fully appear, by reference to the same. Which said agreements thus forming a *Treaty*, were laid before the Senate of the United States during their then session: but were not at said session acted on by that body. Whereupon a further agreement was on the fifteenth day of March, in the same year, entered into for the purpose of preserving the provisions of the treaty, made as aforesaid; by which it was stipulated that the said articles of agreement, concluded as aforesaid, should be laid before the next Senate of the United States, at their ensuing session; and if sanctioned and confirmed by them, that each and every article thereof should be as binding and obligatory upon the parties respectively, as if they had been sanctioned at the previous session. *And whereas* the Senate of the United States, by their resolution of the twenty-fifth day of June, one thousand eight hundred and thirty-two, did advise and consent to accept, ratify and confirm the same, and every clause and article thereof upon the *conditions* expressed in the proviso, contained in their said resolution: which proviso is as follows: "Provided that for the purpose of establishing the rights of the New York Indians, on a permanent and just footing, the said treaty shall be ratified, with the express understanding that two townships of land on the east side of Winnebago Lake, equal to forty-six thousand and eighty acres shall be laid off (to commence at some point to be agreed on) for the use of the Stockbridge and Munsee tribes; and that the improvements made on the lands now in the possession of the said tribes on the east side of the Fox river, which said lands are to be relinquished shall, after being valued by a commissioner to be appointed by the President of the United States, be paid for by the Government: Provided, however, that the valuation of such improvements shall not exceed the sum of twenty-five thousand dollars. And that there shall be one township of land adjoining the foregoing, equal to twenty-three thousand and forty acres laid off and granted for the use of the Brothertown Indians, who are to be paid by the Government the sum of one thousand six hundred dollars for the improvements on lands now in their possession, on the east side of Fox river, and which lands are to be relinquished by said Indians: also that a new line shall be run, parallel to the southwestern boundary line or course of the tract of five hundred thousand acres, described in the first article of this treaty, and set apart for the New York Indians, to commence at a point on the west side of the Fox river, and one mile above the Grand Shute, on Fox river, and at a sufficient distance from the said boundary line as established by the said first article, as shall comprehend the additional quantity of two hundred thousand acres of land on and along the west side of Fox river, without including any of the confirmed private land claims on the Fox river; and which two hundred thousand acres shall be a part of the five hundred thousand acres, intended to be set apart for the Six Nations of the New York Indians and the St. Regis tribe; and that an equal quantity to that which is added to the southwestern side shall be taken off from the northeastern side of the said tract described in that article, on the Oconto creek, to be determined by a commissioner to be appointed by the President of the United States; so that the whole number of acres to be granted to the Six Nations, and St. Regis tribe of Indians, shall not exceed the quantity originally stipulated by the treaty." And whereas, before the treaty afore-said, *conditionally* ratified, according to the proviso to the resolution of the Senate, above recited, could be obligatory upon the said Menominee nation, their assent to the same must be had and obtained.

And whereas the honorable Lewis Cass, Secretary of the Department of War, by his letter of instructions of the eleventh day of September, A.D. 1832, did authorize and request George B. Porter, Governor of the Territory of Michigan, to proceed to Green Bay, and endeavor to procure the assent of the Menominees to the change proposed by the Senate, as above set forth; urging the necessity of directing his first efforts to an attempt to procure the unconditional assent of the Menominees to the said treaty, as ratified by the Senate. But should he fail in this object that he would then endeavor to procure their assent to the best practicable terms, short of those proposed by the Senate; giving them to understand that he merely received such proposition as they might make, with a view to transmit it for the consideration of the President and Senate of the United States. And if this course became necessary that it would be very desirable that the New York Indians should also signify their acceptance of the modifications required by the Menominees.

And whereas, in pursuance of the said instructions the said George B. Porter proceeded to Green Bay and having assembled all the chiefs and headmen of the Menominee nation, in council, submitted to them, on the twenty-second day of October A.D. one thousand eight hundred and thirty-two, the said proviso annexed to the resolution aforesaid of the Senate of the United States, for the ratification of the said treaty: and advised and urged on them the propriety of giving their assent to the same. And the said chiefs and headmen having taken time to deliberate and reflect on the proposition so submitted to them, and which they had been urged to assent to, did in the most positive and decided manner, refuse to give their assent to the same. (The many reasons assigned for this determination, by them, being reported in the journal of the said commissioner, which will be transmitted with this agreement.)

And whereas after failing in the object last stated, the said George B. Porter endeavored to procure the assent of the said chiefs and headmen of the Menominee nation to the best practicable terms short of those proposed by the Senate of the United States; and after much labor and pains, entreaty and persuasion, the said Menominees consented to the following, as the modifications which they would make; and which are reduced to writing, in the form of an agreement, as the best practicable terms which could be obtained from them, short of those proposed by the Senate of the United States, which they had previously positively refused to accede to. And as the modifications so made and desired, have been acceded to by the New York Indians, with a request that the treaty thus modified might be ratified and approved by the President and the Senate of the United States, it is the anxious desire of the Menominees also, that the treaty, with these alterations may be ratified and approved without delay, that they may receive the benefits and advantage secured to them by the several stipulations of the said treaty, of which they have so long been deprived.

The following is the article of agreement made between the said George B. Porter, commissioner on the part of the United States, specially appointed as aforesaid, and the said Menominee nation, through their chiefs and headmen on the part of their nation.

FIRST. The said chiefs and headmen of the Menominee nation of Indians do not object to any of the matters contained in the proviso annexed to the resolution of the Senate of the United States, so far as the same relate to the granting of three townships of land on the east side of Winnebago Lake, to the Stockbridge, Munsee and Brothertown tribes; to the valuation and payment for their improvements, &c. (ending with the words "*and which lands are to be relinquished by said Indians.*") They therefore assent to the same.

SECOND. The said chiefs and headmen of the Menominee nation of Indians, objecting to all the matters contained in the said proviso annexed to the resolution of the Senate of the United States, so far as the same relate to the running of a new line parallel to the southwestern boundary line or course of the tract of five hundred thousand acres, described in the first article of the treaty, and set apart for the New York Indians, to commence at a point on the southwestern side of Fox river, and one mile above the Grand Shute, on Fox river, and at a sufficient distance from the said boundary line, as established by the said first article, as shall comprehend the additional quantity of two hundred thousand acres of land, on and along the west side of the Fox river, without including any of the confirmed private land claims, on the Fox river, to compose a part of the five hundred thousand acres intended to be set apart for the Six Nations of the New York Indians and St. Regis tribe, *agree* in lieu of this proposition, to set off a like quantity of two hundred thousand acres as follows: The said Menominee nation hereby agree to cede for the benefit of the New York Indians along the southwestern boundary line of the present five hundred thousand acres described in the first article of the treaty as set apart for the New York Indians, a tract of land; bounded as follows. Beginning on the said treaty line, at the old mill dam on Fox river, and thence extending up along Fox river to the little *Rapid Croche*; from thence running a northwest course three miles; thence on a line running parallel with the several courses of Fox river, and three miles distant from the river, until it will intersect a line, running on a northwest course, commencing at a point one mile above the Grand Shute; thence on a line running northwest, so far as will be necessary to include, between the said last line and the line described as the southwestern boundary line of the five hundred thousand acres in the treaty aforesaid, the quantity of two hundred thousand acres; and thence running northeast until it will intersect the line, forming the southwestern boundary line aforesaid; and from thence along the said line to the old mill dam, or place of beginning, containing two hundred thousand acres. Excepting and reserving therefrom the *privilege* of Charles A. Grignon, for erecting a mill on Apple creek, &c., as approved by the Department of War on the twenty-second day of April one thousand eight hundred and thirty-one and all confirmed private land claims on the Fox river. The lines of the said tract of land so granted to be run, marked and laid off without delay, by a commissioner to be appointed by the President of the United States. And that in exchange for the above, a quantity of land equal to that which is added to the southwestern side shall be taken off from the northeastern side of the said tract, described in that article, on the Oconto creek, to be run, marked and determined by the commissioner to be appointed by the President of the United States, as aforesaid, so that the whole number of acres to be granted to the Six Nations and St. Regis tribe of Indians, shall not exceed the quantity of five hundred thousand acres.

THIRD. The said chiefs and headmen of the Menominee nation agree, that in case the said original treaty, made as aforesaid, and the supplemental articles thereto, be ratified and confirmed at the ensuing session of the Senate of the United States, with the modifications contained in this agreement, that each and every article thereof shall be as binding and obligatory upon the parties respectively, as if they had been sanctioned at the times originally agreed upon.

In consideration of the above voluntary sacrifices of their interest, made by the said Menominee nation, and as evidence of the good feeling of their great father, the President of the United States, the said George B. Porter commissioner as aforesaid, has delivered to the said chiefs, headmen, and the people of the said Menominee nation here assembled, presents in clothing to the amount of one thousand dollars: five hundred bushels of corn, ten barrels of pork, and ten barrels of flour, &c. &c.

In witness whereof, we have hereunto set our hands and seals, at the Agency House, at Green Bay, this twenty-seventh day of October, in the year of our Lord one thousand eight hundred and thirty-two.

G. B. Porter, Commissioner of the United States, [L. S.]
Kausk-kan-no-naive, grizzly bear, his x mark, [L. S.]
Osh-rosh, the brave, (by his brother fully empowered to act,) [L. S.]
Osh-ke-e-na-neur, the young man, his x mark, [L. S.]
A-ya-mah-ta, fish spawn, his x mark, [L. S.]
Pe-wait-enaw, rain, his x mark, [L. S.]
Che-na-po-mee, one that is looked at, his x mark, [L. S.]
Ko-ma-ni-kin, big wave, his x mark, [L. S.]
Ke-shee-a-quo-teur, the flying cloud, his x mark, [L. S.]
Wain-e-saut, one who arranges the circle, (by his son, Wa-kee-che-on-a-peur,) his x mark, [L. S.]
Ke-shoh, the sun, (by his son, A-pa-ma-chao, shifting cloud,) his x mark, [L. S.]
Ma-concee-wa-be-no-chee, bear's child, his x mark, [L. S.]
Wa-bose, the rabbit, his x mark, [L. S.]
Shaw-e-no-ge-shick, south sky, his x mark, [L. S.]
Ac-camut, the prophet, his x mark, [L. S.]
Mas-ka-ma-gee, his x mark, [L. S.]
Sho-ne-on, silver, his x mark, [L. S.]
Maw-baw-so, pale color, his x mark, [L. S.]
Paw-a ko-neur, big soldier, (by his representative, Che-kaw-mah-kee-shen,) his x mark, [L. S.]

Sealed and delivered, in the presence of—
George Boyd, United States Indian agent,
Charles A. Grignon, interpreter,
Samuel Abbott,
Joshua Boyer, secretary,
James M. Boyd,
Richard Pricket, his x mark, interpreter,
Henry S. Baird,
R. A. Forsyth, paymaster U.S. Army,
B. B. Kercheval,
Ebenezer Childs.

TREATY OF 1832

To all to whom these presents shall come, the undersigned, Chiefs and Headmen of the sundry tribes of New York Indians, (as set forth in the specifications annexed to their signatures,) send greeting:

WHEREAS a tedious, perplexing and harassing dispute and controversy have long existed between the Menominee nation of Indians and the New York Indians, more particularly known as the Stockbridge, Munsee and Brothertown tribes, the Six Nations and St. Regis tribe. The treaty made between the said Menominee nation, and the United States, and the conditional ratification thereof by the Senate of the United States, being stated and set forth in the within agreement, entered into between the chiefs and headmen of the said Menominees, and George B. Porter, Governor of Michigan, commissioner specially appointed, with instructions referred to in the said agreement. And whereas the undersigned are satisfied, and believe that the best efforts of the said commissioner were directed and used to procure, if practicable, the unconditional assent of the said Menominees to the change proposed by the Senate of the United States in the ratification of the said treaty: but without success. And whereas the undersigned further believe that the terms stated in the within agreement are the best practicable terms, short of those proposed by the Senate of the United States, which could be obtained from the said Menominees; and being asked to signify our acceptance of the modifications proposed as aforesaid by the Menominees, we are compelled, by a sense of duty and propriety to say that we do hereby accept of the same. So far as the tribes to which we belong are concerned, we are perfectly satisfied, that the treaty should be ratified on the terms proposed by the Menominees. We further believe that the tract of land which the Menominees in the within agreement, are willing to cede, in exchange for an equal quantity on the northeast side of the tract of five hundred thousand acres contains a sufficient quantity of good land, favorably and advantageously situated, to answer all the wants of the New York Indians, and St. Regis tribe. For the purpose, then, of putting an end to strife, and that we may all sit down in peace and harmony, we thus signify our acceptance of the modifications proposed by the Menominees: and we most respectfully request that the treaty as now modified by the agreement this day entered into with the Menominees, may be ratified and approved by the President and Senate of the United States.

In witness whereof, we have hereunto set our hands and seals, at the Agency House at Green Bay, this twenty-seventh day of October, in the year of our Lord one thousand eighteen hundred and thirty-two.

G. B. Porter, commissioner on behalf of the United States, [L. S.]

For, and on behalf of, the Stockbridges and Munsees:

John Metoxen, [L. S.]

John W. Quinny, [L. S.]

Austin Quinny, [L. S.]

Jacob Chicks, [L. S.]

Robert Konkopa, his x mark, [L. S.]

Thos. J. Hendrick, [L. S.]

Benjamin Palmer, his x mark, [L. S.]

Sampson Medyard, [L. S.]
Capt. Porter, his x mark, [L. S.]
   For, and on behalf of, the Brothertowns:
William Dick, [L. S.]
Daniel Dick, [L. S.]
Elcanah Dick, his x mark, [L. S.]
   For, and on behalf of, the Six Nations and St. Regis tribe:
Daniel Bread, [L. S.]
John Anthony Brant, his x mark, [L. S.]
Henry Powles, his x mark, [L. S.]
Nathaniel Neddy, his x mark, [L. S.]
Cornelius Stevens, his x mark, [L. S.]
Thomas Neddy, his x mark, [L. S.]

Sealed, and delivered, in the presence of—
George Boyd, United States Indian agent,
R. A. Forsyth, paymaster U. S. Army,
Charles A. Grignon, interpreter,
Samuel Abbott,
Joshua Boyer, secretary,
B. B. Kercheval,
Eben. Childs,
Henry S. Baird,
Peter B. Grignon,
Hanson Johnson,
James M. Boyd,
Richard Pricket, his x mark, interpreter.

1836 UNRATIFIED SCHERMERHORN TREATY

Articles of a Treaty, made and concluded at Green Bay, Wisconsin Territory, September 19, 1836 by John F. Schermerhorn, Commissioner on the part of the United States, and the Chiefs and head men of the Stockbridge and Munsee Tribes of Indians, interested in the Lands, on Winnebago Lake, provided for them in the Menomonee Treaty of February 1831 and assented to by them October 27 1832 and who now reside on Winnebago Lake, and those that are still in the State of New York.

Article First. The chiefs and head men of the said Stockbridge & Munsee Tribes of Indians, whose names are hereunto annexed, in behalf of their people, hereby cede, relinquish, & convey to the United States, all their right, title and interest, of and to their lands on the East side of Winnebago Lake, as provided for them in the aforesaid Treaty, for and in consideration of the Covenants, stipulations and provisions contained in the several articles of this Treaty, on the part of the United States.

Article Second. The United States, in consideration of the above Cession, hereby covenant and agree to dispose of and sell the lands above ceded, for the benefit of the Stockbridge and Munsee Tribes of Indians; and after the deducting from the avails thereof, the actual expenses incurred by the United States, in the survey and sales attending the same. And such reasonable sums for the lands assigned to them by this Treaty for their future homes as the President may see fit to fix upon it (should the Senate of the United States require it) then the nett avails shall be disposed of as follows.

First. The Lots and improvements of each individual of the Tribe shall be valued by the Commissioner to be appointed by the President of the United States for that purpose and the fair and just value of the same shall be allowed and paid to the respective owners thereof. The Lot and improvements for the Mission to go to the A.B.C.F.M. who are now in possession of the same.

Second. A sufficient sum is hereby set apart for the removal and subsistence of the whole of said Tribes of Stockbridge and Munsee Indians and for their subsistence for one year after their arrival at their new homes provided for them, by this Treaty.

Third. The sum of Twenty Thousand ($20,000) dollars shall be and hereby is set apart and allowed to enumerate the Stockbridge Tribe for the monies laid out, and expended by said Tribe, and for the services rendered by their Chiefs and Agents in securing the title to these lands, and removal to the Country, the same to be examined and determined and paid out to the several Claimants by the Commissioner and Chiefs as may be deemed by them most equitable and just. The remainder of the nett avails shall be invested by the United States in some safe and productive stock or corporate company in the State of New York, and the interest thereof to be paid to the Chiefs of the Tribe to be applied by them in such manner as may be for the best interest of the Tribes. Whenever either of these Tribes or any portion of them are ready to remove after having selected new homes they shall be furnished with the means for removal by the United States and for their one years subsistence to be reimbursed out of the sales of their lands and any Chief who removes his Tribe or any party not less than 100 persons shall be allowed & paid $500 for his services.

Article Third. This Treaty is on the Express Condition, that the Stockbridge and Munsee Tribes of Indians shall have the privilege first to go and examine the Indian Country Southwest of the Missouri River, at the expense of the United States, and it the aforesaid country, to suit them which has not already been ceded by the United States to any other Tribe of Indians, and if the same equal to two Townships shall be conveyed to said Stockbridge and Munsee Tribes by Patent from the President of the United States according to the provisions of the act of Congress of June 1830. Then this Treaty shall be obligatory upon the Stockbridge and Munsee Tribes of Indians in all respects and in every part and article of the same.

But if upon such examination they cannot find a Country to suit themselves, that then it is expressly understood and agreed that only the East half of the said tract on Winnebago Lake is hereby ceded to the United States and the remaining half shall be held by them in common, but the Munsees shall not be permitted to sell or relinquish their right to the United States without the consent of the Stockbridge Indians, and in the event of the sale of the remaining half the Munsees shall be entitled to a share of the same in proportion to their relative numbers in amount to be invested or divided for the benefit of the whole. If one township only shall be conveyed to the United States then Eight Thousand dollars shall be set apart and is hereby appropriated out of the resources arriving from the sale of the same for the removal of the Munsee Tribe of Indians from the State of New York, and their subsistence one year on their removal to the Indian Country South West of the said Missouri and the balance shall be paid to the Stockbridge Indians according to the third item in the second article of this Treaty.

Article Fourth. Since it is the desire of the Stockbridge Indians, that their lands shall be sold to the best advantage for their tribe. It is therefore stipulated and agreed by the United States, that a special Commissioner shall be appointed by the President by and with the advise and consent of the Senate of the United States, who is hereby authorized to sell and dispose of said lands in any quantity or quantities at public or private sale as may be deemed best for the interest of said Tribe. Providing, however, that the same shall not be sold for less than the Minimum Congress price. It is understood that the said Stockbridge Indians do accept of a country South West of the Missouri River, that then they will remove in two years from the ratification of this Treaty. And if the whole of the lands at that time are not disposed of at public or private sale by the Consent of the Chiefs and head men of the Stockbridge Tribe of Indians the whole shall be disposed of at public or private sale on such terms as may be deemed best for their interest and the said Commissioner shall also superintend their removal and make all the necessary disbursements and pay all the Claims under the provisions of this Treaty and make an account of the same, both to the Government of the United States, and to the Chiefs of the said Stockbridge and Munsee Tribes of Indians. And it is also understood & agreed that no preemption rights shall be granted by Congress on any of these lands.

Article Fifth. Perpetual peace and friendship shall exist between the United States and the said Stockbridge and Munsee Tribes of Indians and the United States hereby guarantee to protect and defend them in the peaceable enjoyment of their new homes and hereby secure to them the right in their new country to establish their own Government, appoint their own officers & make and administer their own laws and regulations, subject however to such Legislation of the Congress of the United States for regulating trade and intercourse among the Indians as they may deem necessary and proper. The lands secured to the Stockbridge and Munsee Tribes of Indians under this Treaty shall never be included within any State or Territory of this Union, without their consent, and they shall also be entitled to all the rights and privileges secured to any Tribe or Emigrant Indians settled in said Territory.

Article Sixth. This Treaty when approved and ratified by the President and Senate of the United States shall be binding on the respective parties.

In testimony whereof the said John F. Schermerhorn and the Chiefs and headmen of the Stockbridge and Munsee Tribes of Indians have hereunto set their hands and seals, the day and year above written.

J. F. Schermerhorn

In the presence of

George Boyd, U.S. Indian Agent
R. S. Settler, Surgeon, U.S. Army
John S. Arndt
John Mextoxen
Austin Quinney

In the presence of

Cutting Marsh	Jacob Chicks
M. L. Martin	T. Jourdan
W. L. Newberry	John W. Quinney
W. B. Slaughter	Hendrick Aupaumut
M. M. McCarthy	Jacob (his X mark) Davids
A. G. Ellis	Jonas (his X mark) Thompson
D. Giddings	Joseph M. Quinney
	Simon S. Metoxen
	Capt. (his X mark) Porter

The aforesaid treaty having been drafted & explained by J. F. Schermerhorn as commissioner. It is hereby expected to be agreed unto, in all its provisions and stipulations, in the presence of John C. Brodhead Commissioner of the State of New York, on behalf of the Munsees now residing in the State of New York. Oct. 15, 1836.

In the presence of John (his X mark) Wilson

J. C. Brodhead
George Turkey interpreter

TREATY OF 1839

Articles of a treaty made at Stockbridge in the Territory of Wisconsin, on the third day of September in the year of our Lord one thousand eight hundred and thirty-nine, between the United States of America, by their commissioner Albert Gallup, and the Stockbridge and Munsee tribes of Indians, who reside upon Lake Winnebago in the territory of Wisconsin.

ARTICLE 1.

The Stockbridge and Munsee tribes of Indians (formerly of New York) hereby cede and relinquish to the United States, the east half of the tract of forty-six thousand and eighty acres of land, which was laid off for their use, on the east side of Lake Winnebago, in pursuance of the treaty made by George B. Porter commissioner on the part of the United States, and the Menominee nation of Indians, on the twenty-seventh day of October eighteen hundred and thirty-two. The said east half hereby ceded, to contain twenty-three thousand and forty acres of land; to be of equal width at the north and south ends, and to be divided from the west half of said tract of forty-six thousand and eighty acres, by a line to be run parallel to the east line of said tract. The United States to pay therefor, one dollar per acre at the time and in the manner hereinafter provided.

ARTICLE 2.

Whereas a portion of said tribes, according to a census or roll taken, and hereunto annexed, are desirous to remove west and the others to remain where they now are; and whereas the just proportion of the emigrating party in the whole tract of forty-six thousand and eighty acres is eight thousand seven hundred and sixty-seven and three-fourths acres of land; it is agreed that the United States pay to the said emigrating party, the sum of eight thousand seven hundred and sixty-seven dollars and seventy-five cents, as a full compensation for all their interest in the lands held by the party who remain, as well as in the lands hereby ceded to the United States.

ARTICLE 3.

Whereas the improvements of the emigrating party are all on that part of the original tract which is reserved and still held by the party who remain in Stockbridge, and it is but equitable that those who remain should pay those who emigrate for such improvements; it is agreed that the United States shall pay to the emigrating party the sum of three thousand eight hundred and seventy-nine dollars and thirty cents, the appraised value of said improvements; and it is hereby agreed and expressly understood, that the monies payable to the emigrating party shall be distributed among the heads of families according to the schedule hereunto annexed, the whole amount to be paid to the emigrating party under this and the preceding article being the sum of twelve thousand six hundred and forty-seven dollars and five cents.

ARTICLE 4.

The balance of the consideration money for the lands hereby ceded, (after deducting the sums mentioned in the second and third articles,) amounting to the sum of ten thousand three hundred and ninety-two dollars and ninety-five cents, is to be paid to, and invested for the benefit of such of the Stockbridge and Munsee tribes of Indians (numbering three hundred and forty-two souls) as remain at their present place of residence at Stockbridge on the east side of Winnebago lake, as follows. Six thousand dollars of said sum to be invested by the United States in public stocks at an interest of not less than five per cent. per annum as a permanent school fund; the interest of which shall be paid annually to the sachem and counsellors of their tribes, or such other person as they may appoint to receive the same, whose receipt shall be a sufficient voucher therefor; and the balance thereof amounting to four thousand three hundred and ninety-two dollars and ninety-five cents, shall be paid to the said sachem and counsellors, or to such person as they may appoint to receive the same, whose receipt shall be a sufficient voucher therefor.

ARTICLE 5.

The monies herein secured to be paid by the United States to the Stockbridge and Munsee tribes amounting in all to twenty-three thousand and forty dollars, are to be paid in manner aforesaid, in one year from the date hereof, or sooner if practicable.

ARTICLE 6.

It is agreed that an exploring party not exceeding three in number may visit the country west, if the Indians shall consider it necessary, and that whenever those who are desirous of emigrating shall signify their wish to that effect, the United States will defray the expenses of their removal west of the Mississippi and furnish them with subsistence for one year after their arrival at their new homes. The expenses of the exploring party to be borne by the emigrants.

ARTICLE 7.

Whereas there are certain unliquidated claims and accounts existing between the emigrating party, and those who remain where they now are, which it is now impossible to liquidate and adjust; it is hereby agreed that the same shall be submitted to the agent of the United States who shall be appointed to make the payments under this treaty, and that his decision shall be final thereon.

In witness whereof we have hereunto set our hands and seals this third day of September in the year of our Lord one thousand eight hundred and thirty-nine.

Albert Gallup,
Commissioner on the part of the United States.

Austin E. Quinny, Sachem,
Thomas T. Hendrick,
John Metoxen,

Jacob Chicks,
Robert Konkapot,
Captain Porter, Munsee chief,
James Rain, Munsee war chief.
  Stockbridges:
Timothy Jourdan,
Benjamin Palmer,
Jno. N. Chicks,
Jno. W. Quinney,
John P. Quinney,
John W. Newcom,
Thomas S. Branch,
Levi Konkapot,
John Littlemon,
Peter Sherman,
J. L. Chicks.
  Munsee:
John Killsnake.
  Stockbridges:
Jeremiah Singerland,
Jonas Thompson,
Eli Hendrick,
Elisha Konkapot,
Henry Skicket,
Simon S. Metoxen,
Samuel Miller,
Gerret Thompson,
Daniel David,
Ziba T. Peters,
Simeon Konkapot,
David Abrams,
Jonas Konkapot,
David Calvin,
Benjamin Pye, sen.
Aaron Ninham.

Signed and sealed in presence of—

S. Kellogg,
Cutting Marsh,
Clark Whitney,
John Deen,
John Wilber.

TREATY OF 1848

WHEREAS by an act of Congress entitled "An act for the relief of the Stockbridge tribe of Indians, in the Territory of Wisconsin," approved on the third day of March, A.D. 1843, it was provided that the township of land on the east side of Winnebago Lake, secured to said tribe by the treaty with the Menomonee Indians of February 8th,1831, as amended by the Senate of the United States, and not heretofore ceded by said tribe to the United States, should be divided and allotted among the individual members of said tribe, by commissioners to be elected for that purpose, who were to make report of such division and allotment, and thereupon the persons composing said tribe were to become citizens of the United States.

And whereas a portion of said tribe refused to recognize the validity of said act of Congress, or the proceedings which were had under it, or to be governed by its provisions, and upon their petition a subsequent act was passed by the Congress of the United States, on the 6th day of August, 1846, repealing the said act of March 3d, 1843, and providing, among other things, that such of said tribe as should enroll themselves with the subagent of Indians affairs at Green Bay, should be and remain citizens of the United States, and the residue of said tribe were restored to their ancient form of government as an Indian tribe. It was also provided that the said township of land should be divided into two districts, one of which was to be known as the "Indian district," the other as the "citizen district;" the former to be held in common by the party who did not desire citizenship, and the latter to be divided and allotted among such as were citizens and desired to remain so.

And whereas it has been found impracticable to carry into full effect the provisions of the act of August 6th, 1846, by dividing the said township of land in the manner specified in said act, without infringing upon private rights acquired in good faith under the act of 1843 hereinbefore referred to, with a view of relieving both the Indian and citizen parties of said Stockbridge tribe of Indians from their present embarrassments, and to secure to each their just rights, articles of agreement and compromise have been entered into, as follows:

Articles of agreement and treaty made and concluded at Stockbridge, in the State of Wisconsin, on the 24th day of November, in the year of our Lord one thousand eight hundred and forty-eight, by and between the undersigned, acting commissioners on the part of the United States of America, and the Stockbridge tribe of Indians.

ARTICLE 1.

The said Stockbridge tribe of Indians renounce any participation in any of the benefits or privileges granted or conferred by the act of Congress entitled "An act for the relief of the Stockbridge tribe of Indians, in the Territory of Wisconsin," approved March 3, 1843, and relinquish all rights secured by said act; and they do hereby acknowledge and declare themselves to be under the protection and guardianship of the United States, as other Indian tribes.

ARTICLE 2.

That no misunderstanding may exist, now or hereafter, in determining who compose said tribe and are parties hereto, it is agreed that a roll or census shall be taken and appended to this agreement, and in like manner taken annually hereafter, and returned to the Secretary of the War Department of the United States, containing the names of all such as are parties hereto, and to be known and recognized as the Stockbridge tribe of Indians, who shall each be entitled to their due proportion of the benefits to be derived from the provisions made for their tribe by this and former agreements; and whenever any of them shall separate themselves from said tribe, or abandon the country which may be selected for their future home, the share or portion of such shall cease, and they shall forfeit all claims to be recognized as members of said tribe.

ARTICLE 3.

The said Stockbridge tribe of Indians hereby sell and relinquish to the United States the township of land on the east side of Lake Winnebago, (granted and secured to said tribe by the treaty with the Menomonee tribe of Indians of February 8, 1831, as amended by the resolution of the Senate of the United States,) and situated in the State of Wisconsin.

ARTICLE 4.

The said township of land shall be surveyed into lots, in conformity with the plan adopted by the commissioners elected under the act of March 3, 1843, and such of said lands as were allotted by said commissioners to members of said tribe who have become citizens of the United States (a schedule of which is hereunto annexed) are hereby confirmed to such individuals respectively, and patents therefor shall be issued by the United States. The residue of said lands belonging to the United States shall be brought into market but shall not be sold at less than the appraised value, unless the Senate of the United States shall otherwise determine.

ARTICLE 5.

In consideration of the cession and relinquishment hereinbefore made by the said Stockbridge tribe of Indians, it is agreed that the United States shall pay to said tribe, within six months after the ratification of this agreement, the sum of sixteen thousand five hundred dollars, to enable them to settle their affairs, obtain necessaries, and make provision for establishing themselves in a new home.

ARTICLE 6.

The United States shall also pay to said tribe, within six months after the ratification of this agreement, the sum of fourteen thousand five hundred and four dollars and eighty-five cents, being the appraised value of their improvements upon the lands herein ceded and relinquished to the United States, and to be paid to the individuals claiming said improvements according to the schedule and assessment herewith transmitted.

ARTICLE 7.

It is further stipulated and agreed that the said Stockbridge tribe may remain upon the lands they now occupy for one year after the ratification of this agreement, and that they will remove to the country set apart for them, or such other west of the Mississipi River as they may be able to secure, where all their treaty stipulations with the Government shall be carried into effect.

ARTICLE 8.

Whenever the said Stockbridge tribe shall signify their wish to emigrate, the United States will defray the expenses of their removal west of the Mississippi and furnish them with subsistence for one year after their arrival at their new home.

ARTICLE 9.

It is further stipulated and agreed, that, for the purpose of making provision for the rising generation of said tribe, the sum of sixteen thousand five hundred dollars shall be invested by the United States in stock, bearing an interest of not less than five per cent. per annum, the interest of which shall be paid annually to said tribe, as other annuities are paid by the United States.

ARTICLE 10.

It is agreed that nothing herein shall prevent a survey of said lands, at any time after the ratification of this agreement, and that said tribe shall commit no waste or do unnecessary damage upon the premises occupied by them.

ARTICLE 11.

The United States will pay the expenses incurred by the sachem and head-men, amounting to three thousand dollars, in attending to the business of said tribe since the year 1843.

ARTICLE 12.

This agreement to be binding and obligatory upon the contracting parties from and after its ratification by the Government of the United States.

In witness whereof, the said commissioners, and the sachem, councillors, and headmen of said tribe, have hereunto set their hands and seals, the day and year above written.

Morgan L. Martin, [L. S.]
Albert G. Ellis, [L. S.]
Augustin E. Quinney, sachem, [L. S.]
Zeba T. Peters, [L. S.]

Peter D. Littleman
* Abram Pye, [L. S.]   Councillors. [L. S.]

Joseph M. Quinney, [L. S.]
Samuel Stephens, [L. S.]
Jeremiah Slingerland, [L. S.]
* Benjamin Pye, 2d, [L. S.]
Simon S. Metoxen, [L. S.]
Daniel Metoxen, [L. S.]
* Moses Charles, [L. S.]
* Benjamin Pye, 3d, [L. S.]
* Jacob Jehoiakim, [L. S.]
John Metoxen, [L. S.]
John W. Quinney,
Samuel Miller, [L. S.]   Councillors. [L. S.]

* David Palmer, [L. S.]
Ezekiel Ribinson, [L. S.]
* James Joshua, [L. S.]
* Garrett Thompson, [L. S.]
* Laurens Yocron, [L. S.]
* Thomas Schanandoah, [L. S.]
* John W. Quinney, jr., [L. S.]
* Nicolas Palmer, [L. S.]
John P. Quinney, [L. S.]
* Washington Quinney, [L. S.]
* Aaron Turkey. [L. S.]

To each of the names of the Indians marked with an asterisk is affixed his mark.

In presence of—

Charles A. Grignon, U.S. Interpreter.
Lemuel Goodell,
Eleazer Williams,
Charles Poreuninozer.

SUPPLEMENTAL ARTICLE.

Whereas the Stockbridge and Munsee Indians consider that they have a claim against the United States for indemnity for certain lands on White River in the State of Indiana, and for certain other lands in the State of Wisconsin, which they allege they have been deprived of by treaties entered into with the Miamies and Delawares, or to the lands claimed by them in Indiana, and with the Menomonees and Winnebagoes, or to the lands in Wisconsin, without their consent; and whereas the said Stockbridge and Munsee Indians, by their chiefs and agents, have continued to prosecute their said claims during the last twenty years at their own expense, except the sum of three thousand dollars paid them in 1821; and whereas it is desirable that all ground of discontent on the part of said Indians shall be removed, the United States do further stipulate, in consideration of the relinquishment by them of said claims, and all other, except as provided in this treaty, to pay the sachems or chiefs of said Indians, on the ratification of this article by them, with the assent of their people, the sum of five thousand dollars, and the further sum of twenty thousand dollars, to be paid in ten annual instalments, to commence when the said Indians shall have selected and removed to their new homes, as contemplated by the seventh article of this treaty.

The President of the United States, within two years from the ratification of this treaty, shall procure for the use of said Stockbridge Indians a quantity of land west of the Mississippi River, upon which they shall reside, not less than seventy-two sections, said Indians to be consulted as to the location of said land, and to be holden by the same tenure as other Indian lands.

UNRATIFIED TREATY OF 1855

PREAMBLE:

Whereas, by an Act of Congress entitled "An act for the relief of the Stockbridge Tribe of Indians in the Territory of Wisconsin, approved on the 3rd day of March a.d. 1843, it was provided, that the township of land on the East side of Winnebago Lake, secured to said tribe and the Munsees by treaty with the Menomonees of the 8th of Feb. 1831, and not heretofore ceded to the United States should be divided and allotted among the individual members of said Tribe; and whereas a portion of said Tribe refused to recognize the validity of said act, or the proceedings had under it or to be governed by its provisions, and a subsequent act, was passed on the 6th day of August A.D. 1846, repealing the above mentioned Act, and restored to their ancient form of Government, as an Indian Tribe, such as should not signify by enrollment their desire to be citizens of the United States; and whereas it was impracticable to carry into effect the provisions of the last mentioned act, all which is fully stated in the preamble to the Treaty, made with said Tribe of Indians, on the 24th day of November 1848; and wherein among other provisions, the Tribal character is again resumed by the Stockbridges, the township of land is sold and relinquished to the United States, and the Tribe obligated to remove to the country west of the Mississippi set apart for them by the amendment to said Treaty; and whereas, difficulties and disagreements among the parties composing the Tribe, have been existing until the present time and they are averse to a removal west of the Mississippi; and whereas the Unite States are willing to exercise the same liberal policy as heretofore, and for the purpose of bringing together and uniting in peace and harmony as one people the several parties of the Tribe, and such Munsee Indians of New York, as were included in the Treaty of September 3, 1839, and to establish comfortably together all such Stockbridges and Munsees, whether they are now residing in the State of New York or Wisconsin or west of the Mississippi or anywhere else in the United States, the following articles of agreement have been entered into:

Articles of Agreement and Treaty made between and concluded at Stockbridge in the State of Wisconsin on the 6th day of June in the year of our Lord one thousand eight hundred and fifty-five, by and between the undersigned Superintendent of Northern Indian Affairs on the part of the United States of America, acting in conformity with the instructions of the Secretary of the Interior and the Commissioner of Indian Affairs, and the advice of the Commissioner of the General Land Office, who was sent by the Government to assist and counsel him, and the Stockbridge Tribe of Indians.

Article I. All the Stockbridge Indians, those who have been heretofore designated as the "Citizen Party" as well as those who have been designated the "Indian Party" do hereby acknowledge and declare themselves to be under the protection of the United States, as other Indian Tribes, and do agree to bury and forget all differences which have heretofore existed among them to remain as a tribal organization and as one people, admitting into their organization or Tribe all Stockbridges and such Munsees as were included in the Treaty of Sept 3, 1839.

Article II. The United States recede to the Stockbridges & Munsee Tribes of Indians the township of land on the East side of Lake Winnebago set apart for the Stockbridge & Munsee Tribes by the Treaty with the Menomonees of February 8t, 1831 and not ceded to the United States by the Treaty with the said Tribes of Sept. 3, 1839, such Township of land to be held by the same tenure as Indian lands.

Article III. The Stockbridges recede and relinquish to the United States the seventy-two sections of land west of the Mississippi, set apart for them by the amendment to the Treaty of November 24, 1848, and do relinquish all claim for moneys to be paid out for their removal and subsistence as well as every other unsettled or pretended claim against the United States which claims are hereby entirely abrogated.

Article IV. The Stockbridges acknowledge that it would be but just and proper that the whites who bought from them lands should be indemnified for the money laid out and their improvements made out of their funds and therefore agree and consent that the twenty thousand dollars stipulated to be paid to them by the amendments to said Treaty of Nov. 24, 1848 shall be paid toward settling their difficulties by paying those white persons the money paid for their lands purchased with interest and the cost of their improvements to deducting for use and occupation.

Article V. To aid and assist in liquidating the liabilities mentioned in the preceeding article, the United States agrees to pay an amount not exceeding twenty thousand dollars which said sum or the portion thereof which shall be applied for the said purpose is considered by the said Stockbridges as a gratuity granted to them by the liberality of the United States.

Article VI. All the moneys to be paid hereafter to the said Stockbridge & Munsee Tribes under the treaties concluded with the Six Nations Nov. 11, 1794, with said Stockbridge & Munsee Tribes Sept. 3, 1839, and with the said Stockbridges Nov. 24, 1848, are to be applied to educational purposes and to improve their condition among the said united nation of Stockbridges and Munsees under the direction of the President of the United States.

Article VII. So much of the Treaties of Nov. 14, 1794, of Sept. 3, 1839, and of Nov. 24, 1848 as is in contravention of or is in conflict with this agreement is annulled.

In witness whereof the said Commissioner and the Sachem, Councilors, and members of said Tribes have hereunto set their hands and seals.

Francis Huebschman, Superintendent of Indian Affairs of the Northern Superintendency
Austin E. Quinney, Sachem
John P. Quinney
Ziba T. Peters
Daniel P. Metoxen
Washington Quinney
Peter D. Littleman
Jeremiah Slingerland
Simon S. Metoxen
Jonas his X mark Thompson
Samuel Miller
Joseph M. Quinney
Thomas S. Branch
John W. Quinney, Jr.
John Hendricks
Jacob N. Konkapot
Cornelius Aaron
Elish his X mark Konkapot

TREATY OF 1856

Whereas by Senate amendment to the treaty with the Menomonees of February eighth, one thousand eight hundred and thirtyone, two townships of land on the east side of Winnebago Lake, Territory of Wisconsin, were set aside for the use of the Stockbridge and Munsee tribes of Indians, all formerly of the State of New York, but a part of whom had already removed to Wisconsin; and

Whereas said Indians took possession of said lands, but dissensions existing among them led to the treaty of September third, one thousand eight hundred and thirty-nine, by which the east half of said two townships was retroceded to the

United States, and in conformity to which a part of said Stockbridges and Munsees emigrated west of the Mississippi; and

Whereas to relieve them from dissensions still existing by "An act for the relief of the Stockbridge tribe of Indians in the Territory of Wisconsin," approved March third, one thousand eight hundred and forty-three, it was provided, that the remaining townships of land should be divided into lots and allotted between the individual members of said tribe; and

Whereas a part of said tribe refused to be governed by the provisions of said act, and a subsequent act was passed on the sixth day of August, one thousand eight hundred and forty-six, repealing the aforementioned act, but without making provision for bona fide purchasers of lots in the townships subdivided in conformity to the said first-named act; and

Whereas it was found impracticable to carry into effect the provisions of the last-mentioned act, and to remedy all difficulties, a treaty was entered into on the twenty-fourth of November, one thousand eight hundred and forty-eight, wherein among other provisions, the tribe obligated itself to remove to the country west of the Mississippi set apart for them by the amendment to said treaty; and

Whereas dissensions have yet been constantly existing amongst them, and many of the tribe refused to remove, when they were offered a location in Minnesota, and applied for a retrocession to them of the township of Stockbridge, which has been refused by the United States; and

Whereas a majority of the said tribe of Stockbridges and the Munsees are averse to removing to Minnesota and prefer a new location in Wisconsin, and are desirous soon to remove and to resume agricultural pursuits, and gradually to prepare for citizenship, and a number of other members of the said tribe desire at the present time to sever their tribal relations and to receive patents for the lots of land at Stockbridge now occupied by them; and

Whereas the United States are willing to exercise the same liberal policy as heretofore, and for the purpose of relieving these Indians from the complicated difficulties, by which they are surrounded, and to establish comfortably together all such Stockbridges and Munsees—wherever they may be now located, in Wisconsin, in the State of New York, or west of the Mississippi—as were included in the treaty of September third, one thousand eight hundred and thirty-nine, and desire to remain for the present under the paternal care of the United States Government; and for the purpose of enabling such individuals of said tribes as are now qualified and desirous to manage their own affairs, to exercise the rights and to perform the duties of the citizen, these articles of agreement have been entered into:

Articles of agreement and convention made and concluded at Stockbridge in the State of Wisconsin, on the fifth day of February, in the year of our Lord one thousand eight hundred and fifty-six, between Francis Huebschmann, commissioner on the part of the United States, and the Stockbridge and Munsee tribes of Indians assembled in general

council, and such of the Munsees who were included in the treaty of September third, one
thousand eight hundred and thirty-nine, but are yet residing in the State of New York, by
their duly authorized delegates, William Mohawk and Joshua Willson.

ARTICLE 1.

The Stockbridge and Munsee tribes, who were included in the treaty of September third, one thousand eight hundred and thirty-nine, and all the individual members of said tribes, hereby jointly and severally cede and relinquish to the United States all their remaining right and title in the lands at the town of Stockbridge, State of Wisconsin, the seventy-two sections of land in Minnesota set aside for them by the amendment to the treaty of November twenty-fourth, one thousand eight hundred and forty-eight, the twenty thousand dollars stipulated to be paid to them by the said amendment, the sixteen thousand five hundred dollars invested by the United States in stocks for the benefit of the Stockbridge tribe in conformity to Article 9 of the said treaty, and all claims set up by and for the Stockbridge and Munsee tribes, or by and for the Munsees separately, or by and for any individuals of the Stockbridge tribe who claim to have been deprived of annuities since the year one thousand eight hundred and forty-three, and all such and other claims set up by or for them or any of them are hereby abrogated, and the United States released and discharged therefrom.

ARTICLE 2.

In consideration of such cession and relinquishment by said Stockbridges and Munsees, the United States agree to select as soon as practicable and to give them a tract of land in the State of Wisconsin, near the southern boundary of the Menomonee reservation, of sufficient extent to provide for each head of a family and others lots of land of eighty and forty acres, as hereinafter provided; every such lot to contain at least one-half of arable land, and to pay to be expended for improvements for the said Stockbridges and Munsees as provided in article 4, the sum of forty-one thousand one hundred dollars, and a further sum of twenty thousand five hundred and fifty dollars to enable them to remove, and the further sum of eighteen thousand dollars, (twelve thousand for the Stockbridges and six thousand for the Munsees,) to be expended, at such time, and in such manner, as may be prescribed by the Secretary of the Interior, in the purchase of stock and necessaries, the discharge of national or tribal debts, and to enable them to settle their affairs.

ARTICLE 3.

As soon as practicable after the selection of the lands set aside for these Indians by the preceding article, the United States shall cause the same to be surveyed into sections, half and quarter sections, to correspond with the public surveys, and the council of the Stockbridges and Munsees shall under the direction of the superintendent of Indian affairs for the northern superintendency, make a fair and just allotment among the individuals and families of their tribes. Each head of a family shall be entitled to eighty acres of land, and in case his or her family consists of more than four members, if thought expedient by the said council, eighty acres more may be allotted to him or her; each single male person above eighteen years of age shall be entitled to eighty acres; and each female person above eighteen years of age, not belonging to any family, and each orphan child, to forty acres; and sufficient land shall be reserved for the rising generation.

After the said allotment is made, the persons entitled to land may take immediate possession thereof, and the United States will thence-forth and until the issuing of the patents, as hereinafter provided, hold the same in trust for such persons, and certificates shall be issued, in a suitable form, guaranteeing and securing to the holders their possession and an ultimate title to the land; but such certificates shall not be assignable, and shall contain a clause expressly prohibiting the sale or transfer by the holder of the land described therein. After the expiration of ten years upon the application of the holder of such certificate, made with the consent of the said Stockbridge and Munsee council, and when it shall appear prudent and for his or her welfare, the President of the United States may direct, that such restriction on the power of sale shall be withdrawn and a patent issued in the usual form.

Should any of the heads of families die before the issuing of the certificates or patents herein provided for, the same shall issue to their heirs; and if the holder of any such certificate shall die without heirs, his or her land shall not revert to the United States, unless on petition of the Stockbridge and Munsee council for the issuing of a new certificate for the land of such deceased person, to the holder of any other certificate for land, and on the surrendering to the United States of such other certificate, by the holder thereof, the President shall direct the issuing of a new certificate for such land; and in like manner new certificates, may be given for lots of land, the prior certificates for which have been surrendered by the holders thereof.

ARTICLE 4.

Of the monies set aside for improvements by the second of these articles, not exceeding one-fourth shall be applied to the building of roads leading to, and through said lands: to the erection of a school-house, and such other improvements of a public character, as will be deemed necessary by the said Stockbridge and Munsee council, and approved by the superintendent of the northern superintendency. The residue of the said fund shall be expended for improvements to be made by and for the different members and families composing the said tribes, according to a system to be adopted by the said council, under the direction of the superintendent aforesaid, and to be first approved by the Commissioner of Indian Affairs.

ARTICLE 5.

The persons to be included in the apportionment of the land and money to be divided and expended under the provisions of this agreement, shall be such only, as are actual members of the said Stockbridge and Munsee tribes, (a roll or census of whom shall be taken and appended to this agreement,) their heirs, and legal representatives; and hereafter, the adoption of any individual amongst them shall be null and void, except it be first approved by the Commissioner of Indian Affairs.

ARTICLE 6.

In case the United States desire to locate on the tract of land to be selected as herein provided, the Stockbridges and Munsees emigrated to the west of the Mississippi in conformity to the treaty of September third, one thousand eight hundred and thirty-nine, the Stockbridges and Munsees, parties to this treaty, agree to receive them as brethren: *Provided,* That none of the said Stockbridges and Munsees, whether now residing at Stockbridge, in the State of Wisconsin, in the State of New York, or west of the Mississippi, shall be entitled to any of these lands or the money stipulated to be expended by these articles, unless they remove to the new location within two years from the ratification hereof.

ARTICLE 7.

The said Stockbridges and Munsees hereby set aside, for educational purposes exclusively, their portion of the annuities under the treaties of November the eleventh, one thousand seven hundred and ninety-four; August eleventh, one thousand eight hundred and twenty-seven; and September third, one thousand eight hundred and thirty-nine.

ARTICLE 8.

One hundred and fifty dollars valuation of the schoolhouse at Stockbridge made in conformity to article 6 of the treaty of November twenty-fourth, one thousand eight hundred and forty-eight, and remaining unpaid, shall be expended in the erection of a school-house, with the other funds set aside for the same purpose by article 4 of this agreement.

ARTICLE 9.

About seven and two-fifths acres bounded as follows: Beginning at the northeast corner of lot eighty-nine, in the centre of the military road; thence west, along the north line of said lot, fifty-four and a quarter rods; thence south, thirty-eight and a quarter rods; thence east twenty-eight and a quarter rods; thence north thirty four and a quarter rods; thence east twenty-six rods; thence north, four rods, to the place of beginning, comprising the ground heretofore used by the Stockbridges to bury their dead, shall be patented to the supervisors of the town of Stockbridge, to be held by them and their successors in trust for the inhabitants of said town, to be used by them as a cemetery, and the proceeds from cemetery lots and burial-places to be applied in fencing, clearing, and embellishing the grounds.

ARTICLE 10.

It is agreed that all roads and highways laid out by authority of law shall have right of way through the lands set aside for said Indians, on the same terms as are provided by law for their location through lands of citizens of the United States.

ARTICLE 11.

The object of this instrument being to advance the welfare and improvement of said Indians, it is agreed, if it prove insufficient from causes which cannot now be foreseen, to effect these ends, that the President of the United States may, by and with the advice and consent of the Senate, adopt such policy in the management of their affairs, as in his judgment may be most beneficial to them; or Congress may, hereafter, make such provision by law, as experience shall prove to be necessary.

ARTICLE 12.

The said Stockbridges and Munsees agree to suppress the use of ardent spirits among their people and to resist by all prudent means, its introduction in their settlements.

ARTICLE 13.

The Secretary of the Interior, if deemed by him expedient and proper, may examine into the sales made by the Stockbridge Indians, to whom lots of land were allotted in conformity to the acts of Congress, entitled "An act for the relief of the Stockbridge tribe of Indians in the Territory of Wisconsin," approved March third, one thousand eight hundred and forty-three; and if it shall be found that any of the said sales have been improperly made, or that a proper consideration has not been paid, the same may be disapproved or set aside. By the direction of the said Secretary, patents to such lots of land shall be issued to such persons as shall be found to be entitled to the same.

ARTICLE 14.

The lots of land the equitable title to which shall be found not to have passed by valid sales from the Stockbridge Indians to purchasers, and such lots as have, by the treaty of November twenty-fourth, one thousand eight hundred and forty-eight, been receded to the United States, shall be sold at the minimum price of ten dollars per acre for lots fronting on Lake Winnebago, on both sides of the military road, and all the lands in the three tiers of lots next to Lake Winnebago, and at five dollars per acre for the residue of the lands in said township of Stockbridge. Purchasers of lots, on which improvements were made by Stockbridge Indians shall pay, in addition to the said minimum price, the appraised value of such improvements. To actual settlers on any of said lots possessing the qualifications requisite to acquire pre-emption rights, or being civilized persons of Indian descent, not members of any tribe, who shall prove, to the satisfaction of the register of the land district to which the township of Stockbridge shall be attached, that he or she has made improvements to the value of not less than fifty dollars on such lot, and that he or she is actually residing on it; the time of paying the purchase-price may be extended for a term not exceeding three years from the ratification hereof, as shall be deemed advisable by the President of the United States, provided, that no such actual settler shall be permitted to pre-empt, in the manner aforesaid, more than one lot, or two contiguous lots, on which he has proved to have made improvements exceeding the value of one hundred dollars. The residue of said lots shall be brought into market as other Government lands are offered for sale, and shall not be sold at a less price than the said minimum price; and all said sales shall be made, and the patents provided for in these articles shall be issued in accordance with the survey made in conformity to said act of March third, one thousand eight hundred and forty-three, unless, in the opinion of the Secretary of the Interior, a new survey shall be deemed necessary and proper.

ARTICLE 15.

The United States agree to pay, within one year after the ratification of this agreement, the appraised value of the improvements upon the lands herein ceded and relinquished to the United States, to the individuals claiming the same, the valuation of such improvements, to be made by a person to be selected by the superintendent of Indian affairs for the northern superintendency, and not to exceed, in the aggregate, the sum of five thousand dollars.

ARTICLE 16.

The hereinafter named Stockbridge Indians, having become sufficiently advanced in civilization, and being desirous of separating from the Stockbridge tribe, and of enjoying the privileges granted to persons of Indian descent by the State of Wisconsin, and in consideration of ceding and relinquishing to the United States all their rights in the lands and annuities of the Stockbridge tribe of Indians, and in the annuities, money, or land, to which said Indians now are or may hereafter be entitled, the United States agree to issue patents in fee-simple to the said Stockbridge Indians to the lots of land, at the town of Stockbridge, described and set opposite their names.

The said Mary Hendrick, and Levy Konkapot, John W. Abrams to have the privilege of joining again the said Stockbridges and Munsees in their new location.

ARTICLE 17.

So much of the treaties of September third, one thousand eight hundred and thirty-nine, and of November twenty-fourth, one thousand eight hundred and forty-eight, as is in contravention or in conflict with the stipulations of this agreement, is hereby abrogated and annulled.

ARTICLE 18.

Upon the contracting parties whenever the same shall be ratified by the President and the Senate of the United States.

In testimony whereof, the said Francis Huebschmann, commissioner as aforesaid, and the chiefs, headmen, and members of the said Stockbridge and Munsee tribes, and the said delegates of the Munsees of New York, have hereunto set their hands and seals at the place and on the day and year herein before written.

Signed and sealed in presence of—

Theodore Koven, Secretary to Commissioner.
Saml. W. Beall,
Adam Scherff,
James Christie,
Lemuel Goodell,
Enos McKenzie,
Elam C. Pease.

UNRATIFIED TREATY OF 1867

Articles of Treaty and Agreement made and concluded at Washington in the District of Columbia this fifteenth day of February A.D. 1867 between Louis V. Bogy, Commissioner of Indian Affairs, and W. H. Watson, Commissioners appointed on the part of the United States, and the Delegates of the Stockbridge and Munsee tribes of Indians Darius Charles, Ziba T. Peters, Jeremiah Slingerland, and John P. Hendricks dully appointed and authorized by said tribes.

Article 1. The Stockbridge and Munsee tribes of Indians, hereby cede and relinquish to the United States, all the rights, title and interests held by them individually or collectively, in and to the two townships of lands in the State of Wisconsin, designated as Townships Twenty eight (28) in ranges thirteen (13) and fourteen (14) east, according to the public surveys and being the same lands set apart and allotted to said tribes, under the treaty made with them on the fifth day of February A.D. 1856.

Article 2. The said tribes, having voluntarily divided themselves into two classes, one class embracing and known as the Citizens Party, composed of two hundred and twenty-four (224) persons, (according to the Roll or Census hereunto annexed); the other class, embracing and known as the Indian Party composed of one hundred and sixty-eight (168) persons (according to the Roll or Census hereunto annexed); it is stipulated and agreed, that the Citizen Party each and every one of them, hereby surrender and relinquish all claims to be hereinafter known or considered as members of said tribes or in any manner interested in any provision heretofore or hereafter to be made by any treaty or law of the United States, for the benefits of said tribes.

Article 3. In consideration of the cession and relinquishment hereinbefore made by the said Citizens Party, and as a full settlement and satisfaction of all claims of said party and of every individual thereof, either against the tribe or the United States, it is agreed that the United States shall, within one year after this treaty shall take effect, pay to said Citizens Party to be equally divided and distributed among them the sum of thirty-two thousand eight hundred and twenty-nine dollars and forty-four cents, being their share or proportion of the estimated value of said two townships of lands; also, to be distributed in like the sum of ten thousand two hundred and fifty-nine dollars and twenty cents, being their share or proportion of the sums of money expended in constructing roads and erecting public buildings on the said two townships of land and of monies invested under former treaties for the benefit of said Stockbridge and Munsee tribes of Indians. Every member of said Citizens Party having improvements upon the lands hereby ceded to the United States shall also receive compensation therefore, as provided in the fifth article of this Agreement.

Article 4. In consideration of the cession herein made on the part of the Indian Party, it is stipulated and agreed that the members of said Indian party and their descendants and no others, shall be hereafter recognized by the United States as composing said Stockbridge and Munsee tribes of Indians, and entitled to all the benefit to be received by said tribes under this and all other treaties heretofore or hereafter to be mad with said tribes. The United States will also procure for said tribesa tract of land suited for agricultural pursuits and have the same surveyed and held in trust for their benefits, and will assign to each of them lots so that each male member of said tribes shall have at least eighty acres and each female at least forty acres of land, for which certificates shall be issued signed by the Sachem and Councilors and countersigned by the Agent or such person as may be appointed by the Secretary of the Interior to superintend such allotments. The lot of lands thus assigned shall be held by the individuals respectively and their heirs, members of said tribes, without power of alienation, except with the sanction and approval of the Secretary of the Interior Department, and whenever any member of said tribes shall have sold and conveyed the lands thus assigned and the conveyance shall have been approved, such conveyance shall operate as a relinquishment of all interests of the grantor in the stipulations made for the benefits of said tribes by this or any other treaty with the United States and of all claims to be further recognized as a member of said tribes. In addition to the lands thus allotted to the members of said tribes, there shall be set apart and appropriated a lot of lands of not less than forty acres, in a central part of the tract, to be held as the common property of said tribes, on which to erect a church, parsonage, school house and other improvement necessary for the accommodation of said tribes.

Article 5. The United States further agree, that in securing the lands provided in the last article (the survey thereof to be at the expense of the United States) and for the expense of removal thereto of the said Indian Party and in the construction of roads and their necessary buildings and improvements in their new location, under the direction of the Commissioner of Indian Affairs or such person as he may be appointed for that purpose, and for the purchase of cattle and farming implements for the use of said Indian Party or such as shall remove within two years after the ratification of this agreement and for the subsistence of such as remove, there shall be appropriated and expended the sum of thirty thousand dollars. The United States will also pay the sum of ten thousand dollars for the buildings and improvements upon the lands ceded by the first article of this agreement, to be divided up among the several persons interested therein, according to an appraisal to be made under the direction of the Agent, by the Sachem and Councilors of said tribes, the estimated value of the public buildings to be first deducted and the amounts thereof to be expended in the erection of others in their new location.

Article 6. The United States will also pay the just debts contracted by the Sachem and Councilors for the benefit of said tribes, amounting to the sum of fifteen thousand dollars, according to the schedule certified by them and returned to the Commissioner of Indian Affairs.

Article 7. The said Indian Party having made provision in this Agreement for such of the Munsees as are resident in the State of New York, it is stipulated and agreed that such of said Indians as shall not remove to and settle upon the land to be obtained for them in pursuance of the fourth article, within two years from the ratification hereof by the Senate of the United States shall forfeit all rights to any allotments or share of said lands, and the lands set apart for their use shall revert to and become the common property of said tribes and may be allotted to any other members of said tribes or their descendants, who may not have received allotments under the provisions of this agreement.

Article 8. For the purpose of reimbursing the sums of money stipulated to be paid under the provisions of this agreement the two townships of land ceded by the first article shall be appraised under the direction of the Secretary of the Inteior, in lots of forty acres, such appraisals to be returned to the Register of the Land Office of the District in which such lands may be situated; and after notice of not less than ninety days, to be published in the several counties of the District. The same shall be offered for sale at public auction to the highest bidder, but shall not be sold at less that the appraised value thereof; none of said lands shall be subject to entry or pre-emption until they shall have been offered as aforesaid, and then only at the price fixed by such appraisal, not less than one dollar and twenty-five cents per acre; all the lands within the said two townships remaining unsold at the expiration of one year after they shall have been offered as aforesaid, shall be again offered at not less than the minimum of one dollar and twenty-five cents per acre, and thereafter shall become subject to entry as other public lands.

Article 9. It is expressly stipulated and agreed that none of the provisions of this agreement shall be binding or obligatory until a suitable location shall have been secured for said Indian Party, in conformity with the fourth article and the approval of the President and ratification of the Senate of the United States.

In testimony whereof, the said Louis V. Bogy and W. H. Watson Commisioners, and the said Darius Charles, Ziba T. Peters, Jeremiah Slingerland, and John P. Hendricks, Delegates of said Stockbridge and Munsee tribes of Indians, have hereunto set their hands and seals, at the place and on the day and year first above written.

Signed and sealed in the presence of
Charles E. Mix
Lewis S. Hayden
Robert Flint
M. L. Martin

Acts of Congress Concerning the Stockbridge-Munsees, 1843–1972

ACT OF 1843

An Act for the Relief of the Stockbridge tribe of Indians in the Territory of Wisconsin.

SECTION 1. *Be it enacted by the Senate and House of Representatives of the United States of America in Congress assembled,* That the township of land, containing twenty-three thousand and forty acres, (or whatever quantity now remains to them), lying on the east side of Winnebago Lake in the Territory of Wisconsin, which by the proviso of a treaty made with the Menominee Indians on the seventeenth day of February in the year eighteen hundred and thirty-one and ratified on the ninth day of July, eighteen hundred and thirty-two, was reserved for the use of the Stockbridge Indians, and which, by a subsequent treaty with the Menominee tribe, bearing date twenty-seventh October, eighteen hundred and thirty-two, and ratified thirteenth March eighteen hundred and thirty-three, was further secured to the said Stockbridge tribe of Indians, may be partitioned and divided among the different individuals composing said tribe of Stockbridge Indians, and may be held by them, separately and severally in fee simple and after such division shall have been made in the manner hereinafter mentioned.

SECTION 2. *And be it further enacted,* That for the purpose of making partition and division of said lands among the individuals of said tribe of Stockbridge Indians, a board of commissioners shall be constituted, to consist of five of the principal or head men of said tribe, a majority of whom shall constitute a quorum to do business, whose duty it shall be to make a just and fair partition and division of said lands among the members of said tribe, or among such of them as, by the laws and customs and regulations of such tribe, are entitled to the same, and in such proportions and in such manner as shall be consistent with equity and justice, and in accordance with the existing laws, customs, usages, or agreements of said tribe.

SECTION 3. *And be it further enacted*, That, for the purpose of electing or choosing said board of commissioners, a meeting of said tribe shall be held at their church or principal public place, on the reservation of land aforesaid, on the first Monday in April, eighteen hundred and forty-three, at which all the male members of said tribe, over the age of twenty-one years, shall be allowed to vote for such commissioners; and the said five commissioners shall then and there be elected or chosen by the said tribe, by a majority of the whole number of such voters then present. And the judge of the district in which said lands are situated (or, in his absence, the register of the land office at Green Bay, or the commanding officer of the United States troops at Fort Howard) shall attend at the time and place aforesaid, and preside at such meeting, superintend the said election, and see that the proceedings are fairly conducted. And the said presiding officer may, in his discretion, prescribe whether the said election shall be by ballot or viva voce, and shall, in other respects, cause the proceedings to be conducted in such a manner as to ensure a fair and proper choice or election; and after the said commissioners shall have been so chosen or elected, the said presiding officer shall immediately certify that fact, setting forth the names of the commissioners who shall be elected, and shall make two copies of said certificate, one of which he shall file in the office of the register of the land district at Green Bay, and the other he shall transmit by mail to the President of the United States.

SECTION 4. *And be it further enacted*, That after the said commissioners shall have been elected or chosen as above prescribed, and as soon thereafter as conveniently may be, they shall proceed to make partition and division of all the lands aforesaid, among the individual members of said tribe, or among such of them as, by the laws, customs, usages, or agreements of said tribe, are justly entitled to the same, and in such way and manner, and upon such principles, and in such proportions, as shall be agreeable to equity and justice, and consistent with the laws, usages, customs, and agreements of said tribe: Provided, however, That the buildings and improvements, and the farms on which the same are situated, which are now held or possessed in severalty by the members of said tribe, shall, so far as the same can be consistently done, be allotted or apportioned to the present occupants; and that no person or individual of said tribe shall be dispossessed or deprived of the improvements or land which they now occupy, unless it shall be found by the said commissioners that such person or persons are in possession of and occupying more land than they are justly entitled to, and then the overplus may be apportioned to others.

SECTION 5. *And be it further enacted*, That after the said commissioners shall have made such partition and division as aforesaid, they shall make, or cause to be made, a full report of their proceedings in the premises, setting forth the name of each person to whom they have apportioned any part of said land, the quantity apportioned or allotted to each, with the metes and bounds, or other definite descriptions of each several piece or parcel of land; and they shall accompany the said report with a fair and accurate map of the whole, showing the divisions and partitions aforesaid; which report and map, or a true copy thereof, shall be deposited with the town clerk of said tribe, on or before the first day of July, eighteen hundred and forty-three, and shall remain open for inspection to all for the space of twenty days thereafter; and if any member or members of said tribe shall object to the partition or division so made by the said commissioners, or shall deem himself or themselves aggrieved thereby, he or they may, within ten days thereafter, give notice thereof to said commissioners, who shall within twenty days thereafter, meet to hear and determine such grievances, and take testimony, if necessary, and, after such hearing, shall have power to alter or modify such partition, if, in their judgment, any alteration or modification is necessary, in order to do equal and exact justice to all parties interested.

SECTION 6. *And be it further enacted,* That, after the said report shall be finally completed, the commissioners shall cause three fair copies of the said report, and of the map accompanying the same, as finally agreed upon and settled, to be made and signed by said commissioners, one copy of which shall be deposited in the office of the Secretary of said Territory, one copy in the office of the clerk of the county within which said lands are situated, and the other shall be transmitted to the President of the United States, who shall thereupon cause patents to be issued to the several individuals named in said report, for the lands so apportioned to them respectively, by which the said persons shall be authorized to hold the said land in fee simple, to themselves and their heirs and assigns.

SECTION 7. *And be it further enacted,* That the said report and map shall be filed with the Secretary of said Territory, and in the clerk's office of said county, and shall also be transmitted to the President, on or before the first day of January, eighteen hundred and forty-four; and after the same shall have been filed and transmitted to the President as aforesaid, the said Stockbridge tribe of Indians, and each and every of them, shall then be deemed to be, and from that time forth are hereby declared to be, citizens of the United States, to all intents and purposes, and shall be entitled to all the rights, privileges, and immunities of such citizens, and shall in all respects, be subject to the laws of the United States and of the Territory of Wisconsin, in the same manner as other citizens of said Territory; and the jurisdiction of the United States and of said Territory shall be extended over the said township or reservation now held by them, in the same manner as over other parts of said Territory; and their rights as a tribe or nation, and their power of making or executing their own laws, usages, or customs, as such tribe, shall cease and determine: Provided, however, That nothing in this act contained shall be so construed as to deprive them of the right to any annuity now due them from the State of New York or the United States, but they shall be entitled to receive any such annuity, in the same manner as though this act had not been passed.

Approved, March 3, 1843.

ACT OF 1846

An Act to repeal an Act entitled "An Act for the Relief of the Stockbridge Tribe of Indians in the Territory of Wisconsin," approved March third, eighteen hundred and forty-three, and for other Purposes.

SECTION 1. *Be it enacted by the Senate and House of Representatives of the United States of America in Congress assembled,* That the act entitled "An Act for the Relief of the Stockbridge Tribe of Indians in the Territory of Wisconsin," approved March third, eighteen hundred and forty-three, be and the same is hereby repealed; and the said Stockbridge tribe or nation of Indians is restored to their ancient form of government, with all powers, rights, and privileges, held and exercised by them under their customs and usages, as fully and completely as though the above-recited act had never passed.

SECTION 2. *And be it further enacted,* That the sub-agent of Indian affairs at Green Bay, under the direction of the Governor of Wisconsin, who shall be a commissioner for this purpose, shall be required to open a book for the enrolment of the names of such persons of the Stockbridge tribe of Indians as shall desire to become and remain citizens of the United States, immediately upon the passage of this law; and three months shall be allowed after the opening of said books for the enrolment, within which time it shall be the duty of all desiring citizenship to come forward in person and file their application. After the expiration of the three months, the said sub-agent shall divide the said township of land now held by the Stockbridges on the Winnebago Lake into two districts, to be known and designated as the Indian District and the Citizen District, according to the strength and numbers of their respective parties, and the laws and usages in said tribe. The lands in the Indian District are to remain and to be held in common; those in the Citizen District are to be divided; and to each Indian who becomes a citizen the said sub-agent shall assign, by distinct metes and bounds, his ratable proportions of land. And, after the division and allotment are completed, it shall be the duty of the said sub-agent to make out three copies of the divisions thus made, one of which he shall file with the clerk of the District Court of the county in which the Citizen District of land may be situated; one other copy he shall file in the land office at Green Bay, in Wisconsin Territory; and the other shall be returned to the Secretary of War. And, upon the receipt of the said return by the Secretary of War, patents may be issued to the individual reservees who become citizens, upon the receipt of which a title in fee simple to the lot of land shall vest in the patentee; and all transfers and assignments of the land made previous to the issuance of the patent shall be null and void: Provided, however, That those Indians who become citizens shall forfeit all right to receive any portion of the annuity which may now or may become due the nation of Stockbridges, by virtue of any treaty heretofore entered into by this government with said Stockbridges.

SECTION 3. *And be it further enacted,* That, in consideration of the moneys paid by said Stockbridge nation of Indians to the Winnebagoes and Menominees in the years eighteen hundred and twenty-one and eighteen hundred and twenty-two, and all other claims, the sum of five thousand dollars to be paid to said tribe of Indians by the Secretary of War; and for this purpose, the said sum of five thousand dollars be, and the same is hereby, appropriated, out of any money in the treasury not otherwise appropriated: Provided, That nothing in this act contained shall be construed to impair any claim which said nation may have upon the Delaware nation to a share of the lands assigned to them west of the Missouri River.

Approved August 6, 1846

ACT OF 1853

An Act for the Relief of John W. Quinney, a Stockbridge Indian
Be it enacted by the Senate and House of Representatives of the United States of America in Congress assembled, That in lieu of all the rights of John W. Quinney in the lands and annuities of the Stockbridge tribe of Indians, and in the annuities, money or land to which said Indians now are or may hereafter be entitled under existing treaties, there shall be paid to the said John W. Quinney, out of the moneys now due and payable to the said Stockbridge tribe of Indians, the sum of one thousand dollars, or so much more or less than that sum as shall be declared to be just and proper by the chiefs and head-men of said Stockbridge tribe; and there shall also be granted to the said John W. Quinney, in fee simple, and to his heirs and assigns forever, the tract or parcel of land now in the possession and occupancy of the said John W. Quinney, in Stockbridge, in the State of Wisconsin, and bounded and described as follows, to wit: bounded on the north by lot number thirty-three, recommended to be patented to Mr. Dinslow, in the Stockbridge treaty of November twenty-fourth, eighteen hundred and forty-eight, and the United States lot numbered seventy-four; south by lots numbered thirty-seven and seventy, recommended to be patented to Mr. John Dick; east by the military road (so called) passing through the town of Stockbridge, and west by the Winnebago Lake—containing three hundred and sixty acres of land, more or less; and it shall be the duty of the Commissioner of the General Land Office to cause the said piece of land to be surveyed, and to issue to the said John W. Quinney a patent therefore, in accordance with such survey.

Approved, January 27, 1853.

ACT OF 1865

An Act making Appropriations for the current and contingent Expenses of the Indian Department, and for fulfilling Treaty Stipulations with various Indian Tribes for the year ending thirtieth June, eighteen hundred and sixty-six, and for other purposes.

SECTION 4. *And be it further enacted*, That each of the chiefs, warriors, and heads of families of the Stockbridge and Munsee tribes of Indians residing in the County of Shawana and State of Wisconsin, may, under the direction of the Secretary of the Interior, enter a homestead and become entitled to all the benefits of an act entitled "An act to secure homesteads to actual settlers on the public domain," approved May twenty, eighteen hundred and sixty-two, free from any fee or charge whatever, and any part of the lands being a part of their present reservation, which may be abandoned under the forgoing provisions, may be sold under the direction of the Secretary of the Interior, and the proceeds applied for the benefit of such Indians as may settle on said homesteads, to aid them in improving the same. The same homestead thus secured shall not be subject to any tax, levy, or sale whatever, nor shall the same be sold, conveyed, mortgaged, or in any manner encumbered except upon the decree of the district court of the United States, as hereinafter provided. Whenever any of said chiefs, warriors, or heads of families of said tribes, having filed with the clerk of the district court of the United States a declaration of his intention to become a citizen of the United States, and to dissolve all relations with any Indian tribe, two years previous thereto, shall appear in said court, and prove to the satisfaction thereof, by the testimony of two citizens of the United States, that for five years last past he has adopted the habits of civilized life, that he has maintained himself and family by his own industry, that he reads and speaks the English language, that he is well disposed to become a peaceable and orderly citizen; and that he has sufficient capacity to manage his own affairs; the court may enter a decree admitting him to all the rights of a citizen of the United States and thenceforth he shall no longer be held or treated as a member of any Indian tribe, but shall be entitled to all the rights and privileges, and be subject to all the duties and liabilities to taxation of other citizens of the United States. But nothing herein contained shall be construed to deprive them of annuities to which they are or may be entitled.

Approved, March 3, 1865.

ACT OF 1871

An act for the relief of the Stockbridge and Munsee tribe of Indians, in the State of Wisconsin

SECTION 1. *Be it enacted by the Senate and House of Representatives of the United States of America in Congress assembled*, That the two townships of land, situated in the county of Shawanaw, and State of Wisconsin, set apart for the use of the Stockbridge and Munsee tribe of Indians, shall, under direction of the Secretary of the Interior, be examined and appraised, by two or more disinterested appraisers to be selected by him, in eighty acre lots, according to public survey; such appraisal shall state the quality of the soil, the quantity, quality, and value of the timber growing on each lot, estimating the pine timber at not less than one dollar per thousand, and the value of all improvements, if any, made thereon, with the name of the owner of such improvements, as certified by the sachem and councillors of said tribe, and, when returned to the land office of the district in which said lands are situated, be subject to public inspection for at least thirty days before the day appointed for the sale of such lands, as hereinafter provided. One copy of said appraisal shall be made and returned to the land office of the district, and a duplicate thereof to the Secretary of the Interior, within six months fromthe passage of this act, and the person[s] appointed to make such appraisal shall be allowed such compensation for their services as may be fixed by the Secretary of the Interior.

SECTION 2. *And be it further enacted,* That the said two townships of land shall be advertised for sale, by notice of not less than three months, to be published in at least three newspapers of the district having general circulation, and shall be offered at public auction, at the nearest Government land office within the Green Bay agency, to the highest bidder, in lots of not exceeding eighty acres each, but shall not be sold for less than the appraised value thereof. None of said lands shall be subject to entry until they shall have been offered as aforesaid, and then only at the price fixed by such appraisal. All of said lands remaining unsold at the expiration of one year after they shall have been offered as aforesaid shall again be advertised and offered at public auction at the nearest Government land office within the Green Bay agency, at not less than the minimum of one dollar and twenty-five cents per acre, and thereafter shall be subject to private entry at the latter price, and shall in all cases be sold for cash only: *Provided, however,* That the Secretary of the Interior is hereby authorized to reserve from sale a quantity of said lands not exceeding eighteen contiguous sections, embracing such as are now actually occupied and improved, and are best adapted to agricultural purposes, subject to allotment to members of the Indian party of said tribe as hereinafter provided.

SECTION 3. *And be it further enacted,* That from the first proceeds of the sale of lands, as provided in the second section of this act, shall be paid the expenses of appraisal and sale of said lands, the amount due to individuals for improvements as returned by the appraisers, and the amount of the debts contracted by the sachem and councillors for the benefit of said tribes, amounting to the sum of eleven thousand dollars, according to a schedule to be certified by them, and returned to the commissioner of Indian affairs.

SECTION 4. *And be it further enacted,* That, immediately after the returns shall be received at the General Land-Office of the last public sale according to the provisions of this act, a statement shall be made up, under the direction of the Secretary of the Interior, exhibiting the gross amount of moneys realized from the sale of the said two townships of land, after deducting therefrom the sums appropriated by the preceding sections of this act, to which said amount shall be added the value of the lands remaining unsold of said two townships, estimating the same at sixty cents per acre; also the sum of six thousand dollars held in trust by the Government of the United States for the use of the Stockbridge and Munsee tribes of Indians, under the treaty of eighteen hundred and thirty-nine; and the total amount thereof shall constitute the entire sum of money due from the Government of the United States to the said Stockbridge and Munsee tribes of Indians, to be paid and appropriated for their benefit as hereinafter directed.

SECTION 5. *And be it further enacted,* That the sum of money thus found due to the said tribes shall be divided between the citizen and Indian parties of said tribes, in proportion to the number of each, respectively, according to rolls thereof, made and returned in conformity with the provisions of this act to the Commissioner of Indian Affairs: That portion of said sum belonging to the citizen party shall be equally divided among them per capita, and paid to the heads of families, and adult members of said party; that portion of said sum belonging to the Indian party shall be placed to their credit on the books of the treasurer of the United States, and bear interest at the rate of five per centum per annum, payable semiannually, and said interest shall be applied to the support of schools, the purchase of agricultural implements, or paid in such other manner as the President may direct: *Provided, however,* That a part of said sum due the Indian party, not exceeding thirty thousand dollars, may, on the request of the sachem and councillors of said tribe, be expended in securing a new location for said tribe, and in removing and aiding them to establish themselves in their new home;and in case of their procuring and removal to such new location, at any time, the said eighteen sections of land reserved for their use by the second section of this act shall be sold in the manner therein provided, and the proceeds thereof be placed to their credit as aforesaid.

SECTION 6. *And be it further enacted,* That for the purpose of determining the persons who are members of said tribes and the future relation of each to the Government of the United States, there shall be prepared, under the direction of the Commissioner of Indian Affairs, or such person as may be selected by him to superintend the same, two rolls, one to be denominated the citizen roll, to embrace the names of all such persons of full age, and their families, as signify their desire to separate their relations with said tribe, and to become citizens of the United States; the other to be denominated the Indian roll, and to embrace the names of all such as desire to retain their tribal character and continue under the care and guardianship of the United States; which said rolls shall be signed by the sachem and councillors of said tribe, certified by the person superintending the same, and returned to the Commissioner of Indian Affairs, but no person of full age shall be entered upon said citizen roll without his or her full and free consent, personally given to the person superintending such enrollment; nor shall any person, or his or her descendants, be entered upon either of said rolls who may have heretofore separated from said tribe and received allotment of lands under the act of Congress for the relief of the Stockbridge tribe of Indians, of March third, eighteen hundred and forty-three, and amendment of August six, eighteen hundred and forty-six, or under the treaty of February five, eighteen hundred and fifty-six, or who shall not be of Stockbridge or Munsee descent. After the said rolls shall be made and returned as herein provided, the same shall be held as a full surrender and relinquishment on the part of the citizen party, each and every one of them, of all claims to be thereafter known or considered as members of said tribe, or in any manner interested in any provision heretofore or hereafter to be made by any treaty or law of the United States for the benefit of said tribes, and they and their descendants shall thenceforth be admitted to all the rights and privileges of citizens of the United States.

SECTION 7. *And be it further enacted,* That after the said rolls shall have been made and returned, the said Indian party shall thenceforth be known as the "Stockbridge Tribe of Indians," and may be located upon lands reserved by the second section of this act, or such other reservation as may be procured for them, with the assent of the council of said tribe, and their adoption among them of any individual, not of Indian descent, shall be null and void

SECTION 8. *And be it further enacted,* That as soon as practicable, after a suitable and permanent reservation shall be obtained and accepted by said tribe, either at their present home or elsewhere, the same shall, under the direction of the Secretary of the Interior, be surveyed and subdivided to correspond with the public survey, and the council of said tribe number the superintendence of the agent of the United States, shall make a just and fair allotment of so much thereof (in compact form) as may be required, among the individuals and families composing said tribe, as follows: Each head of a family consisting of four persons shall receive eighty acres of land, and if consisting of more than four persons, at the discretion of the council, eighty acres more may be assigned to him or her; each male person above the age of eighteen years, not included in any family, shall receive eighty acres; each female person above the age of eighteen years, not a member of any family, and each orphan child, shall receive forty acres; the lands assigned and allotted as aforesaid shall be held inalienable, and in case of the death of any person, his or her right thereto shall descend to his or her heirs, if members of said tribe, and if he or she dies without heirs capable of inheriting, the land shall revert to and become the common property of said tribe; there shall also be set apart and appropriated a lot, not exceeding forty acres, to be held as common property on which to erect a church, parsonage, school-house, and other improvements necessary for the accommodation of said tribe: *Provided,* That if any female shall marry out of said tribe, she shall thereby forfeit all right to hold any of said lands, as if deceased.

SECTION 9. *And be it further enacted,* That the allotments contemplated in the previous sections of this act, shall be made, and a certified copy thereof returned to the Commissioner of Indian Affairs, within one year after the reservation shall have been made and accepted by said tribe; and thereafter the title of the lands described therein shall be held by the United States in trust for individuals and their heirs to whom the same were allotted. The surplus lands embraced in such reservation remaining after making such allotments shall be held in like manner by the United States, subject to be allotted to individuals of said tribe who may not have received any portion of said reservation, or to be disposed of for the common benefit of said tribe: *Provided,* That no change or addition shall be made in the allotment returned to the Commissioner of Indian Affairs, unless the same shall be approved by the Secretary of the Interior.

J. G. BLAINE,
Speaker of the House of Representatives.
SCHUYLER COLFAX,
Vice-President of the United States and President
of the Senate.

Received by the President, January 25, 1871.

[NOTE BY THE DEPARTMENT OF STATE.—The foregoing act having been presented to the President of the United States for his approval, and not having been returned by him to the House of Congress in which it originated within the time prescribed by the Constitution of the United States, has become a law without his approval.]

ACT OF 1874

An Act to provide for the payment of the Stockbridge and Munsee tribe of Indians of Wisconsin

For this amount, to enable the Secretary of the Interior to carry out the provisions of the fourth section of the act entitled "An act for the relief of the Stockbridge and Munsee tribe of Indians in the State of Wisconsin," approved February sixth, eighteen hundred and seventy-one, by causing to be credited to said tribe the estimated value, at sixty cents an acre, of eleven thousand eight hundred and three acres of land remaining unsold of the two townships referred to in said act: Provided, That the expenses of enrollment and payment required by the provisions of said act shall be defrayed from the amount hereby appropriated, seven thousand and eighty-one dollars and eighty cents.

Approved, June 22, 1874.

ACT OF 1893

An act for the relief of the Stockbridge and Munsee tribe of Indians, in the State of Wisconsin

Whereas, a treaty was entered into on the fifth day of February, eighteen hundred and fifty-six, by and between the Government of the United States and the Stockbridge and Munsee Indians, in which the said Indians ceded certain lands to the United States, and accepted in consideration thereof certain lands as a reservation, to which said Indians removed, and upon which they have ever since resided; and

Whereas by the interpretation placed by Government officials on the act of February sixth, eighteen hundred and seventy-one, an act for the relief of said Indians, a large part

of said Indians (and their descendants) who signed said treaty of eighteen hundred and
fifty-six, and have continued with said tribe from the making of said treaty to the present
time, are excluded from participating in tribal funds and the right to occupy said reser-
vation: Therefore, Be it enacted by the Senate and House of Representatives of the United
States of America in Congress assembled,

SECTION 1. That all persons who were actual members of said tribe of Indians at the time of the execution of the treaty of February fifth, eighteen hundred and fifty-six, and their descendants, and all persons who became members of the tribe under the provisions of article six of said treaty, and their descendants, who did not in and by said treaty, and have not since its execution, separated from said tribe, are hereby declared members of said Stockbridge and Munsee tribe of Indians and entitled to their pro rata share in tribal funds and in the occupancy of tribal lands; and all members who entered into possession of lands under the allotments of eighteen hundred and fifty-six and of eighteen hundred and seventy-one, and who by themselves or by their lawful heirs have resided on said lands continuously since, are hereby declared to be owners of such lands in fee simple, in severalty, and the Government shall issue patents to them therefor.

SECTION 2. That it shall be the duty of the Secretary of the Interior, without unnecessary delay after the passage of this act, to cause to be taken an enrollment of said tribe on the basis of the provisions of this act, which enrollment shall be filed, a copy in the Department of the Interior and a copy in the records of said tribe: *Provided*, that in all cases where allotments of eighteen hundred and seventy-one shall conflict with allotments of eighteen hundred and fifty-six, the latter shall prevail.

Approved, March 2, 1893.

ACT OF 1906

STOCKBRIDGE AND MUNSEE TRIBE

That the members of the Stockbridge and Munsee Tribe of Indians, as the same appear upon the official roll of said tribe, made in conformity with the provisions of the act of Congress approved March third, eighteen hundred and ninety-three, entitled "An act for the relief of the Stockbridge and Munsee Tribe of Indians in the State of Wisconsin," and their descendants, who are living and in being on the first day of July, nineteen hundred and four, and who have not heretofore received patents for land in their own right, shall, under the direction of the Secretary of the Interior, be given allotments of land and patents therefor in fee simple, in quantities as follows: To each head of a family, one-eighth of section: *Provided*, That such allotment to the "head of a family" shall be deemed to be a provision for both husband and wife, or the survivor in the event of the death of either. To each single person not provided for as above, one-sixteenth of a section. That where a patent has heretofore been issued to the head of a family (a married man) the same shall be deemed to have been in satisfaction of the claims of both husband and wife, and no further allotment shall be made to either of such persons under this act: *Provided*, That the children of such parents shall be entitled to allotments hereunder in their own right, if enrolled as members of the tribe. That as there is not sufficient land within the limits of the Stockbridge and Munsee Reservation to make the allotments in the quantities above specified, all available land in said reservation shall first be allotted to the heads of families and single persons residing thereon, until said reservation land shall be exhausted, the additional land that may be required to complete the allotments to be obtained in the manner hereinafter specified: *Provided*, That the Secretary of the Interior may make such rules and regulations as he may deem necessary to carry out the requirements of this act as to making and designating allotments. That it shall be obligatory upon any member of said tribe who has made a selection of land within the reservation, whether filed with the tribal authorities or otherwise, to accept such selection as an allotment, except that the same shall be allotted in quantity not to exceed that hereinbefore authorized: *Provided*, That where such selection does not equal in quantity the allotment hereinbefore authorized, the allottee may elect to take out of the lands obtained under the provisions of this act the additional land needed to complete his or her quota of land, or in lieu thereof shall be entitled to receive the commuted value of said additional land in cash, at the rate of two dollars per acre, out of the moneys hereinafter appropriated. That those members of said tribe who have not made selections within the reservation shall be entitled to the option of either taking an allotment under the provisions of this act, or of having the same commuted in cash, at the rate of two dollars per acre, out of the moneys hereinafter appropriated: *Provided*, That the election of any member to take cash in lieu of land shall be made within sixty days after the date of the approval of this act. That for the purpose of obtaining the additional land necessary to complete the allotments herein provided for the Secretary of the Interior is hereby authorized and directed to negotiate, through an Indian inspector, with the Menominee Tribe of Indians of Wisconsin for the cession and relinquishment to the United States of a portion of the surplus land of the Menominee Reservation in said State, or to negotiate with the authorities of said State, or with any corporation, firm, or individual, for the purchase of said additional land: *Provided, however,* That in no event shall any agreement of cession or contract of purchase so negotiated stipulate that a sum greater than two dollars per acre shall be paid for the land so obtained: *And provided further,* That no such agreement or contract shall have any force or validity unless the same shall be approved by the Secretary of the Interior; or said Secretary may, in his discretion, utilize such unappropriated public lands of the United States as may be required to complete the allotments. That certain members of the Stockbridge and Munsee Tribe having made selections of land on tracts patented to the State of Wisconsin under the swamp-land acts, and having made valuable improvements thereon, the Secretary of the Interior is hereby authorized to cause said improvements to be appraised by an inspector or special agent or Indian agent of his department, and to pay to the owners, as their interests may appear, the appraised value of said improvements, in all not to exceed the sum of one thousand dollars, out of the moneys hereinafter appropriated. That the sum necessary to carry out the provisions hereof the Secretary of the Treasury is directed to pay out of the Stockbridge consolidated fund in the Treasury of the United States, which fund on the thirty-first of October, nineteen hundred and four, amounted to seventy-five thousand nine hundred and eighty-eight dollars and sixty cents, under the direction and upon the warrant of the Secretary of the Interior.

ACT OF 1916

An Act Making appropriations for the current and contingent expenses of the Bureau of Indian Affairs, for fulfilling treaty stipulations with various Indian tribes, and for other purposes, for the fiscal year ending June thirtieth, nineteen hundred and seventeen.

Section 25. There is hereby appropriated the sum of $95,000, to be used in addition to the tribal funds of the Stockbridge and Munsee Tribes of Indians, for the payment of the members of the Stockbridge and Munsee Tribes of Indians who were enrolled under the Act of Congress of March third, eighteen hundred and ninety-three, equal amounts to the amounts paid to the other members of said tribe prior to the enrollment under said Act, and such payments shall be made upon the certificate and order of the Commissioner of Indian Affairs upon claims being filed with him, showing to his satisfaction that such claimants, or the ancestors of such claimants, were enrolled tinder the Act of March third, eighteen hundred and ninety-three, entitled, "An Act for the relief of the Stockbridge and Munsee Tribes of Indians of the State of Wisconsin."

ACT OF 1924

An Act Conferring jurisdiction upon the Court of Claims to hear, examine, adjudicate, and enter judgment in any claims which the Stockbridge Indians may have against the United States, and for other purposes.

SECTION 1. *Be it enacted by the Senate and House of Representatives of the United States of America in Congress assembled,* That jurisdiction be, and is hereby, conferred upon the Court of Claims, notwithstanding the lapse of time or statutes of limitation, to hear, examine, and adjudicate and render judgment in any and all legal and equitable claims arising under or growing out of any treaty or agreement between the United States and the Stockbridge Tribe of Indians, or arising under or growing out of any Act of Congress in relation to Indian affairs, which said Stockbridge Tribe may have against the United States, which claims have not heretofore been determined and adjudicated on their merits by the Court of Claims or the Supreme Court of the United States.

SECTION 2. Any and all claims against the United States within the purview of this Act shall be forever barred unless suit be instituted or petition filed as herein provided in the Court of Claims within five years from the date of approval of this Act, and such suit shall make the Stockbridge Tribe party plaintiff and the United States party defendant. The petition shall be verified by the attorney or attorneys employed to prosecute such claim or claims under contract with the Stockbridges approved by the Commissioner of Indian Affairs and the Secretary of the Interior; and said contract shall be executed in their behalf by a committee chosen by them under the direction and approval of the Commissioner of Indian Affairs and the Secretary of the Interior. Official letters, papers, documents, and records, or certified copies thereof, may be used in evidence, and the departments of the Government shall give access to the attorney or attorneys of said Indian nation to such treaties, papers, correspondence, or records as may be needed by the attorney or attorneys of said Indian nation.

SECTION 3. In said suit the court shall also hear, examine, consider, and adjudicate any claims which the United States may have against said Indian nation, but any payment including gratutities which may have been made by the United States upon any claim against the United States shall not operate as an estoppel, but may be pleaded as an offset in such suit.

SECTION 4. That from the decision of the Court of Claims in any suit prosecuted under the authority of this Act, an appeal may be taken by either party as in other cases to the Supreme Court of the United States.

SECTION 5. That upon the final determination of any suit instituted under this Act, the Court of Claims shall decree such amount or amounts as it may find reasonable to be paid the attorney or attorneys so employed by said Indian nation for the services and expenses of said attorneys rendered or incurred prior or subsequent to the date of approval of this Act: *Provided,* That in no case shall the aggregate amounts decreed by said Court of Claims for fees be in excess of $5,000, or in excess of a sum equal to 10 per centum of the amount of recovery against the United States.

SECTION 6. The Court of Claims shall have full authority by proper orders and process to bring in and make parties to such suit any or all persons deemed by it necessary or proper to the final determination of the matters in controversy.

SECTION 7. A copy of the petition shall, in such case, be served upon the Attorney General of the United States, and he, or some attorney from the Department of Justice to be designated by him, is hereby directed to appear and defend the interest of the United States in such case.[1]

Approved, June 7, 1924.

ACT OF 1972

To declare that certain federally owned lands shall be held by the United States in trust for the Stockbridge-Munsee Indian Community, Wisconsin.

Sec. 1. Be it enacted by the Senate and House of Representatives of the United States of America, in Congress assembled. That subject to valid existing rights, all the right, title, and interest of the United States, except all minierals including oil and gas, in the submarginal lands and federally owned improvements thereon, which are indentified below, are hereby declared to be held by the United States in trust for the Stockbridge-Munsee Indian Community, and the lands shall be a part of the reservation heretofore established for this community. Stockbridge Project LI-WI-11 Shawano County, Wisconsin comprising thirteen thousand and seventy-seven acres, more or less, acquired by the United States under Title II of the National Industrial Recovery Act of June 1933 (48 Stat. 200), the Emergency Reliefe Appropriation Act of April 8, 1935 (49 Stat. 750, 781), administrative jurisdiction over which was transferred from the Secretary of Agriculture to the Secretary of the Interior by Executive Order 7868 dated April 15, 1938, for the benefit of the Stockbridge-Munsee Indian Community.

Sec. 2. The Indian Claims Commission is directed to determine in accordance with the provisions of section 2 of the Act of August 13, 1946 (60 Stat. 1050) the extent to which the value of the beneficial interest conveyed by this Act should or should not be set off against any claim against the United States determined by the Commission.

Approved, Oct. 9, 1972.

Photographs, Lists, and Censuses of the Stockbridge-Munsees

A gallery of historical photographs, portraits, and drawings to accompany *A Nation of Statesmen* can be viewed on the Internet at *http:www.mohican-nsn.gov.*

In the research for this book I have transcribed the following manuscript rosters, rolls, lists, and censuses of the Stockbridge-Munsees. Some of the lists are simply that, lists of individuals, but others include important social, political, and demographic information about the individuals. I coded the lists and created data sets in SPSS and MS-Excel format and deposited copies of the computer files in the Inter-University Consortium for Political and Social Research (at www.icpsr. umich.edu) and with the Stockbridge-Munsee Historical Library and Museum. A list of the data sets follows.

1839 List of Emigrant and Wiskonsin Parties
1847 List of Citizens and Indian Parties
1848 Census of the Stockbridges, Indian Party
1856 Census of the Stockbridges-Munsees
1867 Census of the "Citizens" and "Indian" Parties
1893 Census of the Stockbridges and Munsees
1900 Census of Population, Stockbridge-Munsee Indian Reservation
1907 List of Stockbridge-Munsees Allottees
1910 Census of Population, Stockbridge-Munsee Indian Reservation
1913 List of Money–No Land Payees
1920 Census of Population, Towns of Red Springs and Bartelme
1930 Census of Population, Towns of Red Springs and Bartelme

Notes

CHAPTER 1

1. Cooper, *The Last of the Mohicans*, vii; Taylor, *William Cooper's Town*.

2. Davids, *Brief History of the Mohican Nation*.

3. *The West Wing*, NBC Television, episode of November 26, 2001.

4. Brasser, "Mahicans"; Goddard, "Delaware"; Davids, "Stockbridge-Munsee (Mohican)"; Orr and Campana, eds., *The People of Minisink;* "'Last of the Mohicans' Was William Dick, Just Dead," *Milwaukee Journal*, Nov. 8, 1933.

5. Dunn, *The Mohican World, 1680–1750;* Frazier, *The Mohicans of Stockbridge;* Davids, *Brief History of the Mohican Nation*.

6. Davidson, *Muh-He-Ka-Ne-Ok;* Jones, *Stockbridge Past and Present;* Morgan, *League of the Ho-de-no-sau-nee; Constitution of the Stockbridge-Munsee Community*, 1937.

7. Hauptman and McLester, *Chief Daniel Bread and the Oneida Nation of Indians of Wisconsin*.

8. The past decade has seen a flowering of studies in Menominee history and culture. See Davis, *Sustaining the Forest, the People, and the Spirit;* Hosmer, *American Indians in the Marketplace;* Beck, *Siege and Survival;* Bieder, *Native American Communities in Wisconsin;* Grignon, *Menominee Tribal History*.

9. I have been influenced by the following writings on American Indian politics: Cleland, "Economics and Adaptive Change among the Lake Superior Chippewa of the Nineteenth Century"; Fogelson, "The Context of American Indian History"; Fowler, "Local-Level Politics and the Struggle for Self-Government"; Fowler, *Tribal Sovereignty and the Historical Imagination;* Hauptman,

Conspiracy of Interests; Siegel and Beals, "Pervasive Factionalism"; Champagne, *American Indian Societies;* Silverman, *A House Divided?* Albers, "Marxism and Historical Materialism in American Indian History"; DeLoria and Wilkins, *Tribes, Treaties & Constitutional Tribulations;* Prucha, *American Indian Treaties.*

10. I respectfully disagree with the analysis of the late anthropologist James Clifton in his "The Tribal History: An Obsolete Paradigm," especially his lead essay, "The Invented Indian," in his edited volume of the same title. Instead, I have turned to recent works for thinking about researching and writing tribal histories, especially the essays in Mihesugh, *Natives and Academics;* and Meyer, "Native American Studies and the End of Ethnohistory." I am grateful to Ruth Gudinas for sharing her work on the political history of the Ho-Chunk Nation of Wisconsin: "Wisconsin Winnebago Political Organization."

11. Schaefer, *The Winnebago-Horicon Basin;* Savagian, "The Tribal Reorganization of the Stockbridge-Munsee"; Skinner, "Notes on Mahikan Ethnology"; Mochon, "Stockbridge-Munsee Cultural Adaptations."

12. Brasser, "Mahicans"; Goddard, "Eastern Algonquian Languages," esp. table 1; Brasser, "Riding on the Frontier's Crest." For contrast, see Mooney and Thomas, "Mahican," in the Smithsonian's earlier "Handbook of North American Indians" series, and "Munsee" in the same volume; Speck, *The Celestial Bear Comes Down to Earth;* Ruttenber, *History of the Indian Tribes of Hudson's River;* or even Jefferson, *Notes on the State of Virginia,* pp. 205–7. Important recent work on the history of the Wisconsin and western Great Lakes tribes includes Patty Loew, *Indian Nations of Wisconsin;* Bieder, *Native American Communities;* Satz, *Chippewa Treaty Rights;* Cleland and McClurken, eds., *Fish in the Lakes, Wild Rice, and Game in Abundance;* Campisi and Hauptman, *The Oneida Indian Experience;* Hauptman and McLester, *The Oneida Indian Journey;* Beck, *Siege and Survival.*

13. Brasser, "Mahicans," pp. 205–6; Aupaumat, "Narrative of an Embassy to the Western Indians"; Taylor, "Captain Hendrick Aupaumut"; Savagian, "Remembering a Life."

14. Viola, *Diplomats in Buckskin;* Quinney, "Memorial to the Senate and House of Representatives of the United States."

15. Titus, "A Brief Account of the Stockbridges." There is a rich literature on mixed American Indian/African American/Euro-American identities, starting with Woodson, "The Relations of Negroes and Indians in Massachusetts"; Greene, *The Negro in Colonial New England;* Tanner, "The Glaize in 1792"; Thomas, *Rise to Be a People;* McMullen, "Blood and Culture." See also Holzhueter, "Negro Admixture among the Stockbridge and Brothertown Indians of Wisconsin" (copy supplied to the author courtesy of Richard Niemi); see also Mochon, "Stockbridge-Munsee Cultural Adaptations."

16. Report of Special Agent William Parsons, "Stockbridge Indian Troubles," Jan. 16, 1888, in Records of the Senate Committee on Indian Affairs, 51st Cong., 2d sess., Folder 2, Record Group 46, National Archives.

17. Savagian, "Tribal Reorganization of the Stockbridge-Munsee."

18. Mochon, "History of the Wisconsin Stockbridge Indians"; McLaughlin, *Revivals, Awakenings, and Reform.*

CHAPTER 2

1. *Berkshire Eagle, Two Centuries of Stockbridge History;* Jones, *Stockbridge, Past and Present;* Frazier, *The Mohicans of Stockbridge.*

2. R. R. Bowker, "The After History of the Stockbridge Indians," Ayer Manuscripts, Newberry Library; John Sergeant II to Jedidiah Morse, Feb. 27, 1797, Ayer Manuscripts.

3. Blodgett, *Samson Occum;* Appleton, *Gospel Ministers Must Be Fit for the Master's Use;* Belknap and Morse, *Report of a Committee of the Board of Correspondents of the Scots Society for Propagating Christian Knowledge Who Visited the Oneida and Mohekunuh Indians in 1796.*

4. Blodgett, *Samson Occum,* pp. 171–72; Belknap and Morse, *Report . . . in 1796;* Morse, *Report to the Secretary of War on Indian Affairs;* Love, *Samson Occom and the Christian Indians of New England,* p. 207.

5. Davidson, "Coming of the New York Indians to Wisconsin"; Commuck, "Sketch of the Brothertown Indians"; Blasingame, "The New England Indians in the Western Great Lakes Region"; Minutes of Meeting of July 1, 1789, Stockbridge Tribal Records, 1789–1857, Newberry Library.

6. John Sergeant II to Jedidiah Morse, Feb. 2, 1797, in Ayer Manuscripts; John Sergeant II to DeWitt Clinton, July 12, 1819, Ayer Manuscripts.

7. "Stockbridge Nation to Legislature of New York," Oct. 11, 1802, Ayer Manuscripts; Brainerd, *The Life of John Brainerd,* pp. 419–21.

8. "Stockbridge Indian Troubles: Report of William Parsons, Special Agent," in Records of the United States Senate, Committee on Indian Affairs, 51st Cong., 2d sess. (1892), Accession # 51A-F14, Box 56, Folder 2, Record Group 46, National Archives and Records Administration.

9. Belknap and Morse, *Report . . . in 1796.*

10. Oneida Nation to John Taylor, Feb. 27, 1806, Ayer Manuscripts; Belknap and Morse, *Report . . . in 1796;* Ryan, *Cradle of the Middle Class;* Osterud, *Bonds of Community.*

11. Morse, *Report to Secretary of War,* p. 86; Davidson, *Muh-He-Ka-Ne-Ok,* p. 20.

12. Blodgett, *Samson Occum,* pp. 182–85, quote on p. 187.

13. Belknap and Morse, *Report in . . . 1796;* Brasser, "Riding on the Frontier's Crest."

14. Jones, *Stockbridge Past and Present,* pp. 90, 98; "Memorial of John W. Quinney to the Senate and House of Representatives of the United States," in *WHC,* vol. 4, pp. 326–27.

15. "Treaty between the United States and the Oneida, Tuscarora, and Stockbridge Indians," Dec. 2, 1794, in Kappler, ed., *Indian Affairs,* pp. 37–39.

16. Taylor, "Captain Hendrick Aupaumut," p. 451.

17. Jones, *Stockbridge Past and Present*, pp. 87–98.

18. Taylor, "Captain Hendrick Aupaumut"; Hauptman, *Conspiracy of Interests*; Oneida Nation to John Taylor, Feb. 27, 1806, Ayer Manuscripts.

19. "Claim of the Stockbridge Indians," *Senate Report* 166, 16th Cong., 1st sess. (1820).

20. Aupaumut, "Narrative of an Embassy to the Western Indians"; Tanner, "The Glaize in 1792"; Treaty of Aug. 21, 1805, between the United States and the Miamis, in Kappler, ed., *Indian Affairs*, vol. 2, p. 80; Treaty of Sept. 30, 1809, between the United States and the Miamis, in Kappler, ed., *Indian Affairs*, vol. 2, p. 101; "Petition of the Muhheakunuk or Stockbridge Nation of Indians," *House Report* 70, 16th Cong., 1st sess. (1820).

21. Davidson, *Muh-he-ka-ne-ok*, p. 19; Taylor, "Captain Hendrick Aupaumut," p. 437.

22. Davidson, *Muh-he-ka-ne-ok*, p. 19.

23. Treaty of Oct. 3, 1818, between the United States and the Delawares, in Kappler, ed., *Indian Affairs*, vol. 2, p. 170; "Claim of the Stockbridge Indians to Lands in Indiana," *House Report* 311, 16th Cong., 1st sess. (1820), printed in *American State Papers: Indian Affairs,* vol. 30.

24. John Gregg to John Taylor, Jan. 24, 1819, Ayer Manuscripts.

25. "Claim of the Stockbridge Indians to Lands in Indiana."

26. Ellis, "Advent of the New York Indians into Wisconsin."

27. Quinney and Aupaumut, eds., *The Assembly's Shorter Catechism;* Miles, "The Assembly's Catechism, Captain Hendrick Aupaumut, and the Mohican Language"; Berkshire Eagle, *Two Centuries of Stockbridge History.*

28. Morgan, *Ancient Society;* Millar, *Observations Concerning the Distinction of Ranks.*

29. Morse, *Report to the Secretary of War*, p. 86.

30. Colton, *Tour of the American Lakes in 1830,* p. 128.

31. Lewis Cass to Secretary of War, Nov. 11, 1820, in *Territorial Papers of the United States: Michigan Territory*, vol. 10, pp. 69–70, hereafter cited as *TPUS.*

32. Mahon, *The War of 1812;* Hickey, *The War of 1812;* Prucha, *Broadax and Bayonet.*

33. Alexander Dallas to Gov. Lewis Cass, June 19, 1815, in Letters Sent by the Secretary of War, Record Group 107, Microcopy M-15, Roll 3, Frame 120, National Archives; Cass to Dallas, July 15, 1815, *TPUS,* vol. 10, pp. 573–75.

34. John Bowyer to Secretary of War, June 10, 1819, *TPUS,* vol. 10, pp. 834–35; John Calhoun to Bowyer, Aug. 24, 1819, *TPUS,* vol. 10, p. 852; "Speech of Great Wave," copied in Records of the Quarter-Master General, Consolidated Files on Fort Howard, Wisconsin, 1819–1873, Record Group 92, National Archives. See also Grignon, "Seventy-two Years' Recollections of Wisconsin";

Childs, "Recollections of Wisconsin Since 1820"; Baird, "Recollections of the Early History of Northern Wisconsin"; Oberly, "Decision on Duck Creek."

35. Morse, *Report to Secretary of War*, pp. 53, 55; Cass to Calhoun, Nov. 11, 1820, *TPUS*, vol. 10, p. 70.

36. Act of Mar. 3, 1807, 2 *Statutes at Large*, pp. 445–46; Act of May 11, 1820, 3 *Statutes at Large*, p. 572; Act of Feb. 21, 1823, 3 *Statutes at Large*, pp. 724–25; Act of Apr. 17, 1828, 4 *Statutes at Large*, pp. 260–61.

37. DeLoria and Wilkins, *Tribes, Treaties & Constitutional Tribulations*; Hoxie, "Why Treaties?"; Prucha, *American Indian Treaties*; Gates, *Fifty Million Acres*.

38. Ellis, "Advent of the New York Indians," pp. 422–23.

39. Treaty of 1821 between the New York Indians and the Menominees and Winnebagos, Heath Manuscripts, Wisconsin Historical Society.

40. "Memorial of the Stockbridge Nation of Indians in Wisconsin," *Senate Document* 189, 27th Cong., 2d sess. (1842), p. 7.

41. Treaty of 1822 between the New York Indians and the Menominees, Heath Manuscripts.

42. Davidson, *Muh-He-Ka-Ne-Ok*, p. 22; Hauptman and McLester, *Chief Daniel Bread*, chap. 4; Speech of Daniel Bread, Aug. 24, 1830, in "Documents Relating to Ratified and Unratified Treaties," Records of the Bureau of Indian Affairs, Record Group 75, National Archives Microfilm M-668, National Archives; Thomas Dean, "Diary," entries Jan. 10–Mar. 5, 1831, in Thomas Dean Papers, Wisconsin Microfilm Series 22, Roll 1, Wisconsin Historical Society.

43. Taylor, "Captain Hendrick Aupaumut," p. 452.

44. *TPUS*, vol. 11, pp. 508–9. My translation: "In September 1822 Reverend Williams made a treaty between the Stockbridges whom he represented and the Menominees and Ho-Chunks, he wrote it himself without input from these two nations, who were not represented by the right leaders. After learning of the treaty the Menominees refused to ratify it and the Ho-Chunks, too, both denying that the treaty reflected their wishes; neither tribe had an interpreter of their own choosing. This treaty was written by Reverend Williams to take advantage of the situation, and was signed only by a few miserable Menominee low-lifes. No one from the Army was present to witness the council."

For a scholarly treatment of the Green Bay Canadians, see Peterson, "Many Roads to Red River."

45. Jacob Chicks and Austin E. Quinney to Jedediah Morse, Nov. 6, 1824, in Letters Received from the Green Bay Agency, National Archives Microseries M234, Roll 315, frame 8, Record Group 75, Records of the Bureau of Indian Affairs, National Archives (hereafter cited as LR-GB); Ellis, "Advent of the New York Indians," p. 428.

46. Davidson, *Muh-He-Ka-Ne-Ok*, pp. 20, 24.

47. "An Agreement between the Stockbridge Tribe and John P. Arndt," Aug. 20, 1825, in Stockbridge Indian Papers, Huntington Free Library, Museum of

the American Indian, Item No. 9 (hereafter cited as Stockbridge Indian Papers); Ellis, "Recollections of Rev. Eleazer Williams"; "Statesburg Mission Site," *WHC*, vol. 15, pp. 7–13, 39–47.

48. Colton, *Tour of the American Lakes in 1830*, chap. 19; Ellis, "Advent of the New York Indians," p. 430.

49. Davidson, "Coming of the New York Indians to Wisconsin," p. 170.

50. "Reminiscence of Thomas Miner" (1899), Thomas Miner Papers, Wisconsin Historical Society.

51. Colton, *Tour of the American Lakes in 1830*, chap. 18.

52. Col. Brevoort to Thomas McKenny, 1825, in LR-GB, Roll 315, frames 003–004; *Annual Report of the Commissioner of Indian Affairs*, 1829, p. 160 (hereafter cited as *ARCIA*).

53. *TPUS*, vol. 11, p. 113; "Present Condition of the Stockbridge Indians," *House Document* 38, 19th Cong., 2d sess. (1827).

54. Kinzie, *Wau-bun*, p. 329; Colton, *Tour of the American Lakes in 1830*, p. 203.

55. Viola, *Thomas L. McKenny*, chap. 8; Kuasnicka and Viola, *The Commissioners of Indian Affairs*.

56. Viola, *Thomas L. McKenny*, pp. 158–61.

57. Zanger, "Red Bird"; Shrake, "The Winnebago War of 1827"; McKenney, *The Winnebago War of 1827;* "WPA Finds Prison Where Red Bird Died," *Milwaukee Journal*, Oct. 30, 1938.

58. Viola, *Thomas L. McKenny*, pp. 161–65; Treaty of Aug. 11, 1827, between the United States and Chippewas, in Kappler, ed., *Indian Affairs*, vol. 2, p. 281.

59. Zanger, "Red Bird"; Davidson, *Muh-he-ka-ne-ok*, p. 26.

60. "Petition and Appeal of the Six Nations, Oneida, Stockbridge, etc., Nov. 18, 1828, in *Senate Document* 189, 27th Cong., 2d sess., p. 8; Royce, "Indian Land Cessions," Cession #134.

61. Oberly, "Decision on Duck Creek," pp. 39–76.

62. Thomas McKenney to Ogden, Jan. 26, 1829, *TPUS*, vol. 11, pp. 14–15.

63. Davidson, *Muh-He-Ka-Ne-Ok*, pp. 27–29.

64. Petition of Citizens of Brown County, Sept. 24, 1829, *TPUS*, vol. 11, pp. 69–72.

65. John Henry Eaton letter, Jan. 9, 1830, in Thomas Dean Papers, Wisconsin Historical Society.

66. Journal of the Treaty Commissioners, 1830, in LR-GB, Roll 315, frames 456–57.

67. Colton, *Tour of the American Lakes in 1830*, p. 254.

68. Speech of John Metoxen, Aug. 26, 1830, in Colton, *Tour of the American Lakes in 1830*, pp. 252–69.

69. Ibid.

70. Smith, *History of Wisconsin*, vol. 1, p. 380.

71. Thomas Dean Diary, Feb. 8, 1831, entry, Thomas Dean Papers.

72. Treaty of Feb. 8, 1831, between the United States and the Menominee, in Kappler, ed., *Indian Affairs*, vol. 2, p. 319.

73. Thomas Dean Diary, Feb. 12, 1831, entry, Thomas Dean Papers.

74. Cutting Marsh to Presbyterian Board, Aug. 28, 1831, Cutting Marsh Papers, Wisconsin Historical Society.

75. Marsh to Presbyterian Board, July 20, 1831, Cutting Marsh Papers.

76. Marsh to Presbyterian Board, Nov. 25, 1831, Cutting Marsh Papers.

77. Treaty of Oct. 27, 1832, between the United States and the Menominee, in Kappler, ed., *Indian Affairs*, vol. 2, p. 32.

78. Marsh to Presbyterian Board, Jan. 10, 1833, and Feb. 17, 1834, Cutting Marsh Papers.

CHAPTER 3

1. Quoted in Tanner, *History of Kaukauna's Revolutionary Hero*, p. 9; Cutting Marsh to Jeremiah Evarts, Sept. 30, 1830, Cutting Marsh Papers.

2. Viola, *Diplomats in Buckskin*; Quinney, "Memorial to the Senate and House of Representatives of the United States," pp. 321–33.

3. Samuel Stambaugh to Secretary of War, Nov. 8, 1831, reprinted in *WHC*, vol. 15, pp. 399–438.

4. "Report of Secretary of Treasury, Jan. 21, 1839," reprinted in Bogue, ed., *New American State Papers*, vol. 1, pp. 562–64; Agent Boyd to Secretary of War, July 25, 1837, LR-GB, Roll 316, frames 254 and 267.

5. Gates, *History of Public Land Law Development*; Gates, "Frontier Land Business in Wisconsin"; Feller, *The Public Lands in Jacksonian Politics*; Lebergott, "The Demand for Land."

6. "Report of the Secretary of War on Extinguishing Indian Title to Land in Vicinity of Green Bay and north of Wisconsin and Iowa Rivers," *Senate Document* 229, 24th Cong., 1st sess. (1836), Serial Set #281; *ARCIA*, 1836, p. 423.

7. Cited in Satz, *Chippewa Treaty Rights*, chap. 1.

8. Cutting Marsh to Presbyterian Board, Feb. 17, 1834, March 25, 1835, Feb. 9, 1836, Cutting Marsh Papers.

9. James Stryker to Secretary of War, May 17, 1831, in LR-GB, Roll 315, frame 629; Marsh to Presbyterian Board, Mar. 11, 1834, Cutting Marsh Papers; *ARCIA*, 1837, p. 466.

10. Marsh to Presbyterian Board, Mar. 11, 1834, Cutting Marsh Papers.

11. Secretary of War, "Extinguishing Indian Title to Land in vicinity of Green Bay"; Richardson, comp., *Messages and Papers of the Presidents, 1789–1897*, vol. 3, pp. 1390–92, and vol. 4, p. 1475; Remini, *Andrew Jackson & His Indian Wars*.

12. Marsh to Presbyterian Board, Aug. 12, 1836, Cutting Marsh Papers.

13. Marsh to Presbyterian Board, June 17, 1836, Cutting Marsh Papers; Porter, "Relations between Negroes and Indians"; Peterson, "Prelude to Red River."

14. Stambaugh to Secretary of War, in *WHC*, vol. 15, p. 407. Typical in attitude toward mixed-race people at Green Bay was the New York-born Presbyterian missionary Jeremiah Stevens, who disparaged what he called the "motley" people he saw there and at Mackinac in 1827 and 1828, in his "Memoir," pp. 68–69, Jeremiah Stevens Papers, Wisconsin Historical Society; Marsh to Presbyterian Board, Aug. 21, 1837, Cutting Marsh Papers, where he mentions "a Mulatto man living with the Stockbridges and who had married into the Nation"; on Paul Cuffe's relations with the Brothertown Indians and other intertribal groups at New Stockbridge, see Armistead, comp., *Memoir of Paul Cuffe, a Man of Colour;* Cuffe, *Narrative of the Life of Paul Cuffe, a Pequot Indian;* Thomas, *Rise to Be a People.*

15. Prucha, *Broadax and Bayonet,* pp. 216–18.

16. Strong, *History of the Territory of Wisconsin,* pp. 107–14.

17. On Schermerhorn, see Hauptman, *Conspiracy of Interests,* pp. 178–86; Hauptman and McLester, *Chief Daniel Bread,* pp. 91–94.

18. Hauptman, *Conspiracy of Interests,* p. 185; Marsh to Presbyterian Board, Sept. 21, 1836, Cutting Marsh Papers.

19. Unratified treaty between the United States and the Stockbridges, Sept. 17, 1836, in "Ratified and Unratified Indian Treaties," Record Group 75, Microfilm T-494, Roll 8, National Archives; Marsh to Presbyterian Board, Sept. 21, 1836, Cutting Marsh Papers; Chiefs and Principal Men of the Stockbridge Tribe to Governor Dodge, Sept. 1836, Stockbridge Indian Papers, Item 11.

20. Smith, *History of Wisconsin, I,* pp. 143–45; Unratified treaty of Sept. 17, 1836; John W. Quinney to Secretary of War, Apr. 18, 1838, LR-GB, Roll 317, frame 246.

21. "Declaration of the Rights and Frame of Government of the Stockbridge Nation," 1837, LR-GB, Roll 316, frames 702–14. There is a printed copy in J. C. Adams Papers, Wisconsin Historical Society. Electa Jones, writing in 1854, recognized the radical change made by the Quinney constitution. As Jones put it, "The Government of the Stockbridge Tribe was at that time undergoing a change from that of Chiefs to Republicanism." Jones, *Stockbridge, Past and Present,* p. 106. See also "Oath of John W. Quinney," Stockbridge Tribal Records, 1789–1857, Item #7 (1841), Newberry Library.

22. Jones, *Stockbridge, Past and Present,* p. 106; Robert Konkapot and Thomas Hendricks to Secretary of War, Dec. 4, 1837, LR-GB, Roll 316, frames 563–65; Thomas Hendrick and Stockbridge Chiefs and Warriors to President of the United States, Dec. 4, 1837, LR-GB, Roll 316, frame 568; Marsh to Presbyterian Board, Aug. 21, 1837, Cutting Marsh Papers.

23. Marsh to Presbyterian Board, Dec. 13, 1837, May 28, 1838, and July 31, 1838, Cutting Marsh Papers.

24. Marsh to Presbyterian Board, Nov. 28, 1838, Cutting Marsh Papers; "Two Minute Books of Kansas Missions in the Forties."

Reverend Marsh seems to fit the profile that Robert Berkhofer discerned in his 1963 article, "Protestants, Pagans, and Sequences among the North American

Indians, 1760–1860," p. 215: "Given conditions of advanced acculturation and tribal division, missionaries entering a tribe then were thrown into an already existing faction rather than aiding in the creation of one."

25. "An Act for the Relief of the Brothertown Indians, in the Territory of Wisconsin," 5 *Statutes at Large* (1839), p. 349; Strong, *History of the Territory of Wisconsin*, p. 115; Cammuck, "Sketch of Calumet County"; Marsh to Presbyterian Board, July 30, 1839, Cutting Marsh Papers.

26. Colonel Boyd to Secretary of War, Oct. 9, 1834, LR-GB, Roll 317, frame 118; Oberly, "Decision on Duck Creek," pp. 39–76.

27. Wisconsin Territorial Legislature, "Praying that the Right of Citizenship may be extended to the Stockbridge Indians residing on the eastern shore of Lake Winnebago," *House Document* 173, 25th Cong., 2d sess. (1838).

28. Foner, *Reconstruction*, pp. 114–16, 251–61.

29. Power-of-attorney to Austin E. Quinney and John W. Quinney from the Stockbridge Tribe, Nov. 14, 1838, Stockbridge Indian Papers, Item 19; Commissioner of Indian Affairs to Secretary of War, Feb. 26, 1839, in "Report Books of the Office of Indian Affairs," National Archives Microcopy M348, Roll 1, Record Group 75, Records of the Bureau of Indian Affairs, pp. 149–51 (hereafter cited as "Report Books"); Robert Konkapot and Thomas Hendrick to Commissioner of Indian Affairs, Dec. 10, 1838, LR-GB, Roll 317, frame 472; *ARCIA*, 1838, pp. 542–43.

30. Commissioner of Indian Affairs to Albert Gallup, July 3, 1839, in "Ratified and Unratified Treaties," Microcopy T-494, Roll 4; also in Stockbridge Indian Papers, Item 22; *ARCIA*, 1839, pp. 580–81; Marsh to Presbyterian Board, July 30, 1839, Cutting Marsh Papers.

31. Albert Gallup to Commissioner of Indian Affairs, Sept. 26, 1839, in "Ratified and Unratified Treaties," Roll 4; Treaty of Sept. 3, 1839, between the United States and the Stockbridge and Munsee, in Kappler, *Indian Affairs*, vol. 2, p. 529; Marsh to Presbyterian Board, Oct. 22, 1839, Cutting Marsh Papers.

32. "Petition of Emigrant Party," Nov. 9, 1839, in Records of the Wisconsin Superintendent of Indian Affairs, National Archives Microcopy M951, Roll 3, frame 410, Records of the Bureau of Indian Affairs, Record Group 75, National Archives; "Recommending an Appropriation for the Removal and Subsistence of a number of Stockbridge and Munsee Indians," *Senate Document* 42, 26th Cong., 1st sess. (1840); Secretary of War to Senate Committee on Finance, July 1, 1840, in "Report Books," Roll 2, frames 139–40; Commissioner of Indian Affairs to Secretary of War, Nov. 28, 1840, in "Report Books," Roll 2, frames 236–37.

33. Marsh to Presbyterian Board, June 8, 1840, Cutting Marsh Papers.

34. "Two Minute Books of Kansas Missions in the Forties," p. 240; Marsh to Presbyterian Board, June 8, 1840, Cutting Marsh Papers.

35. Marsh to Presbyterian Board, Oct. 22, 1839, Cutting Marsh Papers.

36. Jones, *Stockbridge, Past and Present*, pp. 106–7; Marsh to Presbyterian Board, Sept. 30, 1840, started talking about the new split in the tribe between

the Chicks and Metoxens on the one side and the Quinneys on the other. Marsh blamed Joseph L. Chicks, who had spent two years of study at the New York Oneida Institute (now Hamilton College) but returned to Wisconsin "an enemy to the Cross of Christ." On the importance of Hamilton College in missionary and education work among New York (and Wisconsin) Indian tribes, see Hauptman, *Conspiracy of Interests*, pp. 70–73; Pilkington, *Hamilton College, 1812–1962;* Love, *Hamilton College and Her Family Line.*

37. Austin E. Quinney to James D. Doty, Dec. 12, 1839, Stockbridge Indian Papers, Item 28; Commissioner of Indian Affairs to Secretary of War, Aug. 28, 1841, in "Report Books," Roll 2, frames 495–500; "Petition of the Stockbridge Nation of Indians in Wiskonsin," *House Document* 127, 26th Cong., 1st sess. (1840); "Memorial of the Stockbridge Nation of Indians in Wisconsin," *Senate Document* 189, 27th Cong., 2d sess. (1842).

38. Marsh to Presbyterian Board, Feb. 14, 1840.

39. Smith, *History of Wisconsin, I,* pp. 328–43.

40. "Stockbridge Indians," *House Report* 961, 27th Cong., 2d sess. (1842).

41. Governor of Wisconsin Territory to Commissioner of Indian Affairs, quoted in *House Report* 961, 27th Cong., 2d sess. (1842); *Congressional Globe,* 27th Cong., 3d sess., pp. 83, 377.

42. "An Act for the Relief of the Stockbridge Tribe of Indians in the Territory of Wisconsin," Mar. 3, 1843, 5 *Statutes at Large,* p. 643.

43. Ibid.; Marsh to Presbyterian Board, Mar. 29, 1843, Apr. 10, 1843, June 24, 1844, and Aug. 12, 1844, Cutting Marsh Papers.

44. Miller, *Thirty Years in the Itinerancy,* p. 28. I am indebted to Martin Zank for this reference. On the Methodist missions to various American Indian tribes during Wisconsin territorial and early statehood years, see Bennett and Lawson, *History of Methodism in Wisconsin in Four Parts,* pp. 12–18.

45. For a comparable intratribal split with age as one of the fault lines, see Young, "Tribal Reorganization in the Southeast, 1800–1840"; Anderson, "Comment."

46. Marsh to Presbyterian Board, June 12, 1843, and Mar. 7, 1844, Cutting Marsh Papers; *Congressional Globe,* 28th Cong., 1st sess., pp. 620, 668, 685.

47. Marsh to Presbyterian Board, June 20, 1845, Cutting Marsh Papers; "Petition of Stockbridge Indians," *Senate Report* 302, 28th Cong., 1st sess. (1844).

48. *Congressional Globe,* 28th Cong., 2d sess., pp. 208, 296, 332, 333, 387.

49. Viola, *Diplomats in Buckskin,* pp. 85–86; "Praying for Repeals of Law Passed in 1843," *House Document* 128, 29th Cong., 1st sess. (1846); Jones, *Stockbridge, Past and Present,* pp. 107–8; "Stockbridge Indians," *House Report* 447, 29th Cong., 1st sess. (1846); Marsh to Presbyterian Board, July 28, 1845, Cutting Marsh Papers; Smith, *History of Wisconsin, I,* pp. 366–68.

50. *Congressional Globe,* 29th Cong., 1st sess., pp. 563, 941, 949, 958, 1039, 1179.

51. "An Act to repeal an Act for the Relief of the Stockbridge Tribe of Indians in the Territory of Wisconsin" (1846), 9 *Statutes at Large*, p. 55; *ARCIA*, 1846, p. 158.

52. *ARCIA*, 1846, p. 158.

53. Marsh to Presbyterian Board, Aug. 11, 1846, Apr. 1, 1847, June 27, 1847, Cutting Marsh Papers.

54. Marsh to Presbyterian Board, Apr. 1, 1847, Cutting Marsh Papers; also *ARCIA*, 1847, pp. 177–78.

55. *ARCIA*, 1847, pp. 771–83; Marsh to Presbyterian Board, Oct. 18, 1847, Cutting Marsh Papers.

56. Marsh to Presbyterian Board, Oct. 18, 1847, Cutting Marsh Papers.

57. Marsh to Presbyterian Board, Oct. 18, 1847, and Nov. 18, 1847, Cutting Marsh Papers.

58. Wisconsin Constitution, 1848, Art. III, "Qualification of Electors," in *Wisconsin Blue Book*.

59. Keyssar, *The Right to Vote*, pp. 164–65.

60. *ARCIA*, 1847, p. 787.

61. On Daniel Whitney, see Smith, *History of Wisconsin, I*, pp. 114, 193–94, 278. In the Stockbridge Indian Papers, the following detail Whitney's many financial dealings with the Stockbridges: Items 10 (1834), 12 (1836), 26 (1839), 28.3 (1840), 57 (1850).

62. Commissioner of Indian Affairs to Albert G. Ellis and Morgan L. Martin, Oct. 19, 1848, in Ratified and Unratified Treaties, National Archives Microfilm T-494, Roll 4.

63. Albert G. Ellis to Commissioner of Indian Affairs, Dec. 2, 1848, in Ratified and Unratified Treaties, National Archives Microfilm T-494, Roll 4.

64. Treaty of Nov. 24, 1848, between the United States and the Stockbridges, in Kappler, *Indian Affairs*, vol. 2, p. 745. On the changes in the Taylor-Fillmore administration's federal Indian policy on the question of removal, see Satz, *Chippewa Treaty Rights*, chap. 4; Beck, *Siege and Survival*, chap. 10; Prucha, *American Indian Treaties*, p. 201.

65. "Supplemental Article," in Kappler, *Indian Affairs*, vol. 2, p. 577; Commissioner of Indian Affairs to Senator Sam Houston, Jan. 11, 1849, in "Report Books," Roll 5, pp. 68–85.

66. Robert B. Haines letter, June 11, 1849, in Robert B. Haines Papers, Wisconsin Historical Society; William Bruce to Commissioner of Indian Affairs, June 8, 1849, in Ratified and Unratified Treaties, National Archives Microfilm T-494, Roll 4.

67. "Treaty with the Winnebago," Oct. 13, 1846, in Kappler, *Indian Treaties*, vol. 2, pp. 565–67; "Treaty with the Chippewas of the Mississippi and Lake Superior," Aug. 2, 1847, in Kappler, *Indian Treaties*, vol. 2, pp. 567–69; "Treaty with the Sioux," July 23, 1851, in Kappler, *Indian Treaties*, vol. 2, pp. 588–90; Rasmussen, *Ojibwe Journey*.

68. Art. 7, Treaty of Nov. 24, 1848; *ARCIA*, 1849, p. 946; *ARCIA*, 1850, p. 38; *ARCIA*, 1852, p. 295.

69. *ARCIA*, 1849, p. 947.

70. *ARCIA*, 1850, p. 38.

71. Satz, *Chippewa Treaty Rights*, chap. 5; Beck, *Siege and Survival*, pp. 189–95; *ARCIA*, 1851, pp. 307–8; *ARCIA*, 1852, pp. 346, 364.

72. "Letter from the Sachem and Councillors of the Stockbridge Indians," *House Miscellaneous Document* 69, 32d Cong., 1st sess.; Jones, *Stockbridge, Past and Present*, p. 116; "A List of Claims of J. W. Quinney Re his Share of Monies Due and Payable to the Stockbridge Tribe," Stockbridge Indian Papers, Item 75.

73. Stockbridge Indian Papers, Items 71–75; "An Act for the Relief of John W. Quinney, a Stockbridge Indian," 10, *Statutes at Large*, p. 746 (1853); Francis Huebschman to George Manypenny, June 6, 1853, in Special Files of the Office of Indian Affairs, File 177A, National Archives Microfilm M574, National Archives Record Group 75 (hereafter cited as Special File 177A).

74. "Speech of John W. Quinney, July 4, 1854," in *WHC*, Vol. 4(1859), p. 319; Gienapp, *The Origins of the Republican Party*, pp. 147–61.

75. "Speech of John W. Quinney," pp. 313–20; Quinney's speech is also reprinted in Lauter, ed., *The Heath Anthology of American Literature*; Davidson, *Muh-He-Ka-Ne-Ok*; "Death of John W. Quinney," *WHC*, Vol. 4 (1859), pp. 309–11.

CHAPTER 4

1. Petition of Chicks (Citizens) Party, Feb. 2, 1854, in Special File 177A, Roll 44, frame 603; Bowker, "After History of the Stockbridge Indians."

2. Unratified treaty of 1855, in Stockbridge Indian Papers, Item 86.1; *ARCIA*, 1855, pp. 426–27, 466–67.

3. Manypenny to Huebschman, Jan. 7, 1856, in "Documents Relating to Ratified Treaties," National Archives Microfilm M-668, Treaty #301, Item 6.

4. Huebschman to Manypenny, Feb. 23, 1856, in "Documents Relating to Ratified Treaties," National Archives Microfilm M-668, Treaty #301, Item 6.

5. Treaty of Feb. 5, 1856, between the United States and the Stockbridge and Munsee, and Treaty of Feb. 11, 1856, between the United States and the Menominee, both in Kappler, *Indian Affairs*, vol. 2, pp. 742, 755.

6. Slingerland to Manypenny, Sept. 28, 1856, Special File 177A, Roll 44, frame 687.

7. Calculated from Special Census of Indians, Stockbridge-Munsee Reservation, Census of 1900. For comparative purposes, I drew a sample from the 1900 U.S. Census of 10,934 women born between 1820 and 1840, and of this group, 375 lived in Wisconsin at the time of the census. The women in the sample of between sixty and eighty years of age had the following characteristics: 93.8% were ever-married (97.1% for the Wisconsin subsample), and the mean number of children the women bore was 5.8 for the United States as a whole and 6.2 for

Wisconsin. Calculated from a "Regular" sample (N = 375,930 cases) from the Integrated Public Use Microdata Sample (IPUMS) at *www.ipums.umn.edu*. Although the Stockbridge-Munsee fertility rate of cohorts of women born after 1840 declined steadily, the tribe's mortality dropped even faster, leading to a population rebound at the same time as many other American Indian tribes. See Shoemaker, *American Indian Population Recovery in the Twentieth Century*.

8. Quinney et al., *Petition to U.S. House and Senate;* Huebschman to Manypenny, Oct. 6, 1856, Special File 177A, Roll 44, frames 677–79.

9. Manypenny to Huebschman, Oct. 7, 1856, Special File 177A, Roll 44, frames 681–83; *ARCIA*, 1856, p. 4.

10. Manypenny to Huebschman, Oct. 7, 1856, Special File 177A, Roll 44, frames 681–83.

11. Billinghurst to Manypenny, Feb. 3, 1857, LR-GB, Roll 323, frame 203.

12. Act of Mar. 3, 1857, 11 *Statutes at Large*, p. 176; *Biographical Directory,* "Charles Billinghurst," p. 172.

13. Constitution of 1857, in *Record Book of the Stockbridge Nation of Indians, 1857–1885,* in "Special Case 42," Box 5. [Note: items in "Special Case 42" were removed by the Office of Indian Affairs from the regular files of Letters Received from the Green Bay Agency, Records of the Bureau of Indian Affairs, Record Group 75, National Archives. All subsequent citations to "Special Case 42" are to the originals in the National Archives; there is a microfilm set of "Special Case 42" at SMHLM with six boxes of files placed on five reels of microfilm.]

14. *ARCIA*, 1856, pp. 4, 40–41; *ARCIA*, 1857, p. 41; "Protest of A. Miller, Delegate of the Stockbridge Nation of Indians," *Senate Miscellaneous Document 119,* 48th Cong., 1st sess. (1884), Serial Set #2174.

15. Current, *Pine Logs and Politics,* pp. 72–74; Current, The *History of Wisconsin,* vol. 2, p. 557; *Biographical Directory,* "Philetus Sawyer," p. 1783.

16. Field Notes of Original Survey, Records of the Surveyor General, Bureau of Land Management, Record Group 49, National Archives, Microseries T1280; and Original Plats of T28N R14E and T28N R13E in Cartographic Records of the Bureau of Indian Affairs, Record Group 75, National Archives.

17. Francis Huebschman to Benjamin Hunkins, Sept. 25, 1856, Stockbridge Indian Papers, Item 89; Register of Allotment Selections, 1856–69, Stockbridge Indian Papers.

18. *Record Book of the Stockbridge Nation,* Dec. 11, 1858, and Jan. 17, 1859; *ARCIA*, 1858, pp. 29–30; *ARCIA*, 1859, pp. 39–41; *ARCIA*, 1860, p. 36.

19. *Record Book of the Stockbridge Nation,* Oct. 3, 1862.

20. *ARCIA*, 1863, pp. 346–47; *ARCIA*, pp. 435–36; *ARCIA*, 1865, p. 435.

21. *Record Book of the Stockbridge Nation,* June 13, 1864.

22. Act of Mar. 3, 1865, 13 *Statutes at Large*, p. 541.

23. *ARCIA*, 1865, p. 435. Green Bay Agent to Commissioner of Indian Affairs, Aug. 13, 1872, LR-GB, Roll 328, frames 73–74, gives a history of the

contract logging of the Burnt District awarded to Jenkins & Co. and to Knapp & Co., Wolf River lumbermen.

24. The complete file on the unratified Treaty of Feb. 15, 1867, including the endorsements from the president, the secretary of the interior, and the Commissioner of Indian Affairs is found in the Records of the U.S. Senate, Committee on Indian Affairs, National Archives, Record Group 46, Accession #Senate 40B-C1.

25. Hendricks to Morgan L. Martin, Feb. 12, 1867, Morgan L. Martin Papers (microfilm edition), Wisconsin Historical Society, Reel 14.

26. Darius Charles to Martin, May 2, 1867, Martin Papers, Reel 14; Prucha, *American Indian Treaties,* chap. 12; *Congressional Globe,* 41st Cong., 1st sess., Mar. 5, 1869, p. 9; and Mar. 6, 1869, p. 21. *Congressional Globe,* 41st Cong., 2d sess., May 31, 1870, p. 3942; *Senate Journal,* 41st Cong., 2d sess., May 31, 1870, pp. 732–33; Slingerland and Charles to Senate Committee on Indian Affairs, Mar. 16, 1870, Record Group 46, Accession #Senate 41A-E8, Box 25.

27. James Jenkins to Martin, Nov. 4, 1867, and Dec. 23, 1867, Martin Papers, Reel 14.

28. Current, *History of Wisconsin,* vol. 2, p. 557.

29. The text of the draft treaty of 1868 is in LR-GB, Roll 326, frames 114–23.

30. *Report on the Stockbridge Indians* (1870).

31. *Advantages and Productions of the Counties of Brown, Door, Oconto and Shawano,* p. 19.

32. Current, *Pine Logs and Politics,* pp. 72–74.

33. Philetus Sawyer to Commissioner of Indian Affairs, Oct. 22, 1869, LR-GB, Roll 326, frames 727–29.

34. Charles to Martin, Jan. 7, 1870, Martin Papers, Reel 14; Darius Charles and Jeremiah Slingerland to Sen. James Harlan, Mar. 16, 1870, Petitions to the Senate Committee on Indian Affairs.

35. S.B. 849, Bill Files of the 41st Cong., Records of the United States Senate, Record Group 46, National Archives.

36. S.B. 610, Bill Files of the 41st Congress.

37. "An Act for the Relief of the Stockbridge and Munsee Tribe of Indians in the State of Wisconsin," 16 *Statutes at Large,* p. 404 (1871).

38. Secretary of Interior to Senator Howe, Mar. 1, 1870, Petitions to the Senate Committee on Indian Affairs.

39. Petitions to the Senate Committee on Indian Affairs, 41st Cong., 2d sess., Records of the Senate, Record Group 46, Accession #Senate 41A-E8.

40. S.B. 610, Bill Files of the 41st Cong.

41. *Congressional Globe,* 41st Cong., 2d sess., pp. 1624, 1818, 2984, 3040, 4954, 5594 for the history of S.B. 610; pp. 3014, 3554, 5380, 5411, 5597, 5599 for the Menominee bill, S.B. 849.

42. S. E. Gilbert to Commissioner of Indian Affairs, Mar. 27, 1870, LR-GB, Roll 327, frame 396.

43. There is no printed decision in *U.S. v. Wybro*. The trial transcript and Judge Drummond's ruling are preserved in LR-GB, Roll 327, frames 827–83. A parallel case that Judge Drummond heard from the Oneida Indian Reservation was *U.S. v. Foster*.

44. *Shawano Journal*, Feb. 24, 1870; "Interior Department Appointment Papers, Wisconsin, 1849–1907," National Archives Microfilm M-831, Roll 7, Green Bay Agency.

45. Charles to Martin, Apr. 7, 1870, Morgan Martin Papers, Reel 14.

46. I am indebted to Charles Cleland for this insight, developed at greater length in his "History of the Stockbridge-Munsee Reservation in the Context of Federal Indian Policy," submitted to the Federal District Court for the Eastern District of Wisconsin, Case No. 98-C-0871 (2001), pp. 80–82.

47. *Oshkosh Times*, Oct. 12, 1870.

48. *Marquette Express*, Oct. 22, 1870, as reprinted in the *Oshkosh Times*, Oct. 26, 1870.

49. Petition of Members of the Stockbridge and Munsee Tribes," Senate Committee on Indian Affairs, 41st Cong., 3d sess., Records of the Senate, Record Group 46, National Archives.

50. Slingerland to Martin, Nov. 29, 1870, Morgan Martin Papers, Reel 14.

51. *Congressional Globe*, 41st Cong., 3d sess., pp. 90, 494, 586.

52. Ibid., p. 587.

53. Ibid., p. 588.

54. Gates, *Fifty Million Acres*; Haney, *A Congressional History of Railways in the United States*.

55. "To Inquire into and report to the Senate the effect of the Fourteenth Amendment to the Constitution upon the Indian tribes of the country," *Senate Report* 268, 41st Cong., 3d sess. (1870); DeLoria and Wilkins, *Tribes, Treaties & Constitutional Tribulations*, pp. 141–48; Prucha, *American Indian Treaties*, p. 300; Kerber, "The Abolitionist Perception of the Indian."

56. *Congressional Globe*, 41st Cong., 3d sess., pp. 585–88.

57. Ibid., p. 585.

58. Ibid., p. 588.

59. Ibid., pp. 599, 615, 689, 988. On the president's inaction, see Simon, ed., *The Papers of Ulysses S. Grant*, vol. 21, p. 416.

60. Sachem and Councilors to Philetus Sawyer, Jan. 24, 1871, in Special Case 42, Box 1.

61. *Shawano Journal*, Jan. 26, 1871.

62. W. T. Richardson to Commissioner of Indian Affairs, Feb. 14, 1871, in Special Case 42, Box 1.

63. Philetus Sawyer to Jeremiah Slingerland, Feb. 16, 1871, in J. C. Adams Papers, Box 1, Wisconsin Historical Society.

64. Green Bay Agent to Commissioner of Indian Affairs, Jan. 6, 1871, LR-GB, Roll 327, frames 901–4.

65. Sachem John P. Hendricks and Councilors to President Grant, Mar. 25, 1871, in Special Case 42, Box 1.

66. *Oshkosh Times*, Apr. 26, 1871.

67. *Oshkosh Northwestern*, May 4, 1871.

68. Acting Commissioner of Indian Affairs to Secretary of the Interior, Apr. 18, 1871, "Report Books," Roll 20, frame 140.

69. Commissioner of Indian Affairs to Green Bay Agent, Apr. 24, 1871, "Letters Sent by the Office of Indian Affairs, 1824–1881," National Archives Microfilm M-21, Roll 102, frames 24; May 4, 1871, frame 57.

70. Jeremiah Rusk to John P. Hendricks, Apr. 5, 1871, J. C. Adams Papers, Box 1.

71. "Chiefs and Headmen of the Menominee Nation to Commissioner of Indian Affairs," June 9, 1871, in LR-GB, M-234, Roll 327, frames 1174–82; "An Act making Appropriations for the General Incidental Expenses of the Indian Service," 17 *Statutes at Large*, pp. 190–91 (1872).

72. Huebschman to Secretary of the Interior, July 21, 1879, copy in J. C. Adams Papers, Box 1.

CHAPTER 5

1. "Writer Recalls Episodes in Stockbridge History," *Antigo Journal*, Oct. 27, 1932, accessed through the Wisconsin Local History and Biography site at *www.wisconsinhistory.org/whlba*.

2. Prucha, *American Indian Treaties*, pp. 409–12; DeLoria, *Behind The Trail of Broken Treaties*.

3. Prucha, *American Indian Treaties*, pp. 311–19; Act of Feb. 6, 1871, 16 *Statutes at Large*, pp. 404–7.

4. Myron McCord to Commissioner of Indian Affairs, June 8, 1871, in Special Case 42, Box 1.

5. Agent Richardson to Commissioner of Indian Affairs, Sept. 7, 1872, LR-GB, Roll 328, frame 253.

6. Myron McCord's appraisal is located in "Stockbridge Indians," Special Case 42, Box 6; *Oshkosh Northwestern*, Oct. 5, 1871; *Oshkosh Northwestern*, Jan. 18, 1872; *Shawano Journal*, Jan. 26, 1872; Green Bay Agent to Commissioner of Indian Affairs, July 18, 1873, LR-GB, Roll 329, frames 587–610.

7. *Beecher v. Wetherby; Minnesota v. Hitchcock;* Wilkins, *American Indian Sovereignty and the U.S. Supreme Court*, p. 113.

8. "An Act to Provide for the Disposition of Funds Appropriated for the Indian Department," 18 *Statutes at Large*, p. 174 (Act of June 22, 1874).

9. "The Stockbridge Indians—Internecine War Impending," *Shawano Journal*, Sept. 21, 1871; Agent Richardson to Commissioner of Indian Affairs, Nov. 15, 1872, LR-GB, Roll 328, frames 281–87.

10. Daniel Davids to J. C. Adams, Stockbridge Indian Papers; *Record Book of the Stockbridge Nation,* May 4, 1871, and June 1, 1872.

11. "An Act for the Relief of the Stockbridge and Munsee Tribe of Indians of Wisconsin," 16 *Statutes at Large,* p. 404 (Act of Feb. 6, 1871).

12. J. C. Adams spent twenty years trying to overturn the Act of 1871. He collected documents and sworn affadavits from tribal members about the Wells roll of 1874. Those documents are preserved in two places, the Papers of John C. Adams, Wisconsin Historical Society and the archival records of the Senate Committee on Indian Affairs (see note 39 below).

13. *ARCIA,* 1875, p. 598.

14. "Field Notes of Indian Reservation Surveys," Record Group 75, Records of the Bureau of Indian Affairs, National Archives.

15. Kemble Report, 1877, J. C. Adams Papers, Box 6.

16. Inspector Kemble to Commissioner of Indian Affairs, Aug. 4, 1874, in Reports of Indian Inspectors, Report #637, Records of the Bureau of Indian Affairs, Record Group 75, National Archives Microfilm M-1070, Roll 18.

17. Ibid.

18. *ARCIA,* 1889.

19. Report of Inspector McNeil to Commissioner of Indian Affairs, Apr. 18, 1880, Records of Indian Inspectors, M-1070, Roll 18, frames 639–44; *Record Book of the Stockbridge Nation,* June 26, 1875.

20. *Record Book of the Stockbridge Nation,* Oct. 31, 1881; see also Green Bay Agent to Commissioner of Indian Affairs, Jan. 26, 1880, LR-GB, M-234, Roll 333.

21. *Record Book of the Stockbridge Nation,* July 16, 1883.

22. Act of Mar. 3, 1893, "An Act for the Relief of the Stockbridge and Munsee tribes of Indians in the State of Wisconsin," 27 *Statutes at Large,* p. 744; *Biographical Directory,* "Angus Cameron."

23. *Record Book of the Stockbridge Nation,* Jan. 10 and 26, 1881.

24. Ninth Census of the United States (1880), Town of Herman, Shawano County, Wisconsin, National Archives Microfilm T-1224.

25. "Protest of A. Miller, Delegate of the Stockbridge Nation of Indians," *Senate Miscellaneous Document* 119, 48th Cong., 1st sess. (1884), Serial Set #2171.

26. Albert Miller to Secretary of the Interior, Sept. 29, 1884, in "Stockbridge Indian Papers," Item 301.

27. Memorial of J. C. Adams for and in behalf of the Stockbridge and Munsee Tribe of Indians," *Senate Miscellaneous Document* 61, 48th Cong., 2d sess. (1885), Serial Set #2265.

28. *Congressional Record,* 52d Cong., 1st sess., June 15, 1892.

29. Zachariah Miller to Albert Miller, Aug. 19, 1886, in Stockbridge Indian Papers, Item 336.

30. The testimony before the Senate Committee on Indian Affairs is in Record Group 46, Senate Accession #51A-F14, Box 56. Some, not all, of this

material was published in "Testimony Taken Before the Sub-Committee of the Committee on Indian Affairs for the Relief of the Stockbridge and Munsee Tribe," *Senate Miscellaneous Document* 226, 52d Cong., 1st sess., Serial Set 2907.

31. *Record Book of the Stockbridge Nation,* Jan. 14, 1885.

32. Hagan, *The Indian Rights Association,* pp. 72–73, 137–38.

33. Veto #649 of Senate Bill 712 "For the Relief of the Stockbridge Tribe of Indians in the State of Wisconsin," *Presidential Vetoes, 1789–1976,* p. 139; Hagan, *The Indian Rights Association,* p. 13.

34. *ARCIA,* 1890, 1891, 1892. The last-ditch attempts of Senator Sawyer to have the Citizens Party members evicted from the reservation may be followed in the series "Letters of the Indian Division of the Office of Secretary of the Interior," Records of the Department of Interior, Record Group 48, National Archives Microfilm M-606, Roll 71, Sawyer to Secretary of Interior, Apr. 20, 1891, at frame 320; Secretary of Interior to Commissioner of Indian Affairs, Feb. 15 and Feb. 23, 1892, Roll 74, at frames 427 and 470.

35. "Testimony Taken Before the Sub-Committee . . . for the Relief of the Stockbridge and Munsee Tribe."

36. *Congressional Record,* 52d Cong., 2d sess., Feb. 13, 1893, p. 1512; *Biographical Directory,* "Thomas Lynch."

37. *Congressional Record,* 52d Cong., 2d sess., p. 1512.

38. Ibid., p. 2088; Act of Mar. 3, 1893, 27 *Statutes at Large,* p. 744.

39. In 1892 J. C. Adams deposited his extensive collection of Stockbridge-Munsee documents with the Senate Committee on Indian Affairs. See Committee on Indian Affairs Papers, Record Group 46, Records of the U.S. Senate, National Archives, Sen. Accession #51A-F14, Box 56.

40. The complete file of Painter's census and 1893–94 correspondence with the Commissioner of Indian Affairs is in Special Case 42, Box 5.

41. Albert Miller to Secretary of the Interior, Dec. 1893, in Special Case 42, Box 5.

42. The original of the Painter roll of 1893–94 is in "Stockbridge Indians," Special Case 42, Box 5.

43. Report of Inspector McNeil, Apr. 18, 1880, in Reports of Indian Inspectors, M-1070, Roll 18, frame 639.

44. On the Buffalo Creek Treaty, see Hauptman, *Conspiracy of Interests*; Prucha, *American Indian Treaties,* pp. 202–7; *New York Indians v. United States,* p. 1. The successful plaintiffs recovered more than $1.9 million in the case. See "Judgments Rendered by the Court of Claims," *House Document* 226, 56th Cong., 1st sess. (1900), Serial Set #3974; "An Act to Pay Judgments Rendered in the Court of Claims," 31 *Statutes at Large,* p. 27 (1900); see also "Will Receive Second Payment Soon; Stockbridge Indians to Be Paid in about Two Weeks," *Shawano Advocate,* Aug. 2, 1906.

CHAPTER 6

1. Secretary of the Interior to Commissioner of Indian Affairs, Dec. 6, 1895, Special Case 42, Box 5. On the appointment of Hoke Smith to head the Interior Department, see Woodward, *Origins of the New South, 1877–1913*, p. 271.

2. "Letter from the Secretary of the Interior with the draft of a bill for adjusting matters pertaining to the affairs of the Stockbridge and Munsee Tribe of Indians," *House Document* 405, 56th Cong., 2d sess. (1901), Serial Set 4163.

3. Ibid.

4. Ibid.

5. Ibid.

6. *Congressional Record*, 56th Cong., 2d sess., p. 1874; 57th Cong., 1st sess., p. 466; 57th Cong., 2d sess., p. 1400; 58th Cong., 1st sess., p. 180; 58th Cong., 2d sess., pp. 355, 514, 793, 841, 2961; "Letter from the Secretary of the Interior . . . about the affairs of the Stockbridge and Munsee Tribe of Indians," *House Document* 167, 57th Cong., 1st sess. (1902); "Stockbridge and Munsee Tribe of Indians, *Senate Report* 2699, 57th Cong., 2d sess. (1903), Serial Set #4411; "Allotment of Lands in Severalty to Certain Indians, etc.," *House Report* 3783, 57th Cong., 2d sess. (1903), Serial Set #4415; "Stockbridge and Munsee Tribe of Indians," *Senate Report* 173, 58th Cong., 2d sess. (1904), Serial Set #4570; "Stockbridge and Munsee Tribe of Indians," *House Report* 1420, 58th Cong., 2d sess. (1904), Serial Set #4580.

7. "Allotment of Lands in Severalty to Certain Indians, etc.," *House Report* 3783, 57th Cong., 2d sess. (1903), Serial Set #4415; Stockbridge and Munsee Tribe of Indians, etc.," *House Report* 1420; see also *Congressional Record*, 57th Cong., 1st sess., p. 1372; 57th Cong., 2d sess., pp. 1400, 1485, 2295; 58th Cong., 1st sess., p. 180; 58th Cong., 2d sess., pp. 514, 793, 841, 2961.

8. Act of June 21, 1906, 34 *Statutes at Large*, p. 382. For contrast, see the Act of Apr. 21, 1904, 33 *Statutes at Large*, p. 189, where Congress explicitly dissolved boundaries on several Oklahoma Indian reservations in the process of allotment; but see also Moore, "The Enduring Reservations of Oklahoma."

9. *United States v. Anderson* and the archival record in the case in "United States v. Anderson," U.S. District Court, Eastern District of Wisconsin, Record Group 21, Records of the District Courts of the United States, National Archives—Great Lakes Region, Mixed Case Files.

10. "To Restrict Conveyance of Lands Allotted to Indians of Stockbridge Munsee Reservation, Wis.," *House Document* 471, 60th Cong., 1st sess. (1908), Serial Set #5377; "Condition of Indian Affairs in Wisconsin," *Hearings Before the Senate Committee on Indian Affairs*, 61st Cong., 1st sess.; "Stockbridge and Munsee Indians—Unallotted or Who Failed to Secure Full Allotments Under Act of June 21, 1906," in Records of the Keshena Agency, Record Group 75, Records of the Bureau of Indian Affairs, National Archives—Great Lakes Region.

11. *United States v. Cook.*

12. *United States v. Paine Lumber Company; United States v. Torrey Cedar Company.*

13. *United States v. Gardner.*

14. *ARCIA*, 1905, p. 92; *ARCIA*, 1906, p. 101; Act of Mar. 3, 1899, 30 *Statutes at Large*, p. 990.

15. Secretary of the Interior to Keshena Agent, Central Classified Files, File #21892-1910-371-Keshena, Records of the BIA, Record Group 75, National Archives (hereafter cited as CCF); Act of Aug. 4, 1852, 11 *Statutes at Large*, p. 28; Act of 1875, 18 *Statutes at Large*, p. 482; Cohen, *Handbook of Federal Indian Law*, pp. 358–59.

16. Patent to Laura Mohawk, copy in Shawano County Register of Deeds, vol. 108, p. 27; Deed from Shawano Lumber Company to Green Bay, Oshkosh, Madison & Southwestern Railway Company, May 22, 1906, copy in Shawano County Register of Deeds, vol. 184, p. 487; "Field Notes of Survey of Stockbridge & Munsee Reservation," 1907, Reservation Surveys, Record Group 75, Records of the Bureau of Indian Affairs, National Archives; the patents to the individual allotments are on file in the office of the Shawano County Register of Deeds.

17. "Indian Appropriation Bill," *Hearings Before the Senate Committee on Indian Affairs*, 63d Cong., 3d sess. (1915), p. 253.

18. Appeal No. 19551, Treasury Department, Office of Comptroller of the Treasury, CCF 193709-1912-313-Keshena.

19. "An Act making Appropriations for the current and contiguous expenses of the Indian Department," 39 *Statutes at Large*, p. 123 (1916); *Biographical Directory*, "Thomas Konop."

20. Congressman Browne to Asst. Commissioner OIA, May 11, 1922, CCF 38751-1922-Keshena.

21. H.R. 8493, "Conferring Jurisdiction on the Court of Claims for the Stockbridge Indians," 68th Cong., 1st sess., Bill File, House Committee on Indian Affairs, Record Group 236, National Archives; "Claims of Stockbridge Indians before the Court of Claims," *House Report* 682, 68th Cong., 1st sess. (1924), Serial Set #8228; "Conferring Jurisdiction on the Court of Claims to hear the claims of the Stockbridge Indians," *Senate Report* 567, 68th Cong., 1st sess. (1924), Serial Set #8221; "An Act Conferring Jurisdiction upon the Court of Claims to hear, examine, and adjudicate and enter judgment in any claims which the Stockbridge Indians may have against the United States," 43 *Statutes at Large*, p. 644 (1924). See also *Stockbridge Tribe of Indians v. United States.*

22. "Message of the President of the United States transmitting to the House of Representatives without his approval the bill H.R. 5229," *House Document* 274, 74th Cong., 1st sess. (1935), Serial Set #9928; "Message of the President of the United States transmitting to the House of Representatives without his approval the bill H.R. 5230," *House Document* 269, 74th Cong., 1st sess. (1935), Serial Set #9928.

23. *Wisconsin Blue Book*, 1911; *Shawano County Centurawno, 1853–1953*; Records of the School District of Red Springs, 1915–47, Wisconsin Historical Society.

24. Jacoby and Sharma, "Employment Duration and Industrial Labor Mobility in the United States, 1880–1980"; Galenson and Levy, "A Note on Biases in the Measurement of Geographical Mobility"; Thernstrom, *The Other Bostonians.*

25. Richter, *The Mohican.*

26. Brown, Diary Entry Aug. 24, 1895, in William F. Brown Papers, Wisconsin Historical Society; Putnam, *Christian Religion among the Stockbridge-Munsee Band of Mohican Indians,* p. 38.

27. "Indians Observe their Centennial," *Shawano Journal,* Nov. 2, 1922.

28. Gough, *Farming the Cutover;* Kamphoefner, "German Emigration Research, North, South, and East"; Lubinski, "Overseas Emigration from Mecklenburg-Strelitz."

29. *State of Wisconsin v. Dan Tousey,* in Records of the Shawano County Circuit Court, Box 185, Folder 4, Wisconsin Historical Society—Green Bay Area Research Center; "Narrative Reports from Agencies—Keshena," National Archives Microfilm M-1011, Record Group 75, Records of the Bureau of Indian Affairs, National Archives, 1910, Roll 149, 1915 (hereafter cited as Keshena Narrative Reports). For a discussion of the federal enforcement of liquor laws in Indian Country, see Hoxie, *A Final Promise.*

30. Keshena Narrative Reports, 1918–21.

31. Ibid., 1924–25.

32. Ibid., 1926 and 1930.

33. *United States v. Dan Tousey* (1938), U.S. District Court, Eastern District of Wisconsin, Case #5849, Civil Records of the U.S. District Court, Record Group 21, National Archives—Great Lakes Region. Carl Miller, the frequent chair of the Tribal Business Committee in the 1920s, despaired about the Tousey family. According to Miller, the Touseys were a mixed African-Indian family that was denied membership among the Stockbridges in the 1820s, then admitted by Superintendent Huebschman at the 1856 treaty, removed from the rolls by Commissioner Wells after the Act of 1871, readmitted by Painter in 1894, and, Miller lamented, "still with us today." In Carl Miller Papers, Stockbridge-Munsee Historical Library Museum (hereafter cited as SMHLM).

34. Hauptman, *The Iroquois Struggle for Survival,* chap. 10; Stovey, "Parallel Souls"; Campisi, "Ethnic Identity and Boundary Maintenance in Three Oneida Communities."

35. Hauptman, *Iroquois Struggle for Survival;* Stovey, "Parallel Souls"; Kesehena Narrative Reports, 1925; Bernice Miller Pigeon, discussion with Stockbridge-Munsee Historical Committee, June 2002; oral history interviews with Mr. Tom King and Mrs. Cornelius Nelson, Oneida Oral History Culture Project, 1940–42, Files D-106 and S7, Wisconsin Historical Society—Green Bay Area Research Center; Keshena Narrative Report, 1924.

36. "Rehabilitation/Land Acquisition Project—Stockbridge" (1934), Records of the Bureau of Indian Affairs, Tomah Agency, Record Group 75, National Archives—Great Lakes Region.

CHAPTER 7

1. The most important scholarship on the history of the Mohicans during the 1930s and 1940s is Savagian, "The Tribal Reorganization of the Stockbridge-Munsee." Other important studies of more general interest are Hauptman, *The Iroquois and the New Deal*; Philp, *John Collier's Crusade for Indian Reform, 1920–1954*; Kelly, *The Assault on Assimilation*; Bernstein, *American Indians and World War II*.

2. Undated notes, ca. 1934, Carl Miller Papers, SMHLM.

3. Carl Miller to John Collier, Jan. 2, 1934, Carl Miller Papers, SMHLM.

4. For studies old and new about the workings of allotment, see Meriam, *The Problem of Indian Administration*; Kinney, *A Continent Lost—A Civilization Won*; Sutton, *Indian Land Tenure*; McDonnell, *The Dispossession of the American Indian, 1887–1934*; Greenwald, *Reconfiguring the Reservation*.

5. Occum Miller Diary, entries for January through June 1934, SMHLM.

6. Stockbridge-Munsee Tribal Business Committee to Commissioner of Indian Affairs, Feb. 20, 1934, CCF 9388-1934-310-Keshena.

7. Minutes of the Hayward Indian Congress, Apr. 24–25, 1934, Minnesota Historical Society; Richter, *The Mohican*; Occum Miller Diary, Feb. 24, 1934, and Apr. 24–25, 1934, entries; "Hayward Congress," *Indians at Work*, May 1, 1934, pp. 9–12.

8. Occum Miller diary, May 1934 entries.

9. John Collier to Keshena Agency Superintendent, May 1934, in "Rehabilitation/Land Acquisition Project—Stockbridge," Records of the Bureau of Indian Affairs, Tomah Agency, Record Group 75, National Archives—Great Lakes Region (hereafter cited as SPP, for Stockbridge Purchase Project). There is also a copy of many of the document in this set of records at the SMHLM under the headings "Project Proposal for Stockbridge Indian Project" and "Farm Security Administration Papers."

10. W. A. Beyer to John Collier, June 11, 1934, CCF 28891-1934-313-Keshena.

11. Mary Koonz to Keshena Agency Superintendent Ralph Fredenberg, Oct. 2, 1934, SPP, "Exhibit 11."

12. "Project Proposal for Stockbridge Indian Project, Shawano County, Wisconsin," January 1935, SPP.

13. For the basic workings of the Federal Emergency Relief Administration, see Searle, *Minister of Relief*; McJimsey, *Harry Hopkins*.

14. Draft 1934 Mohican Constitution, Carl Miller Papers, SMHLM.

15. "Results of the Referendum on the Reorganization Act, Dec. 15," *Indians at Work*, Jan. 1, 1935, for a report on the Stockbridge vote of 166–1 in favor of the IRA.

16. John Collier to "Indians of the Stockbridge Reservation," Dec. 16, 1934, CCF 9757-1936-066-Keshena.

17. Tribal Business Committee to Commissioner of Indian Affairs, Oct. 6, 1934, SPP.

18. John Collier to Tomah Agency Superintendent Frank Christy, Aug. 2, 1935, SPP.

19. "Annual Report of the Resettlement Administration, 1936," in *Senate Document* 213, 74th Cong., 2d sess., Serial Set #10007. On the general crisis of northern Wisconsin agriculture in the 1930s, see Gough, *Farming the Cutover;* on the Resettlement Administration, see Cannon, *Remaking the Agrarian Dream;* Namorato, *Rexford G. Tugwell, a Biography.*

20. J. M. Stewart to Tomah Agency Superintendent Peru Farver, May 26, 1938, SPP.

21. Keshena Narrative Report, 1936.

22. Felix Cohen to John Collier, Dec. 27, 1935, CCF 9757A-1936-068-Keshena.

23. Ibid.; also see Cohen, *Handbook of Federal Indian Law,* (for his discussion on tribal government under the Indian Reorganization Act.

24. William Zimmerman to "Chairman, Constitutional Committee," Jan. 29, 1936, CCF 9757A-1936-068-Keshena.

25. Frederick A. Daiker to John N. Chicks, Apr. 28, 1937, CCF 20583-1937-068.

26. "Secretarial Election of 1937" File, Stockbridge-Munsee Legal Department.

27. Fay, comp., *Charters, Constitutions, and By-laws of the Indian Tribes of North America.* Many of the tribal constitutions from the 1930s are now on-line at the University of Oklahoma Law School's American Indian Law and Tribal Sovereignty Project: at *http://thorpe.ou.edu/.* See also Taylor, *The New Deal and American Indian Tribalism;* DeLoria and Lyttle, *Nations Within.*

28. Constitution of the Stockbridge-Munsee Community, 1937, SMHLM, accessible at *http://thorpe.ou.edu.*

29. Ralph Fredenburg to John Collier, Oct. 2, 1936, SPP.

30. Corporate Charter of the Stockbridge-Munsee Community, May 21, 1938, accessible at *http://thorpe.ou.edu.*

31. Carl Miller to Assistant Secretary of the Interior Oscar Chapman, Oct. 20, 1938; Chapman to Miller, Nov. 3, 1938, both CCF 9757C-1936-066-Tomah.

32. Peru Farver to Commissioner of Indian Affairs, Nov. 29, 1938; Oscar Chapman to Harry Chicks, Jan. 17, 1939, both CCF 9757C-1936-066-Tomah.

33. Putnam, *Christian Religion among the Stockbridge-Munsee Band,* pp. 21–27.

34. Ibid., pp. 36–43.

35. "Project Proposal for Stockbridge Indians," p. 12, SPP.

36. "Tomah Agency Emergency Conservation Work, 1933–1937," SPP. There was some dissension in the Stockbridge-Munsee Community in 1937 and 1938 over the way Carl Miller made his hiring decisions on CCC-ID jobs; one critic

went so far as to call him a "Mussolini" for his apparent strong hand in controlling jobs. See also Wisconsin Public Welfare Department, *Relief to Indians in Wisconsin.*

37. F. L. Robinson letter to John Collier, Oct. 10, 1935, Carl Miller Papers, SMHLM.

38. Tomah Superintendent to Wisconsin Conservation Commission, Nov. 4, 1948, Records of the Wisconsin Department of Natural Resources, Box 419, Wisconsin Historical Society (hereafter cited as WCC).

39. Gresham Sportsman Club to Wisconsin Conservation Commission, Jan. 9, 1938, WCC, Box 419.

40. John Collier to H. L. MacKenzie, Feb. 2, 1940, WCC, Box 419; see also the coverage in the *Shawano Leader,* Nov. 25, Nov. 27, and Dec. 2, 1941.

41. Mike Fischer to Wisconsin Conservation Commission, Jan. 23, 1943, WCC, Box 419.

42. The OIA periodical *Indians at Work* changed its focus from work and rehabilitation projects on reservations to the war effort soon after the attack on Pearl Harbor. There are frequent reports on enlistments and casualties from Wisconsin tribes in the series after 1941. Borkowski et al., comps., *Wisconsin Women during World War II Oral History Project,* interviews with Bernice Davids Miller Pigeon and Dorothy Davids; see also Bernstein, *American Indians and World War II.*

CHAPTER 8

1. Fixico, *Termination and Relocation;* Philp, *Termination Revisited;* Loew, *Indian Nations of Wisconsin;* Castile, *To Show Heart;* Lurie, *Wisconsin Indians.*

2. Mochon, "Stockbridge-Munsee Cultural Adaptations," pp. 182–219; Davids, "Our People—Past, Present, Future: The Stockbridge-Munsee Band of Mohican Indians," presented at the 1961 American Indian Conference, University of Chicago (copy in Elmer Davids Papers, SMHLM).

3. Davids, "Our People—Past, Present, Future."

4. Cornell, *The Return of the Native,* pp. 124–25.

5. Taylor, *The New Deal and American Indian Tribalism*; Arvid Miller Biographical File, SMHLM.

6. Barker and Ehrenfeld, *Legislative History of the Indian Claims Commission Act of 1946.*

7. Rosenthal, *Their Day in Court;* Sutton, ed., *Irredeemable America;* Lurie, "The Indian Claims Commission Act"; Scherer, *Imperfect Victories.*

8. *Emigrant New York Indians v. United States,* in *Decisions of the Indian Claims Commission,* Docket 75, Vol. 5, pp. 553–607, vol. 11, pp. 336–86, vol. 13, pp. 560–73; and *Stockbridge-Munsee Community v. United States,* in *Decisions of the Indian Claims Commission,* Docket 300A, Vol. 25, pp. 281–302; Docket 300, vol. 26, pp. 491–512 (hereafter cited as *ICC Decisions*). The Stockbridge-Munsees considered but did not pursue a claim for the value of pine stumpage wrongly seized by the U.S. Indian

agent in 1899 and 1900 from allotments that had been made in 1897 under the Treaty of 1856 and the Act of 1893. These were allotments on more than 2,000 acres of the reservation that preceded the bigger allotment under the Act of 1906. The problem of untangling which logs came from legal allotments and which did not proved too daunting a half century later. See Annie Besaw to Commissioner of Indian Affairs, July 7, 1951, Annie Besaw Papers, SMHLM.

9. *ICC Decisions*, Docket 75, Vol. 5, pp. 568–602.

10. *New York Indians v. United States; ICC Decisions*, vol. 5, p. 626.

11. *ICC Decisions*, vol. 5, p. 631; vol. 11, p. 357; vol. 13, p. 560.

12. *ICC Decisions*, vol. 25, pp. 294–301.

13. *ICC Decisions*, vol. 26, pp. 491–512.

14. Peroff, *Menominee Drums;* Lurie, "The Indian Claims Commission Act."

15. "Investigation of the Bureau of Indian Affairs," *House Report* 2503 (1952), 82d Cong., 2d sess., pp. 205–7, 611–14, 989–91.

16. *Congressional Record*, 81st Cong., 1st sess., vol. 95, p. 3320; 81st Cong., 2d sess., vol. 96, pp. 1827, 2858, 2901; 82d Cong., 1st sess., vol. 97, p. 12572; 82d Cong., 2d sess., pp. 2412, 3189, 3225; "Reid Murray" and "William Van Pelt," *Biographical Directory*, pp. 1573, 1985.

17. "Melvin Laird," *Biographical Directory*, p. 1358.

18. Arvid E. Miller to Melvin R. Laird, Apr. 2, 1953, Box 13, Folder 4, Papers of Melvin R. Laird, Wisconsin Historical Society (hereafter cited as Laird Papers).

19. Secretary of the Interior to Senator Butler and Senate Sub-Committee on Indian Affairs, Apr. 21, 1953, Laird Papers, Box 13, Folder 4.

20. Clarence Otto to Melvin Laird, May 6, 1953, Laird Papers, Box 13, Folder 4.

21. Mrs. Edward La Budde to Annie Besaw, Jan. 28, 1953, Annie Besaw Papers, SMHLM.

22. Arvid E. Miller to Melvin Laird, Nov. 15, 1961, Laird Papers, Box 16, Folder 14.

23. Arvid E. Miller to Congressman Alvin O'Konski, Senator Alexander Wiley, and Congressman Melvin Laird, Jan. 7, 1963, Laird Papers, Box 16, Folder 23.

24. Arvid E. Miller to Melvin Laird, Jan. 22, 1963, Laird Papers, Box 16, Folder 23.

25. Stockbridge-Munsee Tribal Council to Commissioner of Indian Affairs, Dec. 1961, copy in Laird Papers, Box 16, Folder 23.

26. "Stockbridge Development Program," Dec. 20, 1961, Laird Papers, Box 16, Folder 23.

27. Ibid. Of all the proposed development ideas, the only one to take hold on the reservation and earn success was the Arts and Crafts Workshop staffed by women of the tribe. See "Federal Lands in Trust for Tribes in Minnesota and Wisconsin," *Hearing before the Senate Sub-Committee on Indian Affairs,* Mar. 26, 1971, 92d Cong., 1st sess.

28. Mike Fischer to Melvin Laird, Sept. 20, 1961, Laird Papers, Box 16, Folder 14.

29. Melvin Laird to Arvid E. Miller, June 4, 1962, Laird Papers, Box 16, Folder 14.

30. "Federal Lands in Trust for Tribes in Minnesota and Wisconsin," pp. 1–30.

31. Ibid., p. 36.

32. Ibid., p. 50.

33. *Congressional Record*, 92d Cong., 1st sess., pp. 2407, 3657, 6314; 92d Cong., 2d sess., pp. 19264, 20268–69, 20275, 20428, 33180, 33401, 34788.

34. Satz, *Chippewa Treaty Rights*, pp. 83–85; *State of Wisconsin v. Morrin* (1908), p. 136, *Wisconsin Reports*, 552.

35. Satz, *Chippewa Treaty Rights*, pp. 89–90; Wisconsin Attorney General, *Opinions of the Attorney General*, 1964—53, p. 222; Wilkinson, Cragun, and Wilkinson to Great Lakes Inter-Tribal Council, Mar. 20, 1968, as cited in *State of Wisconsin v. Bert Davids* (1991), Shawano County Circuit Court.

36. Wisconsin Department of Justice, *Opinions of the Attorney-General*, 1967–11; Satz, *Chippewa Treaty Rights*, pp. 91–124; Nesper, *The Walleye War; Minnesota et al. v. Mille Lacs Band of Chippewa Indians et al.;* Ferguson, "Indian Fishing Rights"; Krogseng, "Chippewa Treaty Rights"; Cleland and McClurken, eds., *Fish in the Lakes, Wild Rice, and Game in Abundance*.

37. "An Act to Regulate Trade and Intercourse with the Indian Tribes," 4 *Statutes at Large*, p. 729 (1834).

38. Title 18, *U.S. Code* (1948), Sec. 1151.

39. *State of Wisconsin v. Perry Bowman* (1945), Shawano County Circuit Court, copies of case file papers in Records of the Tomah Superintendency, Record Group 75, National Archives—Great Lakes Region; on Joseph McCarthy as a circuit court judge, see O'Brien, *McCarthy and McCarthyism in Wisconsin*, pp. 31–41; Reeves, *The Life and Times of Joe McCarthy*, chap. 4.

40. On Public Law 280, see Fixico, *Termination and Relocation*, pp. 111–33.

41. *State of Wisconsin v. Vincent Malone* (1968), Shawano County Circuit Court, as reported in *Shawano Leader*, June 11, 1968.

42. Ibid.

43. Minneapolis Field Solicitor as quoted in Acting Deputy Commissioner of Indian Affairs to Melvin Laird, Sept. 9, 1968, Laird Papers, Box 64, Folder 15.

44. Acting Commissioner of Indian Affairs Kenneth Payton to Leonard Miller, Apr. 5, 1974, copy in *State of Wisconsin v. Davids* (1991), Shawano County Circuit Court.

45. Ibid.

Works Cited

ARCHIVES AND DOCUMENTS

American Geographical Society Map Collection, University of Wisconsin-
    Milwaukee
Borchert Map Collection, University of Minnesota
Huntington Free Library, New York
    Stockbridge Indian Papers
Minnesota Historical Society
    Hayward Indian Congress minutes
Newberry Library
    Ayer Manuscripts
    Stockbridge Tribal Records, 1789–1857
Oneida Nation of Wisconsin Tribal Museum
    Oneida Oral History Culture Project, 1940–1942
Stockbridge-Munsee Historical Library Museum
    Annie Besaw Papers
    Arvid Miller Biographical File
    Elmer Davids Oral History
    Carl Miller Papers
    Occum Miller Diary
    Stockbridge Purchase Project
Stockbridge-Munsee Legal Department
    Secretarial Election Files

Wisconsin Historical Society
    J. C. Adams Papers
    William F. Brown Papers
    Thomas Dean Papers
    Robert B. Haines Papers
    Heath Manuscripts
    Melvin R. Laird Papers
    Cutting Marsh Papers
    Morgan L. Martin Papers
    Thomas Miner Papers
    Red Springs School District Papers
    Jeremiah Stevens Papers
    Wisconsin Women during World War II Oral History Project (Bernice Davids
       Miller Pigeon and Dorothy W. Davids)

GOVERNMENT DOCUMENTS

Fay, George E. *Charters, Constitutions, and By-laws of the Indian Tribes of North America.*
    16 vols. Greeley: Colorado State College Museum of Anthropology, 1967.
Kappler, Charles. *Indian Affairs: Laws and Treaties.* Washington, D.C.: Government
    Printing Office, 1904. [Vol. II: Treaties. Also available at http://digital.library.
    okstate.edu]
    Treaty with the Oneidas, etc., Dec. 2, 1794, p. 37.
    Treaty with the Miamis, Aug. 21, 1805, p. 80.
    Treaty with the Delawares, etc., Sept. 30, 1809, p. 101.
    Treaty with the Delawares, Oct. 3, 1818, p. 171.
    Treaty with the Chippewas, etc., Aug. 11, 1827, p. 281.
    Treaty with the Menominee, Feb. 8, 1831, p. 319.
    Treaty with the Menominee, Oct. 27, 1832, p. 377.
    Treaty with the New York Indians, Jan. 15, 1838, p. 502.
    Treaty with the Oneida Indians, Feb. 3, 1838, p. 517.
    Treaty with the Stockbridge and Munsee, Sept. 3, 1839, p. 529.
    Treaty with the Winnebago, Oct. 13, 1846, p. 565.
    Treaty with the Chippewas of the Mississippi and Lake Superior, Aug. 2, 1847,
       p. 567.
    Treaty with the Stockbridge Tribe, Nov. 24, 1848, p. 574.
    Treaty with the Sioux, July 23, 1851, p. 588.
    Treaty with the Stockbridge and Munsee, Feb. 5, 1856, p. 742.
    Treaty with the Menominee, Feb. 11, 1856, p. 755.
Richardson, James D., comp. *Messages and Papers of the President, 1787–1897.*
    Washington, D.C.: Government Printing Office, 1896–99.
Shawano County. Mortgage, Patent, and Deed Records, County Register of
    Deeds.

State of Wisconsin. Conservation Commission Records, Wisconsin Historical Society.

Truesdell, L., ed. *The Indian Population of the United States*. Washington, D.C.: Government Printing Office, 1937.

United States. Bureau of the Census. Ninth, Eleventh, Twelfth, Thirteenth, and Fourteenth Censuses of the United States. Population Schedules. National Archives Microfilms T-1224, T-1210, and T626.

United States. Bureau of Indian Affairs. *Annual Report of the Commissioner of Indian Affairs*, 1825–1932. Washington, D.C.

———. Cartographic Records of the Bureau of Indian Affairs, Record Group 75, National Archives.

———. Central Classified Files, 1907–1939. Record Group 75, National Archives.

———. Circulars and Orders, Record Group 75, National Archives Microfilm M-1121.

———. Documents Relating to Ratified Treaties Record Group 75, National Archives Microfilm M-668.

———. Field Notes of Indian Reservation Surveys. Record Group 75, National Archives.

———. Indian Census Rolls, 1884–1940. Record Group 75, National Archives Microfilm M-595.

———. *Indian Land Tenure, Economic Status and Population Trends*. Washington, D.C.: Government Printing Office, 1937.

———. Letters Received from the Green Bay Agency. Record Group 75, National Archives Microfilm M-234.

———. Letters Sent by the Office of Indian Affairs. Record Group 75, National Archives Microfilm M-21.

———. Narrative Reports from Agencies, 1910–1939. Record Group 75, National Archives Microfilm M-1011.

———. Ratified and Unratified Treaties. Record Group 75, National Archives Microfilm T-494.

———. Records of the Keshena Agency. Record Group 75, National Archives.

———. Records of the Tomah Agency. Record Group 75, National Archives.

———. Records of the Wisconsin Superintendent of Indian Affairs. Record Group 75, National Archives Microfilm M-951.

———. Report Books of the Office of Indian Affairs. Record Group 75, National Archives Microfilm M-348.

———. Reports of Indian Inspectors. Record Group 75, National Archives Microfilm M-1070.

———. Special Case 42. Record Group 75, National Archives.

———. Special Files of the Bureau of Indians Affairs, Record Group 75, National Archives Microfilm M-574.

United States. Bureau of Land Management. Records of the Surveyor General. Record Group 49, National Archives Microfilm T-1280.

United States. Congress. *Congressional Globe*. 1833–73.

———. *Congressional Record*. 1873–1972.

———. *Statutes at Large*. Washington, D.C.: Government Printing Office.

"An Act to Prevent Settlements being made on lands ceded to the United States, until authorized by law." 2 *Statutes at Large*, 445–46 (1807).

"An Act to revive the powers of the commissioners for ascertaining and deciding on claims to land in the District of Detroit, and for settling the claims to lands at Green Bay and Prairie du Chien in the Territory of Michigan." 3 *Statutes at Large*, 572 (1820).

"An Act to revive and continue in force certain acts for the adjustment of land claims in the Territory of Michigan." 3 *Statutes at Large*, 724–25 (1823).

"An Act to confirm claims to certain lands in the Territory of Michigan." 4 *Statutes at Large*, 260–61 (1828).

"An Act to Regulate Trade and Intercourse with the Indian Tribes." 4 *Statutes at Large*, 729 (1834).

"An Act for the Relief of the Brothertown Tribe of Indians, in the Territory of Wisconsin." 5 *Statutes at Large*, 349 (1839).

"An Act for the Relief of the Stockbridge Tribe of Indians in the Territory of Wisconsin." 5 *Statutes at Large*, 643 (1843).

"An Act to repeal 'An Act for the Relief of the Stockbridge Tribe of Indians in the Territory of Wisconsin.'" 9 *Statutes at Large*, 55 (1846).

"An Act to grant the Right of Way to all Rail and Plank Roads and Macadamized Turnpikes passing through the Public Lands of the United States." 11 *Statutes at Large*, 28 (1852).

"An Act for the Relief of John W. Quinney, a Stockbridge Indian." 10 *Statutes at Large*, 746 (1853).

"An Act making Appropriations for the Current and Contingent Expenses of the Indian Department." 11 *Statutes at Large*, 176 (1857).

"An Act making Appropriations for the Current and Contingent Expenses of the Indian Department." 13 *Statutes at Large*, 541 (1865).

"An Act for the Relief of the Stockbridge and Munsee Tribe of Indians in Wisconsin." 16 *Statutes at Large*, 404 (1871).

"An Act making Appropriations for the General Incidental Expenses of the Indian Service." 17 *Statutes at Large*, 190–91 (1872).

"An Act to provide for the disposition of funds appropriated for the Indian Department. . . . " 18 *Statutes at Large*, 174 (1874).

"An Act for the Relief of the Stockbridge and Munsee tribe of Indians, in the State of Wisconsin." 27 *Statutes at Large*, 744 (1893).

"An Act to pay Judgments Rendered in the Court of Claims." 31 *Statutes at Large*, 27 (1900).

"An Act making Appropriations for the current and contiguous expenses of the Indian Department." 33 *Statutes at Large*, 189 (1904).

"An Act making Appropriations for the current and contiguous expenses of the Indian Department." 34 *Statutes at Large*, 326 (1906).

"An Act making Appropriations for the current and contiguous expenses of the Indian Department." 39 *Statutes at Large*, 123 (1916).

"An Act Conferring Jurisdiction upon the Court of Claims to hear, examine, and adjudicate and enter judgment in any claims which the Stockbridge Indians may have against the United States." 43 *Statutes at Large*, 644 (1924).

"An Act to provide for the disposition of funds appropriated to pay a judgment in favor of the Emigrant New York Indians in Indian Claims Commission Docket 75." 81 *Statutes at Large*, 229 (1967).

"To declare that certain federally owned lands shall be held by the United States in trust for the Stockbridge Munsee Indian Community, Wisconsin." 86 *Statutes at Large*, 795 (1972).

"To declare that certain sub-marginal land of the United States should be held in trust for certain Indian tribes." 89 *Statutes at Large*, 578 (1975).

United States. Department of the Interior. Letters from the Indian Division of the Office of the Secretary of the Interior. Record Group 48, National Archives Microfilm M-606.

———. Appointment Papers, Wisconsin, 1849–1907. Record Group 48, National Archives Microfilm M-831.

———. *Opinions of the Solicitor of the Department of Interior—Indian Affairs, 1913–1974*. Washington, D.C.: Government Printing Office, 1975.

United States. Department of Justice. Records of the U.S. Attorney for the Western District of Wisconsin. Record Group 21, National Archives.

United States. Department of State. Territorial Papers of the United States: Wisconsin Territory. National Archives Microfilm M-236.

———. *Territorial Papers of the United States: Michigan Territory*. Vols. 10–12. Washington, D.C.: Government Printing Office, 1943.

United States. Department of Treasury. "Report of Secretary of Treasury." In *New American State Papers: Public Lands*, edited by Margaret Bogue. Wilmington, Del.: Scholarly Resources, 1973.

United States. Department of War. Letters Sent by the Secretary of War. National Archives Microfilm M15.

———. Records of the Quartermaster General. Record Group 92, National Archives.

United States. House of Representatives. Bill File. Record Group 243, National Archives.

United States. House of Representatives. *Documents*.

"Present Condition of the Stockbridge Indians." *House Document* 38, 19th Cong., 2d sess. (1827), Serial Set #150.

"Memorial of the Legislature of Wisconsin Territory Praying that the Right of Citizenship may be Extended to the Stockbridge Indians." *House Document* 173, 25th Cong., 2d sess. (1838), Serial Set #327.

"Petition of the Stockbridge Nation of Indians in Wiskonsin." *House Document* 127, 26th Cong., 1st sess. (1840), Serial Set #365.

"Memorial of the Chiefs and Sachems of the 'Indian Party' of the Stockbridge Indians Praying for Repeal of Law Passed in 1843." *House Document* 128, 29th Cong., 1st sess. (1846), Serial Set #483.

"Judgments Rendered by the Court of Claims." *House Document* 226, 56th Cong., 1st sess. (1900), Serial Set #3974.

"Letter from the Secretary of the Interior . . . with the draft of a bill for adjusting matters pertaining to the affairs of the Stockbridge and Munsee Tribe of Indians." *House Document* 405, 56th Cong., 2d sess. (1901), Serial Set #4163.

"Letter from the Secretary of the Interior . . . with the draft of a bill . . . Stockbridge and Munsee Indians," *House Document* 167, 57th Cong., 1st sess. (1902), Serial Set #4331.

"To Restrict Conveyance of Lands Allotted to Indians of Stockbridge-Munsee Reservation, Wis." *House Document* 471, 60th Cong., 1st sess. (1908), Serial Set #5377.

"Message of the President of the United States transmitting to the House of Representatives without his approval the bill H.R. 5230, 'An Act to Confer Jurisdiction upon the Court of Claims to hear claims of the Stockbridge and Munsee Tribe of Indians of the State of Wisconsin." *House Document* 269, 74th Cong., 1st sess. (1935), Serial Set #9928.

"Message of the President of the United States transmitting to the House of Representatives without his approval the bill H.R. 5229 . . . of the Stockbridge and Munsee Tribe of Indians of the State of Wisconsin." *House Document* 274, 74th Cong., 1st sess. (1935), Serial Set #9928.

United States. House of Representatives. *Executive Documents.*

"Letter from the Secretary of the Interior . . . present condition of the Stockbridge and Munsee Indians." *House Executive Document* 61, 37th Cong., 3d sess. (1863), Serial Set #1162.

"To carry out the provisions of . . . 'An Act for the relief of the Stockbridge and Munsee Tribe of Indians in the State of Wisconsin.'" *House Executive Document* 244, 43d Cong., 1st sess. (1874), Serial Set #1614.

United States. House of Representatives. *House Journal.*

United States. House of Representatives. *Miscellaneous Documents.*

"Memorial of the Stockbridge Nation of Indians in Wiskonsin." *House Document* 127, 26th Cong., 1st sess. (1840). Serial Set #365.

"Letter from the Sachem and Councillors of the Stockbridge Indians." *House Miscellaneous Document* 69, 32d Cong., 1st sess. (1852), Serial Set #652.

"Letter from the Acting Commissioner of Indian Affairs—for relief of the Stockbridge and Munsee tribe of Indians, in the State of Wisconsin." *House Miscellaneous Document* 14, 46th Cong., 3d sess. (1881), Serial Set #1981.

United States. House of Representatives. *Reports.*

"Claim of the Stockbridge Indians to Lands in Indiana." *House Report* 311, 16th Cong., 1st sess. (1820). In *American State Papers: Indian Affairs,* vol. 30.

"Petition of the Muhheakunuk or Stockbridge Nation of Indians." *House Report* 70, 16th Cong., 1st sess. (1820), Serial Set #40.

"Stockbridge Indians." *House Report* 961, 27th Cong., 2d sess. (1842), Serial Set #411.

"Stockbridge Indians." *House Report* 447, 29th Cong., 1st sess. (1846), Serial Set #489.

"Stockbridge and Munsee Indians." *House Report* 813, 44th Cong., 1st sess. (1876), Serial Set #1714.

"Stockbridge and Munsee Tribe of Indians, in the State of Wisconsin." *House Report* 1950, 47th Cong., 2d sess. (1883), Serial Set #2159.

"Stockbridge and Munsee Indians." *House Report* 1054, 48th Cong., 1st sess. (1884), Serial Set #2256.

"Stockbridge and Munsee Indians." *House Report* 1339, 50th Cong., 1st sess. (1888), Serial Set #2601.

"Stockbridge and Munsee Tribe of Indians." *House Report* 1856, 51st Cong., 1st sess. (1890), Serial Set #2812.

"Stockbridge and Munsee Indians," *House Report* 558, 52d Cong., 1st sess. (1892), Serial Set #3043.

"Allotment of Lands in Severalty to Certain Indians, etc." *House Report* 3783, 57th Cong., 2d sess. (1903), Serial Set #4415.

"Stockbridge and Munsee Tribe of Indians, etc." *House Report* 1420, 58th Cong., 2d sess. (1904), Serial Set #4580.

"To Adjudicate Claims of Stockbridge Indians." *House Report* 870, 68th Cong., 1st sess. (1924), Serial Set #8229.

"Claims of the Stockbridge Indians before the Court of Claims." *House Report* 682, 68th Cong., 1st sess. (1924), Serial Set #8228.

"Claims of Stockbridge and Munsee Indians." *House Report* 2009, 73d Cong., 2d sess. (1934), Serial Set #9776.

"Declaring that the United States holds certain lands in trust for the Stockbridge-Munsee Community, Inc., of the State of Wisconsin." *House Report* 1654, 81st Cong., 2d sess. (1950), Serial Set #11378.

"Declaring that the United States holds certain lands in trust for the Stockbridge-Munsee Community, Inc., of the State of Wisconsin," *House Report* 1510, 82nd Congress, 2nd Session (1952), Serial Set #11575.

Investigation of the Bureau of Indian Affairs." *House Report* 2503, 82d Cong., 2d sess. (1952). Serial Set #11582.

United States. President. *Presidential Vetoes, 1789–1976.* Washington, D.C.: Government Printing Office, 1978.

United States. Senate. Bill File. Record Group 46, National Archives.

————. Records of the Committee on Indian Affairs. Record Group 46, Records of the United States Senate.

United States. Senate. *Committee on Indian Affairs. Hearings.*

"Stockbridge-Munsee Indians of Wisconsin" (1892).

"Condition of Indian Affairs in Wisconsin." 61st Cong., 1st sess. (1910).

"Indian Appropriation Bill." 63d Cong., 3d sess. (1915).

"Federal Land in Trust for Tribes in Minnesota and Wisconsin." 92d Cong., 1st sess. (1971).

United States. Senate. *Documents.*

"Annual Report of the Resettlement Administration, 1936." *Senate Document* 231, 74th Cong., 2nd sess. (1937). Serial Set #100007.

"Petition and Appeal of the Six Nations, Oneida, Stockbridge, etc." *Senate Document* 189, 27th Cong., 2d sess. (1842). Serial Set #397.

"Report of Secretary of War on Extinguishing Indian Title to Land in vicinity of Green Bay and north of Wisconsin and Iowa Rivers." *Senate Document* 229, 24th Cong., 1st sess. (1836). Serial Set #281.

"Letter from the Secretary of War . . . Recommending an Appropriation for the Removal and Subsistence of a Number of Stockbridge and Munsee Indians." *Senate Document* 42, 26th Cong., 1st sess. (1840). Serial Set #366.

"Memorial of the Stockbridge Nation of Indians in Wisconsin." *Senate Document* 189, 27th Cong., 2nd sess. (1842). Serial Set #397.

United States. Senate. *Senate Journal.*

United States. Senate. *Miscellaneous Documents.*

"Resolution of the Legislature of Wisconsin in Favor of a New Treaty between the general government and the Stockbridge Indians." *Senate Miscellaneous Document* 18, 39th Cong., 2d sess. (1867). Serial Set #1278.

"Protest of A. Miller, Delegate of the Stockbridge Nation of Indians." *Senate Miscellaneous Document* 119, 48th Cong., 1st sess. (1884). Serial Set #2171.

"Memorial of J. C. Adams, for and in behalf of the Stockbridge and Munsee Tribe of Indians." *Senate Miscellaneous Document* 61, 48th Cong., 2d sess. (1885). Serial Set #2265.

"Testimony Taken before the Subcommittee . . . for the relief of the Stockbridge and Munsee Tribe of Indians in the State of Wisconsin." *Senate Miscellaneous Document* 226, 52d Cong., 1st sess. (1892). Serial Set #2907.

"Papers to accompany the bill H.R. 3594 for the relief of the Stockbridge and Munsee Tribes of Indians of Wisconsin." *Senate Miscellaneous Document* 54, 52d Cong., 2d sess. (1893). Serial Set #3064.

United States Senate. *Reports.*

"An Act for the Relief of Jacob Konkopot, and others, of the Nation of Stockbridge Indians." *Senate Report* 166, 16th Cong., 1st sess. (1820). Serial Set #27.

"Petition of a Number of Stockbridge Indians, praying the division among the tribe of six thousand dollars. . . . " *Senate Report* 302, 28th Cong., 1st sess. (1844). Serial Set #435.

"To Inquire into and report to the Senate the effect of the Fourteenth Amendment to the Constitution upon the Indian tribes of the country." *Senate Report* 268, 41st Cong., 3d sess. (1870). Serial Set #1443.

"A bill to amend an act entitled 'An act for the relief of the Stockbridge and Munsee Tribe of Indians in the State of Wisconsin." *Senate Report* 2262, 50th Cong., 1st sess. (1888). Serial Set #2526.

"A bill to amend an act entitled 'An act for the relief of the Stockbridge and Munsee Tribe of Indians in the State of Wisconsin.'" *Senate Report* 1718, 51st Cong., 1st sess. (1890). Serial Set #2711.

"For the Relief of the Stockbridge and Munsee Tribe of Indians in the State of Wisconsin." *Senate Report* 1108, 52d Cong., 1st sess. (1892). Serial Set #2915.

"Stockbridge and Munsee Tribe of Indians." *Senate Report* 2699, 57th Cong., 2d sess. (1903). Serial Set #4411.

"Stockbridge and Munsee Tribe of Indians." *Senate Report* 173, 58th Cong., 2d sess. (1904). Serial Set #4570.

"Conferring Jurisdiction on the Court of Claims to hear the claims of the Stockbridge Indians." *Senate Report* 567, 68th Cong., 1st sess. (1924). Serial Set #8221.

"Individual Claims of Stockbridge and Munsee Indians, Wisconsin." *Senate Report* 1090, 74th Cong., 1st sess. (1935). Serial Set #9880.

"Claims of Stockbridge and Munsee Indians, Wisconsin." *Senate Report* 1091, 74th Cong., 1st sess. (1935). Serial Set #9880.

Wisconsin. *Blue Book*. Madison, 1882–.

Wisconsin. *Laws of Wisconsin*.

Wisconsin. Department of Justice. *Opinions of the Attorney General*. OAG 1904—491; 1931—982; 1964—222; 1967—11; 1980—64.

Wisconsin. Public Welfare Department. *Relief to Indians in Wisconsin*. Madison, 1937.

COURT CASES

Annette Davids et al v. Laura Coyhis et al and *Stockbridge-Munsee Community Band of Mohican Indians v. Bruce Miller et al*, 857, *F. Supp.* 641, 1994, U.S. District Court for the Eastern District of Wisconsin.

Beecher v. Wetherby (1877), 95 *U.S. Reports*, 517.

Minnesota v. Hitchcock (1901), 185, *U.S. Reports*, 373.

Minnesota et al v. Mille Lacs Band of Chippewa Indians et al (1999), 526 *U.S. Reports*, 172.

Emigrant New York Indians v. United States (1964), *Indian Claims Commission*, Docket 75.

New York Indians v. United States (1899), 170 *U.S. Reports*, 1.

State of Wisconsin v. Perry Bowman (1945), Shawano County Circuit Court.

State of Wisconsin v. Bert W. Davids (1991), Shawano County Circuit Court.

State of Wisconsin v. Vincent Malone (1968), Shawano County Circuit Court.

State of Wisconsin v. Morrin (1908), 136, *Wisconsin Reports*, 552.

State of Wisconsin v. Dan Tousey (1915), Shawano County Circuit Court.

Stockbridge-Munsee Tribe of Indians v. State of Wisconsin (1897), 25, *Land Decisions of the Department of the Interior*, 17.

Stockbridge-Munsee Community v. United States (1974), *Indian Claims Commission*, Docket 300 and Docket 300A.

Stockbridge Tribe of Indians v. United States (1926) *U.S. Court of Claims*, Case D-552.

Stockbridge Tribe of Indians v. United States (1927), U.S. *Court of Claims*, Case F-202.

United States v. Anderson (1915), 225 *Fed. Reporter*, 825.

United States v. Celestine (1909), 215 *U.S. Reports*, 278.

United States v. Cook (1874), 86, *U.S. Reports*, 591.

United States v. Foster (1870) 25 *Fed. Cases*, p. 1171

United States v. Gardner (1911), 189 *Fed. Reporter*, 690

United States v. Paine Lumber Company (1906), 206 *U.S. Reports*, 467.

United States v. Torrey Cedar Company (1904), 154 *Fed. Reporter*, 263.

United States v. Tousey (1938), U.S. District Court, Eastern District of Wisconsin.

United States v. Wybro (1870).

NEWSPAPERS AND PERIODICALS

Antigo Journal

Chicago Tribune

Indians at Work (Bureau of Indian Affairs)

Janesville Daily Gazette

Milwaukee Journal

Oshkosh Northwestern

Oshkosh Times

Shawano Advocate

Shawano Journal

Shawano Leader

BOOKS, ARTICLES, AND THESES

Advantages and Productions of the Counties of Brown, Door, Oconto and Shawano. Green Bay: n.p., 1870.

Albers, Patricia C. "Marxism and Historical Materialism in American Indian History. In *Clearing a Path: Theorizing the Past in Native American Studies,* edited by Nancy Shoemaker, pp. 107–35. New York: Routledge, 2002.

Anderson, Gary C. "Comment." In *The Struggle for Political Autonomy,* edited by Frederick Hoxie, pp. 90–93. *Newberry Library Center for the History of the American Indian Occasional Papers* No. 11 (1989).

Appleton, Nathan. *Gospel Ministers Must Be Fit for the Master's Use.* Boston, 1735.

Armistead, Wilson, comp. *Memoir of Paul Cuffe, a Man of Colour.* London: Edmund Fry, 1840.

Aupaumut, Hendrick. "Narrative of an Embassy to the Western Indians." In *Memoirs of the Historical Society of Pennsylvania,* pp. 61–131. Philadelphia: M'Carty and Davis, 1827.

Baird, Henry S. "Recollections of the Early History of Northern Wisconsin." *Wisconsin Historical Collections,* vol. 4, pp. 197–221. Madison: State Historical Society of Wisconsin, 1857.

Barker, Robert W. and Alice Ehrenfeld. *Legislative History of the Indian Claims Commission Act of 1946.* New York: Clearwater Publishing, 1976.

Barrett, S. A. *The Dream Dance of the Chippewa and Menominee Indians of Northern Wisconsin.* Milwaukee, Wis.: Milwaukee Public Museum, 1911.

Beals, Alan. "Pervasive Factionalism." *American Anthropologist* 62, no. 2 (1960: 394–417.

Beck, David R. M. *Siege and Survival: History of the Menominee Indians, 1634–1856.* Lincoln: University of Nebraska Press, 2002.

Belknap, Jeremy, and Jedidiah Morse. *Report of a Committee of the Board of Correspondents of the Scots Society for Propagating Christian Knowledge Who Visited the Oneida and Mohekunuh Indians in 1796.* Boston: Samuel Hall, 1798.

Bennett, P. S., and James Lawson. *History of Methodism in Four Parts.* Cincinnati: Cranston & Stowe Printers, 1890.

Berkhofer, Robert. "The Political Context of a New Indian History." *Pacific Historical Review* 40, no. 3 (1971): 357–82.

———. "Protestants, Pagans, and Sequences among the North American Indians, 1760–1860." *Ethnohistory* 10, no. 3 (1963): 201–32.

Berkshire Eagle. *Two Centuries of Stockbridge History.* Pittsfield, Mass.: Berkshire Eagle Publishing, 1939.

Bernstein, Alison R. *American Indians and World War II.* Norman: University of Oklahoma Press, 1991.

Bieder, Robert E. *Native American Communities in Wisconsin, 1634–1960.* Madison: University of Wisconsin Press, 1995.

Biographical Directory of the American Congress, 1774–1996. Alexandria, Va.: Congressional Quarterly Staff Directories, 1997.

Blasingham, E. J. "The New England Indians in the Western Great Lakes Region." *Proceedings of the Indiana Academy of Science,* vol. 66, pp. 193–224. 1957.

Blodgett, Harold William. *Samson Occum.* Hanover: Dartmouth College Publications, 1935.

Borokowski, Kathryn, comp. *Wisconsin Women during World War II Oral History Project.* Madison: Wisconsin Historical Society, 1992.

Bowker, R. R. "The After History of the Stockbridge Indians." Ayer Manuscripts, Newberry Library.

Brainerd, Thomas. *The Life of John Brainerd and his Mission to the Indians of New Jersey.* Philadelphia: Presbyterian Publications Committee, 1865.

Brasser, Ted J. "Mahicans." In *Handbook of North American Indians: Northeast,* vol. 15, edited by Bruce Trigger, pp. 192–239. Washington, D.C.: Smithsonian Institution, 1978.

———. "Riding on the Frontier's Crest: Mohican Indian Culture and Cultural Change." *National Museum of Man, Mercury Series, Ethnology Division,* Paper 13 (1974).

Campisi, Jack. "Ethnic Identity and Boundary Maintenance in Three Oneida Communities." Ph.D. diss., State University of New York, Albany, 1974.

Campisi, Jack, and Laurence M. Hauptman. *The Oneida Indian Experience: Two Perspectives.* Syracuse: Syracuse University Press, 1988.

Cannon, Brian. *Remaking the Agrarian Dream: New Deal Rural Resettlement in the Mountain West.* Albuquerque: University of New Mexico Press, 1996.

Castile, George. *To Show Heart: Native American Self-Determination and Federal Indian Policy, 1960–1975.* Tucson: University of Arizona Press, 1998.

Champagne, Duane. *American Indian Societies: Strategies and Conditions of Political and Cultural Survival.* New York: Cambridge University Press, 1990.

Childs, Ebeneezer. "Recollections of Wisconsin since 1820." *Wisconsin Historical Collections,* vol. 4, pp. 153–95. Madison: State Historical Society of Wisconsin, 1857.

Cleland, Charles. "Economics and Adaptive Change among the Lake Superior Chippewa of the Nineteenth Century." In *Ethnohistory and Archaeology: Approaches to Postcontact Change in the Americas,* edited by J. Daniel Rogers and Samuel L. Wilson, pp. 110–22. New York: Plenum Press, 1993.

———. "History of the Stockbridge-Munsee Reservation in the Context of Federal Indian Policy." Report to the Federal District Court for the Eastern District of Wisconsin, Case No. 98-C-0871, 2001.

Cleland, Charles, and James McClurken, eds. *Fish in the Lakes, Wild Rice, and Game in Abundance: Testimony on Behalf of Mille Lacs Ojibwe Hunting and Fishing Rights.* East Lansing: Michigan State University Press, 2000.

Clifton, James. "The Tribal History: An Obsolete Paradigm." *American Indian Culture and Research Journal* 3, no. 4 (1979): 81–100.

———, ed. *The Invented Indian: Cultural Fictions and Government Policies.* New Brunswick, N.J.: Transaction, 1990.

Cohen, Felix. *Handbook of Federal Indian Law.* Washington, D.C.: Government Printing Office, 1942.

Colton, Calvin. *Tour of the American Lakes in 1830.* London: Frederick Westly, 1833.

Commuck, Thomas. "Sketch of the Brothertown Indians." *Wisconsin Historical Collections,* vol. 4, pp. 291–98. Madison: State Historical Society of Wisconsin, 1857.

———. "Sketch of Calumet County." *Wisconsin Historical Collections,* vol. 1, pp. 103–6. Madison: State Historical Society of Wisconsin, 1857.

Cooper, James Fennimore. *The Last of the Mohicans: A Narrative of 1757.* 1826; Albany: State University of New York Press, 1982.

Cornell, Stepehn E. *The Return of the Native: American Indian Political Resurgence.* New York: Oxford University Press, 1988.

Cuffe, Paul, Jr. *Narrative of the Life of Paul Cuffe, a Pequot Indian: During Thirty Spent at Sea.* Vernon, N.Y: Horace Brill, 1839.

Current, Richard. The *History of Wisconsin, Volume II: The Civil War Era, 1848–1873.* Madison: State Historical Society of Wisconsin, 1976.

———. *Pine Logs and Politics: A Life of Philetus Sawyer, 1816–1900.* Madison: State Historical Society of Wisconsin, 1950.

Davids, Dorothy W. *Brief History of the Mohican Nation, Stockbridge-Munsee Band.* Bowler, Wis.: Stockbridge-Munsee Historical Committee, 2001.

———. "Stockbridge-Munsee (Mohican)." In *Encyclopedia of North American Indians*, edited by Frederick E. Hoxie, p. 611. New York: Houghton Mifflin, 1996.

Davidson, John N. "Coming of the New York Indians to Wisconsin." *Proceedings of the State Historical Society of Wisconsin,* vol. 5, pp. 153–85. Madison: Democrat Printing Co., 1899.

———. *Muh-He-Ka-Ne-Ok: A History of the Stockbridge Nation.* Milwaukee: Siles Chapman, 1893.

Davis, Tom. *Sustaining the Forest, the People, and the Spirit.* Albany: State University of New York Press, 2000.

DeLoria, Vine, Jr. *Behind the Trail of Broken Treaties.* New York: Delacorte Press, 1974.

DeLoria, Vine, Jr., and Clifford M. Lyttle. *Nations Within: The Past and Future of American Indian Society.* New York: Pantheon, 1984.

DeLoria, Vine, Jr., and David E. Wilkins. *Tribes, Treaties & Constitutional Tribulations.* Austin: University of Texas Press, 1999.

Dunn, Shirley W. *The Mohican World, 1680–1750.* Fleischmanns, N.Y.: Purple Mountain Press, 2000.

Ellis, Albert G. "Advent of the New York Indians into Wisconsin." *Wisconsin Historical Collections,* vol. 5 p. 416. Madison: State Historical Society of Wisconsin, 1856.

———. "Recollections of Rev. Eleazer Williams." *Wisconsin Historical Collections,* vol. 8, p. 338. Madison: State History Society of Wisconsin, 1859.

Feller, Daniel. *The Public Lands in Jacksonian Politics.* Madison: University of Wisconsin Press, 1984.

Ferguson, Karen. "Indian Fishing Rights: Aftermath of the Fox Decision and the Year 2000." *American Indian Law Review* 23, no. 1 (2000): 97–154.

Fixico, Donald. *Termination and Relocation.* Albuquerque: University of New Mexico Press, 1986.

Fogelson, Raymond. "The Context of American Indian History." In *The Struggle for Political Autonomy,* edited by Frederick Hoxie, pp. 129–32. *Newberry Library Center for the History of the American Indian Occasional Papers* No. 11 (1989).

Foner, Eric. *Reconstruction: America's Unfinished Business, 1863–1877.* New York: Harper, 1988.

Fowler, Loretta. "Local-Level Politics and the Struggle for Self-Government." In *The Struggle for Political Autonomy,* edited by Frederick Hoxie, pp. 129–32. *Newberry Library Center for the History of the American Indian Occasional Papers* No. 11 (1989).

———. *Tribal Sovereignty and the Historical Imagination: Cheyenne-Arapaho Politics.* Lincoln: University of Nebraska Press, 2002.

Frazier, Patrick. *The Mohicans of Stockbridge.* Lincoln: University of Nebraska Press, 1992.

Galenson, David, and Daniel Levy. "A Note on Biases in the Measurement of Geographical Mobility." *Historical Methods* 19 (1986): 171–79.

Gates, Paul W. *Fifty Million Acres: Conflicts over Land Policy in Kansas, 1854–1890.* Ithaca: Cornell University Press, 1954.

———. "Frontier Land Business in Wisconsin." *Wisconsin Magazine of History* 53 (1969): 306–27.

———. *History of Public Land Law Development.* Washington, D.C.: Government Printing Office, 1968.

Gienapp, William. *The Origins of the Republican Party, 1852–1856.* New York: Oxford University Press, 1987.

Goddard, Ives. "Delaware." In *Handbook of North American Indians,* vol. 15: *Northeast,* edited by Bruce Trigger, pp. 213–39. Washington, D.C.: Smithsonian Institution, 1978.

———. "Eastern Algonquian Languages." In *Handbook of North American Indians,* vol. 15: *Northeast,* edited by Bruce Trigger, pp. 70–77. Washington, D.C.: Smithsonian Institution, 1978.

Gough, Robert J. *Farming the Cutover: A Social History of Northern Wisconsin, 1900–1940.* Lawrence: University Press of Kansas, 1998.

Greene, Lorenzo. *The Negro in Colonial New England.* New York: Columbia University Press, 1942.

Greenwald, Emily. *Reconfiguring the Reservation: The Nez Perces, Jicarilla Apaches, and the Dawes Act.* Albuquerque: University of New Mexico Press, 2002.

Grignon, August. "Seventy-two Years' Recollections of Wisconsin." *Wisconsin Historical Collections,* vol. 3, pp. 197–295. Madison: State Historical Society of Wisconsin, 1856.

Grignon, David. *Menominee Tribal History Project.* Keshena, Wis.: Menominee Historical Preservation Department, 1998. Available at *www.menominee.nsn. us/History/HISTORYHOME.htm.*

Gudinas, Ruth. "Wisconsin Winnebago Political Organization: Structure/Culture Incompatibility and Organizational Effectiveness." Ph.D. diss., University of Chicago, 1974.

Hagan, William T. *The Indian Rights Association: The Herbert Welsh Years, 1882–1904.* Tucson: University of Arizona Press, 1985.

Haney, Lewis. *A Congressional History of Railways in the United States.* Bulletin of the University of Wisconsin Economics and Political Science Series, vol. 6, 1910.

Hauptman, Laurence. *Conspiracy of Interests: Iroquois Dispossession and the Rise of New York State.* Syracuse: Syracuse University Press, 1999.

———. *The Iroquois and the New Deal.* Syracuse: Syracuse University Press, 1981.

———. *The Iroquois Struggle for Survival: World War II to Red Power.* Syracuse: Syracuse University Press, 1986.

Hauptman, Laurence, and L. Gordon McLester III. *Chief Daniel Bread and the Oneida Nation of Indians of Wisconsin.* Norman: University of Oklahoma Press, 2002.

———. *The Oneida Indian Journey: From New York to Wisconsin, 1784–1860.* Madison: University of Wisconsin Press, 1999.

Hickey, Donald. *The War of 1812: A Forgotten Conflict.* Urbana: University of Illinois Press, 1991.

Holzhueter, John O. "Negro Admixture among the Stockbridge and Brothertown Indians of Wisconsin." Unpublished seminar paper, 1966.

Hosmer, Brian. *American Indians in the Marketplace: Persistence and Innovation among the Menominees and Metlakatlans, 1870–1920.* Lawrence: University Press of Kansas, 1999.

Hoxie, Frederick. A *Final Promise: The Campaign to Assimilate the Indians, 1880–1920.* New York: Cambridge University Press, 1984.

———. "Why Treaties?" In *Buried Roots and Indestructible Seeds: The Survival of American Indian Life in Story, History, and Spirit,* edited by Mark Lindquist and Martin Zanger, pp. 85–105. Madison: University of Wisconsin Press, 1995.

Jacoby, Sanford, and Sunil Sharma. "Employment Duration and Industrial Labor Mobility in the United States, 1880–1980." *Journal of Economic History* 52, no. 1 (1992): 161–79.

Jefferson, Thomas. *Notes on the State of Virginia.* 1787; Chapel Hill: University of North Carolina Press, 1955.

Jones, Electa F. *Stockbridge Past and Present, or, Records of an Old Mission.* Springfield, Mass: S. Bowles and Co., 1854.

Kamphoefner, Walter D. "German Emigration Research, North, South, and East: Findings, Methods, and Open Questions." In *People in Transit: German Migrations in Comparative Perspective, 1820–1930,* edited by Dirk Hoerder and Jorg Nagler. Washington, D.C.: German Historical Institute, 1995.

Kelly, Lawrence C. *The Assault on Assimilation: John Collier and the Origins of Indian Policy Reform.* Albuquerque: University of New Mexico Press, 1983.

Kerber, Linda K. "The Abolitionist Perception of the Indian." *Journal of American History* 62, no. 2 (September 1975): 271–95.

Keyssar, Alex. *The Right to Vote: The Contested History of Democracy in the United States.* New York: Basic Books, 2000.

Kinney, J. P. *A Continent Lost—A Civilization Won: Indian Land Tenure in America.* Baltimore: Johns Hopkins University Press, 1937.

Kinzie, Juliette. *Wau-bun, the Early Days in the Northwest.* Philadelphia: J. B. Lippincott, 1873.

Krogseng, Kari. "Chippewa Treaty Rights." *Ecology Law Review* 27 (2000): 771–97.

Kuasnicka, Robert, and Herman Viola. *The Commissioners of Indian Affairs.* Lincoln: University of Nebraska Press, 1979.

Lebergott, Stanley. "The Demand for Land: The United States, 1820–1860." *Journal of Economic History* 45, no. 2 (June 1985): 181–212.

Loew, Patty. Indian *Nations of Wisconsin: Histories of Endurance and Renewal.* Madison: Wisconsin Historical Society Press, 2001.

Love, William Deloss. *Hamilton College and Her Family Line.* Hamilton, N.Y.: n.p., 1963.

———. *Samson Occom and the Christian Indians of New England.* 1899; Syracuse University Press, 2000.

Lubinski, Axel. "Overseas Emigration from Mecklenburg-Strelitz." In *People in Transit: German Migrations in Comparative Perspective, 1820–1930,* edited by Dirk Hoerder and Jorg Nagler. Washington, D.C.: German Historical Institute, 1995.

Lurie, Nancy. "The Indian Claims Commission Act." In *The Rape of Indian Lands,* edited by Paul W. Gates, pp. 56–70. New York: Arno Press, 1979.

———. *Wisconsin Indians.* Madison: State Historical Society of Wisconsin, 1971.

Mahon, John. *The War of 1812* New York: Macmillan, 1972.

McDonnell, Janet. *The Dispossession of the American Indian, 1887–1934.* Bloomington: Indiana University Press, 1991.

McJimsey, George. *Harry Hopkins: Ally of the Poor and Defender of Democracy.* Cambridge, Mass.: Harvard University Press, 1987.

McKenney, Thomas L. *The Winnebago War of 1827.* Madison, 1868.

McLaughlin, William G. *Revivals, Awakenings, and Reform: An Essay on Religion and Social Change in America, 1607–1977.* Chicago: University of Chicago Press, 1978.

McMullen, Ann. "Blood and Culture: Negotiating Race in Twentieth Century Native New England." In *Confounding the Color Line: The Indian-Black Experience in North America,* edited by James F. Brooks, pp. 261–92. Lincoln: University of Nebraska Press, 2002.

Meriam, Lewis C. *The Problem of Indian Administration.* Washington, D.C.: Brookings Institution, 1928.

Meyer, Melissa. "Native American Studies at the End of Ethnohistory." In *Studying Native America: Problems and Prospects,* edited by Russell Thorton, pp. 182–216. Madison: University of Wisconsin Press, 1998.

Mihesugh, Devon A., ed. *Natives and Academics: Researching and Writing about American Indians.* Lincoln: University of Nebraska Press, 1998.

Millar, John. *Observations Concerning the Distribution of Ranks.* Edinburgh, 1771.

Miller, W. G. *Thirty Years in the Itinerancy.* Milwaukee: I. L. Hauser & Co., 1875.

Miles, Lion G. "The Assembly's Catechism, Captain Hendrick Aupaumut, and the Mohican Language." Paper delivered to the 2001 Many Trails of the Mohican Nation Conference, Bowler, Wis.

Mochon, Marion Johnson. "History of the Wisconsin Stockbridge Indians." *Wisconsin Archaeologist* 49, no. 3 (1968): 81–95.

———. "Stockbridge-Munsee Cultural Adaptations: 'Assimilated Indians.'" *Proceedings of the American Philosophical Society* 112, no. 2 (1968): 182–219.

Mooney, James, and Cyrus Thomas. "Mahican." *Bulletin of the Bureau of American Ethnology*, vol. 30, pt. 1, pp. 787–89. Washington, D.C.: Smithsonian Institution, 1907.

———. "Munsee." *Bulletin of the Bureau of American Ethnology*, vol. 30, pt. 1, pp. 957–58. Washington, D.C.: Smithsonian Institution, 1907.

Moore, John H. "The Enduring Reservations of Oklahoma," In *State and Reservation: New Perspectives on Federal Indian Policy*, edited by George Pierre Castile and Robert L. Bee, pp. 92–109. Tucson: University of Arizona Press, 1992.

Morgan, Lewis Henry. *Ancient Society: Researches in the Lines of Human Progress from Savagery through Barbarism to Civilization.* Chicago: Charles H. Kerr, 1877.

———. *League of the Ho-de-no-sau-nee, or Iroquois.* 1851; New York: Corinth Books, 1962.

Morse, Jedidiah. *Report to the Secretary of War on Indian Affairs.* New Haven, Conn.: S. Converse, 1822.

Namorato, Michael V. *Rexford G. Tugwell, a Biography.* New York: Praeger, 1988.

NBC Television. *The West Wing.* Nov. 26, 2001.

Nesper, Larry. *The Walleye War: The Struggle for Ojibwe Spearfishing and Treaty Rights.* Lincoln: University of Nebraska Press, 2002.

Oberly, James W. "Decision on Duck Creek: Two Green Bay Reservations and their Boundaries, 1816–1996." *American Indian Culture and Research Journal* 24, no. 3 (fall 2000): 39–76.

O'Brien, Michael. *McCarthy and McCarthyism in Wisconsin.* Columbia: University of Missouri Press, 1980.

Orr, David Gerald, and Douglas V. Campana. *The People of the Minisink: Papers from the 1989 Delaware Water Gap Symposium.* Philadelphia: National Park Service, Mid-Atlantic Region, 1991.

Osterud, Nancy Grey. *Bonds of Community: The Lives of Farm Women in Nineteenth-Century New York.* Ithaca: Cornell University Press, 1991.

Peroff, Nicholas C. *Menominee Drums: Tribal Termination and Restoration, 1954–1974.* Norman: University of Oklahoma Press, 1982.

Peterson, Jacqueline. "Many Roads to Red River: Metis Genesis in the Great Lakes Region, 1680–1815." In *The New Peoples: Being and Becoming Metis in North America,* edited by Jacqueline Peterson and Jennifer Brown, pp. 37–71. Lincoln: University of Nebraska Press, 1985.

———. "Prelude to Red River: A Social Portrait of the Great Lakes Métis." *Ethnohistory* 25, no. 1 (winter 1978): 41–67.

Philp, Kenneth R. *John Collier's Crusade for Indian Reform, 1920–1954.* Tucson: University of Arizona Press, 1977.

———. *Termination Revisited: American Indians on the Trial to Self-Determination, 1933–1953.* Lincoln: University of Nebraska Press, 1999.

Pilkington, Walter. *Hamilton College, 1812–1962.* Clinton, N.Y.: Hamilton College, 1962.

Porter, Kenneth W. "Relations between Negroes and Indians within the Present Limits of the United States: Contacts in Other Parts." *Journal of Negro History* 17, no. 3 (July 1932): 359–67.

Prucha, Francis Paul. *American Indian Treaties: The History of a Political Anomaly.* Berkeley: University of California Press, 1994.

———. *Broadax and Bayonet: The Role of the United States Army in the Development of the Northwest, 1815–1850.* Madison: State Historical Society of Wisconsin, 1953.

Putnam, Thelma. *Christian Religion among the Stockbridge-Munsee Band of Mohican Indians.* Bowler, Wis.: Muh-he-con-neew Press, 1978.

Quinney, Austin. *Petition to U.S. House and Senate.* Stockbridge, Wis., 1856.

Quinney, John W. "Memorial to the Senate and House of Representatives of the United States (1852). In *Wisconsin Historical Collections*, vol. 5, pp. 321–33.

Quinney, Joseph, and Hendrick Aupaumut, eds. *The Assembly's Shorter Catechism.* Philadelphia, 1796.

Rasmussen, Charles Otto. *Ojibwe Journeys: Treaties, Sandy Lake & the Waabanong Run.* Odanah, Wis.: Great Lakes Indian Fish & Wildlife Commission Press, 2003.

Reeves, Thomas. *The Life and Times of Joe McCarthy.* New York: Stein & Day, 1982.

Remini, Robert. *Andrew Jackson & His Indian Wars.* New York: Viking, 2001.

Report on the Stockbridge Indians. Boston: State Printer, 1870.

Richter, Walter G. *The Mohican: A Century of Lutheran Indian Missions.* n.p., 1998.

Rosenthal, Harvey D. *Their Day in Court: A History of the Indian Claims Commission.* New York: Garland Publishing, 1990.

Royce, Charles C. "Indian Land Cessions." *Bulletin of the Bureau of American Ethnology* 18, pt. 2 Washington, D.C.: Smithsonian Institution, 1898.

Ruttenber, E. M. *History of the Indian Tribes of Hudson's River.* Albany, N.Y., 1872.

Ryan, Mary P. *Cradle of the Middle Class: The Family in Oneida County, New York, 1790–1865.* New York: Cambridge University Press, 1981.

Satz, Ronald N. *Chippewa Treaty Rights: The Reserved Rights of Wisconsin's Chippewa Indians in Historical Perspective.* Madison: Wisconsin Academy of Sciences, Arts, and Letters, 1991.

Savagian, John. "Remembering a Life: Hendrick Aupaumut's Return to the Historical Record." Paper delivered to the 2001 Many Trails of the Mohican Nation Conference, Bowler, Wis.

———. "The Tribal Reorganization of the Stockbridge-Munsee: Essential Conditions in the Re-creation of a Native American Community, 1930–1942." *Wisconsin Magazine of History* 77, no. 1 (1993): 39–62.

Schaefer, Joseph. *The Winnebago-Horicon Basin*. Madison: State Historical Society of Wisconsin, 1937.

Scherer, Mark. *Imperfect Victories: The Legal Tenacity of the Omaha Tribe, 1945–1995*. Lincoln: University of Nebraska Press, 1999.

Searle, Charles F. *Minister of Relief: Harry Hopkins and the Depression*. Syracuse: Syracuse University Press, 1963.

Shattuck, George C. *The Oneida Land Claims: A Legal History*. Syracuse: Syracuse University Press, 1991.

Shawano County Centurawno, 1853–1953. Shawano, Wis., 1953.

Shoemaker, Nancy. *American Indian Population Recovery in the Twentieth Century*. Albuquerque: University of New Mexico Press, 1999.

Shrake, Peter. "The Winnebago War of 1827." M.A. thesis, University of Wisconsin-Eau Claire, 1827.

Siegel, Bernard, and Alan Beals. "Pervasive Factionalism." *American Anthropologist* 62, no. 2 (1960): 394–417.

Silverman, Marilyn. *A House Divided? Anthropological Studies of Factionalism*. Toronto: University of Toronto Press, 1977.

Simon, John. Y., ed. *The Papers of Ulysses S. Grant*. 24 vols. Carbondale: Southern Illinois University Press.

Skinner, Alanson. "Notes on Mahikan Ethnology." *Bulletin of the Milwaukee Public Museum* 2, no. 3 (1925): 87–119.

Smith, Alice E. *History of Wisconsin*. Vol. 1: *From Exploration to Statehood*. Madison: State Historical Society of Wisconsin, 1973.

Speck, Frank G. *The Celestial Bear Comes Down to Earth: The Bear Sacrifice Ceremony of the Munsee Mahican Nation in Canada as Related by Nekatcit*. Reading, Pa.: Reading Public Museum, 1945.

"Statesburgh Mission Site." In *Wisconsin Historical Collections*, vol. 15, pp. 39–47. Madison: Democrat Printing Co., 1900.

Stovey, Patricia Ann. "Parallel Souls: Studies in Early Twentieth Century Native American Leaders in Relation to Black Activists W. E. B. DuBois and Marcus Garvey, 1900–1934." M.A. thesis, University of Wisconsin–Eau Claire, 2002.

Strong, Moses. *History of the Territory of Wisconsin, from 1836 to 1848*. Madison, Wis.: Democrat Printing Co., 1885.

Sutton, Imre. *Indian Land Tenure*. New York: Clearwater Publishing, 1975.

———. *Irredeemable America: The Indians' Estate and Land Claims*. Albuquerque: University of New Mexico Press, 1985.

Tanner, Helen Hornbeck. "The Glaize in 1792: A Composite Indian Community." *Ethnohistory* 25, no. 1 (1978): 15–39.

Tanner, Herbert Battles. *History of Kaukauna's Revolutionary Hero*. Kaukauna, 1926.

Taylor, Alan. "Captain Hendrick Aupaumut: The Dilemmas of an Intercultural Broker." *Ethnohistory* 43, no. 3 (1996): 431–57.

———. *William Cooper's Town: Power and Persuasion on the Frontier of the Early American Republic*. New York: Alfred A. Knopf, 1995.

Taylor, Graham D. *The New Deal and American Indian Tribalism: The Administration of the Indian Reorganization Act, 1934–1945*. Lincoln: University of Nebraska, 1980.

Thernstrom, Stephan. *The Other Bostonians: Poverty and Progress in the American Metropolis, 1870–1970*. Cambridge, Mass.: Harvard University Press, 1973.

Thomas, Lamont D. *Rise to be a People: A Biography of Paul Cuffe*. Urbana: University of Illinois Press, 1986.

Titus, W. A., "A Brief Account of the Stockbridges." *Wisconsin Magazine of History* 30, no. 4 (1947): 423–32.

"Two Minute Books of Kansas Missions in the Forties." *Kansas Historical Quarterly* 2, no. 3 (spring 1934): 227–50.

Viola, Herman. *Diplomats in Buckskin: A History of Indian Delegations in Washington City*. Washington, D.C.: Smithsonian Institution, 1981.

———. *Thomas L. McKenney, Architect of America's Early Indian Policy, 1816–1830*. Chicago: Sage Books, 1974.

Wilkins, David E. *American Indian Sovereignty and the U.S. Supreme Court: The Masking of Justice*. Austin: University of Texas Press, 1997.

Woodson, Carter G. "The Relations of Negroes and Indians in Massachusetts." *Journal of Negro History* 5 (1920): 45–57.

Woodward, C. Vann. *Origins of the New South, 1877–1913*. Baton Rouge: Louisiana State University Press, 1951.

Young, Mary E. "The Cherokee Nation: Mirror of the Republic." *American Quarterly* 33, no. 5 (winter 1981): 502–24.

———. "Tribal Reorganization in the Southeast, 1800–1840." In *The Struggle for Political Autonomy*, edited by Frederick Hoxie, pp. 59–82. *Newberry Library Center for the History of the American Indian Occasional Papers* No. 11 (1989).

Zanger, Martin. "Red Bird." In *American Indian Leaders: Studies in Diversity*, edited by R. David Edmunds, pp. 64–87. Lincoln: University of Nebraska Press, 1980.

Index